INTO
THE
SUNRISE

CHRIS
POUNTNEY

Copyright © 2018 Chris Pountney

ISBN-13: 978-1724471215
ISBN-10: 172447121X

Cover Design: © Chris Pountney
Interior Maps: © Chris Pountney

Also by Chris Pountney:

NO WRONG TURNS: Cycling the World, Part One: Paris to Sydney

For more from the author, please visit:
www.differentpartsofeverywhere.com

To view photographs that accompany the book, please visit:
www.differentpartsofeverywhere.com/book/photos
or
www.flickr.com/photos/into-the-sunrise/albums

DEDICATION

For Mum and Dad.

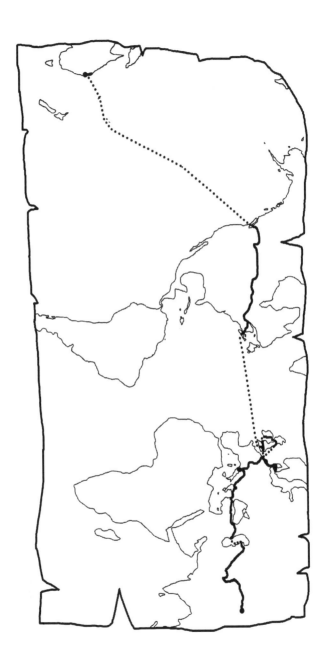

THE ONLY WAY WAS EAST, THE ONLY WAY WAS INTO THE SUNRISE

This book is a true story.

A few names have been misspelt, some of them quite badly, but it all really happened, honest.

Also, *Into The Sunrise* continues on from the first book in the series, *No Wrong Turns*. If you haven't read that, stop, what are you doing? This book isn't going to make any sense.

Due to printing costs, this book is once again lacking in photographs.

If you would like to view the photographic evidence that supports this book, please go to:

www.flickr.com/photos/into-the-sunrise/albums

I know that's quite a lot to type, but I got a better camera than last time, so it might be worth it.

Now, on with the story...

The Challenges

1. Circumnavigate the planet

Once again, I mean Earth.

2. Do so using only my bicycle and boats

No planes, no buses, no trucks, no trains, no cars, and definitely no more blue pick-up trucks!

3. Pass through antipodal points

Opposite spots on the planet.

4. Visit all of the inhabited continents

Antarctic researchers and penguins excluded.

5. Cycle at least 100,000 kilometres

Otherwise known as 62,137 and a bit miles.

6. Cycle in 100 countries

Full United Nation members only.

7. Return with more money than I start with

So I won't have to get a proper job.

PART ONE

SYDNEY TO HONOLULU

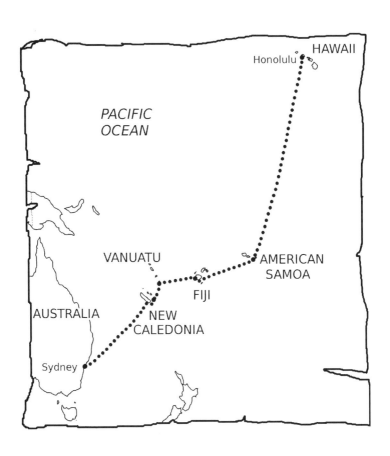

There are moments in life when everything just feels right. When everything seems to have fallen into place. When you feel like the luckiest person in the world. When you feel really, truly happy.

There could be no doubt that this was just such a moment. I was standing on the upper deck of the MS Noordam, a giant cruise ship, leaning upon the railings and looking around in wonder at the scene before me. Dominating the view was the mighty Sydney Harbour Bridge that stretched out across the bay. Far beneath it little ferry boats spluttered about, looking like toys compared with the gigantic steel bridge and the behemoth of a ship I stood upon. I swivelled my head to the right and the Opera House gleamed back at me across the water. The finishing line for the first leg of my journey was now the starting post for the second, and the iconic roofs still took my breath away every time my eyes fell upon them. But as I turned my head just a little further to the right my eyes found an even more breath-taking sight. Looking back into them were two bright blue eyes that seemed to sparkle and fizz with the excitement of the moment. I loved those eyes so much.

Eighteen months had now passed since I'd first seen those eyes, when Dea had ridden into my life on a Mongolian motorcycle. And it had been almost eight months since we'd first cycled into Sydney together, at the culmination of my two-year ride from Paris. Now Australia was at an end, and we'd achieved exactly what we wanted to. Dea had completed her final thesis with a top grade and earned her freedom, and after six months of working on the pedicabs in Surfers Paradise we'd made enough money to pay for this cruise and fund another two years of cycling. Everything had gone according to plan. In fact, it seemed that everything since Paris had, with the exception of one kilometre between Siberia and Mongolia, gone quite remarkably according to plan.

Now it was time for us to begin writing the script for the sequel (and, as anyone who has seen *Speed 2: Cruise Control* will tell you, sequels set on cruise ships are *always* a good idea). The MS Noordam would, over the next twenty-four days, sail to Vancouver, Canada. From there we intended to spend the next two years cycling south through the Americas, visiting as many countries as possible along the way, before finding another boat eastwards from somewhere in South America. It was a prospect that had us both excited, especially Dea, who would be undertaking her first long journey by bicycle. As she put her arms around me and looked at me with those perfect eyes I just felt so incredibly lucky to have found her. We'd grown so close during our time together in Australia. Far below us in a park a couple were getting married, and I was growing ever more confident that one day that might be happening for Dea and me.

The ship was delayed and as it grew dark we decided to investigate the outdoor sports court. It was at the highest point of the ship and as a consequence we had the most extraordinary backdrop for our games. We played basketball and football, and I didn't even mind losing the football five goals to nil, for it was such a magical experience to see the joy on my girlfriend's face with the lights of the city's skyscrapers, the Harbour Bridge, and the Opera House surrounding us in a 360 degree panorama. It was one of those special moments when everything just seemed to have come together. Everything felt right.

The ship blasted its horn and we watched spellbound as it carefully manoeuvred away from the dock, slipped past the Opera

House, and continued on out of the harbour into the darkness. The diamond lights of the Sydney skyline grew smaller and smaller behind us, gradually shrinking away to nothing. The Pacific Ocean had us. A new adventure had begun.

§

What a complete moron this guy was. He ran after my pedicab, laughing like a maniac and grabbing for the back of the seat, hoping for a free ride. My three paying passengers, only slightly less intoxicated themselves, looked back at the idiot nervously as we made our way along the esplanade. He was no doubt under the influence of something more than just alcohol if the crazed look in his eyes and the way he howled as he jumped aboard were anything to go by. I sighed. Just another Saturday night in Surfers Paradise. I kept turning the pedals, cursing under my breath at having to haul four fully grown men behind me now. But then the idiot lost his grip and fell, landing smack upon his face on the tarmac. It was a moment of light relief, to be sure, but only a brief one, for he rose once again to recommence his pursuit. I couldn't outpace him, not with so much cargo. Once again he jumped aboard and my frustrations grew. It was the early hours of the morning, I was exhausted, and this just wasn't fun any more. I strained at the pedals until, near to the destination of my three paying customers, I ground to a halt. "I'm not going any further!" I declared. "Not with this muppet."

The three men understood and willingly departed to walk the final few metres, even tipping me for my troubles. Then I turned to face my tormentor. The madman grinned, wild pupils dilated, and raised a hand. In it was a crisp fifty dollar note. "Let's go for a ride!" he said, jumping into the back seat.

"Yes sir," I said.

That fifty pushed me over 500 dollars for the night. The previous evening I'd made only 140 in twelve hours. But that was just how it was, and it was why I loved pedicabbing. It was all about being in the right place at the right time, saying the right things. It was a game, the money just a way of keeping score. Sometimes it was amazing and sometimes it wasn't, and sometimes you just got lucky, like the time that someone handed me a fifty for cycling them twenty metres to a kebab shop, and like this night, my thirty-first birthday. It had been all go, and I hardly stopped from six in the evening until six in the morning, when Dea and I sat in our pedicabs and watched the sunrise over the ocean, exhausted, but with another 850 travel points in the bank.

We'd been in Surfers Paradise for three weeks, and we'd just signed a six month lease on an apartment, which I thought was probably the maximum amount of time I was going to be able to handle living in a place with such a glaringly obvious apostrophe missing from its name. We'd moved in with Matt, the short little bearded chap I met in Mongolia about ten seconds before I met Dea. I really do owe Matt a lot for his decision to stop his motorbike to talk with me, because it led Dea to stop her motorbike to talk with me, and therefore led to everything that followed. I should probably stop describing him as a short little bearded chap, for a start. After their bike trip Dea and Matt had remained friends and he'd decided to come and join us in Surfers Paradise. He'd been in Australia for a little while, having achieved his aim to travel all the way from the UK without flying, and, keen to earn some more travel points himself, he joined us working on the pedicabs.

The three of us soon hatched a plan to get across the Pacific without flying. It was an idea that had originally formulated in the bizarre world of my mind during my long cycle across Australia, and it seemed to everyone to be a brilliant one. We would simply use our savings to buy a sailing boat, sail it to North America, sell it again, and use that money to continue travelling. Dea, who looked a bit terrified, and Matt, who I think might well have been stoned, both said it was a great idea, and it was settled. It didn't really matter that our collective sailing experience was close to zero, because Matt had once lived on a boat (it wasn't entirely clear if it had ever sailed anywhere, but I imagined he had a good idea of where things were) and, what was more, Dea had for my birthday presented me with a book entitled 'Sailing Essentials'. I read a few pages of it, and, as I recall, even went so far as to make notes. The plan seemed foolproof.

For months we went on with this happy existence, pedicabbing by night, dreaming of sailing by day. We had a nice, bright apartment complete with a pool, just a short walk from the beach. I'd long dreamt of living and working in Australia just like this, and it felt good to spend some time in one place after two years of constant travel. Matt became a good friend, something that I missed having during all the time I moved around. Given his stature I put forth Elijah Wood as the actor I thought best suited to portray him in the movie series, but Matt did not agree, and instead made his own suggestion.

"Do you know Bret from *Flight of the Conchords*?"

"Yeah. He's the slow, dim-witted one isn't he?"

"Yeah. I'd like to be played by him."

To be honest, I think this choice probably says more about Matt than I can.

Surfers Paradise, however, was a peculiar place, and not only because the surf in Surfers Paradise was rather tame, with not many surfers to be seen on its beaches. The name actually originated as a means of attracting tourists, and that had certainly worked. With its beautiful sandy beaches and grand watery inlets it was now the holiday destination for many from Australia and abroad. Everything was geared towards tourism, from the multitude of nearby theme parks to the tacky gift shops that lined every street. It was a strange place, something of a cross between Las Vegas, the French Riviera, and Blackpool. It wasn't the sort of location that either Dea or myself would have thought we would have enjoyed living in, but somehow we came to love it. The other pedicabbers, a diverse group of travellers and students from countries as far afield as Brazil, France, and South Korea, were for the most part a fantastic bunch who we had a lot of fun working with. And even though the weekends tended to get messy out on the streets (imagine a scene from a zombie movie, but with drunken Australians staggering around left, right and centre, occasionally taking swings at one another) for most of the week the job involved pedalling families and couples around on tours. It was good fun and easy enough work for someone with 45,000 kilometres of training, and the money began to pile up.

With our savings growing I began to research the sailing boat idea a little more thoroughly. What I discovered was not so encouraging. It seemed that the prevailing winds blew consistently from east to west, so we would unfortunately have to sail the entire journey into the wind. Trying to remain positive I opened up my 'Sailing Essentials' book and figured out how to sail into the wind. "I've figured out how to sail into the wind Dea, don't worry!" All was okay for a while. I even found a blog written by some people who had sailed from west to east. They'd gone up to Vanuatu, Guam, and Japan, then across to Alaska. That sounded terrific. We'd just do that. So I e-mailed them and thought everything was going rather well. But then one of them wrote back.

Apparently, according to this experienced sailor, crossing the Pacific this way was not only extremely difficult, but also extremely dangerous. Only a dozen or so boats attempt it each year, and some don't make it. Given our level of experience with the Pacific (so far we'd been out on a whale watching trip, but the boat was motorised, and we weren't in charge) I couldn't help but admit we might be one of the unlucky ones. He strongly advised us against the idea. In fact he suggested we would be much better off flying to North America and then sailing back to Australia, which I admitted sounded nice, but rather defeated the object.

So I changed the focus of my research and found that there was a cruise ship heading from Sydney to Vancouver that was reasonably priced and stopped in Hawaii. It seemed like an ideal solution. "Dea, it turns out that we might genuinely die if we try to sail across the Pacific, do you want to just take a cruise ship instead? It stops in Hawa-"

"Oh God! Yes please!"

As well as Hawaii the cruise itinerary also featured stops at several South Pacific islands, something we were all looking forward to (apart from Matt, of course, who was no longer invited). But after our departure from Australia Dea and I first had two very relaxing days at sea to enjoy. Having used this time to become extremely laid-back, relaxed, and chilled out, on the second evening we thought we might get up and do something. We'd had the foresight to go to a charity shop before leaving to buy some smart second hand clothes, and so we got ourselves dressed up and headed to the main dining room for dinner. Dea had bought a flowing orange dress and when she put it on that evening and did her blonde hair all nice, my God, she was about the most beautiful thing I'd ever seen in my whole entire life. It was a shame, then, that the blue shirt I'd bought came out of my bags all creased and I looked barely more respectable than usual. Still, we went to the restaurant and I was as pleased as anything to have this girl on my arm. I knew that all of the other men in the restaurant were jealous of me; I had the most stunning girl in the room, and everyone knew it. The fact that everyone else in the room was over the age of sixty, besides the point.

"Are you on your honeymoon?" asked the waiter after he'd taken our order.

"No," we both smiled. "Not yet."

Dea's smile was as wide as I'd ever seen it. Her eyes sparkled. "I can't believe we're really here," she said, looking around the fancy restaurant. "I'm so glad we didn't sail. I couldn't imagine being out here on a tiny sailing boat."

"I know. And tomorrow we'll be in New Caledonia. Then Vanuatu. Then Fiji. Then Hawaii. And then after all that, Canada."

"I know. I can't wait to cycle in Canada with you."

"You're going to love it, I know you are. And then the United States, Mexico, South America."

"I just can't believe it, Chris. There are so many good things ahead of us."

We awoke the next day to find that the ship had arrived in New

Caledonia, anchoring a few hundred metres from an island of small green hills. It looked to me like a good place for a bike ride, but Dea couldn't see it so well. She was complaining of a painful and itchy eye that had apparently kept her up most of the night. It was sufficiently bad for her to consider going to the onboard medical centre, but we had a busy day planned riding our bikes around the island and she decided she would wait and see if it improved.

Because the cruise ship could not navigate the shallow waters close to the island it was necessary to use some of the ship's lifeboats to transport people to shore. Dea and I pushed our bikes down the ship's hallways and into the elevators, gaining admiring glances and comments of "I wish we'd thought of that" from other passengers. I was confident we'd be allowed to take our bicycles off the ship because I'd gone and checked at front reception the night before, and it was going to be a great place to use them. The island was not heavily populated, and our research told us we could expect a nice quiet ride along the coast to a beach and some caves.

We got our bikes down to the lower deck and I carried mine down some steps to the temporary dock next to one of the lifeboats. Greeting me there was none other than the captain of the MS Noordam himself. It seemed he was about to abandon his ship, and go ashore himself for the day.

"What ish thish?" he asked, in a thick Dutch accent. "You cannot take your bishycle on the tender boat."

"Erm," I said, "we were told that we could."

"No, you can't. I'm shorry. The tender boat ish for people, not bishycles. I've been doing thish job twenty yearsh. Nobody hash ever taken bishycles on tender boatsh. Out of the queshtion!"

Well, that didn't seem like a very Dutch attitude to me. We retreated back inside, waited until the lifeboat with the captain on had left, then tried to sneak down onto a different boat. It was no use, the staff stopped us. There was no way we were going to be allowed to take our bikes off the ship, not after the captain had spoken. His word was final.

So we reluctantly left our bikes behind and headed to the island without them. We arrived in a small village, where a few Pacific Islanders loitered beside simple homes, and hundreds of white tourists with cameras around their necks jumped on buses. That was the easiest way to get to the beach and the caves fifteen kilometres away, but I couldn't do that. My aim was still to travel around the world using nothing more than my bicycle and boats, and that meant that I couldn't allow myself to use motorised transport on land at any point, not even for a side trip. So Dea and I started to walk.

Initially it felt so nice to be off the ship and wandering through a lush green landscape next to a sea that shimmered in various shades of turquoise and blue. Our goal was just to find somewhere to get in and snorkel, but the shoreline was made up of sharp rocky outcrops which would have made it impossible to climb out again. We kept walking and walking, hoping to find somewhere. The sun rose high in the sky and Dea's eye was bothering her more and more, so it was a relief when we finally found a secret little spot where we could get into the sea. With Dea undecided on whether she should snorkel I dived in first. Immediately I put my head back up again and said, "You must come in Dea, it's amazing!" And it was too, with such a variety of coral and tropical fish, it was really fantastic.

We gave up on the beach and the caves and set out on the return journey. I found the long walk back to be quite arduous, so for Dea it really must have been a form of torture. She'd gone in the water briefly and it had done nothing to help her poor left eye. It was itching constantly and she had to keep it firmly closed most of the time while doing her best to resist the temptation to rub it. I felt so sorry for her, and regretted that we had walked such a long way under the hot sun.

Back on board the ship Dea retired immediately to bed, keeping the lights down low and putting a cold flannel over her eye, while I went about organising some other business. The following morning we would be in Vanuatu and it was another tender port where we'd need to take lifeboats to get ashore. I didn't really mind about not having cycled in New Caledonia, what with it being a mere French territory, but Vanuatu was a fully fledged member of the United

Nations. I was aiming to cycle in one hundred countries during this trip, and Vanuatu was a potential number forty-six. I was determined not to miss out on it.

"So the problem," I confirmed with the front desk staff, "is that we can't take our bicycles ashore because they would block the passageways on the lifeboat?"

"Yes, that's right sir."

"Okay, thank you."

I'd had another one of my cunning plans.

2

Mystery Island, Vanuatu
13th April 2016

Dea's eye was no better in the morning and she decided to just stay on the boat and rest while I implemented my quite brilliant cunning plan. The previous evening, working by head torch in our cramped room while Dea slept, I'd taken my bicycle entirely apart, and now I intended to take it across to Vanuatu piece by piece. The tender boats went back and forth all day long. I'd take the frame across first, then come back for the wheels, and then finally the fork and handlebars. I'd rebuild the bike on the island, cycle a few hundred metres or so, and then take it all apart again to bring back in a similar fashion. It would only take me all day. It was pure genius.

As soon as the announcement was made that the first boat was ready I rushed downstairs with my bicycle frame in my hands, this time getting some very confused looks along the way, until I made it down to the staff manning the tender boats.

"No bicycles," they said, and a hand was held up to bar my progress.

"This is not a bicycle," I protested. "It's a bicycle frame."

Despite the unquestionable accuracy of this statement, I was still not permitted to pass.

"I was told that I couldn't take the bike because it would block the passageways. This is just a frame, I can hold this on my lap."

Understanding now that they had a madman on their hands, I was asked to wait while one of the staff members made a call on his radio. I was half expecting some men in white coats to arrive, but instead he returned with interesting news. "The captain has said that you can take your bicycle today. But you must go on the first tender boat, and come back on the last tender boat. Okay?"

While this was good news, it would have been much, much better news had it been given to me before I took my bicycle apart. I could hardly believe it as I now stood with just my frame in my hands as the first tender boat reached full capacity and set sail for Vanuatu.

I took my frame and my increasingly vehement protests back to the front reception desk. Fortunately my vexation was appreciated by the front desk staff and I was soon talking with a more senior woman, the head of customer relations or some sort. After listening patiently to my story she said, "You know this is a very small island. In fact it is just sand. You won't really be able to ride your bike anywhere."

"I know, but I'm cycling around the world and I want to ride my bike in one hundred countries, so I'd really like it if I could cycle in Vanuatu."

She turned to the lifeboat staff and spoke for a moment, before turning back to me and sighing. It was the sigh of a woman keen to avoid any more of a scene being made. "Okay, you can put your bike back together and take it on another tender boat."

Success!

I took my frame back up to the room to rebuild the bike and found Dea lying in bed taking eye drops and looking all adorable and sick. While I'd been trying to get off the boat she'd visited the ship's onboard doctor. The price for this consultation was ninety-five dollars, which frankly should have been enough to make anyone's eyes water, but just to be safe he'd also given her the eye drops. His diagnosis was conjunctivitis, and hopefully it would clear up soon.

I put my bike back together. With the cramped conditions and feeling a little rushed I did a spectacularly bad job of it and managed to break my bike in several different ways, but it didn't matter; so long as I could still cycle it a little bit it didn't need to work very well. I took it back down to the lifeboats and walked forwards to board. "No bicycles," they said. No, not really. They let me through this time. And finally I was on a lifeboat with my bicycle. Blocking the passageway a little bit, true, but it was a lifeboat. If we had to evacuate from a lifeboat we really would be in trouble. We sailed over to the very flat Mystery Island, a tiny piece of paradise which appeared to be all sand where I couldn't cycle. Luckily a local man came to my rescue. His name was Tony and after watching my desperate attempts to pedal in the sand he offered to show me a better place to ride. He then led me through some palm trees and we emerged, much to my surprise, on an airstrip. It was a runway of compacted grass that had been built to service the Allied forces in the Second World War. Indeed it was because of this that Mystery Island got its name – the island was so small and flat that it appeared the planes were mysteriously taking off and landing right out of the sea.

I cycled up and down the length of the airstrip. It was about a kilometre long and stretched the entire length of the island. Somehow even on this short trip I managed to bend my derailleur all out of shape having not put it back together properly. So I leant my malfunctioning bike against a palm tree and explored the rest of the island on foot. This did not take long. There was a market selling sarongs and bracelets that had obviously been set up just for the cruise ship passengers, most of whom were by now lounging around on the beaches that circled the island. There wasn't much to do here, but I did make it into the water to snorkel again and saw some fish, but it wasn't as good as in New Caledonia, and I kept bumping into old people.

Back on the ship there was a worrying development. While I was messing about on Vanuatu, Dea had noticed that a pale yellow spot had appeared over the middle of her left eye. It looked extremely unpleasant, and surely more serious than mere conjunctivitis. The next day, which was another sea day, I accompanied Dea back to the medical centre. The onboard doctor was a young South African man (played no doubt by Leonardo DiCaprio with his unforgettable

Blood Diamond accent), of only about our age, who looked concerned by the spot. It was right over the front of Dea's pupil and seriously affecting her vision. At first the doctor tried to remove it with a swab, but this didn't work as it was below the top layer of the cornea and, perhaps realising that he was a bit out of his depth with this one, he told Dea that she needed to get to a specialist eye doctor as soon as possible.

The next morning our ship arrived in Lautoka, Fiji. It was the second largest settlement on the island, but as I looked down on the overcast town early in the morning I was not convinced that its dilapidated corrugated roofs hid any world class eye specialists. In all probability the capital city, Suva, was the only place Dea could get the treatment she needed. It was 250 kilometres away and the staff at the onboard medical centre had promised to make all of the necessary arrangements for us. As we made our way there at eight a.m. we were confident they would have everything in place ready to whisk Dea away to Suva, or wherever she needed to be. No such luck. Instead we sat there on the hard chairs of the waiting room for an hour, being told that the port agent, who was apparently the one responsible for such things, was busy doing the hundred other things the port agent must be responsible for.

As we sat there waiting I grew increasingly anxious. If Dea could not get the help that she needed before the ship set sail again then she would have to disembark, and I would of course go with her. It would ruin everything. As the clock ticked past nine a.m. I could sit twiddling my fingers no longer, and decided to take things into my own hands, hurrying off to the dock to make my own arrangements. I asked one of the taxi drivers lined up at the port how long it would take to drive to Suva and back.

"It's a three and a half hour drive. What time does the ship leave again?"

"Four thirty."

"Oh. It's very difficult to get to Suva and back in time. Especially because the road is wet."

"Okay. How much does it cost?"

"It doesn't matter. You can't do it."

I was pretty annoyed to say the least, and my mood was not improved when I got back to the medical centre and found Mr DiCaprio conducting a Google search (something which could easily have been done the day before). "Looks like all the eye doctors are in Suva," he said. I threw my hands up in despair. Had we been readied to go at eight o'clock when the ship arrived, Dea could have got there and back in time. Now she couldn't, because we'd wasted the first hour and a half of the day in a waiting room. I was fuming. This was really serious. Dea needed to see an eye doctor, and now it seemed like the only way to do it was going to be for us to disembark the ship completely. Which also meant that my attempt to travel around the world continuously by bicycle and boats was pretty much over.

With the medical team still saying that they needed to wait to hear from the port agent, but having no actual idea where he was, I went off to look for him myself. I needed to get away from there and try to do something. I was really very angry about everything potentially being ruined by their incompetence. The port agent was nowhere to be found, however, and when I returned inside I discovered that he'd finally been in contact with the medical centre, and by some miracle an eye doctor had been found in the nearby town of Nandi, only thirty kilometres away.

It was a lucky break and a massive relief, and with it being so close Dea said she was happy to go alone in a taxi so that I could keep up my record of not using motor vehicles. When the taxi arrived I was a little concerned by the driver, who certainly did not give the impression he knew where he was going, but I packed Dea off with him anyway. With the drama suddenly passed I went to get my bicycle. Not being a tender port it was easy for me to get the bike off the ship here, and I thought I might as well nab another country while I had the chance.

It was strange to cycle through the streets of Lautoka. It had that chaotic, run-down appearance that had been so common across Asia. I'd almost forgotten such places existed after the orderliness of Australia. I didn't ride too far. Just through the busy Lautoka streets and

out the other side far enough to get a glimpse of the Fijian countryside. The rolling hills merged with low-hanging clouds on this day
of uninspiring weather, but the road ahead promised plenty of a
country that I'd loved to have had the chance to explore. But the
necessity of returning to the boat to see how Dea had got on, not to
mention my broken derailleur (which made it impossible to change
gears) encouraged me to turn back.

Back on board the boat I sat and waited in our room for Dea's
return. She soon burst in with a smile on her face. The doctor in
Nandi, though working in rather primitive conditions, had been a
really nice woman. She'd diagnosed it as an infected corneal ulcer,
and prescribed some different medications, but the prognosis had
been good. Hopefully it would clear up soon. Another eye doctor
would check the progress during our next stop in American Samoa,
and until then all we should do was proceed with the hourly eye
drops and not worry too much. It was the best possible outcome. We
had come so close to having to leave the ship, close perhaps to the
abrupt end of my continuous journey, but somehow, sailing away
from Fiji that evening, it seemed like everything was going to be just
fine after all.

The next day, Saturday the 16th of April, we were supposed to be
stopping at a smaller Fijian island, but instead we were awoken by an
annoying voice over the ship's public address system. "Thish ish your
captain shpeaking. Unfortunately due to strong windsh and bad
weather we will not be able to shtop at Dravuni Island today, and we
will instead prosheed onwardsh towardsh our next shtop of American Shamoa."

Now that we weren't stopping in Fiji, Saturday the 16th of April
became a rather unremarkable day at sea, during which we did very
little. Dea rested, I administered eye drops, we watched a movie, ate
some food, that kind of thing. Then we went to bed.

We awoke on the morning of Saturday the 16th of April. "If the
captain had any kind of sense of humour," I said to Dea, "he'd
announce on the public address system that we weren't able to stop
in Dravuni today." He didn't of course, because this wasn't the same

Saturday the 16th of April, but a different one. Crossing the International Date Line brought with it the very special experience to live the same day twice. It felt like a great opportunity. An extra day at life, what could be better than that? So Dea rested, I administered eye drops, we watched a movie, ate some food, that kind of thing. Then we went to bed.

After our two Saturdays we finally got to Sunday at about the same time that the ship got to American Samoa. I should have very much preferred it if we could've stopped just a little further to the west, in Samoa, because that would have counted as another country, but I thought it might be pushing my luck to request such a thing of this particular captain, and so I had to make do with this small American territory instead. We docked in a horseshoe bay at a place called Pago Pago, surrounded on all sides by hills that I felt sure must be green but that looked blue as I watched our arrival in the early morning light. It looked like a really nice place and one that I was looking forward to exploring.

Over the previous two days Dea had been in good spirits after her positive visit to the nice doctor in Fiji. However, the yellow spot over her eye didn't yet seem to have improved, and she needed to get the opinion of the eye doctor here too. So our day started once again in the medical centre, and then with me waving her off in another taxi to another morning in a hospital, before I got my bike to go for a little ride.

American Samoa was lovely. Pago Pago was of course overrun with old white tourists fresh from the cruise ship, but once I'd cycled a few kilometres I was free from that and able to get a better feel for the place. I rode around the bay, following its natural curve until I was looking back across the water to the ship and the hillsides beyond, which I could now see were clearly bright green (as I'd suspected). The road was not busy and was dotted with basic concrete houses and a surprising number of churches. Local people walked around in bright Hawaiian shirts, which seemed to be quite the fashion here. A few dogs chased me, no doubt pleasantly surprised by the rare appearance of a cycle tourist on this remote island. After a while

I came to a beach where I stopped and sat for a while to reflect on how jolly nice it was here.

I decided next to cycle up into the hills. The road was very, very steep. Too steep for a man without gears really. By the time I was halfway up I was a physical wreck and needed to sit down. Had circumstances been different I would have liked to continue up and over the pass to see the ocean views on the other side, but I wanted to be back at the ship to meet Dea and see how she'd got on at the doctor (that was my excuse, anyway). Another good reason for my retreat was that I had no water with me, a bit of a mistake given the hot and humid conditions, and I wanted to buy a bottle from a shop back at the bottom of the hill.

As I sat on a bench outside the store to rehydrate a group of boys of about ten or twelve approached and began to talk with me. Their English was excellent, although they spoke to one another in their native Samoan tongue. They told me that they had just come from church, this being a Sunday, and in fact I could see a great many more people spilling out of the place of worship across the street. The men and boys all wore long skirts, many with floral designs on them similar to the Hawaiian shirts that most of them sported. I thought it a most excellent Sunday best. The boys were very friendly, asking me what I was doing and teaching me some Samoan, including all the most important words, like hello, goodbye, sun, moon, stars and bicycle wheel. It was a special moment, to catch just a little glimpse of their culture as we sat looking at the beach, the bay and the mountains. A thought struck me about how very good it felt to be here. It was not a thought that was destined to last long.

I cycled back to the ship and went up to our room, but there was no sign that Dea had yet returned from her appointment. I wanted to get online as I hadn't done so for some time. I'd noticed that there was one place in Pago Pago that offered access for half an hour for five dollars, but I wanted to wait for Dea, and so I decided to log on with the ship's onboard Wi-Fi. This cost an extortionate seventy-five cents per minute, but I only wanted to quickly check my e-mails, and

I guessed I wasn't popular enough for that task to come to more than five bucks. So I logged on and, as anticipated, had very little mail. There was one comment on my blog that caught my eye, however. I read it through a couple of times, kind of froze in horror for a bit, then said a very rude word.

Hi Chris

I recently noticed that the US changed their visa rules so that if you have travelled to Iran before, you are not eligible for a visa waiver anymore and instead have to apply for a full visa.

Stephan Teusch

This was a bit of a problem, to put it mildly. Our plans to cycle from Canada down to South America were kind of dependent on being allowed to cycle through the United States. In fact it was effectively impossible to do it any other way. Now it seemed, at least if Stephan Teusch knew what he was talking about, that the great big Iranian stamp in my passport was going to provide us with one great big problem.

I scribbled a note for Dea letting her know where she could find me and then hurried over to the five dollar Wi-Fi place to do some more research. And it quickly became apparent that Stephan Teusch did know what he was talking about. The United States had introduced a new rule, only three months earlier, that no one who had visited Iran since 2011 could qualify to enter their country via the visa waiver system. Thanks to my visit there two years earlier I would have to apply for a full United States visa, which might not have been a problem, were it not for the rather inconvenient fact that to do that I would have to attend an interview, in London. Kind of a logistically complicated thing to do without flying.

Quickly coming to terms with this new irritating obstacle placed in our path, I began to look for a plan B. My first thought was that I could try to get a new passport while we were in Vancouver. That was a bit of a gamble, because I didn't know how much information the United States might have on me, or if the fact that I'd been to

Iran would be stored on my passport's biometric chip (which would presumably be information that would be transferred to a replacement passport). But it might work. There was an additional consideration, however. In five days time we were going to arrive in Hawaii and face a mandatory border control inspection. If the United States didn't already know that I'd been to Iran, they probably would soon. So I looked for a plan C. The only other way out of Canada was another boat. This led me back to looking for cruises, not that this cruise had really lived up to our expectations as of yet. I found only one ship that might work, a September sailing from Montreal to Liverpool. It wasn't ideal, but it would at least keep alive my hopes to circumnavigate the planet using only my bicycle and boats, which was the most important thing. I would just have to see what Dea would say about such a massive change to our itinerary, and if she'd be happy to come back and cycle the rest of the Americas another time, perhaps.

With all of these thoughts still spinning around in my head I began to head back towards the ship. I looked up and saw Dea walking towards me. She must have got my note. I gave her a wave, but she didn't wave back. She just shook her head. This didn't look too good. I hurried over to her. She was shaking.

"It's not good," she said, looking distraught. "The doctor said I have a really serious infection, and I need to get to a corneal specialist as soon as possible. He said my eye could burst. I need to fly somewhere, Chris. The medical centre on the ship say there is a flight to Hawaii tomorrow, or maybe there is one to New Zealand."

I hugged her close to me. Tried to calm the shaking. Tried to tell her it would be okay.

"Chris, I'm so scared. I'm so scared. I can't do this alone."

"I know, I'm coming with you, don't worry."

3

This was not turning out to be a great day. Now I knew that I was going to have to break my continuous journey. It wasn't even an option. I loved Dea, she needed me, and I had to stand by her. I had to get on a plane. I felt bad enough for not having been with her today. The doctor, who clearly wasn't the kind of man who thought things through, had told her that her eye was like a balloon, and it might burst like one, but that being stressed was more likely to make this happen, so best not to worry. Astonishingly enough this statement had the effect of making Dea rather stressed. In fact she was understandably terrified, and this was not a great time to be stuck on a remote island in the middle of the Pacific Ocean.

I knew that I needed to be strong for Dea, reassure her, try to get things organised, even with a hundred million thoughts spinning in my own head. We returned to the Wi-Fi place and started to look for a way off the island. This turned out to be frustratingly difficult. The airport in Samoa clearly stated on its website that it had several flights scheduled to depart, most of them to New Zealand, but there was no way to book them, and nothing appeared on any booking sites. We would also need to organise a first flight from American Samoa to Samoa, but this was similarly difficult to do.

With nothing working we hurried back to the ship. There were only a few hours left before it would set sail again, and there would be five long sea days before it reached Hawaii. Clearly we needed to disembark here to try and save Dea's eye, but we had so many things to organise in those few short hours. Dea went off back to the medical centre, where the staff were also trying to find us the necessary flight details, while I returned to our room to begin packing. I was a bit of a mess. Everything had fallen apart and, while the ending of my continuous circumnavigation was a side note compared to the serious situation that Dea was in, it still came as a bit of a body blow to know that the mission I'd put years of my life into was coming to such a dramatic end. The packing did not go well. I was just stuffing bits and pieces in randomly, and I had absolutely no idea what we were going to do with the bikes. And then it struck me, what if the best option was to fly to Hawaii? I wouldn't even be able to do that, because of the stupid Iranian stamp in my passport. Dea needed me, and I wouldn't even be able to go with her. Before all this I thought I was pretty good at keeping my head in a crisis, but right now I was crying.

Dea came up to the room and told me that the medical centre and front office were doing what they could to help, but they still hadn't found us any flights. The clock was ticking. It was getting perilously close to the time at which the ship was scheduled to leave, and our world was still pretty much in chaos.

We both went down to the medical centre once again, and the port agent came in to see us. All of us crowded into the doctor's room – Dea and myself, the doctor, the nurse, and the port agent. He was a large Samoan man, whose sombre face was ill-fitting with his bright red floral shirt. He was still trying his best to get new information for us, and would occasionally make and receive calls relating to our case, but he soon laid out the bare facts for us. "I'm sorry," he said, "but there is a holiday time now in American Samoa. There are no flight seats available off the island for the next four or five days, and all of the hotels are fully booked."

The seriousness of our situation was clear. Dea had a major problem with her eye and needed to get treated by a corneal specialist as soon as possible, but we were literally stuck in the middle of the

Pacific Ocean. If we got off the boat now we'd have nowhere to stay (and wild camping with a serious eye infection, not recommended) and we wouldn't be able to fly anywhere for days. Were there any other options? The nurse, who had been so nice to us throughout, suggested the only alternative was to call for an air ambulance. That would cost somewhere in the region of 50,000 dollars, and we could not be certain that our insurance would cover it, particularly as we had no insurance.

It was a dire situation, and Dea and I decided that the only thing we could really do now was to stay on board this ill-fated, godforsaken cruise. At least on the ship she could relax without having to worry about flights or arriving in a new city, and she'd have a big bed to lie in, a dark room to rest her poor eye. But boy, was it ever going to be a long five days at sea before we reached Hawaii.

After all the stress of this nightmare day, Dea retired to bed to nap and I went for a walk around the ship. I found myself back up on the sports court, mostly because it was the one place I felt confident nobody else would go, so nobody would see the tears that rolled down my cheeks. It was here that I sat and watched as the ship slipped out of the harbour and through those hills that just a few hours earlier had seemed so bright. The sky was turning dark and the long stretch of empty ocean, so lacking in corneal specialists, loomed ominously ahead. The continuity of my journey had been saved again, this time by a Samoan holiday, but under the circumstances I felt no consolation at all.

I looked around the sports court and thought of the first night, when the bright lights of Sydney had filled the view, when we had both been so happy and our future had seemed so promising. I thought of how full of joy Dea had been, throwing a basketball around, kicking goal after goal past me on the football pitch, waving her arms around in joyous celebration. How had it come to this? How could our dream have so quickly descended into this nightmare?

But there was no more time to dwell on the events of this dramatic day. I had a patient to look after.

The following days were inevitably long and difficult. Dea spent most of her time lying in bed praying her eye wouldn't burst, and every hour I administered eye drops or creams into it. After hearing that we were stuck on the ship and unable to get to a corneal specialist, the doctor from American Samoa had advised our doctor on board to prescribe antiviral and antifungal treatments alongside the antibiotics already being taken. Nobody knew what this thing was, so it seemed the strategy was simply to attack it from all possible angles. It sounded logical enough, but the number of different potions going in Dea's poor little eye only appeared to be making it look more bloodshot and unhealthy, and the spot certainly wasn't getting any smaller.

It pained me so much to see the girl that I loved going through this ordeal. It seemed so intensely unfair. This cruise was supposed to be our reward for our hard work in Australia, and I knew that Dea had been looking forward to it so much. Now it had turned into nothing more than a floating prison. I did what I could to try and make things easier – bringing food down for Dea to eat, promising her things would be okay – but the truth was I felt woefully inadequate.

We started to talk about our options for Hawaii. In another unfortunate twist we would be there on a weekend, and the medical centre told us that they were unable to book an appointment with a corneal specialist. They did manage to get an appointment with what might be the next best thing, however, and told us we would be visiting an eye doctor by the name of Dr. Chee. With the expenses from this whole episode already in the hundreds of dollar, seventy-five cents a minute for Wi-Fi no longer seemed that bad, so we googled Dr. Chee. Although he didn't specialise in corneal treatment it was at least listed among his many areas of expertise. We hoped he might well have seen something like Dea's condition before, at the very least, given that he was seventy-nine years old, with a total of fifty-four years' experience.

Although Dr. Chee's experience was certainly considerable, I was concerned that he might be past his best, and we were both concerned about the cost of American medical treatment. Clearly this was not a problem that was going to go away quickly, and Dea was probably going to need long-term treatment and monitoring, with corneal replacement surgery also having been mentioned. In reality she was going to have to fly out of Hawaii, either to Vancouver, or more likely home to Denmark. The question was, would I be going with her? By now Dea had calmed down, no longer distraught from the immediacy of meeting with a doctor talking of over-the-top worst-case scenarios, and she assured me that she would be alright to go on alone. If, for example, she flew to Vancouver, she would be able to stay with my friend, Gabi, who I knew would look after her, until I arrived five days later. If she were to fly home to Denmark she would be surrounded by friends and family who would of course take the very best care of her. She might even then be better in a month, and able to fly back to Vancouver, by which time I might have a new passport and a chance to continue with our journey exactly as planned. But I wasn't so sure.

"I don't want to leave you, Dea."

"Chris, I know how important this journey is to you."

"You're the most important thing to me. If you want me to come with you, I will."

"I know Chris, but I really don't want to be the reason for you ruining your trip. I'll be okay, seriously."

Dea's spirits were improving with every day that her eye didn't explode, and as the week went on she began to venture out of the room from time to time. One evening we went up and watched the sunset, on another we celebrated crossing the equator, one time we even managed some games of table tennis (which I won, by the way; I take my victories where I can). But it was never very long before she had to retire back to bed. Every morning I checked Dea's swollen eye hoping to see some improvement, but the spot just never got smaller. Finally, having watched an extraordinary number of movies (and concluded with some degree of certainty that George Clooney really isn't much of an actor) the five sea days were over and we reached Hawaii, ready to face our fate, and placing it firmly in the hands of a seventy-nine-year-old Chinese man.

But before we could get off the ship it was necessary for every single person on board to meet with a United States border official. They actually came onto the boat, and we all had to file through into one of the lounges in order to pass the inspection. Of course I wasn't at all sure that I was going to be allowed to enter the States, but I hoped that I'd have a better chance in this relatively informal border procedure than I might otherwise have. There were four or five officials flicking through passports and I did my best to join the line of the one who looked to be checking the least thoroughly. The previous night I'd folded out every page of my passport except the one with the Iranian visa, in the hope that this page would not fall open during the inspection, and now my moment of truth had arrived as I stood before a stern looking man. He flicked through my passport and to my dismay his finger soon landed on the Iranian visa. I held my breath for a moment, but he soon moved past it and continued to flick through while asking me some general questions about my travels. Then to my great relief he gave me an entry stamp and welcomed me to Hawaii.

I was very happy that I would be able to at least accompany Dea to the doctor. We got off and walked the short distance through downtown Honolulu to the clinic of Dr. Chee. We arrived with time to spare, which was lucky, because Dea had to fill in a large number of different forms, detailing all of the medication she'd been taking, which was a lot. After all the forms were completed she was allowed through into a worryingly dilapidated room to wait for Dr. Chee. A little while later he showed up and, apparently not having had the time to check the forms Dea had patiently filled in, he asked what was wrong and what medications she'd been taking. He was a small Chinese man, bald, with sort of shrivelled, wrinkled skin, you know how people get when they're almost eighty. Dea answered his questions and he quickly examined her eye. With a shake of his head he delivered his verdict.

"You need to go home," he sighed. "You need to go home."

120 dollars well spent.

While Dr. Chee's expert opinion wasn't ideal, it did seem that Dea somehow welcomed the news. As we walked back to the ship it seemed like at least some weight was off her shoulders, as if she'd now been given permission to go back to Denmark and get this thing sorted out properly. The doctors there would really know what they were doing, and with all her friends and family around her she would have a settled base. Dr. Chee had confirmed it was likely to take months to heal, whatever demonic little being it was that had so rudely invaded her eye. There was no question that going home was the best option for Dea now. But what about me? What about my trip? Somehow, without either of us actually saying it out loud, it had been mutually agreed that I was staying. That I'd given too much to this project to abandon it now, and that Dea did not want to be the reason for that abandonment. So the plan we now agreed on was for Dea to fly to Denmark, and for me to get to Denmark as fast as I could by bicycle and boat, which, considering we were pretty much on the opposite side of the world from Denmark, was a bit of a challenge. Still, cycling across Canada didn't look that hard, and I already knew of at least one cruise ship heading across the Atlantic that could get me back to Europe by September, and I desperately hoped I'd be able to find one earlier than that.

After a quick bite to eat on the ship I grabbed my laptop and we headed back into Honolulu to look for a place to use Wi-Fi This wasn't as easy as I'd hoped, and the streets were more run-down and filled with homeless people than I would have ever expected to see in the United States. But finally we located a crepe shop with Wi-Fi, where the young waiter even gave Dea a free coffee, a moment of light in an otherwise dark day. There were once again many things for us to organise, most urgent of which was a flight for Dea. This turned out to be a monumentally difficult task. We tried first to book one for seven that evening, but the booking did not go through. We had to wait four hours for this failure to be confirmed, by which time it was too late to try and book again for that flight. So we tried to book a different flight, but again it failed. I phoned the booking agent and, after a great deal of time spent on hold, eventually found out that the problem was that my bank in England was blocking the payment.

Using Dea's card we finally succeeded in making a booking after about nine hours of trying (no exaggeration), on a flight that would leave Honolulu at seven the next morning. As it happened the ship was spending the night docked in Hawaii, so Dea could get a few hours of sleep, much deserved after another extremely stressful day.

After a few hours of rest we awoke sometime between three and four in the morning. After a quick breakfast of smuggled food, I escorted Dea and her backpack down the gangway of the ship, and she stepped off the MS Noordam for the last time. The great hulk of the sleeping ship dwarfed us as we walked along the dock, Dea no doubt feeling some relief to be leaving the cursed boat behind. Through a cold hangar we walked and out into the street, where a taxi sat idling, ready and waiting. Dea loaded her backpack into the back and then asked the driver to wait for a moment. Then it was time for the tears to roll again as I held Dea in my arms and did not want to let go. This was a gut-wrenching, totally unfair, absolutely not-in-the-script what-is-going-on-with-this-crappy-movie goodbye. It was the worst of goodbyes. But it was goodbye. Dea slipped out of my arms and into the cab. It drove off into the night, and I was alone once more.

Progress Report
Honolulu, April 2016

1. Circumnavigate the planet

The Eiffel Tower is at a longitude of: 2.3° E.
Honolulu is at: 157.9° W.
199.8° out of 360° around the planet.
(55.5 % of the way around.)

2. Do so using only my bicycle and boats

Mori: 90.3° E. Honolulu: 157.9° W.
111.8° out of 360° around the planet.
(31.1 % of the way around.)

3. Pass through antipodal points

Starting to think maybe this isn't such a great way to ensure a circumnavigation after all.

4. Visit all of the inhabited continents

Hawaii makes four.

5. Cycle at least 100,000 kilometres

48,612 kilometres completed. Just the 51,388 to go.

6. Cycle in 100 countries

Forty-seven down, fifty-three more needed.

7. Return with more money than I start with

After pedicabbing, about ten grand to the good.

PART TWO

HONOLULU TO HALIFAX

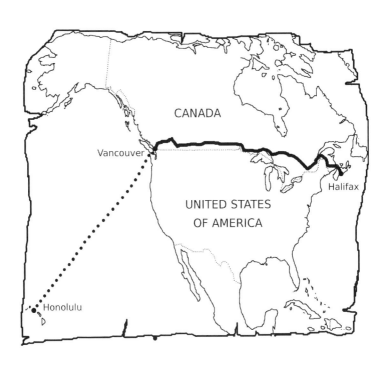

4

Vancouver, Canada
1st May 2016

I awoke for the last time on board the MS Noordam. It was five in the morning and under normal circumstances I'd have rolled over and gone back to sleep, but knowing where we were I climbed out from under the duvet and pulled on some clothes. I hurried up to the top deck at the front of the boat. The sky ahead was a deep, dark orange, glowing like the embers of a fire behind the black, silhouetted shape of mountains. There was no one else around. As twilight continued the ship closed in on land and I spied the outline of the tower blocks and skyscrapers of a major city, although they looked tiny in comparison to those grand mountains. As the light increased I picked out the heavily forested area that I remembered as Stanley Park and as we manoeuvred around it I saw the huge Lions Gate Bridge reaching out across the water, linking city with mountains. I looked on as the ship continued straight under the mighty bridge, and I twisted my head up to watch in awe. As I brought it down again I could clearly see the city. The sun was just rising over the mountains to my left, and the skyscrapers glistened, shining turquoise in this grand light as we made our final approach. I'd made it at last to Vancouver, and sailing into it was as magnificent an ending as departing Sydney had been a beginning, minus one thing of course. I felt a tremendously empty sadness that Dea was not with me to share this moment. But at least she was now in a safe place.

Upon her arrival in Copenhagen she'd been rushed to the best eye doctors in Denmark, who had finally been able to correctly diagnose her condition. Apparently, after barraging her eye with antibacterial, antiviral, and antifungal eye drops, it turned out that her infection was caused by an amoeba. So she was now taking antiamoebic eye drops, and the yellow spot was finally starting to shrink. Even so, the doctors had warned her that she might well need up to six months of treatment, and potentially she could still require corneal replacement surgery after that. I felt so bad that I wasn't with her to comfort her through this, but I knew that her family in Copenhagen was looking after her, and as I stepped off the MS Noordam for the last time I knew that my only task was to get back to her as fast as I could.

I'd been to Vancouver several times before and I had a good friend to stay with in the city. Gabi, a French Canadian girl who I'd worked with tree planting during my first long trip in 2011 put me up on her sofa bed for a few days. It was good to spend time with a familiar face and Vancouver was an ideal place for me to detox from the cruise. With its parks and beaches, and the mountains and forests that look down over it, it's a very picturesque city. It's also a young, hip city, with a lot of millennials riding bicycles around, with such a good vibe that I would probably rank it as my second favourite city in the world, after Barcelona. So it was a good base for me for a few days while I sorted out a long to-do list. Dea's bike needed to be shipped back to Denmark, and my bike needed quite a bit of repair work before it was going to be ready for a 7,000 kilometre cross-country ride, but it was what I was going to do when I got to the other side of the continent that was the most pressing issue. Having just got off a cruise that was such a terrible, horrifying, unenjoyable experience, the last thing I wanted to do was to book another cruise. That is the logic of a masochistic madman, obviously. But what choice did I have? I had made a promise to the girl that I loved that I would get back to Europe as quickly as possible (by bicycle and boat) and the simple reality was that the quickest way to do that was by cruise ship (or global ferries, as I was starting to think of them). I was desperate to be on one sooner than September, and after a fair bit of searching I found one, the Queen Mary 2, that sailed from New York to Southampton in late July. The only slight problem was that with my Iranian stamp I very likely could not get to New York. There was a solution, however, provided by a tremendously helpful travel agent named Deanna in West Vancouver, who arranged for me to be able to board the ship during its scheduled stop in Halifax, Nova Scotia. It was a perfect solution. I now had just eleven weeks to cycle across Canada, and the race was on.

It was a beautiful spring morning and the ride out of Vancouver was an absolute pleasure. I was able to follow shoreline bicycle paths all of the way around the city centre towards Stanley Park. It was a Saturday and there were lots of people out enjoying the sunshine, jogging, walking, or riding bicycles. Some road cyclists went fast in the road, others cruised along with me in our own dedicated bicycle lane. In the distance snow-topped mountains across the bay set a magnificent backdrop, and the atmosphere was just wonderful. I went on through the big forest that is Stanley Park and crossed over the Lions Gate Bridge that a few days earlier I'd been sailing under, into North Vancouver. From there I turned west into West Vancouver (how did they come up with these names?) and continued until I reached a place called Horseshoe Bay. There I made a ceremonial stop, and walked down to the harbour. I bent down to touch the waters of the Pacific Ocean for the last time. The cold water on my fingers marked my furthest west. From now on, the only way was east.

Beyond Horseshoe Bay I was on a road that rose and fell as it wound along the coast, through scenery that was achingly beautiful. The blues of the sky and the sea were intense, and were complimented perfectly by the green of the conifers and the vibrant yellow and purple of wild flowers in full bloom.

That first night I made camp in the forest and became terribly worried about bears as I went about finding a place to sleep in amongst the big evergreen trees. As I sat and ate my dinner I looked around nervously in all directions, my mind playing tricks on me and imagining tree stumps and shadows to be bears. What was it that Sasha had said to me way back in Siberia when I'd cycled there in August 2014? "Bears might attack people, but only in early spring or late autumn when they are hungry." In August such words had been intended to calm my fears, and they had. Remembering them now, in early spring, I found them less reassuring.

I made it through the first night unmauled, and continued on uphill to Whistler, a picturesque ski resort town surrounded by snowy mountains and criss-crossed by bicycle trails. I followed these trails around lakes and past wooden chalets amid the fresh mountain air and I thought to myself, *'people actually live here,'* and I couldn't believe it, to think of some of the poverty I'd seen in other parts of the world and the horrid places some people called home. Whistler seemed like a perfect place to live. Or at least it did until I turned a corner and got a bit of a surprise. I was about to go down a short downhill section when ahead of me I noticed two black bears, a mother and her cub, sauntering along the trail in my direction. It was lucky that I'd spotted them when I did, for had I started on that little downhill I might have been bumping into them, which, as I under-stood it, was not advisable. Instead I froze on the spot and stared at the magnificent creatures. It was slightly worrying that they were walking towards me, and I briefly wondered if the thing to do here wasn't to turn around and cycle back the way that I'd come as fast as possible. That seemed a cowardly act though, and going the wrong way wasn't conducive to getting back to Dea, and before I had the time to do it the mother looked up and noticed me. I stood my ground. For a second or two we held each others' stare, and there was a brief tense moment when it wasn't clear who would back down first. I tried to remember what to do in the event of a bear attack. I knew that you were meant to behave differently for black bears and grizzlies. With one of them you should play dead, the other you should bop on the nose, but I couldn't remember which was which. But it didn't matter in the end, because these particular bears had no interest in attacking me, and just wandered off into a nearby cul-de-sac. I cycled on, thinking perhaps Whistler wasn't the perfect place to live after all. Sure the views are great, high living standards too, but the neighbours... bit too bear-like for me.

For a few days I continued on through snowy mountain scenery that was so breathtakingly beautiful that I struggled to comprehend that it was real. Crystal white peaks and mirror-like lakes, the smell of pine, there was so much to like about Canada. But one thing ruined it – the traffic. As lines of oversized four-wheel-drive pick-up trucks and motorhomes the size of buses zoomed past me I was reminded of my first long bicycle trip through North America, and the way that it had shaped my way of thinking and had led me into living this life completely devoid of motor vehicles. Indeed, it was near this very spot that I had last ridden in a car of my own volition, almost five years earlier when I'd needed to use them for my work as a tree plant- er. Back then there had been an obvious contradiction I'd found in the great outdoors of this continent, that I'd really struggled with. The magnificent nature here was an example of the incredible beauty of the world, but the lifestyle of the people appeared in so many ways to be stuck on an unstoppable course against it. I was so shocked by the size of the motor vehicles, and the affluent lifestyles of many here, that it led me to become something akin to an envir- onmentalist during that first trip. I never intended to become like that, and I hated the idea of preaching about it, but more often than not my conversations with people would stray onto the topic, with me saying annoying things like, "Do you know that the average American emits twenty-five tonnes of CO_2 into the atmosphere each year, compared with a global average of just four tonnes?" and, "Infinite growth on a planet of finite resources is impossible," and, "We can't go on living unsustainably, the clue is in the word. It's not sustainable, either we change the system or the system's going to break."

And the reaction of the people I spoke to would generally always be one of agreement. It would always start with "You're right..." which was of course nice to hear, but it would almost always end with, "...but I need my car." And in most cases that was actually true.

North America is built around the personal motor vehicle and I could understand that in such an environment people leading busy lives benefited greatly from the convenience provided by cars. It was simply a way of life for everyone here, so steadfastly ingrained within society and within individuals that it was impossible for these people, these good, honest, hard-working people, to seriously conceive of any alternative.

After a while I stopped having these kind of conversations. My own views hadn't changed, but I realised that most people already knew about climate change, they knew about resource depletion, they knew that driving their car everywhere was bad for the planet, but they were going to do it anyway. They had to go to work, their kids had to get to school, they needed their cars and nothing I was going to say was going to be able to change that. So I stopped talking about the issue, realising that I wasn't responsible for anyone else other than me. I decided that I would just take accountability for my own actions, and simply practice what I'd preached. I would live my life completely without cars. I would make that *my* way of life.

It wasn't just the environmental impacts that turned me off cars, in fact it isn't even the main reason I don't use them. They're also expensive to run, and not exactly the best way to maintain a healthy lifestyle (in North America I had been shocked to find that they not only have drive-though restaurants, but also drive-through pharmacies, so you don't even need to get out of your car between picking up your Big Mac and your obesity medicine), but my strongest instinct against cars came about by how dangerous they are. In the time it has taken you to read this far through this chapter a child somewhere in the world has almost certainly lost their life because of a car. And if you stop to think about that, to really think about who that child might have been, what their hopes and dreams were for the future, how much life was just stolen from them by that car, if you really pause and imagine that for a few moments, well, by the time you're done another child will probably have been killed. The world accepts this loss of life as collateral damage because the world needs its cars, but as I pedalled along with so much time to think I built an imaginary alternative in my head. A different world, one where the transport system was based around bicycles and trains. I even thought about how it could happen, if I were only allowed to be President of the World some day. I'd start by lowering every speed limit for motor vehicles, which would have the double effect of instantly saving lives, and making driving a whole lot less attractive. Then I'd make an extensive and efficient network of railway lines, with trains that could easily accommodate bicycles. In this world short journeys would be made on foot or bicycle, long ones by train. Of course there would still be some good reasons for having a few motor vehicles, emergency vehicles for example, but how much quicker they would be able to get where they needed to go with the streets no longer clogged with traffic. And how much nicer this world seemed in my imagination, with less pollution, less stress, a world full of happier, healthier people, and fewer funerals. But this was always just a utopian vision. I was not ever going to be President of the World, and there wasn't much I could do to bring my imaginary world to life. But there was one thing I could do. I was passionately against cars, and it didn't matter if I was the only person in the world who felt this way, it was what I believed in. And that is why I stopped using them.

Over the intervening years of travelling under my own power, my opinions on motor vehicles had only hardened. Moving through a world so dependent on cars only added to my own satisfaction in knowing that, wherever I was, I had got there with my own legs, and that was one of the many reasons why I was so determined to make it all of the way around the planet by bike and boat. It was for the challenge, yes, and to see the world in a most rewarding way, but it was also to demonstrate what it's possible to do without motorised transportation if you really try. And that was also why I wasn't allowing myself any side trips, as other adventurers have done when undertaking long human-powered journeys. I did not want to break my continuous line for anything, because it was something I felt so strongly about – if I wanted to get somewhere, I was going to get there with my own legs.

Of course I knew that there had to be exceptions to that rule. When Dea really needed me with her, I had been ready to get on a plane with her in a heartbeat. Some things *are* more important. But if that had happened, if I had flown out of Samoa that afternoon, there would have been no flying back again, no carrying on like nothing had happened.

The cars and motorhomes continued to whiz past me on the Canadian highway, stealing my concentration away from the mountains. I knew that I was going to miss Dea so much during the months that it was going to take me to get back to her. But I also knew that she, more than anyone else, understood me, and understood why it was that I lived this way, why it was that I was undertaking this seemingly crazy challenge. We both needed to be patient now, but my bicycle had got me this far, and I knew that it was all that I really needed to get me back to her again.

5

Kamloops, Canada
12th May 2016

One cold morning I arrived in Kamloops, a town with a special meaning for me. Back in 2011 I'd spent three months working as a tree planter, and it was Kamloops that had been our urban base. Most of the time we were working and camping in the woods, but two days out of seven we'd head back to Kamloops for our days off. So I knew the place well enough and I particularly enjoyed returning to Real Canadian Superstore, a giant supermarket that perhaps constituted my happiest memories from Kamloops. I went inside and was so excited to be back that I spent forty dollars and almost couldn't fit everything on the bike.

But then it was time to really roll down memory lane, or memory hill as it were, seeing as Kamloops is situated in a big valley. It was *that* hill, which took me past *that* bus stop and *that* motel, until I was drawn almost magnetically to turn down *that* road to *that* creek. I walked, as I so often had five years earlier, along a trail beside the creek on which you could almost leave the city behind. It was a nice place full of trees and birds and nature. It looked just the same as I remembered. It even smelt the same. It almost began to feel the same. But it didn't. I could remember the feelings I'd had here, but I looked upon them now with a fresh perspective. The summer of 2011 was when Rachael, the Canadian girl I'd fallen for on my first trip, had left me with a broken heart. And this was the place I had come every week of that intense period of my life, seeking some sort of refuge from the torment. How strange it felt to be back, after so many years, and to remember those emotions. But more than that it made me appreciate how lucky I was to have found Dea, someone I loved so much, someone I dared to trust wouldn't hurt me like that. I didn't need to stay here any longer. It was time to get back to the road, back towards Dea.

Beyond Kamloops there was a break from the big mountains and I struggled to find anywhere to sleep as the land became more agricultural. I eventually found an unused field and had a pretty good night down at the bottom of it, before waking up to a beautiful morning. I got out of the tent, stretched, then walked away from my campsite to answer the call of nature. I was in behind some trees and bushes, well hidden from the road, so I had no concerns as I went through the routine I like to refer to as 'digging a hole'. I'd never been disturbed during this private time before, except on one memorable occasion when a fox came and stared at me, which was probably more memorable for the fox than for me. But on this particular morning I was startled to see a man walking through the field not far from me, fortunately just after I'd pulled my trousers up.

"Morning," I said, trying to act casual.

"Hi. How's it going?" came the young man's jovial response.

"Good. I'm just camping here. I'm bike touring. Do you live here?"

"Yeah, I live next door. I've just been for a walk up the hill over there. It's fine you're here. I'm not the landowner, but I know him. He'll be alright with it."

The conversation was going surprisingly well, and I was pleased he hadn't asked me what I was doing coming out of the bushes a hundred metres from my tent, but apparently I'd been the one to take him by surprise.

"I thought you were a bear!" he said, making me rather relieved he wasn't a hunter. Then he went on: "Actually, you should watch out. There is a bear den down there." With that he pointed to a spot that could not have been more than fifty metres from my tent. My tent which was full of the food I hadn't thought necessary to remove the night before.

"Just right there?" I asked.

"Yeah, three brown bears living there. Have a nice day. See you."

This was an interesting turn of events, and what was particularly interesting about it was that the stage was now perfectly set for the most rapid taking down of a tent and evacuating a field that the world has ever seen. I folded up the poles faster than ever. I clipped my bags back onto my bike with an efficiency quite unlike me. It was not yet seven in the morning and yet this, it already seemed, was going to be a tough Friday the 13th to survive.

Within ten kilometres I had arrived in the small town of Chase. I wanted to hide in the library here but it was not yet open, so first I sat down in a park and decided to go for a swim in a lake. I knew this was a bit of a gamble on a Friday the 13th, but I was quietly confident there were no sharks, piranhas, alligators, or other dangerous creatures in the lake and, what was more, I thought it less likely I'd bump into any brown bears underwater. So I stripped down and dived in. It was ice cold. Hypothermia seemed likely. I got out again, put my clothes back on, and told myself not to be so damn stupid.

I went to the library to warm up. In fact I was visiting the library a lot these days, for I had myself an unexpected goal. Not only was I aiming to cycle across Canada, but also to be the first person to cycle across Canada and visit a library in every single town along the way, without reading any books. My purpose of course was to use the Wi-Fi to connect with Denmark, and Canada's excellent system of libraries meant Dea and I were able to keep in touch, and talk often online.

Thankfully Dea's eye was responding well to the treatment and she was in good spirits. It was such a relief after the ordeal of the cruise, and to keep the positivity levels high we began to discuss our future plans. For me that involved getting to Mori as soon as possible, the little town in China that I'd made the official restart point for my bike-and-boats circumnavigation attempt after I'd been forced to use a motor vehicle at the Mongolian border back in

August 2014. Coming so close to breaking my continuous journey again on the cruise had only reaffirmed just how important this was to me, and how easily things could go wrong. Getting to Mori would make me perhaps the first person ever to go all of the way around the world in one non-stop journey without using any motorised propulsion on land, and I wanted to make getting back there the main priority, before anything else could go wrong. My other goals, to visit all of the continents and one hundred countries, could wait, could be completed after Mori. And Dea also thought heading east was a great idea. She'd often talked of wanting to cycle in Turkey and through Central Asia, and this new plan would give her the chance. It was a terrible shame that she wasn't with me in North America, but I was a hundred percent sure our time to cycle together would come yet. Talking about this exciting new dream helped to kept both of our spirits up.

But I couldn't hide in the library all day, so I left after a couple of hours and cycled on the Trans-Canada Highway for about fifty nerve-racking kilometres until I arrived in Salmon Arm. I remembered how another girl at tree planting, Dani, had told me that they were talking about building a Walmart in this smallish town, her home town, and how it had divided opinion. Some had wanted it, some had not. Now, five years on, I cycled past the 'Welcome to Salmon Arm' sign and was met almost immediately with a massive brand spanking new Walmart. I thought I'd better stop.

I did a bit of shopping and then came back outside to my bicycle to load on the quality merchandise that I'd just purchased, when two teenagers of First Nation ethnicity came along. They were a boy and a girl and they were pushing a shopping trolley. They were both a little fat and, if the way they were staggering along giggling was anything to go by, a lot drunk. I was naturally delighted when they stopped to talk with me.

"Excuse me," started the boy, who seemed a little camp and quite harmless. "Do you work here?"

Now this was an intriguing question. I certainly did not think that I looked like a Walmart employee at that moment, with my dirty second hand clothes and heavily loaded bicycle. I told him that I did not.

"Oh. Do you shop here?"

"Yes. I have just shopped here, yes."

"Do you live here then?"

I was not sure if he was still referring to Walmart, or more generally Salmon Arm, or perhaps just Canada, but it didn't matter, because the answer was the same.

"Where are you from then?" asked the girl.

"England."

"India?"

"No, England."

"Do you want a shot? Let's give him a shot!" The boy was excited, and began to rummage in a bag in the trolley. They really did seem like very friendly drunk teenagers.

"No, no. It's okay, thank you."

"Okay. It was nice meeting you. We're off to steal stuff now. We're gonna steal from Walmart. See you."

Having survived another Friday the 13th my composure returned, and over the next few days I climbed confidently into the Rockies. I went past Mount Revelstoke National Park, through Glacier National Park, and on into Yoho National Park. As you may have guessed from the number of national parks, the scenery here was consistently breathtaking. It was so consistently breathtaking, in fact, that in these areas it is sometimes necessary to close ones eyes every now and again so as to avoid passing out from a lack of breath. You know what I'm talking about here – blue skies, green trees, grey rocks, white snow, and bright yellow flowers lining the road. It was like cycling through a giant three-dimensional postcard.

In Yoho National Park I made a worthwhile detour to visit Emerald Lake. It was a pretty lake, with snowy peaks all around it and a turquoise sheen to its surface that had clearly been a major factor in the name giving process. I was so pleased with this detour, in fact, that I considered making another. I'd heard about another stunning lake hidden in the depths of the national park, Lake O'Hara, that limits the number of tourists that visit it by only allowing a certain number on daily shuttle buses to it. It was too early in the year for the buses to run, and I hadn't got a ticket, and of course I couldn't use a bus without ruining my life, but I'd heard that it was also possible to hike to the lake. A long hike to a hidden lake sounded like a tremendous adventure, so back on the main road I stopped at the small community of Field to make enquiries at the visitor centre there. Unfortunately my hopes were soon shut down by the visitor centre staff, who told me that there was too much snow up on the trail for any hikers to get through.

I went outside and sat on a bench to eat some lunch. I was disappointed to miss out on Lake O'Hara, but this stop at the visitor centre was not destined to be a complete waste of time. Just as I was about to leave I noticed that another touring bicycle, a very small one, was now leaning against the building. A moment later the owner came out. It was a short girl dressed in pink. She smiled when she saw me, then immediately explained, with a voice working at one hundred miles per hour, all the trouble she was having trying to cycle across Canada.

"My front wheel keeps coming loose, I don't know why, my bike just keeps on breaking, a creepy man was harassing me, I ran out of water, I saw a bear, I nearly got hit by a truck, I lost all my food, people keep refusing to cycle with me, or they agree to cycle with me and then abandon me, I don't know why they do that..." she paused very briefly for a breath, "...so, do you want to cycle with me?"

I had just met Vivian.

Field, Canada
16th May 2016

Vivian was a petite girl in her twenties who looked Asian but sounded North American, the result of being born and bred in Ontario to parents from China and Hong Kong. Her goal, she explained, was to cycle right across Canada from Vancouver to St. John's, Newfoundland. I thought she was doing quite well so far, considering she had previously never really ridden a bike before.

"Why are you going all the way to Newfoundland?" I asked.

"Well, I thought if I'm gonna do it, I might as well do it properly," she said, before adding without the slightest hint of irony that she had just taken a lift in a car for ten kilometres after losing all of her food. She looked (and sounded) like she was quite hungry, so I gave her some of my food to eat while I fixed her front wheel for her.

Seeing as Vivian and I were going the same way I thought it made sense to go along together for a while. From first impressions it seemed like she complained a lot, but she also smiled a lot, and cycling with her would, if nothing else, be a lot more entertaining than cycling alone. She told me that she had already had several other cyclists turn down her pleas to accompany her, including a brother and sister cycling across the country together who had actually agreed to cycle with her, but then rode off quickly never to be seen again.

"I'm very slow," Vivian said to me several times. "Are you sure you want to cycle with me? I'm very slow." Well, I'd never yet in all my years met a cycle tourist who rode as slow as me, so I hoped she'd live up to that promise.

We began to cycle, with me just in front, and it dawned on me how perfect this actually was. It sounded like Vivian was having a real hard time of it and maybe I could help her out. Maybe this was going to give my ride a bit of purpose. Hell, maybe this was it, maybe this was the big plot twist for the sequel. Yes, yes, I could see it now. Vivian (Lucy Liu) and I (Ryan Gosling) would form a quirky and unlikely friendship as we made our way together across this huge country, with me helping her to overcome every obstacle and finally reach her goal of St. John's. Yes, that was surely it, the plot of the sequel was going to be all about that, with Vivian finally standing triumphantly at the end of the country looking poignantly out to sea. Wow, maybe I wasn't even going to be in the final scene of this movie.

All went well for a few kilometres, until we arrived at the first climb, and behind me I saw Vivian immediately step off her bike and begin to push. "The hills are too steep for me," she said. "I have to push."

I couldn't believe it. Had she been doing this all the way since Vancouver? I stopped and checked her bike, and saw that she was in completely the wrong gear. "You're in completely the wrong gear," were my exact words, I believe, and so I offered to ride her bike and put it in the right gear for her. This was an offer I had not really thought through, and I laughed as I tried to cycle the miniature bicycle up the steep hill, flicking at the gears and looking for all the world like a clown as I did so.

My efforts were somewhat in vain as, even in the lowest gear, Vivian cycled the bike for only a short time before resorting to walking and pushing again. I went on ahead and then stood and waited for her at the top, secretly delighted to have finally found myself a hapless sidekick slower than me. When Vivian caught up to me we paused for a moment so she could catch her breath and I looked over her bike.

"You really should have a mirror," I told her. "It's so useful for staying safe in traffic."

"I had one, but I threw it away. I threw a lot of stuff away."

"Okay. Well, you're very bright at least."

"I don't think so," replied my new companion, screwing up her face. "If I was bright I wouldn't be doing this trip."

"No Vivian, I meant your hi-vis jacket."

After a lot more cycling/walking we ended the day making camp at the turn-off for Lake O'Hara, where we found a great spot in a clearing with views of snowy peaks. At least *I* thought it was a great spot. Vivian seemed extremely concerned about the risk being presented by wildlife, particularly bears.

"Oh come on Vivian," I said, "there's no reason to worry about bears!"

I was putting on a bit of a brave face. Secretly I was just pleased that I would no longer have to outrun a bear, I would only have to outrun a Vivian.

"Before now I've been camping out the front of gas stations," Vivian revealed.

"Are you serious?"

"Yes. I thought it was safer."

"Well there aren't any gas stations around here, but I'm sure we'll be fine."

Vivian wasn't happy, but she nevertheless began to put up her tent and unpack her things. I did the same, somewhat faster, and then started to cook us dinner on my stove. We had to use my stove, because Vivian's stove was one of the many things she had thrown away in order to save weight. Then, as I stirred the pasta in the pot, I heard a sudden cry echo around the clearing: "Oh, look, here's my food! I didn't lose it after all!"

Vivian came and joined me and we ate our dinner. She was still looking around nervously for wild animals, but she seemed happy about the day, as if relieved to have found some company at last. I asked her why it was that she was making this trip.

"My grandfather has dementia. I want to raise awareness of dementia, and I also want to raise money to send my grandfather to Hong Kong to see his brother who he hasn't seen for thirty years."

It was undoubtedly a good cause, but I felt like there was more to her trip than that. It wasn't long before Vivian revealed what it was.

"I'm also going through a separation from my husband."

"You're married?" I asked, surprised.

"Yeah, but we got married too soon. It's not a good situation. This is just something I need to do, I think, to regain some confidence. It's really hard. My husband wants me to go home. My family want me to go home. Nobody is supporting me, but I need to do this."

It seemed to me that completing this trip would give Vivian more confidence and self-belief, help her to find out who she was and what she wanted from life. My resolve to help her grew stronger.

I woke up the next morning to the pained cry of, "Oh my God! A spider!" soon followed by, "Ahh! What is that?" and finally, "Eww! Is that a slug?" I rushed over to help poor Vivian, by which I mean I laid in my tent and ignored her. I suppose these were not the kind of critters that one usually had to deal with while camping on gas station forecourts, but I figured she'd find a way to cope. The wild back country was not Vivian's natural setting. She frequently described herself as a typical 'Toronto-girl' which was interesting because she actually hailed from Sudbury, a four hour drive from Toronto. Nevertheless, she was a city girl, plucked out of her usual setting and thrust into the scary and difficult world of long distance cycle touring. It would understandably take a little while to adapt.

We cycled on together into Banff National Park and rode along the Bow Valley Parkway, a less frequented small road that runs parallel to the main highway through thick forest. Information boards at the start of the road reminded us that this was bear country, as if we needed any reminding. Another cyclist, heading the other way, had told us she'd been held up by a grizzly around here. By which I should clarify, I do not mean that a grizzly pointed a gun at her and demanded cash, but that a grizzly bear was not something she had wanted to cycle past. I wouldn't have minded seeing one though. It was a grey day with the clouds blocking out the mountain views so I would have appreciated having something interesting to look at, safe in the knowledge I could cycle faster than Vivian. But no bears showed themselves, so I instead entertained myself by chatting with my new friend. She was an interesting person indeed. On the one hand she came across as, and I'll use her word here, 'scatter-brained', and yet on the other revealing that she had run her own business, and run marathons, and one cannot help but admire anyone who can cycle through the Rocky Mountains pushing up every hill.

The day passed quite uneventfully, until at ten to eight in the evening we came to an open road barrier and a sign declaring that this road was closed to all traffic after eight. We guessed this must be because of wildlife and so we decided to stop and go off to camp in the forest. Technically this was illegal, what with us being in a national park, but the campsites were still closed for the season so we actually had little choice in the matter.

I found a good place to get in and began to push my bike into the trees, with Vivian following. Just then I heard a car coming along what had been an almost completely empty road. I instinctively quickened my pace to avoid being seen, but this was an utterly futile act because Vivian was dawdling along behind me in a bright orange hi-vis vest. I heard the car slow to a stop and looked back to see the white vehicle with green stripe running down its side. It was a park warden. "Are you serious?!" I said aloud, turning my bike around and pushing back to the road. "What are the odds?!"

The warden got out of the car and told us that we were not allowed to be camping in here. I pointed out that the campground was shut and the road ahead was closing at eight. It seemed fair enough, we really didn't have anywhere else to go. "You've got three minutes to get through that barrier," he said, "and you'd better make your way to Banff tonight."

The warden was a bit of an ass, but we'd been caught red handed, fair enough, best get on with it I thought, but Vivian continued to remonstrate. This, believe it or not, did not help the situation, and the man told us that he would surely have fined us or sent us to court had we been caught with our tents up.

Although we now needed to cycle another twenty kilometres in the rain my mood was soon improved when we saw some elk grazing at the side of the road. Life really wasn't so bad. I hoped we might get away with just going on a bit and finding another place to sneak off and hide, but the terrain became less inviting for it, and I was naturally worried about being caught. Those fears only increased when the warden's car appeared again behind us. There was nothing for it. He was following us to make sure we left. I worried about Vivian's mood now. I'd hoped to make life better for her, but this situation – cycling in the rain at nine o'clock at night with no idea where we would sleep, while being pursued by an overzealous park warden who took his job just a teensy bit too seriously – was far from the ideal picture of cycle touring bliss I'd have liked to have painted.

We finally made it to the end of the Bow Valley Parkway and ducked under the barrier to rejoin the Trans-Canada Highway, leaving our park warden friend sitting in his car watching us wave goodbye. We were now just a few kilometres from the town of Banff, but neither of us could afford to stay in accommodation there, and finding a place to sleep was our top priority in the fading light. At least we had a segregated cycle path all to ourselves, and when this veered away from the highway into the forest we had to take our chance. With no possibility of any warden cars following us here I guided us off the path and into the ever-darkening forest. It was not ideal, but it was going to have to do. I pitched my tent and slept soundly, feeling exhausted but relieved to have made it. Vivian, as she would tell me the next morning, spent the whole night lying there wide awake with a whistle between her lips, can of bear spray in one hand, hunting knife in the other.

We woke again at first light. Or at least I did, I don't think Vivian had actually slept. Had I known she was so well prepared to ambush any unwanted creature that should intrude upon our campsite I probably wouldn't have worried so much about being discovered by the park warden. But as I didn't know about Vivian's array of self-defence weapons I was still worried about being caught camping, and I got us up before six in the morning. Vivian didn't need much encouragement to get her tent down and to get out of those woods, mind you. I've never seen such a look of relief as she rejoined the cycle path and sped away to safety.

The path led us into the small town of Banff where we stopped briefly to admire another herd of wild elk that were grazing at the side of the road. They weren't at all bothered by the traffic, because there wasn't any. It was very early in the morning, it was absolutely freezing, and I was worried that we weren't going to find anywhere on the quiet streets of Banff to warm ourselves. But luckily I was wrong about this, for there before us, like the great Canadian beacon of hope that it is, stood a 24-hour Tim Hortons.

Tim Hortons, if you have never been fortunate enough to set foot in this great country, is a true Canadian institution, and when I use the word 'institution' please understand that I really just mean 'fast food chain'. It is something of a cross between McDonald's and Starbucks, I think. To be honest this was only the second time I'd been in one. I'm not a big fan of such places, but under the circumstances the warmth this one offered was a little too hard to resist. Plus it had free Wi-Fi. We made ourselves comfortable.

Vivian went off to the toilet, or as they are known in Canada, the washrooms, and came back with an aghast look on her face, declaring to me that "the worst thing has just happened!" She then challenged me to guess what this thing was. "Seriously," she said, "what is the worst thing you can imagine?"

Now Vivian did not look like she had been mauled by any bears in the washroom. In fact she looked very much to have returned in perfectly good health, and I remained flummoxed. Luckily she did not really expect an answer. "My phone just broke!" she wailed, holding up her iPhone, which had long vertical stripes blurring the screen. This did not seem like the worst thing in the world to me. My own phone was a Nokia 3310, some fifteen years old, and I had not switched it on since Australia. It might very well have been broken. I could not have cared less. But for Vivian this was a problem. A very big problem.

As Vivian sat there with her head in her hands trying to work out what she was going to do, a young guy walked in and came over to our table to ask if we had an iPhone charger that he could borrow. The fact that Vivian did have an iPhone charger that was effectively of no use to her any more pleased me on some level, and she was happy to lend it to the young fellow who himself seemed to be in quite a distressed state. He then told us that "the worst thing has just happened" but before I could interrupt him and shout out "wait, I know this one!" he told us what it was, and it didn't involve his iPhone. "I've just been done for DUI!" he blurted out, which, if you're not familiar with American acronyms, means he'd been caught driving under the influence of alcohol.

The guy was in his early twenties and after running off to plug in his phone somewhere came back to sit in the booth right next to me. I was not so happy about this. Ever since witnessing the terrible accident in Mongolia I had no time whatsoever for drink-drivers. His breath absolutely reeked of alcohol and he was almost certainly still drunk. Annoyingly Vivian was being nice and encouraging him as he told us his story. He'd only just got out of the cell where he'd spent most of the night. *'God, how drunk must he have been when he was behind the wheel?'* I wondered.

"I refused to give a breath sample," he said. "Man, I really hope there is a way I can get off. I'm gonna lose my licence. Gonna have to sell my truck. Dang, this is the worst."

I just sat and stared blankly out of the window. My mind was carrying me back to Mongolia. I could see those men again. I could see those lifeless bodies lying in the dust. I could see the blood, see the despair.

"So, what are you doing here?" The young guy interrupted my thoughts. He was being nice. He wanted to know about my trip, but I couldn't find the words. I wanted to shout at him. I should have. I should have told him all about Mongolia. I should have let him know that getting caught by the cops drink-driving was definitely not the worst thing that could have happened to him, not by a long shot, and I knew, because I had seen the worst.

But I didn't. Instead I made up some excuse and I got up and I left to the room next door, which was a bus station waiting room, and in there I sat and I cried. I just burst into tears and I couldn't stop. I cried and I cried and I cried some more. There was some pent-up emotion inside of me that I hadn't even known was in there. I'd rarely thought about the accident in the eighteen months since I'd witnessed it, but now it all came back to me – those men dying in front of me, my own helplessness, the whole pointless stupidity of it – and it all came out, brought about by some naïve kid who had no clue how lucky he really was.

Fortunately Dea came online at that moment and I had someone to talk to about it. She was as patient and understanding as always. Oh, how I missed her. Vivian was many things – an entertaining sidekick, hapless to a tee – but she was certainly no substitute for Dea.

We needed to get back on the road. It had warmed up by now and Vivian and I left Tim Hortons behind with me hoping I'd never have to see one again (an ambitious wish with 5,000 kilometres of Canada still to go). The bicycle path carried us out of Banff and Vivian, in what was a worrying development for her hapless sidekick status, shot off ahead of me.

It was quite a while before I caught up to her at the larger town of Canmore, where we stopped to resupply at a large supermarket. In the latest tragedy to befall her, the poor girl had now lost her hi-vis vest, which was bad timing as we had to navigate a busy road with a narrow shoulder out of Canmore.

"Don't you having anything else bright?" I asked, worried that she was no longer visible enough.

"Oh, I have my hunting jacket!" she remembered, fishing around in her pannier and pulling out a luminous orange coat.

"That's perfect. Why do you have a hunting jacket?"

"Oh, I have a hunting licence. I've got a gun as well you know."

"Really?" This girl was full of surprises.

"Don't worry, I've never killed anything." Then she looked a bit confused and added, "I don't want to shoot animals!"

I decided that it was better for everyone not to pursue Vivian's logic further, and we rode on. Beyond Canmore the traffic thinned out and so did the mountains. This was it, the end of the Rockies. The road still went up and down for a while, but the big snowy mountains no longer dominated the skyline on either side of us as they had before and soon we were pedalling past the last of them. On the very last of the steep hills Vivian strained every sinew to cycle all of the way up. Reaching the summit she declared triumphantly, "It's the first time I got up one without walking!" and that was it, the mountains were over.

7

Alberta, Canada
20th May 2016

I stared ahead at the flat grasslands that would form the view for
the next two thousand kilometres east and shuddered. This was
the start of the vast Canadian prairies, and I knew that they were
likely to provide a far sterner mental test than anything the mountains had thrown at us. But how unbelievably monotonous and boring the prairies were going to be was not something that had yet
occurred to Vivian, and she hollered and cheered to be out in the
open landscape. I could only guess this was because it was so completely devoid of bears.

Our first night in the prairies was as cold as any in the mountains
and we woke up to more dreary weather. But such weather gave
Vivian an extraordinary zeal. It seemed nothing motivated her to
cycle more than the thought that doing so might get her to somewhere warm and indoors. So we got up early again, and set our sights
firmly on the town of Cochrane.

By nine thirty we were there and hunting its streets for my favourite refuge, the library. We stopped a passer-by to ask directions.
Hume was a nice man of around fifty, and, after informing us of the
location of the library, he asked us about our trips. This was nice,
although it was good to have Vivian with me, for she enjoyed
answering these questions much more than I did. The problem I had
with such friendly encounters was simply that after so many years it

had become a little tedious being asked the same questions over and over. Just hearing the words, "How far do you cycle in a day?" was by now enough to make me cringe. I was thinking that I should really get a T-shirt made up with words on the front saying, 'It depends where I am, but usually around 80-100 kilometres', because if I heard those words come out of my mouth one more time I was quite likely going to scream.

Just as we were talking with Hume a group of three joggers stopped to see what we were all up to. The friendliest was a slim, bald man of about sixty who invited us to come for a coffee. With it still being very cold, the library not yet open, and the people being so nice, it was an offer we could not very sensibly refuse.

The coffee shop was just around the corner and it felt exceedingly pleasant to step in out of the cold and into such an authentic small-town place. It was so much cosier then Tim Hortons and was clearly a popular local hangout, buzzing with people as it was. Hot chocolate was generously bought for Vivian and me, and not just any hot chocolate, it was hot chocolate with cream on top. This was the sort of luxury that I rarely got to enjoy with my frugal lifestyle, which was a shame, because in this little coffee shop there was a real slice of Canadian life. Everybody knew each other, smiles and laughter were being shared; it was homely and warm and all the things the cold road was not.

But the biggest pleasure came with the opportunity for me to sit and chat with Martin, the friendly jogger who had invited us in. I soon came to realise that Martin Parnell was no ordinary man. In fact, he was one of the most extraordinary men I'd ever met. I'd overheard him mention to someone earlier that he was soon running a marathon in Calgary, so I asked him about it, and then he told me something unbelievable. He had run his first marathon just a few years earlier, but he'd enjoyed running so much that soon after that, while in his mid-fifties, he had ran 250 marathons in a single year. I was flabbergasted. Having run a few marathons in my twenties (three or four, I mean, over a decade) I had some idea of just what an achievement this was, for running a marathon is so much harder than riding a bike all day. So much harder. What this man had achieved was nothing short of incredible.

But there was more. Martin was a humble man, but as I probed him further my every question revealed something else extraordinary. He'd completed ultra-marathons, climbed mountains, broken world records. All of this was in aid of his 'Quest for kids' – ten challenges he'd set himself to complete over a five year period to raise money to help children in need around the world find hope through sport. "Oh, and I climbed Kilimanjaro," he said, almost as an afterthought, which didn't even seem all that remarkable for such a man, until he added, "in twenty-one hours." And the result of all this astonishing effort? 1.3 million dollars raised for charity. This guy was an inspiration.

I enjoyed chatting with Martin so very much, and so I was a bit disappointed when a young journalist showed up and asked if there was someone cycling around the world. It seemed like news travelled fast in Cochrane. Martin introduced me to him and unexpectedly took his leave, and with his sudden goodbye I was left sitting opposite the journalist, who opened up his notebook and asked if it was alright to put some questions to me for the local paper. I agreed, though with a little apprehension. I rarely enjoyed interviews and this guy did not seem to have much genuine interest in me, but was merely going through the motions of getting a story. It was one thing being asked the same questions over and over again by people who actually cared, but facing them in a forced and slow interview process was too much.

"And how much do you cycle in day?"

"Right, I'm sorry, I can't do this. I'll get my friend Vivian, she's got a much better story."

And so Vivian was interviewed instead, which was much better for everyone, because, like Martin, she was actually doing all this for a good cause and wanted the publicity. While I'd been chatting with Martin she had been going around the coffee shop talking to anyone and everyone about dementia. And she had by now already achieved her financial goal of raising enough money to send her grandparents to Hong Kong, although sadly this was only because her family had donated all of the money in the hope it would make her give up and return home. She wasn't ready to give up yet, however.

At some point she had also spoken again with Hume, and he had invited us to stay at his home for a couple of nights. He'd gone off to run some errands, but in a remarkable show of trust he'd left his front door key with Vivian and told her we were both welcome to go round, take a shower, and make ourselves at home. Once Vivian's interview was over we did just that. No one was home and it felt odd to go into a stranger's house like that, even more so because I was only in it for the free shower. I wasn't going to be staying the night. Vivian was. Although we were through the mountains it had always been my intention to head south from Cochrane and dip back into them at the less well-known but apparently very beautiful Waterton Lakes National Park. In the original plans I had with Dea we would have been crossing from there into the United States in order to continue south. Obviously that wasn't going to be happening any more, but Waterton sounded so fantastic that I decided I would still go down there before turning east again. It was only a slight detour, adding a mere 200 kilometres onto the trip. Out of a total of 7,000 that seemed like no big deal to me, but for Vivian 200 kilometre detours were out of the question. She would continue east to Calgary and then off across the prairies alone. But as she waved me off down the driveway it was not necessarily our goodbye; there was every chance, and I certainly felt it inevitable, that we would meet again soon.

A nice tailwind pushed me along south for a few days through grassy plains that stretched endlessly away to my left, the Rocky Mountains still making up the view to my right. As I got further south more snowy peaks appeared ahead of me, that grew and grew steadily out of the horizon as I pedalled on. Towards the end of the day the sun cast them in various hues ranging from sky blue to golden pink. It was a beautiful sight, as fine a setting for a bike ride as you can imagine. I had made it to Waterton Lakes.

The next morning I awoke early to an equally stunning view from my tent, having pitched it the night before on a ridge overlooking the national park. It was a beautiful sunny day and I was looking forward to this opportunity to enjoy the mountains of western Canada one last time before the prairies really began. I found a place to lock up my bike and headed off for a hike. The trail climbed slowly at first past lakes and meadows of brightly coloured wild flowers, but soon grew steeper as I headed deeper into the mountains. It felt so good to be wandering freely through nature. I loved cycling so much, but the reality of it was that most of the time I needed to be on roads, shared with cars and civilization. Hiking like this gave me an opportunity to really appreciate the natural world in a way I couldn't always do on a bike. After a few hours the trail brought me to a tranquil lake surrounded by snow high up in the mountains. I breathed in deeply, savouring the fresh air, and smiled. It sure felt good to be in Canada. There was only one thing could've made it better. I vowed that one day I would return, and show all this to Dea.

From Waterton I resumed my eastward course, leaving behind the mountains for good. I watched ruefully as they shrank in my mirror until eventually they were gone completely. Now I was out in the flat grasslands of the Canadian prairies, looking around at a whole load of nothing. After a day I was bored. After two days I was bored out of my mind. I needed something to keep me entertained, for I knew it was likely to be three weeks before I saw so much as a tree, and I was therefore pleased to get a message from Vivian. She had much good news to share, for not only did she have a new phone, but she was keen to meet up and ride together again, and was waiting for me in a place with the unlikely, confusing, and some might say ridiculous name of Medicine Hat.

Because I was approaching Medicine Hat from the south I could easily bypass the busy urban centre, and so I suggested to Vivian that we meet at a gas station just past the city that was right on the main (and only) highway going east. I thought it was an obvious rendezvous point, a big red gas station on the only road. It seemed to be completely foolproof.

We had arranged to meet at eleven thirty a.m. but, once again buoyed by a nice tailwind, I was there an hour early. As I stood outside waiting, a slightly peculiar old man named William came to chat with me.

"I've seen you guys riding around with all this gear before," he said in a cheerful manner, "and I've always wanted to ask this…"

William paused for quite a long time. During this pause I found myself thinking, *'Don't say it. Don't you dare say it.'*

"How far do you cycle in a day?"

Luckily for William I was in a good mood, and he was much bigger than me, so I told him, then quickly turned the tables and asked him questions. He said he had hitchhiked from Winnipeg (a thousand kilometres away) in order to buy a pick-up truck and he was now driving it home again. That's a bit like someone in London hitchhiking to Italy to buy a new car and drive it home, but everything in North America happens on a grander scale, and I liked William. He was nuts.

William left and almost as soon as he did another pick-up truck rolled up next to me on the gas station forecourt. From the passenger seat jumped a small and very bright orange bundle of smiling energy. It was Vivian. As the male driver hauled her bike out of the back of the truck I greeted her and enquired as to why she was arriving via motorised transportation.

"I got lost," she explained, "and I didn't want to be late."

"You're forty-five minutes early."

"I know, but I was really scared I'd miss you and you'd go on without me. The last few days have been awful!"

I was still a bit confused as to how she could have had so much trouble finding a bright red gas station on the only road east out of town, but after a barely believable conversation during which I established that Vivian could not read a map, follow GPS directions, nor tell me how many metres there are in a kilometre, I began to understand.

As the conversation continued I realised Vivian really could use some help if she was going to get across Canada. It seemed like she'd been brought close to quitting by the fresh list of things that had gone wrong since I'd last seen her. Her tales of woe included cycling into constant headwinds and terrible rainstorms which had brought her close to breaking point. Even in Medicine Hat her bad luck had not abated. A solar battery that was supposed to have been mailed to her had not arrived and the woman in the post office had apparently been ever so mean to luckless Vivian.

As the trail of complaints flowed at a hundred miles an hour from this little girl, I wondered just what I'd gotten myself into. Would it not have been easier to go on alone? Perhaps, but that would not make for much of a movie script and goodness, at least I would have some company for the long empty prairies ahead. I waited for my new sidekick to pause for a short breath and quickly chipped in with "So, shall we do some cycling?"

Luckily our first day back together was a great one. We had an awesome tailwind, which Vivian seemed to attribute somehow to me, and when we stopped for a break in a little village after twenty kilometres we were fortunate enough to find a little park with a picnic bench. "This is so much better than sitting at the side of the highway to eat," Vivian noted, quite correctly.

We soon crossed into the province of Saskatchewan and with the wind strong at our backs continued to make great progress. Hundreds of prairie dogs (which are in fact not dogs, but buck-toothed rodents) popped their heads out of roadside burrows to watch as we zoomed past. Our only concern was where we might end up camping, the barren terrain offering precious few opportunities to shelter from the wind. The solution arrived finally with a rare patch of trees not quite big enough to constitute being called a wood. For security reasons I insisted we make our way to the back of them, hidden from the road, although whether this location was really more secure was called into question when a herd of bulls wandered over from the field behind us. They didn't seem to enjoy our presence and one or two of them made rather scary and aggressive noises at me as I walked around setting up my tent. There was a short barbed wire fence between us, but that looked wholly inadequate once one of the bulls started lowering its head and kicking the dirt as if preparing for a charge. I couldn't work out what was making it so angry. "Maybe it's because you're wearing red?" Vivian pointed out.

I put on a different coloured jacket and perhaps as a result of that neither of our tents were trampled overnight, and by morning the bulls had departed to the other side of the field, leaving us to pack up in peace. It was a nice morning too, the temperatures warming as spring advanced, and the wind was once again kind to us as we set off across the seemingly infinite plains. The shoulder of the highway was perfectly smooth tarmac and as wide as a lane. It was really very safe, so I stuck in my headphones and listened to some comedy shows on my MP3 player. As I chuckled out loud Vivian, with nothing to entertain herself, eyed me jealously.

At a gas station we noticed two touring bikes leaning against a wall and went to investigate. Inside we found the owners, and were a little surprised that they were two men of about seventy years of age. Ben and Walter were seasoned cross-Canada cyclists. One was completing the ride for the fifth time, the other his seventh. Vivian and I were both pretty astonished. This road was definitely not one that I would like to cycle seven times.

In a scene that I would like to see cut from the movie, the two septuagenarians then cycled on ahead much faster than us, never to be seen again. But the tailwind kept our progress reasonable, and by evening we were on the streets of Swift Current, a town in which Vivian had organised some hosts for us through the *warmshowers* website. They were a surprisingly young couple named Sheldon and Jennifer who, despite only being about my age, had two boys, twelve-year-old Hayden and seven-year-old Lanni, as well as proper jobs, and a house. It was interesting to see how different my life could have been, had I only been a bit more sensible. Of course they were wonderful people and because of their location they hosted cross-Canada cyclists all the time. They didn't have much space inside, however, and so could only offer us their garden. I pitched my tent and Vivian, who is very small remember, curled up in the boys' treehouse.

Vivian and I offered to cook to say thank you, and over dinner I asked the boys what they wanted to do when they grew up. I was hoping they might say they wanted to cycle around the world, but Lanni quickly answered that he wanted to own and run a campground. Hayden, the older boy, thought for a moment, then in a very serious tone revealed, "I want to be an engineer... or... a shoe shop owner."

They were really good kids, and before we left they even told us that we were their favourite ever guests, "Because you cooked *and* played games with us!" Both Vivian and myself could be described as young at heart, so it wasn't like we'd needed a second invitation to join in with those games. After a soccer match in which I realised that I cannot outrun a seven-year-old, we'd moved to the trampoline, where we played a truly, truly epic game of Blind Goat. If you don't know how to play Blind Goat then may I recommend that you put down this book right now, and go and find yourself a young child and a trampoline, because it really is tremendous fun.*

*Please note that I accept no responsibility for any legal issues that may arise from you following that advice.

8

For weeks Vivian and I rode on together, following the long, unbending highway across Saskatchewan and then Manitoba. The empty green scenery remained mind-numbingly monotonous, but the two of us were getting on surprisingly well and sometimes we'd chat or play games to pass the time. A favourite was Twenty Questions. One of us would think of a celebrity, and then the other would have twenty yes or no questions to work out who it was. For example one time I thought of George W. Bush, and Vivian asked a load of questions, then deduced that I was most probably thinking of the skateboarder Tony Hawk. When that got boring I'd return to listening to my MP3 player and Vivian would put on music she'd downloaded to her new phone, and the long, boring kilometres gradually passed by. In the evenings we camped together, in occasional patches of trees or in fields of dandelions. Then each morning Vivian would return to the road, look left, look right, look confused, and then about fifty percent of the time start cycling in the wrong direction.

Finally we began to see trees. At first they were sporadic but before too long they grouped together and called themselves forests. We had made it across the prairies, and it felt like a significant achievement for both of us. I considered us fortunate with our crossing. Beyond the initial cold start things had warmed up and we'd been blessed with good weather and generally favourable winds. An old tree planting friend of mine had once given up on cycling across Canada because of a relentless headwind in the prairies, so I was relieved we'd got off lightly in that regard. And while it was a sad day indeed when I realised that Vivian's fitness had improved to such an extent that, like all the hapless sidekicks that had gone before her, she was able to cycle faster than me, I was glad we had stuck together and made it all of the way across to her home province of Ontario.

The road began to rise and fall more, cresting peaks that revealed new combinations of trees, rocks, and lakes. It became hot and humid, and as a consequence horse-flies and fruit flies started to annoy us, orbiting around us with infuriating persistence as we rode. This of course provided Vivian with more material to moan about and she remained cautious of many of nature's critters, with a particular phobia of ticks. We began to see them more and more frequently, and Vivian became so scared of being bitten that she refused to remove any layers of clothing, even while out on the highway, and cycled along in the midday heat in a long-sleeved top, with leggings tucked into her socks.

For the majority of Canada the highways had good, wide shoulders, but we found that Ontario lagged behind the rest of the country in this regard, so when we had the chance to get off the Trans-Canada at a place called Kenora we did. Our alternative road added about a hundred kilometres onto the route distance, but for the peace and quiet it was definitely worth it. The heavily forested area we cycled through was also broken up by many different bodies of water, and this gave me hope that I might spot an elusive Canadian creature that I'd never seen before. After a few hours carefully scanning the lakes and rivers and ponds we passed I struck gold. For the first time in my life I saw a beaver. As soon as it became aware of my presence it smacked the water with its tail with a loud thunk and disappeared beneath the surface, but I was really happy. The beaver had been one of the few missing from my collection of Canadian animals, and I was pleased to be able tick it off the list. With my previous visits to the country included, I had now spotted black bears, grizzly bears, moose, elk, deer, wolves, coyotes, a lynx, a cougar, bald eagles, and now a beaver. All I needed was for a wolverine to cross my path and I would have the full set.

It wasn't the last beaver I would see. A few days later we found a perfect place to camp at a rest area close to a big lake. After putting up my tent I walked down to the lake for a swim. The water felt so refreshing after a long day on the bike and the surroundings were just incredible. There's something simply wonderful about being away from the rest of the world, surrounded by endless forests and wildlife, and almost feeling like you're a part of it. I thought this, at least, Vivian didn't really agree, and in fact never made it down to the lake because she was up on the road trying desperately to get a signal for her phone. I didn't mind. I was quite content to be alone with my thoughts as I sat on a rock by the water, with the sky turning purple in a beautiful, colourful farewell. I spotted anther beaver, floating effortlessly out into the lake where I myself had just swam. It was going about its business, as it no doubt did every evening, oblivious to my curious, watching eyes. At moments like this the whole bicycle trip all made sense, and I felt like I was living my life just exactly the way I wanted.

The next day it rained, and we spent much of the afternoon hiding from a thunderstorm in a village supermarket. By early evening it eased off, but we knew, thanks to Vivian's phone (which was useful sometimes), that more heavy rain was on the way. We could only make it another fifteen kilometres before the dark clouds rolled in again, but that was enough time for us to meet two extremely interesting cycle tourists coming the other way. I'm not sure I remember their names correctly, but I think the taller, thinner one said his name was Austin Healey, and the shorter, odd-looking one, we'll call Bryan. They were somewhat nerdy in appearance, and I could envisage them being played rather well by Sheldon and Leonard from *The Big Bang Theory*. They came from Michigan, where they had started cycling just two weeks earlier, but they were in the early stages of an eighteen month journey. I was a little jealous, for they still had that excited buzz that being in the first days of a long trip brings. I was also seriously impressed, particularly with Bryan, who revealed that he had built their bikes himself. And I don't just mean that he'd stuck the components together, he had actually built the bikes, including the frames. "Yeah, I had to learn to weld," he said modestly, while hitching his trousers up too high like Simon Cowell.

They were fascinating characters, these two guys. How I would have loved to roll along with them for a few days. They were definitely doing things a different way. They didn't even have a tent, just hammocks, that they planned to string up between trees each night. "Good luck with that in the prairies," I joked. I wanted to ask more, but the dark clouds were gathering menacingly. Austin Healey looked at his futuristic watch and said something about the atmospheric pressure that made us all panic, and with regrettably hurried goodbyes we left them to their own madcap adventures.

Vivian and I rushed to find a place to pitch our tents and soon located a suitable spot on an abandoned little track in the forest. I raced around and got my tent up just in time before the deluge from above began. Vivian, I'm sorry to say, was not so lucky, but the rain hammering down on my tent muffled out her whines, and I drifted off to sleep.

Several hours later I was awoken by a loud, shrill whistle. I tried to remember where I was. It was dark. The rain had stopped. It was the middle of the night.

"Chris!" Vivian shrieked. "There is an animal! It's blowing its horn, I think it's calling other animals!"

It appeared the poor girl was having terrible visions of all of the animals of the wood ganging up on us in the darkness, preparing a coordinated assault, like a poorly scripted Pixar movie. She gave another long blast on her whistle. I sighed. I felt so tired and did not greatly appreciate being woken up at such an hour for this. I lay there and listened for some time, but I could hear nothing, except, maybe, a frog. I rolled over and went back to sleep.

I was beginning to lose my patience with Vivian. Conversations like the one we had before leaving Fort Frances for Thunder Bay on 300 kilometres of very remote and empty road didn't help.

Chris: "Do you have enough food for three days?"

Vivian: "Yes."

Five minutes later:

Chris: "Are you sure you have enough food for three days?"

Vivian: "Yes."

Ten minutes later:

Chris: "You're absolutely sure you have enough food for three days?"

Vivian: "Yes."

Fifteen minutes later:

Chris: "Right Vivian, let's get going. Are you sure you have enough food for three days?"

Vivian: "Well, maybe not enough for *three* days."

A hundred kilometres past Thunder Bay our onward routes would differ, with Vivian wanting to take a more southerly route than me to pass through her home town of Sudbury. It was okay with me. I liked Vivian and I'd enjoyed my time with her, but I was getting frustrated with some things and just about ready to go my own way again. We only had three or four more days together, and I resolved to make them work.

The road from Fort Frances was indeed a remote one. It was quite remarkable to travel through mile after mile of pristine forest and think about how far it stretched in all directions. Having lived most of my life on a densely populated island in a densely populated continent, being in a place like Canada was both humbling and hopeful. It was so vast, so natural, so unspoilt.

The next morning I had a bit of a lie-in. It had been another rainy night and I was annoyed to find my tent covered in hundreds of slugs. As I stooped to flick them off, Vivian was in an unusually good mood as she chirped, "I've never heard you complain before. And you're not really complaining, you're just grunting. You remind me of my dog."

Vivian was ready before me and she left first. As she got to the road I saw her flag down a car. "Which way to Thunder Bay?" I could hear her asking the car's occupants. I shook my head in disbelief. There was literally only one road.

My grumpy mood continued as I set off into a strong headwind. Then it started to rain. My legs felt so tired and it seemed like I was forever cycling uphill. Canada was starting to get the better of me. I felt like I'd been riding here forever, but I was only halfway across, and the Atlantic was feeling like a long way off.

I finally caught up with Vivian in Atikokan, the only small town for a hundred kilometres in either direction. She'd made her way to the library to escape the bad weather and I joined her there, collapsing into a seat quite exhausted. Vivian, by contrast, was in good spirits. She was looking at something on her phone and laughing out loud. "This is how much of an asshole people are!" she exclaimed, rather inappropriately loudly for a library. "Aries 60%, Virgo 80%, Sagittarius 25%, Capricorn minus 400%! Hey, this is pretty accurate!" she said, with complete sincerity. Then she continued, "Libra 9000% asshole!"

"I'm a Libra," I sighed.

"Oh… yeah…" She looked a bit confused for a moment. Her brow furrowed, as if she was trying to justify my outrageous asshole score in her mind. "Well, you do like politics!"

"Erm, Vivian, what exactly makes you think I like politics?"

"You talk about it all the time."

"No, I'm pretty sure I don't."

"Yeah, you do. Remember you said George Bush that time?"

"What? When we were playing Twenty Questions?!"

Although the rain had eased by the next day there were other things irritating me. Being out in the wild in close proximity to so much water there were predictably lots of mosquitoes. This meant that packing up and getting on our way quickly in the morning was important. Annoying, then, to see my rear tyre deflated.

I pumped it up and made it five kilometres to an extremely isolated little motel and restaurant. With so little else on the road we had to stop here to get water anyway. The female owner greeted us and offered us some free toast and jam for breakfast. She was a nice woman and Vivian wanted to talk to her, as well as everyone else who stopped by at the restaurant, at length. I took the chance to fix my tyre, and then, with Vivian still busy, thought I might try and watch a football match that was taking place between England and Wales. I streamed it on my laptop, but the connection was poor, and it kept cutting out at the wrong times, meaning I missed both England goals, including their late winner.

I was still in a pretty foul mood, so it was bad timing when, just as the match cut out at a crucial moment, I overheard Vivian behind me talking with some men about our ride.

"Why are you leaving each other?" I caught one of the men asking, referring to the fact that we would soon be going our separate ways.

"We're not leaving each other. He's leaving me!" Vivian replied, with an accusatory tone.

My blood boiled. I had done everything that I could to help Vivian across three provinces, sticking by her all the way from the Rockies to the Great Lakes, and now, just because our preferred routes differed and we were to part ways, she was painting me as the bad guy. Just another heartless cyclist abandoning her.

I had to bite my tongue, and even more so when a little later the man came over to me and told me to "take good care of this girl." I should have liked to have told him that if he cared so much, perhaps he would like to get a bicycle and escort her the rest of the way.

I tried very hard not to react. There were only two more days to Thunder Bay and really no need for me to say anything. But I wanted some space, so as we went back outside to our bikes I said that I would like it if we could cycle separately for the rest of the day. I only meant it so that I would have some time to think, so that we could meet up later and still be friends, but Vivian asked me why and the floodgates opened. I told her how annoying I'd found her comment, that I did not appreciate being made out to be the bad guy now that I was no longer of any use to her, and plenty more besides. She'd never even mentioned me in her Facebook updates about her trip. Did she appreciate me at all?

For a moment it felt good to have got all these things off my chest, things which had been building up inside me over the past few days. Only for a moment, however. Then I saw how shocked and hurt Vivian looked by my rebuke, and I felt terrible. What had I done? She looked like a scolded puppy. But before I could offer an apology she was back on her bike and I was helpless to do anything more than watch on as she stormed off alone.

9

Ontario, Canada
16th June 2016

I felt terrible about parting with Vivian on such bad terms. The truth was that for all our differences I had greatly enjoyed cycling with her. We had come at the ride across Canada from completely different backgrounds, we were completely different people, yet we had formed an unlikely friendship. She had constantly astounded me, and not just with her baffling statements, but also with her determination not to quit despite the odds. If I could have only kept my mouth shut for a few more days everything would have been alright. Trying to make amends, I wrote her an e-mail saying how sorry I was and that I'd really liked to meet up again in Thunder Bay to patch things up before going our separate ways.

Vivian had gone off at quite a pace (fortunately in the right direction) and I held out little hope that I could catch her. She was by now much faster than me, I'd sadly come to realise, and so I rode alone for the rest of the day. By evening I'd reached a main road and civilisation, and I scanned the front of a couple of gas stations hoping to see Vivian's tent standing on the forecourt. There was no sign of it and so for the first time in a while, I camped alone (not on a gas station forecourt).

It felt strange to wake up all alone in the forest, with no one to wake me up complaining about the mosquitoes and other bugs, no one to amuse me by cycling the wrong way or by saying something unintentionally funny. I wondered where Vivian was, and hoped she was doing okay.

The next morning I found some Wi-Fi and went online to discover Vivian's fate. Her messages made me feel even worse for reacting the way that I had. She apologised for her comments to the man in the café, which had apparently just been a joke, and thanked me for having stuck with her for so long. She also explained that the reason she didn't mention me in her online updates was because it would likely have made her husband upset. I'd known this, but I probably hadn't appreciated just how bad the situation was for Vivian in her relationship, or how important this trip really was to her, until now. I had a bit of a lump in my throat, especially as it now appeared very unlikely that I would see her again. After our falling out she had ended up hitchhiking the rest of the way to Thunder Bay in a truck. She'd heard that a group of cyclists, The Canadian Coasters, were there, and she wanted to catch them up so that she would still have someone to ride with. They were a group of five older riders who had been a day or so ahead of us almost the whole way across the prairies. We'd caught sight of them a couple of times, met them once, but generally they had been pulling ahead of us and we would just hear reports of them having passed through places, unmissable in their matching bright yellow cycling jerseys. I was pleased to hear that Vivian would continue her mission and have others to cycle with. I felt like I had done my bit to help, and passed on the baton. The reality, however, was not so much that I had helped Vivian across the prairies, but that we had helped and supported each other. I'd probably benefited from the company, and the distraction from the boring ride, every bit as much as she had. I would remember our time together fondly.

But I was alone as I entered the shockingly big city of Thunder Bay and made my way to the home of Frank, my *warmshowers* host. It was strange to think that Vivian had been in Frank's home, enjoying dinner with The Canadian Coasters just the previous evening, before moving on a few hours before I arrived. Frank was an exceptionally kind and generous host, although he regretted that I hadn't arrived with Vivian the previous evening, for that would have meant him getting his personal best ever record for the most cyclists staying in his house on one night. This night he only had four – myself and three young lads from Quebec, themselves riding across Canada. I offered to prepare dinner, and the guys were assigned to go to the shops and pick up some missing ingredients. "How about picking up some beers too?" Frank suggested. The boys looked at each other, then said that they couldn't buy alcohol. They were only seventeen.

They were really nice guys, going the opposite way unfortunately, but good company for the evening. Frank was a great host too, and an inspiring one. He was technically clinically blind, but that didn't stop him from doing the things he wanted to, like cycling around the world. He actually had a form of tunnel vision, and despite lacking peripheral vision he could still ride his bike, and, no doubt against doctors' orders, he'd spent a year riding it around the world. This story was particularly inspiring for Dea when I passed it on to her. She was still in the process of recovering from her own eye troubles, of course, but there was also great news from her as the vision in her left eye, which had dropped as low as ten percent at the time she'd flown home, was now back up to eighty percent. With her recovery going so well, and no doubt inspired by the news that someone declared as clinically blind could cycle around the world, she was about to set off on her own cycle tour in Denmark. It was such a relief that her eye was so much better. And this bike tour was only a practice run for her; if all went well she would soon be cycling west across Europe to come and meet me as I pressed on ever eastwards. Motivation for me to keep going, if ever there was some.

From Thunder Bay I followed the northern shore of the massive Lake Superior. The only option for a while was the Trans-Canada Highway, and I'd heard that this was going to be a very busy and dangerous section of it too, with no shoulder to cycle on. Thankfully this was not quite true. There was no paved shoulder, but there was a gravel one, and as I was happy to ride on gravel I found things were nowhere near as dangerous as I'd feared. Unfortunately, however, following a lake didn't mean my route was flat and the road climbed and fell over a disheartening number of big hills, with occasional picturesque views of the massive lake providing some consolation for the effort. Along the way I met another cycle tourist heading west to Vancouver. He was a friendly man named Al, who informed me that he'd met Vivian a day and a half earlier. She was apparently no longer riding with The Canadian Coasters, possibly because she was too fast for them. Al confirmed she was cycling 150 kilometres per day now, leaving all other cyclists, including me, in her dust.

I got a reminder of the perils of the Canadian wilderness one evening when I went into the forest on a muddy track to look for a camping place. The track was lined with dense vegetation, and there was nowhere to get in, so I went on and on, deeper and deeper into the darkening forest. I'd already noticed some animal tracks in the mud that were round and hoof-like, perhaps from a moose, without worrying too much about it, but further along I saw something that made me hit the brakes. Much larger prints that undoubtedly belonged to a bear. A pretty big bear at that, from the looks of them. They looked freshly made, and the bear was moving in the same direction that I'd been heading. I wasn't heading that way any longer, of course, and I quickly turned my bike around and got the hell out of there as fast as I could.

Even though I was happy to ride on the gravel shoulder I really didn't enjoy how busy the highway was, so I was looking forward to getting away from Lake Superior on a quieter route. This road started at a place that, and I think this name might possibly have been chosen by a newborn infant, was called Wawa. I knew that I was taking a much more remote alternative, so I made enquiries at the information centre in Wawa about places along the way where I might be able to find water. They told me that there was a motel in twenty-five kilometres where I could fill up and as a result I ended up leaving town without too much water.

Twenty-six kilometres later I was beginning to regret my decision. There had been no sign of any motel and in fact no real sign of anything along this road other than forest. I felt like I was truly heading into the wilderness here, and doing so without water was silly, especially as the next settlement of any kind was still over a hundred kilometres away. I had only half a litre of water left, and I was beginning to seriously consider how I was going to ration that for a full day. But then I remembered that I had a stove, and so I could boil river water and drink that if I needed to. My brain really did need congratulating, I thought, as I clambered over slippery rocks and almost fell into a fast flowing river to get myself something to boil.

Around the very next corner I came to a set of cabins. I couldn't be bothered with boiling anything, so I stopped at the cabins to ask for some fresh water. They were advertised as hunting and fishing cabins, which made sense as there wasn't much else to be done out here. The owner was very welcoming. He was a big fellow with a lumberjack-style check jacket and long grey hair sprouting out from under a well worn baseball cap, a real man of the woods. He invited me into the reception area and I accepted, mostly because I wanted to get away from the flies for a moment. Inside I noticed (it was hard to miss) a big bear head hanging on the wall. The man saw me staring.

"Oh yeah, lot of bears around here son. We mostly run bear hunts from here. Lotta bears, yes sir."

"That's interesting," I gulped.

"Not just bears. Lotta wolves too. So many wolves. That's what we got around here in these forests, bears and wolves."

It seemed like I was in for an interesting couple of days.

Despite being nervous about the wildlife, the rest of the day turned out to be pure cycling bliss. There was almost no traffic at all, the sky was blue, the forest was pure and wild, everything was good (apart from the flies). This felt like the real Canada – endless forests, wild animals, and no signs of human habitation. I felt like I could just cycle on this road forever, but it would soon be dark and I wanted to be tucked up in my sleeping bag before the animals all came out to play. I found a good place for camping down an abandoned logging road. It was a great site because it was flat but there was no access for vehicles any more, so there was no chance of me being run over. The only slight concern I had was that I thought it might be used as a sort of transport corridor by certain animals, particularly as there seemed to be rather a lot of faeces around. I just told myself it would be okay and set up camp. Shortly after I'd retired to bed I heard the sound of panicked hooves running around outside. It was pitch black and there was nothing I could do. It was too late to move, so I fell asleep, to dreams of being trampled in the night.

I slept surprisingly well, and woke up feeling rather silly with myself for getting so worried about wild animals. They meant me no harm. I climbed out of my tent and into the early morning air of what looked like being another fine and clear day, then wandered twenty metres down the track to retrieve my food pannier. Of course in bear country it would be extremely foolhardy to sleep with food inside the tent, lest it tempt in unwanted visitors. When I'd first arrived in Canada back in 2010 I had been advised that the best thing to do would be to hang my food in a tree, and on my first night wild camping in the country I'd made a farcical attempt at doing so. I'd found some rope at the side of the road that looked like it might do, which I tried to fling over a branch with no idea of the correct technique. After repeated attempts that I could only honestly describe as pathetic, I eventually resigned myself to just leaving my food bag outside on the ground, a safe distance from my tent. I'd been doing that ever since, and in more than a hundred nights of wild camping in Canada my food had never been touched.

You can imagine my dismay, then, to reach the location where I had left this pannier of food the previous evening to discover that it was no longer there. I looked around, confused, thinking at first that perhaps I was in the wrong place. It was then that I noticed my yellow jacket, which I'd wrapped over the top of the pannier as a hopeless extra layer of protection, now hanging from a low branch in the forest beside the trail. As it dawned on me what had happened here I studied the ground again, and saw that, in close proximity to where my food pannier once stood, there now resided a steaming great pile of bear poop.

Now, I'm not a detective. Never have been, probably never will be. But I was nevertheless fairly confident who the chief suspect was in this mystery. And now that I had no food, stranded in the middle of nowhere, eighty kilometres from the next town, I thought it worth my while to try and solve the crime. The jacket was my only clue as to the route by which my food had disappeared, and so I boldly decided to enter the forest in that direction. Perhaps, however, 'boldly' is too strong a word, considering I was grasping a frying pan in one hand and my heavy chain lock in the other, clanging them together to make a tremendous din as I stepped tentatively over fallen logs. The undergrowth was thick, and I could hardly believe that a bear could have made its way through. I was certainly struggling, and it wasn't long before I decided to concede defeat and turn back. There was no sign of the bag, and I didn't really know what I was hoping to find anyway. It was not as if the bear was going to be sitting there fiddling with the buckles. My pannier was surely in tatters by now, wherever it was. And if I did find the bear, looking up at me with a guilty expression and peanut butter and jam smeared around its chops, was I really going to have the tenacity to bop it over the head with my frying pan for half a bag of cookies? No, no, better to let nature run its course on this one, I decided, and I beat a hasty retreat.

Having given my food pannier up for dead, I next had to work out how to carry all of my remaining possessions and I was fortunate enough to find a simple solution. The backpack that I usually carried on the top of the rear rack could be made to fit well enough on the side of the bike in place of the pannier simply by attaching its straps through the rack. With this solved, my only remaining problem was that I still had eighty kilometres to cycle and nothing to eat, save for a 100 gram bar of chocolate that I had miraculously forgotten about and left in one of my other panniers. I made a plan to ration this very carefully, and headed back to the highway.

I cycled onwards on the quiet road, still a little in shock about what had happened, thinking excitedly about how I'd had a bear within twenty metres of my sleeping head last night, and wondering, more practically, what I was going to do about getting just one replacement pannier. The lost item was an Ortlieb pannier and so came with a five year warranty, but no doubt there was some cheeky little thing in the small print about theft by bear not being covered if the pannier was filled with food and then left unattended in the middle of bear country. But I was also secretly delighted, because Canada had not always been the most exciting of countries, and now at last I had a good story to tell. I had no one to tell it to, of course, being out in the forest on an empty road. But just as I was thinking this another cyclist appeared in my mirror, and cycled up beside me.

The cyclist was a middle-aged French Canadian from Quebec named Jean. I resisted my hungry stomach's demands to immediately request he give me food, my brain correctly deciding that I should make a little small talk first. In any case he was on a road bike with almost nothing in the way of bags, so he very likely had no food with him. Jean seemed a little eccentric, and his English was not very good, but I managed to establish that he was on a tour across Canada, and that he was on his way from Quebec to Vancouver.

"You're going the wrong way," I told him.

"No, I go zis way."

"But you are cycling to Vancouver?"

"Yes. I go Vancouver."

"You're going the wrong way then."

"No."

"Well, one of us is."

"No."

This was getting us nowhere. I changed the topic, and asked how it was that he had no stuff on his bike. Surely he could not really be cycling to Vancouver with so few possessions.

"I 'ave a support car."

Ah, that explained it.

"And where is your support car?" I asked, hoping to soon have myself some breakfast.

"Just up 'ere. In ze trees."

"Great. And who is driving your support car?"

"I am."

Now the jaw-dropping explanation as to why Jean was going the wrong way was revealed. He was crossing Canada, with a support car, alone. He would park the car somewhere, cycle thirty kilometres west, then turn around and cycle the same thirty kilometres back east, fetch the car, then drive himself thirty kilometres west, covering the same ground for a third time. I could not believe what I was hearing. I was alone in the woods in the presence of a clinically insane lunatic.

"So you are cycling everything twice?"

"Yes. I would like to cycle 'ome again."

"You're going to cycle back from Vancouver as well?"

"Yes."

"With the car?"

"Yes."

"So really you are going to cycle everything four times?"

"No. Twice."

"But you are doing it four times, because you are doing it twice in each direction."

"No. I am doing it twice. I would not do it four times! Are you crazy!? It iz too much!"

Thankfully bringing an end to this bizarre conversation, we reached a trail leading into the trees where Jean told me that his car was parked. Under normal circumstances I probably wouldn't have wanted to follow such a madman into the woods, but my stomach was pressing an increasingly convincing case for trying to gain some of the man's food.

We soon came to an orange car parked in a little clearing. On the roof was a luggage container, the back rack held a spare bicycle, and a third bike was wedged in the back seats amongst a cluster of boxes and cycling paraphernalia. "I don't know about mechanics," Jean explained. "So when one bike breaks, I just take another."

I was naturally pretty stunned by all this, but I was also terribly hungry, so I asked Jean if he could spare me some food. I'd already told him my bear story a couple of times, but he hadn't seemed to grasp what I was saying, so now I skipped the niceties and just asked straight out for some food. He gave me a couple of peanut butter sandwiches, the cycle tourist staple, which I devoured with something like grateful impoliteness.

As my stomach settled towards contentment and I stood there batting away the flies, Jean revealed more of his story to me. There were originally five of them that were planning to cycle across the country together, with one of them acting as the support driver. Over time each of these other fellows had made their excuses and dropped out, until finally there was only Jean left. To his credit, Jean had not been deterred, and he'd decided to continue with the ride anyway. And not wanting to lose out on the support driver, with all the luxury and convenience that would bring, he'd simply adapted to take on the role himself. It certainly gave a new meaning to the term 'self-supported'.

It was almost beginning to make sense, but I did have to wonder if he was really going to keep this routine up all of the way across the mundane prairies, which had been bad enough to do once. But Jean next revealed that the prairies and Vancouver had never even been part of the original plan. He was only supposed to cycle across Quebec, but after successfully doing that, he'd liked the lifestyle so much that he thought he'd carry on all the way across the country. The only slight issue with this, so far as I could tell, was that he hadn't informed his wife. "She doesn't know about Vancouver," Jean confirmed. "She keeps calling and asking where I am."

Strangely when it was time for us to say goodbye and exchange contact details, the only number Jean gave me was that of his wife. I wondered if perhaps this was secretly a call for help. Maybe I was meant to phone her, tell her that I'd found her husband and I was worried that perhaps he might have escaped from somewhere.

But when I finally reached the small town of Chapleau a few hours later, the only oasis of civilisation on this long road, I completely forgot about Jean. Despite his sandwiches I was starving hungry once again and I hurried to the supermarket. It wasn't one of the cheap ones, but under the circumstances it was going to have to do. As I was in the middle of locking up my bike outside, a friendly man came over to say hello, which was something that happened an awful lot in Canada. We had a little chat, and of course he asked me where I was from, so I told him.

"England?" he said earnestly. "Well, of course they have been in the news today. They've chosen to go it alone. Fifty-one percent to forty-nine. It's a funny old world isn't it?"

I was in shock. I wandered around the supermarket in a daze. This was a disaster. Dea and I had put all of our savings from Australia into British pounds. With our plans to spend all of this money in other currencies, we'd effectively just lost somewhere between ten and twenty percent of our money overnight, as the value of the pound plummeted post-Brexit. I really did not believe this would happen. How could this have happened? I tried to do my shopping, but I'd completely lost my appetite. The slightly more expensive groceries now seemed trivial. What was a couple of dollars more? We'd just lost thousands.

I went to the library and sat on my laptop, and tried to digest the fallout from my country's decision to leave the European Union. I was in such a state of disbelief that I didn't even eat anything, and my stomach raised no objections thanks to the sickly feeling that now resided within it. As well as losing so much money, the future implications for Dea and myself, the potential complications we might face in the future as a result of her being a citizen of the European Union and me not, weighed heavily upon both of us as I did my best to reassure her, while feeling quite un-reassured myself. My country appeared to have descended into chaos overnight, and quite aside from our own losses, we both feared what this might mean on a larger scale. I could not see how this was going to turn out to be anything other than a backward step for Britain, Europe, and the world in general.

After a few hours I pulled myself away from the computer, my stomach telling me that it could probably hold down a little food now if I wouldn't mind forcing some down. I did that, then got back on my bike and rode out of Chapleau. I felt like the whole world had just been turned upside down, but heading back out into the wild, on the long, empty, tree-lined road, I felt calmed. Whatever madness there was in the world, there would always be places like this, places to escape to on my bike. I was still free, still living my life the way that I wanted, a travelling vagabond, mostly unaffected by all that political nonsense. I decided against my original plan to spend my evening constructing an effigy of Boris Johnson, and instead relaxed and enjoyed where I was. And then, as I cycled along, a huge mother moose suddenly lumbered out of the trees just ahead of me and crossed the road with two calves in tow. The calves looked the size of horses, the mother an elephant. It was an incredible sight, this giant creature going about her motherly business, completely unaware of all our human troubles. I smiled. Life was still good.

10

I was very excited to arrive in Montreal for the second time in my life. Almost six years had passed since my previous visit, during the early days of my first, ultimately unsuccessful, attempt at a journey around the world by bike. On that occasion I had arrived from the opposite direction, having cycled from Halifax, before turning south towards Toronto. Arriving now from the west was a significant moment then, for I knew for sure that the distance left to Halifax was not insurmountable. I had ridden it before, and I also knew from experience that it would be more interesting than the long kilometres I had left behind me. Weeks of prairies had been followed by weeks of repetitive forest, but the province of Quebec, with its network of incredible off-road bicycle paths, promised something a little more interesting. And what was more, by the time Quebec was over I would practically be within sight of the finishing line in Halifax.

But being a tangible distance from the end of Canada was not the only reason for my excitement about being in Montreal. There was also an opportunity to meet up with an old friend, the first of several that I planned to see in Quebec. It was Daniel, the man who was supposed to have been joining me on this trip, who was supposed to have been my hapless sidekick, but who was sadly too hapless to make it to the start line. Three years earlier he'd declined, at the very last minute, to join the great adventure, for a variety of extremely questionable reasons, including the fact that his car had broken down and he'd lost his glasses.

"You don't need a car to cycle," I had protested, but his mind was made up, and he'd chosen to remain in Canada.

And so it was after three long years that it was in Canada where I finally tracked the man down. He had been living in Montreal for a couple of years, settling down with a girl, studying, doing normal life things. I wondered what it would be like to see him again, whether he would have any regrets. But most of all I looked forward to cycling with him, as he planned to ride with me for a few days up to Quebec City. A chance to glimpse what might have been, perhaps.

There was light rain in the morning as I cycled through the outskirts of Montreal's metropolitan area, past overly ornate homes of wealthy suburbanites, where I noticed the latest trend was to add castle-like turrets to one's home. Being in a developed nation sometimes felt like too much when I knew how people in other parts of the world lived, but I nevertheless appreciated the well-maintained cycle paths that guided me. They led me all the way over a bridge into Montreal proper, a city interestingly enough built on a large island in the middle of the great Saint Lawrence River. Here I came across by far the most bicycles I'd seen since Vancouver, on gridded streets that reminded me more of Melbourne, Australia, than anywhere I'd seen in Canada. I made my way to Daniel's address and rang the bell.

He opened the door with a broad smile. His shock of strawberry blonde hair was as I remembered it, and I was delighted to see that he had some new glasses; he would not be able to use that as an excuse to get out of our ride to Quebec City together. We greeted one another and set about becoming reacquainted, not having seen each other for over four years.

That evening we walked to the centre of Montreal to see a big jazz festival that was taking place, and talked about how it was a shame that Daniel had never joined the trip. Ultimately, of course, his failure to do so came down to money. He thought he couldn't afford it, like all of the other people who had turned down my invitations to join me from the start. I hoped he wouldn't be too upset to learn that after three years on the road, 50,000 kilometres cycled, forty-nine countries, four continents, and after paying for three cruises, I presently had more money than when I started. He wasn't, he had no regrets. By staying home he'd met the love of his life, Lucy. Everything happens for a reason, and it seemed everything had worked out pretty well for both of us, in different ways.

The festival was great. We started off by watching two female street performers as they danced with fire, swallowed fire, and generally did lots of entertaining things, with fire.

"Where do you think they're from?" I asked.

"They look Eastern European. Romania maybe," Daniel guessed, and as I watched them I got carried away imagining their life stories. How interesting their lives must be, living as street performers, travelling all over the world breathing fire, and what had they come from, what had they grown up with, and what had brought them here, to the other side of the world? Then the performance came to an end and one of them spoke to the crowd, in French, with a Quebec accent, and the fantasy was ruined.

We moved on and spent the rest of the evening watching a variety of musicians perform on several stages set up throughout the city centre for this free annual public festival. It was very entertaining, and as I watched and listened my mind wandered, and I thought back on who I was the last time I was in this city. I'd spent the past six years on my bike and a lot of things had changed so much in that time. I looked at Daniel and I thought about how differently things could have gone, for both of us. The forks in the road that we all come to, the choices we make, the gambles, and the outcomes, all leading us places, yet forever leaving us mystified as to what else might have been.

I'd arrived in Montreal on a Thursday, under the assumption that Daniel and I would start cycling together on the Saturday. Unfortunately he informed me that he simply could not get out of working at the Syrian restaurant he was employed at over the weekend. But he was sure he would have Monday, Tuesday, and Wednesday free, giving us just enough time to get to Quebec City, and I was welcome to sleep on his and Lucy's sofa until then. That meant I got to enjoy three whole days off the bike in succession. My tired body was ecstatic about this first break since Vancouver, but the downside was that it made the task of cycling every inch to Halifax in time for the boat a little more difficult. I was putting myself behind schedule, but I thought the chance to finally cycle with Daniel made it worth the risk.

Monday morning arrived and at last Daniel and I were going off on a bicycle tour together. Granted, a three day ride from Montreal to Quebec City was a far cry from the ride around the world we'd originally planned, but it was going to have to do. Daniel emerged from his bedroom into the living room somewhat bleary eyed. Understandable, as he'd been working late in the restaurant the night before. "I'm sorry," he said, "but against all the odds I've been scheduled to work Tuesday. I'm never usually, but someone is off this week and there's no way around it."

It looked like our three day tour had been reduced, thanks to those annoying responsibilities that I've heard come with real life, down to a single day ride.

"I'm really sorry about that," Daniel repeated.

"That's okay, really," I laughed, "I learnt a long time ago what a promise from you means!"

We resolved to make the most of it and fortunately it was a bright, clear morning as I loaded up my bike again outside the apartment. It was quite exciting, for I was clipping onto my bike two brand-new bright-red Arkel panniers. Arkel are a Canadian company who had heard about my misfortune with the bear thanks to a reader of my blog, Lorriane, and very generously sent me some free replacements, presumably as a form of apology on behalf of the disgraceful behaviour of their country's wildlife. The panniers looked more robust than my old ones and I was very happy with them, but whether they would prove themselves more bear-proof than the Ortliebs, I did not yet know.

Daniel was not so lucky. Not only did he not have any brand-new bright-red Arkel panniers, he did not even have a bike. This was something of a handicap, even on a one day bike tour. So our long awaited ride together began with a walk to one of the city's many bike rental stations, where he was able to make a short term loan of a bike. These could not be removed from the city, nor rented for more than thirty minutes, and I was worried our tour together was about to be curtailed still further. But no, Daniel insisted he was one hundred percent committed this time, at least for the next seven or eight hours, and so we went to a bike rental shop in town where he got a slightly better model.

We asked a man who might or might not have been homeless to take a photo of the two of us together, and then we were off. Through the city we rode, on fairly decent cycle lanes, then over a huge bridge that offered us great views back over Montreal as we left the island behind. It was a gorgeous day and we were both in high spirits to finally be making this dream a reality. Finally my movie had its long lost co-star. (Daniel, by the way, was supposed to be being played by the guy who played Ron Weasley in Harry Potter, but I'm not sure he'll be up for such a pitifully small part now, maybe a red-headed extra can be found?)

Beyond the bridge we linked up with La Route Verte 1, one of the so-called green routes, the network of cycle paths that make Quebec by far the best province in Canada for cycling. At the start of it we were slightly unsure of where to turn and as we stopped momentarily to check our directions an old man on a road bike coming the other way stopped to see if we were okay. He came from an Italian family and had a cool white beard, but otherwise he just asked the usual questions about what we were doing and where we were going, and we had a pleasant chat for a few moments before heading our separate ways. As we rode off I prepared to think nothing more of it, it was the kind of encounter that happened all the time. But Daniel burst out with, "Whoa! What a crazy character! Amazing!" and I realised that for him all of this was new and exciting, and he saw everything from a different perspective. He showed a similar level of enthusiasm for the incredible cycle paths that we followed all day. "This is amazing!" he kept exclaiming. These bike paths were a few hours from his home and he'd lived in Montreal for two years, but this was the first time he'd seen them.

We were now clear of the city, and the path guided us through open farmland to the small town of Chambly. Daniel had been going on about wanting to find a place to enjoy a swim, an excellent idea given the hot weather, and it looked like we were in luck as we crossed a bridge on our way into town. On our right was a river, to the left it opened up into a big lake. I suggested that we go for a swim in the lake if we could, but Daniel turned his nose up and said, "I don't think it is a lake, I think it's just where the river gets wider." And so I laughed at him, and asked what he thought a lake was.

We found a beach and I dived in. Daniel did not join me, declaring the water to be too dirty. He was also too busy making phone calls about renting apartments and all that real life stuff he had to deal with, all the stuff he would be going right back to very soon.

We pedalled on east, still revelling in the fantastic bike paths. Daniel continued to be amazed by them, and by the countryside that he seemed to have no idea existed so close to his front door. He was excited by everything. "I have to say, I do enjoy the smell of manure," was a particularly enjoyable quote of his that summed up this point. Actually, maybe it was good he didn't cycle around the whole world, it might have been too much for him.

Then he got a flat tyre. He had literally no idea how to go about fixing it. He didn't even know how to get the tyre off the rim. I shook my head ruefully. A fine hapless sidekick he would have made, and no mistake. I took over and did it for him. We didn't have much time to spare, as he had to make it to Granby in time to catch an eight thirty bus back to Montreal. Daniel was capable of going a lot faster than me, due to the fact that a) he had practically no luggage on his bike, b) I had everything I owned on mine, and c) literally every cyclist in the world is faster then me. With him beginning to panic about making it on time for the bus I told him that he was welcome to go on ahead, and he said he thought he'd better. So we fist bumped goodbye without pausing from cycling and then that was it, he went off ahead, slowly but surely disappearing into the distance. Our cycle together had been ever so brief, especially compared to what it might have been, but it had been very enjoyable, and it ended, perhaps fittingly, with him rushing off to get back to real life, and with me plodding slowly along all by myself, just like I'd been doing for the last three years.

11

Quebec, Canada
12th July 2016

The excellent cycle paths continued for the next couple of days. In places they were well-used, by a variety of riders ranging from families to serious Lycra-clad road cyclists. At one point where the path crossed a road I noticed a car park with dozens of cars parked up that had bicycle racks on them, some people pulling their bikes off their car in order to go for an out-and-back ride on the path. This led me to reflect on the irony that the existence of the cycle path was actually *increasing* the traffic on the roads slightly. This didn't matter much to me, though, because I wasn't on the roads, I was on the path, and it was never long before it became more remote and I had it almost entirely to myself. I camped at the frequent rest areas that appeared all along the trail and very much enjoyed the easy cycling experience. These traffic-free routes made Quebec so much more relaxed and pleasant than the rest of Canada had been.

Eventually the cycle routes took me out of the forests and back into civilisation, and across a rusty steel truss bridge over the Saint Lawrence. I remembered that fantastic old bridge from my last visit, all rusting and creaking and magnificent, and it made for a very fine welcome to Quebec City. I rode on to VéloCentrix, a non-profit bicycle workshop where I had arranged to meet a man named Julien. Back in 2010 I'd been cycling south towards Montreal on the same paths I'd just followed, when I'd encountered a local cycle tourist by the name of Meghan. She cycled with me for a few days and we became friends. Now that I was back in Quebec we'd arranged to again cycle together for a few days, north from Quebec City this time, with Meghan's boyfriend Julien also joining us. As luck would have it Julien was a bit of a bike mechanic and volunteered at this workshop, so I'd stopped by as my overworked bike was once again in need of a little TLC.

As I'd cycled out of Montreal with Daniel I'd noticed that my bottom bracket was loose. It was still possible to cycle on, but with a tough time schedule to make it to Halifax a mechanical breakdown was not something I could afford, and Julien's offer of a used-but-functional replacement was most welcome. He helped me fit it and then tightened up the crankset much tighter than I would have done by myself. "You don't want it falling off," he said. He seemed like a nice guy, and I was really looking forward to cycle with him and Meghan, especially now I had a working bike again.

I would meet up with Julien and Meghan in the morning, but first I rode off alone to find more old friends.

Meggie was a lovely girl who on my first Canadian visit had seen me cycling past and invited me to stay with her and her friends in Quebec City. That was back in 2010, but we'd also seen each other in 2012, when she'd stayed with me in Munich and we'd downed pitchers of beer together at Oktoberfest. Another four years had now slipped by and it was time to rekindle our friendship once more. Times had very much changed, however. Last time I'd seen her she had been single, but now she lived in a really nice house with her boyfriend, Martin, and their young baby, Isaak.

I pulled up to her big house and she came out to greet me, although our moment of reunion was interrupted by one of her neighbours, who spotted me and came over to ask me about my brand-new bright-red Arkel panniers.

"Are they good for food?" he asked.

"What?" I was a bit confused.

"Are they good for storing food?"

"Well, yes, I suppose so."

"We just have a container."

I literally had no idea where this conversation was going, but fortunately he noticed that Meggie was standing there waiting to say hello to me after four years, and he stepped aside.

"Meggie! It's so good to see you again. Do you own this house? Wow. You must have been working hard."

And she had. It was a fantastic house. It even had a pool. For days I had been cycling in intense heat, occasionally noticing pools in backyards and only wishing I could jump in one. Now I had my chance.

I was still relaxing in the pool when Simon and Marie-Claude arrived. They had been Meggie's flatmates when I'd stayed there and had come over this evening for the big reunion. Simon was still his usual humorous self, joking around and playing the fool. But things had also changed for them, and Marie-Claude arrived looking much fatter than I remembered her. So fat, in fact, that I was worried about giving her the traditional Quebec greeting of a kiss on each cheek, lest I get too close and bounce right off. She was nine months pregnant, and due any day.

It was a fantastic evening, which included a tofu burger barbecue, nine percent Quebec beer (though not for Marie-Claude), and a lot of fun and games. First up was a round of boules. Meggie was busy putting Isaak to sleep, so it was just me, Simon, and Marie-Claude taking part. I'd imagined that Simon would be my major competition, but in a surprise result it was Marie-Claude who triumphed. Quite convincingly actually. Next up was another throwing game, this one involving hurling a string with two balls on either end so that it would land successfully on a rack at the other end of the garden. Well, once again it was Marie-Claude who proved the victor, and by this stage I was frankly getting a little fed up of losing at sports to a heavily pregnant lady. The final game required teams, so I joined forces with Marie-Claude to take on Simon and Meggie. It was yet another throwing game, the object this time to get metal rings into a box. With the reigning champion on my side I was confident of securing victory. We lost.

It was October 2010 when I first met Meghan, on a bridge in the middle of nowhere, where she introduced herself as "Meghan the vegan."

"That doesn't rhyme," I said, but the truth was I was intrigued. I'd never met a vegan before, didn't know what one was actually. But over the following few days as we cycled together I found out, and I think many of the environmental beliefs and principles that Meghan held must have rubbed off on me, for within a few weeks I'd stopped eating meat myself.

Knowing what kind of person Meghan was, it wasn't any surprise when she pulled alongside me at our present-day rendezvous point and the first thing she did was to tell me that she had a bicycle garden ready for me. She then pulled out several bundles of wheatgrass that she'd already started growing and asked where I'd like to attach them to my bike. I must admit that this wasn't a question I'd really given much thought to before. "You can put them on the frame, on mudguards, in water bottles, your wheels, anywhere really," Meghan reminded me. I settled for wrapping one around my headset, and another on my front wheel hub.

"All we have to do now is water it and watch it grow!" Meghan beamed.

"Can we eat it afterwards then?" I asked.

"Well, you could. But I don't. It's kind of disgusting after it's been on the bike, to be honest."

Just then Julien pulled up. Even if we hadn't already met it would have been easy to identify him as Meghan's boyfriend, due to the phenomenal amount of wheatgrass on his bike.

To save ourselves a detour we took a ferry back across the Saint Lawrence. On board a friendly worker came over and asked about the grass. "You can eat it," I told him. "Go on, try some, I haven't cycled anywhere with it yet." And he did, and he liked it too, and then another woman came over to ask about it as well. It certainly did provide a talking point. As Meghan took over explaining how you really can grow food anywhere, I went upstairs to watch the beautiful city slowly shrinking as we headed over to the eastern bank of the river. Quebec City is the most European of North American cities, and it sure made for a lovely picturesque sight as we glided away from it.

We rolled off the other side, but none of us had had the good sense to eat more than a handful of wheatgrass on the ferry, and so after just two kilometres we stopped to have some food. Then it was time to get down to the serious business of cycling. But two kilometres later Meghan spotted some Saskatoon berries growing wild at the side of the path, and we had to stop to pick some. Then it really was time to get down to the serious business of cycling. But two kilometres later we saw a big waterfall on the other side of the river, and stopped to admire it.

This was all very pleasant. I was very happy to have company, and to be taking our time. The only problem was that I didn't have a lot of time to spare, what with needing to average a hundred kilometres per day to reach Halifax on time. This was more than Meghan and Julien would usually cycle on their tours, and I certainly didn't want to push the pace too much either.

"I hope you won't blame us if you miss your boat though," Meghan said, aware that we weren't moving as fast as we might.

"Don't worry," I said, "I've already decided I'll blame Daniel."

But soon our cycle path ended and we had to cycle on the shoulder of the highway for a while. This was far less idyllic, but it at least meant we stopped to chat less frequently, and our rate of progress improved.

We followed the road for most of the day, making occasional detours through quaint riverside towns. It felt great to be with company, to catch up with Meghan after so many years, and to get used to her little quirks again. At one point she was cycling just ahead of me and I saw her right arm move out. Without slowing down she plucked an orange flower from the roadside, raised it to her mouth, and swallowed it in one swift motion.

We were mostly travelling through farmland and there were no really good options for wild camping, leading us to eventually throw up our tents in a little area of overgrown grass at the side of the road. We soon retired for the night, having already eaten our dinner at a rest area with picnic tables a little earlier in the evening. There had also been a boardwalk that led out into the river a little way there. I'd walked down there on my own and looked at the vast river, the marsh beside it, the sun closing in on the horizon, half hidden by clouds, and I'd realised that I felt really good. The thought just came to me, strong and real, that *'I really love travelling!'* It was so nice to have that positive feeling, which had sometimes been forgotten during the weeks of repetitive cycling. The past few days it had been so good to meet again with friends that I'd met years ago, when travelling was still new and exciting, and to have this timely reminder. It was still true. I knew it. *'I love travelling! I love this!'*

I did not sleep particularly well in our lumpy patch of grass, but given the fact that we were camping right next to a 'no camping' sign, we were all three of us happy to get up early and move on. Early morning cycling is almost always nice, and it was good to be on the highway before the traffic started. Within a couple of hours we reached an outdoor sculpture park that Meghan insisted we must stop at. "This was where Julien was conceived!" she said gleefully as we walked around the sculptures. How exactly she came to know that information was not clear, but I thought it a suitable location for such an event, with the swirling rock patterns down by the river being rather romantic. The sculptures themselves were pretty good too. Most of them were carved from logs and stood upright staring down on us. My favourite was of a wizard whose face was coming through a book. There was also an artist working, carving a new piece with a chainsaw and disturbing the serenity completely. It seemed unlikely anyone could be conceived with that sort of racket going on, but, so far as I understood it, none of us was keen to do any conceiving here this day anyway, so we moved along.

The river was getting ever wider as we followed it north, gradually turning from fresh water to salt as it opened up slowly towards the ocean. On the far side a row of mountains made for a scenic backdrop, while on our side the going remained relatively flat and easy. We took another break in a riverside park, where Meghan and I enjoyed a game of one-a-side volleyball. It was, and I don't use this term lightly, epic fun, not least because I won. I was having such a good time these days. Volleyball is just better with more than one player, isn't it?

Later on we took yet another break, this one at an ice cream place that happened to have free Wi-Fi. I went online to share my good mood with Dea, but the news from Denmark was not so positive. Her eye was giving her problems again. It was itching a lot, the spot was not yet completely gone, and she was concerned that the treatment wasn't working any more. She was sad and afraid, and that made me sad and afraid, and I was in a bad mood by the time the three of us got back on our bikes. I'd been having such a good time cycling with Meghan and Julien and now I felt guilty about that. What was I doing here, merrily cycling in Canada having a jolly time, when I should really be in Europe supporting my sick girlfriend? Not for the first time I wasn't sure if I'd made the right choice to continue alone. But I was almost at the end of Canada now. My boat back to Europe was leaving in just ten days. There was nothing else for it but to keep pushing for that goal.

The next day I started cycling before my companions. Meghan and Julien were slower than me packing up so I went on ahead, before waiting for them to catch up at a rest area. We were not getting close to a hundred kilometre days, but this was our last full day cycling together, so I decided to just relax and enjoy it. There would be the chance for me to put in some longer days to make up the ground when I was alone again. So when my friends arrived at the rest area instead of insisting we cycle on, I insisted we play some more games.

After a while we found the collective motivation to cycle onwards to the big town of Rivière-du-Loup, which I was interested to learn translates as Wolf River. We went shopping and stocked up, for this was the point at which our association with the now very wide Saint Lawrence would end and we would resume heading east. This unfortunately meant we started with a very, very steep climb out of town. It was a big test for three cyclists who had gotten used to cycling merrily along on the flat, but once we were over the hump we connected to another fantastic cycle trail that was much more kindly graded. Now we were back having a good time, cycling along through the forest, chatting and laughing together on this traffic-free route. As ever Meghan had to make occasional stops to pick nature's edibles, including a long break to collect wild mushrooms for dinner. It was interesting for me to see how abundant the food sources were, having cycled in nature so often, yet never having taken the time to forage before.

A little later we sat on a bench beside a lake to eat our dinner. It was an implausibly picturesque scene. The sky was turning golden orange behind the lake, the darkening firs and pines reflecting in the water, where beavers swam around, diving down and doing beaver-like things. It was a magical thing to see. This was absolutely the real one hundred percent Canadian experience.

For some reason over dinner the conversation got onto the topic of making up jokes, and how difficult it is to do. To prove this point I challenged Meghan to try and make up a joke about beavers. She responded smartly with:

"What's a beaver's favourite curse word?"

"Dam!"

This was impressive, if a little too easy. But she kept at it and continued to try and refine the joke, until she came up with something quite brilliant:

"What did the river say when a family of beavers moved in on its banks?"

I struggled to think of a witty answer, so Meghan excitedly revealed it:

"Well, I'll be dammed!"

The punchline was delivered with a smile and a swing of the arm, and we all laughed heartily, in a way that made me quite sure I would be telling that joke for years to come. I congratulated Meghan because, to be fair, it was a quality gag.

In the course all this merriment it had grown late, and we needed to cycle a few more kilometres to get to a nature campsite that we knew of. It was getting dark, but we were on a trail in the forest, with no one else using it, so it didn't seem to matter all that much that visibility was reduced. At least it didn't until the moment when Julien and Meghan screeched to a halt just in front of me, forcing me also into a sudden stop.

"Did you see that?!" a startled Meghan asked. I had not seen anything. I had been too busy trying to think of a joke involving Justin Beaver. "That was a bear. A bear cub. It just ran across the trail right in front of us."

Now we were in a potentially tight spot. Bears only really get aggressive towards humans if you get between them and their cubs. The trouble was, we didn't know where the mother was, and it was too dark to see much. It was a tense moment. We remained still at first, talking, banging things, dinging our bells to let everyone know where we were. When there was no further movements from the trees we decided to continue cautiously onwards, Meghan and Julien still just ahead. Then I got a fly in my eye. Talk about bad timing. I stopped to try and remove it, crying out to my companions, "Please, wait a minute, don't leave me with the bears!" to which Meghan shouted back, "What?" without slowing down.

But I caught them up at the camping place, two kilometres along the trail. We were relieved to have made it away from the bears, until it dawned on us that we were going to be spending the night two kilometres from them, which didn't really seem that far. Meghan was worried about being disturbed in the night, while I was more concerned about a bear making off with one of my brand-new bright-red Arkel panniers. For a moment I wasn't sure what to do, but then I noticed that this campsite had a wood-burning metal stove thing, and I put my bag in there and locked it tight.

Once we'd all made it through to morning I went to retrieve my food pannier. On the plus side it was untouched by any bears, but on the other hand it now had quite a smokey smell to it, that I worried might attract more bears in the future.

We rode onwards towards Témiscouata, where we would be saying our goodbyes and going our separate ways. It was an overcast morning with occasional light rain, but it was alright really, and quite nice to have a break from all the sun. I rode alongside Meghan and Julien for the last time, sad that our ride together was coming to an end.

"What did the beaver say when he found himself in the River Styx?" Meghan asked.

"I don't know."

"Dam it all to hell!"

She had gone too far.

12

Témiscouata, Canada
18th July 2016

We arrived in Témiscouata. From here Meghan and Julien were going north to explore a national park before looping back to Quebec City. For me it was, as ever, necessary to push on east. I was practically on the home straight, but I needed to sprint it now. It had been such a fantastic few days, and I didn't relish the prospect of being all alone again, but that was certainly how it had to be. It was time. It was also time to compare our bicycle gardens. Julien's was flourishing. Meghan's was struggling. Mine was wilted and yellowing. I couldn't work out why, but I think it was probably because I'd forgotten to water it for three days.

Before going our separate ways we stopped for one last break in a big park in town and I was delighted to the point of ecstatic to find a beach volleyball court. Here was one last chance to have some fun together. I started by challenging Meghan to a game, which I won. Then Julien stepped up, but I dispatched him with a comfortable victory too. In the final, enthralling contest, my dominance of the beach volleyball arena was challenged by both Meghan *and* Julien, taking me on two against one. With twice as many hands they won the first set. It was best of three sets though, as is so often the case when I lose the first set, and so I still had a chance. I was determined, I was agile, I was focused, I threw myself around the court like a maniac, I wanted it bad. I was sure I had more desire to win than my opponents, and perhaps that was why I was able to save match points in the second set before coming back to clinch an incredible 9-11, 14-12, 11-8 triumph.

I think it was probably for the best that I won in the end. Meghan and Julien accepted the narrow loss with much better grace than I would have, and we parted on good terms. For some reason as we were saying "goodbye" and "see you in another six years" Meghan asked if I had yet learnt any Danish. I told them that I had not really, but I mentioned the one three-word phrase that I had been taught, and so then as I cycled away from them for the last time it was with us shouting back and forth to each other, in Danish, "I love you!" "I love you!" "I love you!"

I was alone again. My time with Daniel and Lucy, Meggie, Simon and Marie-Claude (who around this time was giving birth to a healthy baby girl, by the way), and Meghan and Julien, had made the past week so great, but now I was on my own and without distractions. This was a good thing, because I had fallen behind schedule, and making sure I reached Halifax on time for my boat back to Europe was now the only thing that mattered.

I hadn't gone far when an old man on the path beckoned for me to stop. Of course I didn't have a lot of time to spare, but it would have been rude to cycle past and he looked like an interesting character. He was leaning on a walking stick, his shirt unbuttoned to reveal a wrinkled chest. He looked old and wise but he soon proved otherwise as he cocked his brow and asked, "Vancouver? That way?" while pointing east, as if he were after directions.

"No, it's the other way," I corrected him.

"Are you sure?"

"Yes, I've just come from Vancouver."

"Oh. How long did that take?"

"Two and a half months. I'm on my way to Halifax."

"Halifax is further than Vancouver?"

Was this man really from Canada? He was, he told me he was from Quebec. He couldn't have travelled much.

"No, no. Halifax is closer than Vancouver."

"Well how long will it take you to get to Halifax?"

"One week. I've got to be there in one week."

"Oh, you'll have to take a bus!"

Determined that I would not have to take a bus I pulled myself away from the old fellow and continued, and before long I was at the border with a new province, New Brunswick. I was sad to be leaving Quebec. It had been my favourite province, thanks to the great cycle paths and the friends I'd shared it with. It had given me a big boost, and carried me almost effortlessly to within range of the finish line. Now I just had the relatively small Maritime provinces of New Brunswick and Nova Scotia ahead of me. The only problem was that this was Canada, and so relatively small things were still pretty big.

In the town of Grand Falls I stopped at a supermarket and bumped into yet another cycle tourist. This time it was a girl called Stephanie, although she wasn't quite a solo female cyclist, as she was riding across Canada with her dog. She had the funny-looking Gadmo sat in a trailer behind her bike. He looked like he was enjoying himself, peering out at the world through his big brown eyes that sat beneath a messy mop of hair. "Actually," Stephanie said, "he doesn't really like it that much."

Stephanie and I went together to the waterfalls that give Grand Falls its name and spent a few minutes admiring them, for they were quite... erm... grand. Gadmo was allowed out of his trailer for a little while and he did not seem like he wanted to go back in again afterwards. He went and laid down under a picnic bench and it took quite a bit of effort on Stephanie's part to coax him back out again.

From Grand Falls I knew that there was another multi-purpose trail and we cycled off together to find it, as it seemed to offer the chance to ride once again off-road for the next 200 kilometres or so. But sadly it was immediately obvious that it was not going to be in the same league as the bike paths of Quebec. There were bumpy, grassy sections and bumpy, rocky sections. It was far from ideal, especially for poor Gadmo, who didn't enjoy the bumps. Stephanie told me a story about how a few days earlier she'd been taking a break and let him run around. Someone had left their car door open nearby, and Gadmo ran over and jumped in the seat.

"Ha ha," I laughed, "I think he's trying to tell you something."

We made it as far as the indecisively named Perth-Andover together, then went our separate ways. It would have been nice to cycle more with Stephanie and Gadmo, but she wanted to stop early at a campground. She was stopping around three in the afternoon every day to give the dog a break. Of course with my schedule I had no choice but to wish them well and press on.

Despite the difficulties I persevered with the rough trail. During the course of the day I encountered a few motorbikes, some quad bikes, even one or two joggers, but no cyclists. It seemed a terrible shame. Quebec had done such a fantastic job of converting their old railway lines into paved bike paths. Here in New Brunswick it felt like they'd done half a job, and it just wasn't good enough for any-one to want to make use of it.

I myself did not really mind the bad surface too much, and man-aged 150 kilometres that day after a last couple of hours of mad bumpy sprinting. It was late by the time I did call it a night, and I had to make do with camping in a disused plot of land next to a river, as there were really no other options. I was next to some trees and bushes and, just after I'd got my tent up, I heard an animal rust-ling about in there. It sounded big and after all my experiences with them across this country, I instantly imagined it to be a bear. I scrambled around for my torch, genuinely feeling quite scared. I flashed the torchlight on the bushes but could see nothing, so I shouted and made noise and told it to go away. I hoped it would run away, startled by me, but it did not. Instead I heard it again, moving closer now. It was not afraid of me. I was in big trouble. I flashed the torch around again, desperate to see what I was up against. Finally my light settled on a pair of eyes. They belonged to a racoon. I breathed a sigh of relief, and decided that my brand-new bright-red smokey-scented Arkel panniers would be staying safely in my tent this night.

The trail ended and I stuck to the shoulder of the highway for the rest of New Brunswick, putting in 150 kilometre days all of the way to Nova Scotia. I was flying along, spurred on by thoughts of what awaited me – a relaxing six days at sea, then the chance to see my family for the first time in three years, and then, finally, a reunion with Dea. It was all the motivation I needed to keep putting in the hours, and Halifax drew near. Once I passed the airport I knew I was getting close. The first time I'd ever entered Canada I had flown into that airport and then cycled into Halifax, so I knew for a fact that I was only forty kilometres from my goal, forty kilometres from the Atlantic Ocean.

There was time for one last night of camping and I found a nice spot on a flat area of grass beside a little stream. I set up camp and as I did so I reflected on how the next time I'd do it, I'd be back in my own country, having been around the world. It was a crazy thought.

The next morning I felt great. I put on some music and, as I cycled alone through a forest park, I thought back on how far I'd come. Almost all of Canada was behind me. 7,000 kilometres had gone by, only a handful remained. Then I emerged beside some water and a small passenger ferry carried me across the bay to Halifax waterfront. I walked along the pedestrianised area pushing my bike through the crowds, past oyster stalls and restaurants and a hundred million dollar yacht, until I found myself at the cruise terminal. A huge cruise ship rested there but it was not mine. I checked carefully to make sure it was not the Queen Mary 2. It would have been a grave error indeed to get my dates wrong. But no, it was another ship, and mine would arrive the next day as planned. I had made it with twenty-four hours to spare, and I could finally relax.

I continued on along the waterfront until I reached Point Pleasant Park. This large park is at the end of the peninsula on which Halifax is built, and I'd decided I must visit to mark the official end point of my cross-country ride. Reaching it was a moment of triumph, although my moment of glory was slightly hijacked by yet another old man asking me where I had come from. This one, George, was very old and very friendly, and I answered him with pride. He was very interested, at first, but our conversation soon deteriorated into him listing countries and what he thought about them. Oh, old people, you've got to love them, haven't you?

Eventually George ran out of countries and I was free to go on alone to the very end of the peninsula. I rested my bike up and we congratulated one another on a job well done. We were at the end of Canada at long, long last. I would have liked to swim, but the water was thick with seaweed and it was crashing in against the rocks a bit aggressively, so I settled for just touching the water. Then I sat back on the grass and looked out at the Atlantic. I thought back on everything that it had taken over the previous eleven weeks to get me to this point. Those wonderful early days riding through the Rocky Mountains, and then the long and boring prairies, made more interesting of course by Vivian, and then the great boreal forest, filled with bears and flies, that had been so tough. Reaching Montreal had been the beginning of the end, and the company of friends had carried me through to the Maritimes and the final stretch. It had been an epic eleven weeks, a real adventure. I had, in truth, underestimated Canada. It was bigger than I had given it credit for, and much tougher. Having to go on alone without Dea had been a hard decision, and missing her had made the ride even more difficult. But it was the thought of getting back to her that kept me going, and I knew she was doing well enough again now to start cycling west from Denmark to come and find me. We would be reunited somewhere in Europe soon. But I would miss Canada. I would miss the mountains, the animals, and the forests. I would miss the smell of pine and the great lakes and the fresh air. Mostly I would miss the sense of being in the middle of endless nature, and those moments when the forest seemed to stretch on to eternity in every direction, and how in such moments that natural world seemed so strong, and capable of resisting man's continued attempts at domination. I loved cycling across Canada. And here I was now at the end. One way or another I had made it.

At almost that exact same moment, several hundred kilometres to the northeast, a short girl (Lucy Lui) was standing beside her own bicycle in Saint John's, Newfoundland, wind flapping at her bright orange hunting jacket, as she stared out at the same ocean. It was the final scene of an incredible and inspiring tale. A city girl with no experience of the wild, no experience of cycling, no experience of camping, with no clue how to read a map nor follow directions, she had against all the odds made it right across Canada with her bicycle, despite wanting to quit every single minute of every single day. An inspiring achievement, and one that proves that just about anything is possible in this world with enough stubborn determination and will-power.

It will make for a great movie, I'm sure.

Progress Report
Halifax, August 2016

1. Circumnavigate the planet

The Eiffel Tower: 2.3° E. Halifax: 63.6° W.
294.1° out of 360° around the planet.
(81.7% of the way around.)

2. Do so using only my bicycle and boats

Mori: 90.3° E. Halifax: 63.6° W.
206.1° out of 360° around the planet.
(57.2% of the way around.)

3. Pass through antipodal points

Not going down to South America meant I wouldn't be
doing this before getting back to Mori, but other criteria
would still qualify it as a circumnavigation...

4. Visit all of the inhabited continents

Still four out of six.

5. Cycle at least 100,000 kilometres

55,699 kilometres completed. Just one more kilometre, and
then there would be only 44,300 to go.

6. Cycle in 100 countries

Canada was number forty-nine, almost halfway.

7. Return with more money than I start with

Damn you Boris.

PART THREE

HALIFAX TO EDINBURGH

13

Halifax, Canada
26th July 2016

I sensed right away that my voyage back to my homeland aboard
the Queen Mary 2 was not going to be like my previous cruises,
for this was a real luxury liner, following in the great transatlantic traditions of the Queen Mary, the Queen Elizabeth, and the
QE2. People (all the people apart from me, anyway) took this particular vessel with expectations of a certain standard of elegance and
extravagance. Like on all cruises, there would be formal and informal
nights, but the standards were a little higher this time, with even the
informal nights described as 'Jacket required, tie optional', and I had
a funny feeling that my bright red rain jacket wasn't going to cut it.

Given such policies I did not feel entirely certain that I was even
going to be allowed on board, and my concerns grew during a long
period of waiting, albeit sat alongside a few other passengers that
were also getting on in Halifax, on some plastic seating in the cruise
terminal. Our passports had all been taken from us and we had been
told by a nice lady to wait until it was time for us to be checked in. I
sat impatiently next to my panniers and bike, now boxed up, worried that something might still go wrong. It wasn't until I was actually on the ship that I would feel safe.

We waited for an hour or so, my anxiety increasing with every
passing minute, until finally another member of staff, this one an
older, more official-looking woman, approached me and spoke in a

harsh, irritated tone: "I'm sorry, but this is the main embarkation area. We have got passengers coming back and forth through here all day. I'm going to have to ask you to go somewhere else!"

"But... but..." I stammered, taken aback by the woman's tone and the fact that my worst fears appeared to be coming true. "Isn't this... isn't this where I'm supposed to board the ship?"

Now it was her turn to look alarmed. "You're a passenger?! Oh, I'm terribly sorry. I didn't realise. I do apologise!"

The woman scooted away with an air of embarrassment and confusion, before eventually another staff member returned with my passport and I was welcomed on board. I let out a huge sigh of relief as I finally stepped onto the ship. It felt so, so good to be on my boat home. I had made it! Arriving in my stateroom I wasted no time at all in popping open the complimentary bottle of sparkling wine that was waiting for me there, swigging it straight from the bottle. I had surely earned myself the right to a little celebrating, and in that moment I felt triumphant, quite euphoric. All of that effort cycling across another continent was now vindicated, as I drank my bubbly and considered how frigging awesome it was going to be to spend the next six days doing absolutely nothing.

The next six days were hideously boring. The strict dress code meant that I could not eat in any restaurants, nor go to any of the shows. I was not even really supposed to leave my stateroom after six in the evening, lest I risk ruining the other passengers' experience as they swanned around in their tuxedos. I shuffled only between my room, the frankly quite disappointing buffet, and the outside walkway on Deck 7. On the bright side, at least the television in my room played some good movies, and I soon discovered the relative joy of room service. But the lack of any company made the whole thing monumentally boring. I wished I had Dea with me, I really did. In my very darkest moments, I even found myself longing for Tom.

The days slipped by and I grew ever more desperate to reach our destination, for there was only one vegetarian meal on the room service menu, and I was beginning to pine after a peanut butter and jam sandwich. We had departed Halifax in thick fog which had stuck with us for several days. The limited visibility meant that we had needed to blow the loud foghorn every few minutes just in case, and I use the word 'we' quite wrongly, I had nothing to do with it. I still spent much of my time outside, just staring out at the sea. By our last full day in the Atlantic the fog had cleared, and around two in the afternoon, as I sat out on deck, I spotted land. It was just a thin sliver of an island, but it was clearly visible on our port side (that's right, I know nautical terms now). Another island soon appeared next to it. It occurred to me that I was looking at the Isles of Scilly, better known to me in my youth as the silly isles, a small cluster of islands off the southwest tip of Cornwall. These were British Isles. For the first time in over three years I could see England. I did not know how to feel.

Later on we passed Land's End, though in this instance it would have been more appropriately titled Land's Start. This was, from my perspective, the beginning of the British mainland. I stared at it from the boat, just faint grey hills on a horizon that held so much meaning for me, and I listened to some music, and I felt sad. I did not know why I felt sad. Maybe it was because I hadn't had a conversation for five days that hadn't involved me saying the phrases "vegetarian quesadilla" or "two double fudge cakes." I felt like an outsider on this ship. I felt like I did not belong. But more than that, I think I was nervous that that was also how it would be for me in England now. It had been my home for the first twenty-five years of my life, and yet, after so long away, now I had no confidence that it would still feel like home. And if it did not feel like home, then where could feel like home for me now? Had I travelled too far? Did I belong anywhere any more, or was I, as I had been on this ship, little more than a lost, wandering soul? I reflected on this, and the irony that I was probably more nervous about returning to my homeland than I'd been about entering any country over the past three years.

I packed my bags so that I would be ready to disembark in the morning, then went back outside and watched a beautiful sunset. More land was visible now, some part of Devon, as we slowly made our way east towards Southampton. The blue distant hills, at least from such a distance, could have been in any part of the world. They reminded me of similar hills I'd gazed at from boats when I'd been sailing past Malaysia, Australia, Fiji. And with this thought it suddenly struck me just how far I'd come. I was on the verge of making it back home after travelling all of the way around the world without flying. I tried to think back on all the places I'd been to since I'd left England, all the things I'd witnessed and all the people I'd met, and my head nearly exploded there was so much good and amazing stuff in there. The T.S. Elliot quote came to mind – *We must not cease from exploration and the end of all our exploring will be to arrive where we started and know the place for the first time'* – and I felt much better than I had earlier in the day. Sure, arriving back in England still caused me anxiety, but maybe that was a good thing. If I approached this right, I realised, this was merely an opportunity for one more adventure.

I awoke at seven in the morning and for the first time in six days there was no gentle pitching from side to side. The Queen Mary 2 had docked safely. I had partly wanted to get up early to witness our five a.m. arrival, but I'd overslept and missed it. That was alright though. I mean, with the best will in the world, Southampton is no Vancouver. I got up now and made my way to Deck 7 to look out on England. On one side was a large port area with the town of Southampton behind it. Far below me I could see my boxed bike being unloaded. I wandered around to the other side of the ship, where across the harbour I saw low green hills, a country manor, and the tiled red roofs of a little fishing village. This was it. This was England. As I looked out over it, waiting for the call to finally disembark this boring boat, another cruise ship sailed in alongside us. It had a gigantic smiley face painted on the front of it, and a big water slide curving around between two floors on the outside of the ship. It looked amazing fun. *Why couldn't I have been on that one?!'* I sighed.

There was a delay in getting off the boat, and then I had to spend some time rebuilding my bike, but by midday I was ready to return to England. I got on my bike and, being careful to align myself on the left side of the road, cycled into Southampton. Within minutes I realised that I did not know where I was, and I got off and pushed my bike along a footpath while I tried to get my bearings. I was looking for a road that I had intended to take, but I could not work out where it was, so I decided to just get back on and cycle in what felt like the right direction. This did not work. My mind was still on the Canadian model of the world, and a part of me was just looking for the long, straight road out of town that I could follow for days. But that was clearly not how things worked here. The streets were not even remotely sticking to a grid system; they twisted and turned and intersected in bizarre and confusing ways. I was soon hideously lost, all sense of direction gone. The streets were busy with people of all races, there were shops that were not big Canadian chain stores. It all seemed so strange and unfamiliar to me. I was lost and I was confused. My worst fears had been realised. I did not know this country.

I eventually stumbled upon a library and went inside to use a computer in order to try and establish where I should head next. I had to register first, and found it almost impossible to even speak with the librarian during this process. I felt really, really weird. But that was nothing to what I felt next, when I wandered into a Sainsbury's supermarket, and found it to be genuinely one of the strangest experiences of my life. It was almost like an out-of-body experience, floating down the aisles, catching snippets of conversations from the everyday lives of English folk. Goodness, they talked funny, they really did.

At least the jam was still cheap, and thanks to the library I was able to find Sustrans Route 23, and I began to regain my composure and confidence a little. I knew these cycle routes so well from my previous life, and I knew they would guide me now, all I had to do was follow the little blue signs. They first led me on a path beside a river and through a park where I saw swans and people playing cricket in the rain. *'How very English,'* I thought. Then I looked closer, and saw that they were all Indian. Already I had heard German, Spanish,

Polish being spoken, and seen people from all over the world in one place like I'd seen nowhere else. England really is extraordinarily multicultural. Or, at least, Southampton is.

I was completely blown away by how condensed everything was. One moment I was on a tree-lined path, the next I was going through a housing estate, a minute later I'd be on a canal towpath, then suddenly in a town centre. After such a long time in Canada this seemed like complete madness to me, as I struggled to comprehend how so many people could live in such close proximity, and within such a diversity of environments.

I followed the cycle route to Windsor, still somewhat in shock. As I had feared, I did not recognise my homeland, and I worried that it might never really feel like home again. But beyond Windsor the constant habitation eased, and for the first time I was out in the British countryside. The narrow roads, high hedgerows, open fields, crooked fences, little villages, country pubs, and red phone boxes all felt more familiar. It was starting to come back to me.

The rain continued to fall, growing heavier as the day went on, a fitting welcome home perhaps. With all the people and the farmland I never believed I would find somewhere to wild camp, but I did; just a patch of ivy-covered trees beside a country lane, but it was all I needed. As I put up my tent I reflected on the day. It had been a truly surreal one, no doubt about it. I still didn't really remember this country as my own, but one thing was for sure, it was not a boring place to ride a bike. I looked forward to the morning.

I slept very badly. Maybe I'd spent too much time in the big, comfortable bed on the ship, but the cold, hard ground just wasn't doing it for me any more. To make matters worse, all night long rain had been pounding down on my tent. With all the noise I just tossed and turned the whole night, having fitful dreams of being caught up in a flood. Morning came and I got up early, feeling weary and tired, but grateful that the rain had downgraded from torrential downpour to light drizzle. Summertime in England.

I cycled on small roads for another twenty kilometres all of the way to Basingstoke. Pleased to be adding another exotic town to the many I'd visited over the years, I followed the trusted blue arrows of the Sustrans cycle route into a park. The next sign told me to turn right, but as I did so my front wheel skidded out from beneath me. I knew at once I was going down. It all seemed to be happening in slow motion. Memories of a previous accident when I'd broken my arm by putting my hand out to cushion my fall flashed into my mind, and in a split second I remembered to reverse my instincts, and pull my arms back, taking the impact instead with my shoulder. I crashed, I rolled, and then I lay dazed on the ground. A woman walking in the park came over to see if I was alright. It was a hard fall, but other than a sore shoulder, hip, and thumb, plus being a little shaken, I seemed to be okay. I'd been lucky. The woman told me she'd slipped in the same spot the other day. Then as I stood up to recover my bike my feet skidded and slipped around even more. The paving slabs at the entrance to the park were like ice. It was extraordinarily dangerous. I thought it very irresponsible that a public path should have paving that became so incredibly slippery when wet, particularly in a country where it rains so much, and I resolved to write a stern letter to Basingstoke City Council saying as much (at the time of going to press, I still haven't quite got around to this).

Another twenty kilometres and I was in my next glamorous location, the town of Reading. I went to the library to investigate if anybody had taken advantage of the tremendous play-on-word opportunities, and to talk with Dea. There was fantastic news from her, that actually made me forget all about play-on-word opportunities. Not only was she feeling good with an almost fully recovered eye, but she was on her bike and cycling west, riding towards me. Our reunion would take place very soon in the Netherlands. I booked my ferry from Harwich to the Hook of Holland and everything was in place. It was all becoming so real, and I couldn't wait to see her again.

But my visit to Reading also had a special meaning for another reason. I had made the Eiffel Tower in Paris the official starting point for my ride around the world, because it was so iconic, and pointy, but I had actually cycled down from Edinburgh to Paris beforehand in something of a warm up ride. And that meant that at some point in Reading I must have crossed my route down to Paris of three years earlier. I had therefore now actually circumnavigated the entire planet, using nothing but my bicycle, boats, and a pick-up truck driven by a relatively attractive yet ever so moody Mongolian woman. Reading was an underwhelming location to reach this milestone (hence why I had passed it up for the official starting point) and none of the people walking around with their heads buried in their smartphones could have cared less, but still, I allowed myself to be a bit pleased with my accomplishment.

I carried this pride with me onto Sustrans Route 5 north towards Oxford, and this too was interesting, for I was now following the exact roads that I'd taken on my first days out of London on my earlier, ill-fated trip, when I'd set off to cycle around the world for the first time way back in 2010. How strange it felt to see the same signs, the same paths, to recognise little things from then, from a completely different time, even longer ago, when I'd just been setting out, with so much anticipation of the world but so little clue as to what I was doing, knowing nothing at all about bikes, with no real plan even about where I was going, no idea what I would find. And to be back now, more than a hundred thousand kilometres of cycling later, having actually done the thing, having been right around the world, having seen so much, and yet to still have no real clue what I was doing, well, that was a pretty special feeling too.

But they do say that pride comes before a fall, and so it should come as no surprise that I was soon lost. The Sustrans routes are great, but miss one sign and you're in trouble. I missed one sign, and began to wish I had some sort of plan B, like a map, or a GPS, or a compass. *'Come on Chris, you've made it around the world, you can do this.'* And with a combination of this positive thinking and blind luck I spotted Didcot Power Station over the fields far away. I remembered from six years earlier that the bike route went right past the cooling towers, so I blundered my way towards them until I was reunited with the cycle route again. But I was tired, and I was tired of the English country lanes, which were ever so hilly and had many drivers on who I felt drove too fast for the narrow, winding roads.

But there were at least some sections on traffic-free paths, like the one that carried me past the power station and on to a nice private campsite. Another very good thing about England was that I no longer had to worry about mosquitoes, and I thought I might even be able to sit outside to eat my dinner. This simple wish was not destined to come true, however, as no sooner had I lit the stove than it started to rain again, and I was forced to retreat into the tent. My body felt bruised from my fall, my legs tired from the hills, my mood tested by the weather and the traffic. For all the places I'd been, everywhere I'd travelled, I'd rarely felt so exhausted and battered after a day on the bike. *'England is really a brutal country,'* I thought, as I drifted off to sleep.

I was up again at four thirty in the morning. There was no more time to waste sleeping, for this was a special day. I was on my way home, to my parents' house in a quiet village straddling the border of Buckinghamshire and Bedfordshire, the place where I had spent my entire childhood. My sister was also visiting with her two children and would only be there for a couple of days, so I'd been hurrying to make it from Southampton as fast as I could. Another early start gave me hope I would be there by the afternoon.

I passed through Oxford at first light, a historic British treasure that left me a little underwhelmed. For me the best sight was the appearance of the sun, most unexpected but certainly very welcome. Relieved that the weather had shown me some mercy I pressed on towards my family along more small roads and cycle paths. I was following the signs for Milton Keynes, a city I knew so well. Through Steeple Claydon, where I'd played football as a kid sometimes. More villages I recognised. Then Milton Keynes itself, where the famous (in Milton Keynes at least) redways, a great network of walking and cycling paths, guided me to Furzton Lake. Across the lake I could see a restaurant that I'd worked at some ten years earlier. I stopped my bike briefly and stared across at it. I remembered how I'd served drinks there for minimum wage, and how I'd stared out of the window and wished that I could travel, wished that I knew how, wished I could leave behind the boring job and see the world. I shook my head. Somehow I'd found the way.

I rode on into the city centre, which brought back more and more memories. I cycled past The Point, a pyramidal building where my mum had taken me to the cinema as a kid, past the shopping centre where I used to work and hang out, past the exact spot outside of Halifax bank where I'd had a fight with my seventeen-year-old girlfriend. Oh, she'd been so mad at me, she really had. How silly that seemed now, and how strange to be back. Then I recognised a guy crossing the road in front of me. We'd gone to school together, been friends, but I'd not spoken to him in fifteen years. He was wearing a suit, staring down at his phone as he walked. I didn't even try to speak to him, for I knew that our lives had diverged too far.

I got lost around an area of the city called Tongwell. I was fifteen kilometres from home and I was lost. What made this even more ridiculous was that I'd used to work in Tongwell. Countless hours in a warehouse to finance the first trip. In a sense, this was where it had all begun. How ironic to be lost here of all places. I found my way eventually, when I noticed a gas station where I used to fill up my car when I was a teenager driving my car too fast over to my girlfriend's house. How much I'd changed since then. How we'd all changed.

At Tongwell Lake I sat to take one last break before home. There was no bench so I just sat on the grass and watched swans floating across the water, trying to make sense of everything as I stuffed my face with biscuits one more time. Then a man approached.

"Where are you going with all that stuff?" he asked. It was the first time anyone had asked me this since I'd arrived back in England. I cleared my throat.

"Actually, I'm from a place ten miles away..." I paused for effect, before adding, "...but I've just cycled around the world."

Argh, I hated the way that sounded. So arrogant somehow, too boastful. I'd waited six years to be able to say I'd cycled around the world, and now I realised that saying it just made me sound like a twat. I decided not to say it again.

The rest of the route was so familiar to me, having ridden it hundreds of times before, yet somehow it felt much shorter than I remembered. The corners of the final winding country lane disappeared behind me quickly and before I knew it I was in a place I knew very well. Three years and two months had gone by since I'd last cycled out of this village. This village where I had first learnt to ride a bike. This village that I had for so many years called home.

I was absolutely exhausted by the time I arrived at my old front door to be greeted by everyone, but I found more energy when I met my niece and nephew. Neither Summer nor Finley even existed when I'd first set off to cycle the world in 2010, and when I'd last been in England in 2013 Finley had been a gurgling baby, but now they had both grown into walking, talking human beings with their own distinct personalities. This included in both of them a strong desire to play, something I could very much associate with. But my own energy reserves were no match for those of a four or a five-year-old, and after losing a few too many games of tag in the garden I suggested a Lego helicopter building competition instead. And I'll tell you what, it's a damn shame there aren't photographs in this book, because I absolutely nailed it.

It was good to see everyone again after so long, for I had always been aware of the irony as I travelled the world meeting families and being invited into family homes, that in doing so I was missing out on time with my own relations. But I'd never been very close with my family, at least not in adulthood. Whether intended or not, I'd always felt a certain amount of pressure, a certain expectation that I should be making something of my life in terms of getting a good job, having a sensible career, just like my father had. In order to break away and follow my own path I had somehow needed to distance myself from my parents, to distance myself from those expectations. Obviously they only ever wanted what was best for me, but I had developed into such a different person from them that I think for a long time it was difficult for them to understand my preferred way of life, and I'd needed space from their perspective in order to fully embrace my own way of doing things. I knew that my parents followed my blog and their understanding of my life choices had evolved, but even now, six years after I'd first left on my bicycle, months could sometimes slip by without us talking to each other.

There was no great fanfare about my arrival home, either. I had not expected it, it was really just not my family's style. My dad actually asked me if I had cycled around the world now. "Well, yes, Dad, that's why I'm back," I had wanted to say, but to be fair to him there was that one kilometre with a moody Mongolian to disqualify the claim. So I settled for a conversation with my parents about why they had voted in favour of Brexit despite having a son for whom it would have calamitous consequences, which made a nice change from discussing why my dad just isn't convinced by the idea of man-made climate change. It remained an enduring fact that me and my parents were just very different people. They read The Daily Mail, after all. But family is family, and it was good to see them again, especially as they seemed to have given up on asking me when I might get a job. And in any case my dad really should take a lot of credit for this whole story, for he was the man who had first taught me to ride a bicycle, and he'd also left a world atlas lying around for me to flick through as a child. A decade or so later he'd tried somewhat to correct things by buying me a Citroën AX and paying for me to go to university, but it was too little, too late, and my path in life as an unemployed cycling vagabond had been set.

After a couple of days my pregnant sister gathered up her growing collection of children and returned to her home in Malvern, near the Welsh border. I spent one more day with my parents, but I could not stay for longer than that, for I had my ferry booked, and someone waiting for me on the other side of it. No, no, this return home was never destined to be the end of the journey. Not the end of the story. Not even close. Sorry if you thought I was wrapping things up already, but as you probably noticed, there are lots of pages left.

"Mum, I'm just going out for a little bike ride."

She looked a bit sceptical. I guess I wasn't going to get away with that one again.

"Don't worry, I won't be long this time. Just a few months. I'll be back for Christmas."

And that was a promise I intended to keep, for I'd actually

enjoyed returning home, seeing my family, and viewing the place where I'd grown up and lived most of my life with new eyes, almost from the perspective of a traveller. I could understand its place in the world better now somehow. And I would be back before too long, but first I had to go and meet someone else special. Someone I would be bringing back with me.

The ride east to Harwich was mostly very pleasant, thanks to better weather, good cycle routes, and being in a much flatter part of the country. The biggest issue I had was that my bike was in a very sorry state. The gears were skipping terribly, all of the components of the drivetrain on their last legs. I should have ordered new parts to replace them at my parents' house. It was a mistake I paid for every time that my chain slipped and clanked. I also should have got new tyres, for there was a gash in the front one that caused me frequent punctures. On top of all this I also had a wobbly front wheel, and I had to stop and buy cone spanners to tighten it up just to keep moving. I was limping along, as if my bike, having made it around the world, thought it might be about to get a rest. "Sorry, old buddy. Just a few more tens of thousand kilometres to go. Hold it together now."

Despite the technical difficulties, I actually felt good about being back in England now. It had slowly all come back to me, and, in contrast to how I'd felt when I first stepped off the Queen Mary 2 in Southampton, I felt like I once again knew and liked this country. The Sustrans bicycle routes were great, the countryside and landscapes so varied that it never got boring, and the people along the way were simultaneously reserved and eccentric. This had only been a brief visit but I would look forward to returning. For now, however, I only had mainland Europe on my mind. Because the reason for my long ride across Canada, the transatlantic cruise, and the dash through England, was waiting for me there on the other side of the North Sea, and I couldn't wait any longer.

14

Hook of Holland, Netherlands
9th August 2016

As the ferry made its final approach towards the Hook of Holland I looked down and was pleased to see that the Netherlands was still as flat as I remembered. It promised easy cycling, and the lack of hills was sure to be of benefit given my dysfunctional bike. I was also happy to spot the many bicycle paths, a most welcome change from the narrow British country lanes. But there was one thing I enjoyed observing far more than those two things. From the deck of the big ship it was a mere speck of red and orange, but I knew exactly what it was the moment that I laid eyes upon it. I dropped my backpack behind me and started jumping up and down, waving my arms furiously. A lump formed in my throat. My eyes began to well up. The red and orange speck waved back.

It took an eternity to get off the ship. I was blocked in by all of the cars, my panniers too wide to allow me to squeeze through as the other cyclists had. I was forced to wait, but I was ever so impatient. I'd already waited so long for this moment, and I didn't want to wait any longer. Once I was finally off the ship I cycled around the outside of the queue of cars at passport control and cut in ahead of them. This was no time for good manners. My passport was checked and I was allowed through. I cycled on around the corner, out of the gate, and finally I reached my goal. Two beautiful blue eyes looked back towards mine. I dropped my bike and moved towards the owner of those amazing eyes, and we fell into each others' arms. We squeezed each other tight, my hands grasping at the supple curve of a back they knew so well, grateful and eager to have this body returned to them to hold once again. We looked at one another and cried tears of disbelief and joy, kissing passionately. Dea and I were reunited at long last.

Our embrace only ended when Dea remembered that she had a bottle of sparkling apple juice with her, and she handed it to me as a gift.

"Congratulations," she said.

"For what?"

"For cycling around the world!"

"Oh... yeah."

I'd already forgotten about that. Sure, I'd been around the world now, but it didn't *really* feel like I'd done it. I hadn't finished what I'd set out to do. That solitary kilometre in a pick-up truck between Siberia and Mongolia still tarnished the achievement, and I knew I would not be truly satisfied until I returned to the west of China and stood in a square in Mori looking up at an odd sculpture. But Dea and I were now going to be doing that together, and there was certainly plenty to celebrate about being reunited. So I popped the cork, sending it rocketing over the car park with a loud bang as Dea let out a whoop of delight, and we toasted our success in getting here, in making it back to one another.

Our immediate plan now was to cycle back to Denmark together. Although Dea's eye was looking so much healthier she still needed to continue with her treatment for a couple more months and visit the doctors in Copenhagen again, so we'd decided to spend September and October living there. That gave us three weeks to ride across Holland, Germany and Denmark. But it was already late afternoon, so we wouldn't be riding further than Rotterdam on the first night. We'd booked a room through AirBnb, and the place where we stayed was a bit unusual, with graffiti on the bedroom wall and a glass door on the bathroom so that you could see right inside. I'd never seen a glass door on a bathroom before. The Dutch can be a bit odd like that though, can't they? It didn't matter, the bedroom had a solid door, and a bed, and we ordered takeaway pizza, and I had everything I could wish for. The long ride back, all those thousands of kilometres across Canada and England, the boats, the lonely nights, it had all been worth it for this moment, this night. Pizza and the most beautiful girl in the world, what more could a man ask for?

We spent most of the next morning in bed, before summoning the energy to begin our cycle to Denmark. I had been looking forward to returning to the fantastic network of segregated bicycle paths that make the Netherlands such an amazing place to cycle, so I was extremely disheartened by the number of mopeds that whizzed past us at speed. I thought it a great shame. I knew that these mopeds were allowed to use the bicycle lanes, but they did so with such reckless abandon that I felt like I had to keep my wits about me almost as much as I did on the roads. It seemed a bit daft to me that the Dutch, having invested so much into creating cycling infrastructure that is the envy of the world, had also permitted mopeds to also use it, and ruined the whole enjoyment of cycling.

We passed through Rotterdam quickly without really seeing it, and headed north. Beyond the industrialised regions the number of mopeds thankfully decreased, and we could better enjoy our cycling together.

"It's so good to be doing this again," Dea said.

"I know. Can you believe I rode all of the way across a whole continent to get back to you?" I asked as we pedalled along next to one another. "Not many boyfriends would do that, you know!"

Dea looked over at me, a smile breaking out on her face. "No," she laughed, "they'd fly!"

That night we found somewhere to camp in some woods and I made a vegetarian spaghetti bolognaise on the camping stove which, even if I do say so myself, was very delicious indeed.

"This is very delicious indeed," I said, as we sat eating.

"It really is good, well done baby," Dea agreed, wiping spaghetti sauce from her chin. "It feels great to be camping with you again. I missed all this so much."

The next morning we again put off getting up, this time because of the pitter-patter of rain on our tent. It really didn't seem like it was going to stop, so finally we gave in and rode on in the drizzling rain. Along the way we played my old favourite game, the classic Dutch pastime of spotting windmills.

With Dea well ahead in the windmill spotting we stopped in a bus shelter to hide from the weather and take a break eating stroopwafels – sweet, flat, caramel-filled waffles that were by far our favourite Dutch snack. Before long a local man came along and we made space for him to sit alongside us. He was about fifty and wore wellies, and I thought him a slightly odd sort of man from our small talk, but a most endearing one. We offered him a stroopwafel and he took it and said he'd save it for the bus. "Extraordinary weather isn't it?" he mused. This was a bit of a strong word, it wasn't all that terrible. It was grey and cold and drizzly, but nothing extraordinary. "It is the coldest 11th of August for twenty-five years," he pointed out, which seemed a fantastically specific thing to be sure of. Impressed by what we were doing cycling on such a day, he turned to us and added, in a very serious tone of voice, "If you can survive this, you can survive anything!"

The man got on a bus, giving us a wave goodbye from the window, and we continued, confident that if we could make it through this chilly summer's day then nothing would stop us getting back to China. We reached the big area of dunes that run up the west coast of the Netherlands, a beautiful and interesting part of the country, even in the rain. We were in a densely populated nation, but this area gave a feeling of being somewhere much more remote as we rode on the paved path through shrubby dunes. Along the way we even spotted many deer, the stags standing proudly with large antlers, protecting their harems with watchful eyes as we passed by.

The weather improved as we moved towards the north of the country, and it was during these carefree days in the Netherlands that a new and exciting game was invented. It evolved from our windmill spotting game. That was basically just spotting windmills, which was fun for a day or two, but didn't have much global appeal, and in fact wouldn't be a very good game at all anywhere else in the world. What it evolved into, however, was a game that would keep us entertained for weeks, months, and indeed years to come. The new game was... drumroll please... The Spotting Things Game.

In a similar vein to the windmill spotting game, The Spotting Things Game involved spotting things. It worked like this: Dea and I each wrote down ten things in the morning, things that we thought might be observable during the course of the day. Twenty pieces of paper would then go into a hat, or a bag, or an empty crisp packet, and we'd take it in turns to select ten out at random. These were the things that we each had to spot. It was a really fun game. I might spot a green car, Dea a white flower, me an old woman on a bike, Dea discarded fruit peel, and so the game would go. We played almost every day, and we loved it, introducing new rules involving bonus swap items, where one player could steal the other's best things, and occasionally breaking spontaneously into a frantic round of 'spotting everything that has ever been part of The Spotting Things Game'.

The games continued as we made our way into Germany. Beach volleyball was a popular favourite whenever we could find somewhere to play, and there was a fantastic court just across the German border. It was the first we'd seen with real sand, which to my delight allowed for much diving and throwing myself around. Dea won the first set 16-14, and then had two match points in the second, before I came back to win it 18-16. In the decisive set I was determined, focused, agile, all those things that I had been back in Quebec, but Dea is of course very tall, and in the end I couldn't handle her superior net-play and she won the third set 15-11.

It was not her only victory in the sporting arena. We'd also stop whenever there was a football goal and play a game of penalty kicks, and Dea usually won these too, much to my disappointment. I tried ever so hard, diving theatrically to try and save Dea's kicks but almost always they would slip past me. Then it would be my turn to shoot, and she'd stick out one of her long legs and save half of my efforts, adding comments like, "Oh sorry! You try so hard!" which I believe was intended to make me feel better.

Even less enjoyable was when we stopped to play mini golf, and Dea beat me by a scarcely believable twenty-one shots. The mental scars are still yet to heal.

But for all my losses, I still found it tremendous fun to be able to stop and play like this. The long summer days meant we had the time, and it was nice to take a break from cycling to relax and enjoy ourselves and just appreciate being back together. And cycling across Germany in general was always going to be great. We pedalled on flat cycle paths that ran alongside the roads in the shadow of wind turbines. It was easy cycling, in a place I had dreamed of returning to so many times on my way around the world. On hectic roads in China, on steep climbs in Tajikistan, and on sandy tracks in Mongolia, I had secretly fantasised about what it would feel like to ride on the flat, safe cycle paths of northern Germany once again. And here I was now. I'd made it back. And with Dea alongside me, boy did it ever feel good.

Arriving at the Danish border was something of a poignant moment. Here we were entering Dea's home country together. After meeting in Mongolia, cycling in Laos, and living in Australia, our relationship to this point had taken place far away from home. Now I was being invited to experience the place that had made Dea who she was. I was going to see where she came from, and that was a great and exciting thing.

During the day and a half it took us to ride from the border to Dea's home town of Grindsted I was reminded that Denmark was a nice, peaceful country that was a real pleasure to cycle in. As we rode I tried to prepare for the challenges that awaited me in Grindsted. First there was the small matter of meeting the parents. Nervousness about being introduced to the potential in-laws is common, I'm sure, but tends to be multiplied when you're essentially a thirty-one-year-old homeless man who cuts his own hair and hasn't had a real job since the age of twenty-three. Perhaps sensing this, Dea's father had arranged for me to give a talk about my journey and lifestyle in front of 500 students at Grindsted High School, where he'd worked for many years. This sounded suspiciously like a test to me.

But my nerves were soon eased when we cycled up Dea's old street and found her parents outside waving us in. They both gave me a big hug and seemed genuinely pleased to meet me, and to welcome me into their home and family with their friendly smiles. Dea's father had cooked us dinner, and we sat down together and everything just felt right. They had done some travelling themselves, most notably a family trip along the Norwegian coast when Dea was a child that everyone had fond memories of, and they seemed enthusiastic and impressed by what we had achieved and what we had planned. I felt so relieved to get along so well with Dea's parents, and it was also really nice to see the house where Dea had grown up, and to really understand for the first time where it was that she came from. Watching Denmark win the men's handball competition at the Olympics, all of us sitting together around the television waving little red and white flags, sealed the deal. I felt completely at home here.

After a rest day gave me time to cobble something together I found myself standing nervously in a big school hall, gulping as row after row of seats filled up with teenagers. 500 of them were present to sit and listen to me for an hour as I talked about my journey around the world. Luckily I'd found a fun landmark-filled map to put up on the projector to show my route that I was able to make a pretty good joke about a windmill from, and they were on my side after that. I did my best to condense three years of events into an hour ("I cycle, I camp, people are good, I met a girl, got hit by a kangaroo, bear stole my food, took three cruises, didn't like China but I've got to go back") and then left them, obviously, with a quote from Bob Dylan. The quote was:

'A man is a success if he gets up in the morning, and goes to bed at night, and in between does what he wants to do'.

I felt so very fortunate to have been able to do that for the past three years, and I wanted to leave them with the thought that perhaps the 'normal' definition of success – to have a good job, a big house, and lots of money – wasn't necessarily always the one to strive for.

Giving the talk to so many students was surprisingly enjoyable, and gave me some sense of satisfaction in thinking that maybe I had a story worth telling now. This thought was compounded by immediately being whisked away by a local journalist to give a two-hour interview along with Dea. I actually quite enjoyed this interview as the journalist was such a friendly woman, and the next day we were front page news, albeit the front page news of a newspaper with very limited circulation.

It felt like this was the moment when I had achieved something, in a way that hadn't really happened passing so briefly through England. I had made it around the world, and for a short while that was being celebrated. But far better than that, I felt welcome in Dea's home town, and I felt welcome in Dea's family. I felt a strong sense of belonging in Denmark. All of the pieces of our jigsaw seemed to have come together, and it was all making perfect sense. I held Dea's hand in mine, in the place where she'd grown up, and I could see our future together. It was a special time.

15

Dea's parents, maybe feeling a little inspired by my speech, cycled with us along a bicycle path out of Grindsted. It was a beautiful summer's day and nice to ride together for a while along the heather-lined trail, where Dea had ridden horses in her youth. After a few kilometres the path ended, and we said farewell, Dea's parents turning for home and Dea and I continuing on alone. We were now heading back south, towards a special sort of high school in Rødding, where I'd been invited to repeat my speech by a young teacher named Jakob. And we weren't long into the day when I found an unexpected chance to practise. As I cycled past a field of cows they all started to follow me, and by the time I was at the end of their field a large crowd had gathered, their intrigued bovine heads leaning over the fence towards me. They appeared to be waiting for a show, so to amuse Dea, myself, and perhaps even them, I started giving them my speech. Before I'd got very far into it, however, the cows started to lose interest. Some turned away, others returned to munching on grass, and one even took to showing her disinterest by urinating. It wasn't too good for my confidence, if I'm honest.

By mid-afternoon we were at the school where we were met by Jakob, a very welcoming young man with big frizzy hair. He was a friend of Dea's sister, and by coincidence also knew of my journey from my online blog, so he'd been keen to extend this invitation to come and talk at the school. It was a special type of voluntary boarding school, where students around the age of eighteen go to learn certain skills. Jakob was teaching an outdoor class and was planning on taking this year's students (who had only just arrived) on some bicycle trips. So we all hoped my talk would provide some inspiration, but it would not be taking place until the next morning, which left the rest of the day free for playing games. Jakob had been paying attention to my blog and so understood how important this was to me, and we played several rounds of volleyball and table-tennis together, until he had to go off and organise a challenge for the new students. They would be divided into teams, given some planks of wood and some water balloons, and tasked with constructing catapults to fire on each other. "You can watch if you want?" Jakob said.

"Watch? I want to play!"

And so Dea and I were permitted to take part as the real adults watched on, and terribly good fun it was too, helping to construct and fire the water balloon catapults. I was growing to like Denmark more and more, high school in England had never been this much fun.

But this was supposed to be a business trip, and the next morning I gave my speech again. Having done it once in front of 500 students, the eight or nine that sat before me this time was quite a different sort of challenge, but everything turned out fine, by which I mean they laughed at at least some of my jokes. After the talk we all went on a bike ride together, stopping in the woods for a question and answer session. The students were very interested and had lots of things to ask, which made me feel pretty good. So did receiving my payment. For the two one-hour talks I'd given I was paid a lot of money, more than I'd spent in eleven weeks cycling across Canada, in fact. Yep, Denmark was definitely alright by me.

Next we cycled southeast to the town of Haderslev, to visit Dea's half-sister Sara and her partner Flemming. It was lovely to be introduced to more of Dea's family, people that I'd been hearing about for so long. Now I was finally meeting them. We stayed for a couple of days, and as well as proving great hosts, there was an additional benefit – Sara, as a qualified dentist with her own surgery, offered to help me out with a troublesome tooth of mine. It was the tooth that had originally caused me such agony in Iran, only for half of it to then fall out in China. We'd been through a lot, me and this tooth, or what was left of it anyway. So I was pleased that in Denmark they have very competent dentists (or one, at least, probably more) and Sara finally sorted this damned tooth out once and for all, by which I mean she pulled it out and put it in the bin.

After a couple of days Dea and I pressed on towards Copenhagen in the warm sunshine. We hadn't gone far when we stopped to take a break in the town of Christiansfeld, a UNESCO World Heritage Site thanks to its well preserved architecture and Moravian church. We had just found a quiet bench in a park to enjoy some sandwiches, when a Chinese girl came past with a look of astonishment at our loaded bikes. "Wow, where are you going?!" she asked. We told her, and Dea casually mentioned where I'd already been.

"You cycled around the world?! That's amazing! I can't believe it! Can I take a photo with you?" The girl's name was Jia, she was as sweet as a stroopwafel, and fascinated by the concept of travelling by bike. She was with her young Danish husband, although he was as shy as she was outgoing and mostly just stood in the background while Jia talked. She told us how it was for her to try and settle in Denmark as a foreigner, and how she also loved to travel. Her enthusiasm was infectious, and before leaving we exchanged contact details, and made plans to meet again in Copenhagen.

We resumed our ride there, and it was generally very pleasant cycling on small, quiet roads. On one of these we stumbled upon something most intriguing. At the side of the road there was a large collection of puzzles built on wooden posts. It was not obvious why they were there, but they seemed to be free for anyone to try and solve. As you may have gathered by now I am a man who likes a challenge, so we leaned down our bikes and got stuck in.

Alas, they were all frustratingly difficult. Most of them involved trying to free rings from being stuck on ropes that were tied in knots, with balls and other obstacles around them. We found it was quite impossible to get any of the rings off. Before long we gave up, me thinking maybe they really were impossible and the whole thing was all just a big trick, and turned our attentions to a smaller puzzle that just involved rearranging wooden blocks. Just then an old man appeared as if from nowhere offering to help. He solved the puzzle in moments.

"Can you do these ring ones?" I asked him.

The man nodded and shuffled over to them. His aged hands moved rapidly, twisting and turning a ring and freeing it within seconds. He moved on to the next puzzle and repeated the trick. It was all very impressive.

The man could not speak English, but luckily that wasn't really a problem, because Dea's Danish is excellent. She asked him some things and then translated for me that his name was Arne, that he lived just down the road, and that he had been the man who had made all of these puzzles. He was keen to show us something else, so we followed him back to his house. He led us to a round conservatory in his garden and to step inside it was to step into a magical little wonderland. There were dozens of shelves all around filled with hundreds of little wooden puzzles, others sat on the floor, and still more hung down from the ceiling. The majority of them had been hand built by Arne himself. It was an amazing place, and Arne was an amazing man. He stumbled about and his hands shook as he showed us some of the puzzles. "I'm not drunk," he joked, "I've just got Parkinson's."

Arne was such a wonderful character. His daughter came out to tell him that his dinner was ready, but he refused to go without first showing us his 'orange cannon'. He then went off to his garden and found a long tube. It looked a little bit like a cannon, but I was disappointed to see that it was grey. Just as I was considering pointing out that what he had there was not an orange cannon, but a grey cannon, he put on some ear-protectors, sprayed something that looked like hairspray into the tube, and pulled out a satsuma. He then rammed the satsuma into the end of the tube, and, just as I was considering pointing out that what he had now was not an orange cannon, but a satsuma cannon, he let the damn thing off. There was an almighty noise, and the citrus fruit shot out at 190 kilometres per hour, soaring off over the trees and possibly killing a bird. Arne was one hell of a guy.

As we crossed Denmark we would often camp at the fantastic shelters that are all over the country. These are public spaces in the countryside with wooden sheltered areas where it is possible to sleep, that often also come with fire pits, basic toilets, and running water. All of this was for free, and was providing another reason for me to fall more in love with the Danish lifestyle.

One night we'd stopped early at one of these shelters and took a walk around the area. We came across a little lake and I thought about going in for a swim. There was a bit of a chill in the air, and I couldn't decide if I really wanted to. So I sat out on a jetty thing that stretched out into the lake and stared down at the water. "I don't know if I want to go in," I said. "It's a bit cold. But, I know I'll enjoy it if I do." I talked myself into it, imagining how nice it would feel to dive into all that water, so I stripped down to my shorts and moved to the end of the jetty and looked out. "Actually, it is a bit cold, isn't it? Maybe I won't. But I should though shouldn't I? No, maybe not. Oh, I don't know."

Dea got bored and started to walk away around the lake. My chance to impress her was slipping away. I decided to just go for it. Yes, yes, I would jump in and make a big splash. She'd be ever so impressed by my bravery. I took a deep breath and threw myself into the water, feet first, and with a thud landed on the ground. The water was only a foot deep. Dea turned around and laughed at me, as I stood there foolishly with water around my ankles.

We were traversing the islands in the south of Denmark, and at Spodsbjerg we had some time to kill waiting for a ferry. That was alright though, because not far from the ferry terminal was Spodsbjerg Mini Golf. My record against Dea in this particular sport was atrocious, but I rolled up my sleeves and vowed to try my very hardest this time. This was my moment to shine, I was quite sure of it. It was a twelve hole course, and I really, really, really, really, really, really wanted to win.

I lost by fourteen shots.

And Dea's good fortune continued on the ferry as she received a phone call that pretty much guaranteed that she would have a job waiting for her when we got to Copenhagen. We were planning to try a different sort of lifestyle, settling down in the city for a couple of months, and it was great to know there would be some money coming in straight away. But it also meant that we had to be in Copenhagen the very next evening, so as soon as we were off the ferry we resumed cycling quickly.

Along the way we passed through Maribo, a fairly insignificant little town that had some significance for me. I had passed through it three years earlier, and I remembered I'd sat taking a break, watching some women packing up market stalls. It was a little moment, one of millions of little moments that made up my journey. But returning to Maribo now was significant, for it was the first time since I'd left the Eiffel Tower that my route connected. For the first time since I started this story of cycling around the world, I had actually cycled around the world (apart from that one kilometre of course). The first of the seven targets I'd left Paris with could now definitely be crossed off. I had successfully circumnavigated the planet. As we cycled around a roundabout that connected the lines Dea let out a whoop behind me and offered her congratulations. One challenge was complete, but there were still six to go.

As we cycled out of Maribo towards our new life in Copenhagen our shadows rode alongside us in the fields. The sun was setting on another day, and everything felt good at that moment.

"I think it's been a perfect day," Dea said to me.

But then she would, after that round of mini golf.

16

Copenhagen, Denmark
1st September 2016

In many ways Copenhagen was the perfect city for us to live in
for a couple of months, what with it being so bicycle-friendly. In
fact, while we were there it was reported that for the first time
more journeys were being made by bicycle in Copenhagen than by
car. With the world fretting simultaneously about climate change
and an obesity crisis, here was a city that was providing a simple,
blindingly obvious answer to both – proving that if you create the
right infrastructure and atmosphere, people will get on their bikes.

That being said, I didn't get on my own bike too much in Copenhagen. For me the novelty of having our own apartment to chill out
in was far more exciting. It belonged to a friend of Dea's who rented
it out to us, and it was small and cosy and everything that we needed.
It was really nice to play at being a normal couple for a while. Dea
would go out to work each day – she'd got a job at the airport doing
very important security work, i.e. taking people's toothpaste away
from them lest it contain a bomb – and then she'd return home each
night to find me having made her dinner, like any house-husband
worth his salt should. But Dea's income was only just enough to cover our expenses. With her eye fiasco having cost us quite a lot of
money and Brexit devaluing our savings further, I needed to figure
out a way to try and bring in some extra cash myself to contribute to
our onward travels. Ideally I would have given more of those talks,

what with them having proved so lucrative, but despite Dea's best efforts as my manager it proved a hard sell to the Copenhagen schools. It was the middle of term and most of them had booked all their speakers well in advance, and I got no more gigs.

So Dea and I tried going back to what we knew, and rented pedicabs one Saturday night. But the Copenhagen scene was far different from that of Surfers Paradise. Almost all of the Danish pedicabs had electric motors on them and were brightly lit up with neon lights. With us not willing to ride a motorised vehicle, the only bikes we could find to rent that were entirely pedal-powered were sorry looking things. They were black, had no lights, and came with something like a bucket at the front which two people could just about squeeze into. I rode around Copenhagen all night on this thing and made almost no money at all, the evening only saved by Flemming, who was visiting from Haderslev, and Dea's brother Johan. They were out for a night on the town and requested a lift home, for which they paid me generously, I think largely out of pity.

The pedicab idea was shelved, and I decided to instead focus my time on the writing of my first book. I knew book writing was not known for paying well, especially as I planned to self-publish, but it had been a dream of mine to write a book about cycling around the world for almost as long as it had been a dream of mine to cycle around the world. Reading books by people like Alastair Humphreys had been a big inspiration for me to travel the world by bike, and I'd always liked the idea that I too could share my journey and maybe even inspire one or two future cyclists myself.

For the first couple of days the writing went well, but it wasn't long before my days descended into procrastination sessions, including long internal mental debates as to whether watching a TED Talk about procrastination, in order to better understand why one procrastinates, so as to eventually stop procrastinating, should in itself really count as procrastinating. Actually I watched a lot of TED Talks (to stimulate my mind), and got pretty good at the Rubik's cube, and in between I occasionally got a bit of writing done.

To be honest the writing was boring and difficult, so I was thankful to be given other distractions, like spending time with Dea's sister and brother who both lived in Copenhagen. Barbara, a tall blonde who looks a lot like her sister, and Johan, an even taller redhead, who doesn't, were good company, and we'd often hang out with them and their partners, Niels and Sasha. The six of us would play football in the park, or meet for dinner together. It was so nice to feel a part of the group, to take part in social activities that I missed out on when travelling, and to be drawn even further into Dea's life.

I liked it a lot in Copenhagen and it was easy to imagine us settling in Denmark someday, but for the time being the road still called out to us both, most emphatically from a big map of the world we'd hung on the wall above our bed. One day we decided to use it to plan out the route that we intended to cycle together, using bits of coloured string and Blu Tack.

We knew that first we should return to England, so that I could keep my promise to spend Christmas with my family, and to introduce them to Dea. Spending winter there would also hopefully give me the time to complete my book, which was certainly not going to be done before we left Copenhagen so long as I was spending my afternoons standing on our bed fiddling with coloured string and Blu Tack. But by the time spring and warmer weather was in the air we would hopefully have a clean slate. We could go anywhere we wanted to. But there was only one place I wanted to go, and that place was Mori, the little town in western China famous for absolutely nothing. But that was alright with Dea, she was herself very keen to cycle through Turkey and the Stans, which were conveniently positioned on the way to Mori, and the first stage of our new joint world tour was easily decided. We stuck on the coloured string and then added on some dates too. Europe in spring, Turkey and Central Asia through the summer months, and we'd be through the Pamir mountains and on to China long before winter, no trouble at all.

What we were going to do after reaching Mori was something we were less sure about. We both wanted to cycle in places we hadn't been to before, like India, Africa, and South America, but how to connect them up was a problem. Neither Africa nor South America were particularly close to the west of China, and India was difficult to get to overland, being surrounded as it was by countries with travel restrictions that made it almost impossible to cycle through. Going through Tibet would have been our first choice, but independent travel there was not allowed and in any case the border to Nepal had been closed since the 2015 earthquake. Going through the mountains of Pakistan instead would make for a fantastic ride but it was dangerous, and getting a visa in the time frames we had was simply not possible. That left going the long way around, via Thailand and Myanmar, but even this route had recently become blocked by Myanmar's decision to only allow travellers to exit via the same border that they had entered, making a traverse of the country impossible. Effectively then, it was not possible for us to continue to India by bicycle. So what would we do? We couldn't cycle south from Mori, we didn't want to go back west the way we had come, going north would only lead us to Siberia and the Arctic, and going east would mean cycling all of the way across China again, an experience I had no great ambition to repeat. Sea routes were also out of the question, what with Mori being just about the furthest it is physically possible to be from the sea. Our only option, it seemed, would be to fly. If I made it to Mori I would have completed my target of circumnavigating the planet using only my bicycle and boats, so I guessed it would be okay to start using other transport again. The thought of it really didn't sit well with me, but I think there was a little part of me that was of the opinion that it might not be such a bad idea to at least try transitioning back towards being a normal human being again post-Mori. Having run out of different string colours, we put up a piece of dental floss to mark out a flight down to Kathmandu. Then with pink string we rode on through India, flew along more dental floss to Africa, cycled there, flew again to South America, did a loop there, then finally dental flossed it back to Europe. It was a world tour, going not around the world in a circumnavigational sense, but in a big, round, circular movement nonetheless. We stared up at it and smiled. It looked amazing. From that moment on to glance up from our bed was to dream of all of the great adventures we had ahead of us.

Our two months in Copenhagen passed quickly. The park where I went to sit, read, and think (i.e. procrastinate) had changed. The leaves had been green when I'd first sat there at the start of September. Within weeks they had turned to dazzling yellows and reds. By the last week of October they were beginning to fall to the ground. And it was during that final week in October that Dea and I cycled together to the hospital where she'd been receiving treatment for her sick eye ever since she'd flown back from Hawaii six months earlier. The course of eye drops she'd been taking had come to an end, and this was a final check-up to make sure that the amoeba was not showing any signs of returning. It was therefore an important day, and an anxious wait sitting together, watching doctors and nurses walk past us for half an hour, not knowing if Dea was going to get the green light to return to normal life or not. Eventually we were called through and a reassuring female doctor examined Dea's eye. She looked at it through a big microscope for a few minutes and asked Dea to perform a couple of tests. Then she offered her verdict. "Everything seems to be fine."

It was such a massive relief to hear those words, and to celebrate on the cycle back to our apartment Dea and I stopped in a big park and went over to a children's playground. Next to the kiddies' slides and climbing frames I had noticed a big swing-thing, similar to a big swing-thing I had once swung around on with a friend in London, and I knew that this was no kids' toy. The construction was essentially a wooden pole three metres high, with a see-saw on top of it, and from each end of the see-saw dangled a rope with a small sitting platform. I encouraged Dea to sit upon one of these little platforms and get a firm grip in the rope. I then went around to the other side, jumped up, and hoisted myself up onto the other side of the see-saw. Dea was suddenly lifted high up into the air with a scream of surprise and delight. Then gravity brought her down and it was my turn to head for the skies. Each time we were raised a frightening distance above the ground, and to add to the thrill the see-saw not only went up and down but also from side to side, and so we spiralled around, colliding sometimes with the central pole, and having a hell of a time with it all. What this crazy contraption was doing in a children's play area I had absolutely no idea, but it sure was a lot of fun for us two young adults. I looked over at Dea. She was laughing uncontrollably as she boinged up and down. She was relaxed and she was free, a look of pure happiness shining out from her two perfect blue eyes.

17

A chill wind whipped our faces, the dark air speckled with icy sleet. The faint light of our cheap torches barely lit the path in front of us. This was certainly proving to be a tough introduction to cold weather cycling for Dea. Eight hours earlier we'd pedalled out of Copenhagen on sunny cycle paths, waved off by Dea's siblings and friends with optimistic fanfare. But the weather had turned, and as we finally reached the home of Dea's cousin in Sorø, eighty kilometres from the capital, both of us were beginning to have our doubts.

Dea became ill, suffering bad migraines, but she wanted to continue cycling. We were following a more northern route back west across the country, and a ferry took us to the small island of Samsø. In the summer this peaceful isle apparently makes for a lovely place for a bike ride, but in November it didn't, and Dea become even more unwell. A long night camping wasn't great for her health, and by the time another ferry carried us back to the mainland and Denmark's biggest region, Jutland, Dea had had enough. The cold, the wind, and the rain was too much in her condition, and she decided she would take a train to her sister's house in Haderslev to recover. Waving her off at the train station I was concerned by how soon Dea had resorted to using other transport. China suddenly felt like a long way off, but the words Dea later used when she wrote about the experience on our blog reassured me that she understood exactly how important not using other transport remained to me:

And finally, I had nervously repeated "Don't go on the train" to Chris as he helped me with my bags. I was afraid the doors would close and it would start moving. This once happened to my mum when she helped a ten-year-old version of me going on a train ride alone for the first time. To most people cycling around the world, going on a train by mistake would have been an inconspicuous incident that could easily be ignored. But Chris isn't like most people. He means it literally, when he says 'I am cycling around the world'. It is spelled out in the words, there are no implicated buts or exceptions. And that can actually be hard to truly understand for most people, and even for me sometimes. Being taken just a few metres by a motorised vehicle would ruin the wholeness of his continuous bike ride. One mistake and it would all be lost. Like it did that one time at the Russian-Mongolian border. It is a project he has been fully dedicated to for the last 3.5 years, and the longer it goes on the more crucial it seems to finish it successfully. The higher grow the stakes. And even though it is his project and not mine I am deeply involved in it too. Both because it influences my life and our trip in various ways. But mostly because it forces me to approach our life and way through the world in a different way. To think new thoughts, to go alternative ways. It is provoking and inspiring. It is just another of his many games, and yet it is so seriously undertaken, so heartfelt, that it reveals the particular purity in him that intrigues me.

I followed along behind the train on my bicycle. Not literally of course, trains are fast, but I got there the next day. Sara and Flemming were once again very welcoming hosts, Flemming taking me to see a local football match that was taking place at the top of a hill in strong winds, where I was greatly entertained by the sight of a goalkeeper forced into a save from his own goal-kick. Flemming's generosity also extended to gifting me one of his old smartphones to help me navigate. I'd always resisted having a smartphone, but I'd also spent quite a lot of time getting lost, and I thought the in-built GPS might be a worthwhile feature to have.

After a few days of rest in Haderslev Dea was feeling much better, and well enough to cycle 200 kilometres back north to Aarhus, where we had both been invited to the wedding of one of her old university friends. The ride there was more successful, with better weather allowing us to settle into a proper routine and appreciate the aesthetic advantage of cycling at this time of year, the trees burning spectacularly in all manner of reds, oranges and yellows.

The wedding was the first I had been to as an adult, for while the majority of my old friends from home were married, spending so little time in England over the years I'd managed to miss all of their special days. Even so I knew enough about weddings to be sure that my usual cycling attire wasn't going to be suitable for the occasion. Thankfully another of Dea's old friends, Andreas, had stepped in and offered to lend me a shirt and tie, as well as smart trousers and shoes. Dea and I cycled to the church and waited outside for him to arrive. Not long before the ceremony was due to begin he walked up clutching a bag and handed it to me, smiling. I looked inside.

"Where are the shoes?" I asked.

His face dropped. He'd forgotten them, and there was no time to go back and get them now.

"It'll be okay," Dea reassured me, "no one will be looking at your feet."

We hurried into the church toilets and got changed, Dea emerging looking stunning in her orange dress. I looked unusually close to a respectable member of society myself, but the look was slightly ruined by the footwear. My filthy, smelly trainers were coming apart at the seams, but there was nothing to do about it now. We walked into the church. Some close friends and family were sitting up at the front on a raised area near to the altar where the groom stood waiting. To my relief instead of going up there, Dea and I slid into one of the pews in the main part of the church. My feet were safely hidden away, and I breathed a sigh of relief about that. My relieved sigh was premature, however, as some of Dea's friends that were sitting up in the raised area waved at us to come up.

"Oh, we can go up there!" Dea said to me, taking me by the hand.

"But, but, but..." I tried, but it was too late, we were heading for the front. Dea sat down on the penultimate chair, leaving me with no choice but to take the end seat. All of me, and particularly my feet, were now in full view of everyone sat below us in the pews. The organ burst into life and a moment later the bride walked in escorted by her proud father, no doubt the most special moment of her life being greatly enhanced by the sight of me, a man she'd never met before, and my filthy footwear, directly in front of her as she walked down the aisle.

Having spent six years studying in Aarhus, Dea still had many friends in town, and I got to meet with a few of them, the most memorable being a visit to a guy named Esben. He quite brilliantly lived in a Mongolian yurt, which he'd set up in an area of the city close to the train tracks, an area which had been semi-abandoned but left open to be used for interesting cultural projects. It was amazing to step inside Esben's cosy home and to see a Mongolian yurt in the middle of a Danish town, so delightfully out of place. It had a special significance for me and Dea too of course, reminding us of our first meeting out in the Mongolian steppe. It brought fond memories to mind of sitting in a yurt that night, looking properly at Dea, the most beautiful girl in the world, for the first time, and wishing that the short little bearded chap (played by Bret from *Flight of the Conchords*) wasn't in the way.

As we left Aarhus behind, cycling back towards Dea's home town of Grindsted, we both felt inspired by our little trip to see Esben.

"Maybe we could live in a yurt in Denmark ourselves one day."

"It would sure be cheaper than a house."

"It would be nice to continue with this sort of lifestyle, even after this trip, wouldn't it?"

"Yes, it really would."

Back in Grindsted we stayed with Dea's parents again for a couple more days, where once again I was made to feel very welcome. The speech I'd made at the high school seemed to have convinced them of the joys of cycling the world, and they were about as enthusiastic and excited as Dea and I were about the journey we had ahead of us.

The short break here also gave me a chance to do some work on my bike. It really needed it, for my exceptionally worn crankset meant that it had become almost impossible to ride. Somehow I'd made it to Grindsted, clunking noisily along, but I knew I wasn't going much further without replacing the drivetrain which had been skipping all of the time since Canada. And it wasn't that I hadn't wanted to replace it earlier, just that I couldn't. I had all the right new parts, and all the right tools, I just couldn't get the damn crankset off. The thread on the crank arm was all worn down, meaning that I was completely unable to screw my crank-removal tool into it. Since we'd left Copenhagen I'd been cycling without the crank bolt, hoping that the crank arm would come loose and just fall off of its own accord, but no such luck. I thought back to when the cranks had last been fitted, back in Quebec City by Julian, Meghan's bike mechanic boyfriend. I remembered him using his special tool to tighten them and tighten them. "They have to be very tight," he said. "You don't want them to fall off."

Well, that's what you get for listening to bike mechanics, I suppose. Now I had a problem, and the only way to solve it was to fall back on my own bike mechanical skills, forged over my many years of cycle touring, and honed by this point, even if I do say so myself, to a very fine art. So I picked up the biggest hammer I could find from Dea's father's collection, and started to whack the crankset as hard as I could with it.

SMACK! BANG! WALLOP!

I hit it about as hard as I could, but there was no movement.

SMACK! SMACK! SMACK!

Not budging.

BANG! BANG! BANG!

Nothing doing.

WALLOP! WALLOP! WALLOP!

It didn't even seem to be coming loose.

SMACK! SMACK! SMACK! SMACK! SMACK! SMACK! BANG! BANG! BANG! WALLOP! WALLOP! WALLOP!

And then suddenly it came off. My old, and now extremely deformed crankset was finally free. "YAAAARGGHHHH!!!!" As it clattered to the garage floor I let out a primeval roar of relief and masculine joy of such volume that it had Dea running from the other end of the garden frantically crying out, "What happened Chris?! Are you okay?!"

But a new crankset was not the only thing I fitted to my bike in Grindsted. On my ride across Canada I had encountered another cyclist who had a front basket on his bike, and ever since then I'd wanted one of my own. It was such a genius idea that I couldn't believe I hadn't thought of it myself, what with all the thinking time I'd had over the years. He had everything he needed, right there in front of him. He'd even had a packet of crisps on the go when I met him, no need to stop cycling to eat for him. I wanted one of my own, and what better place to find one than in Denmark, where so many people go about on bicycles (including old grannies with baskets). And sure enough, there was a basket for sale in Dea's local bike shop, and I bought it for my bike. My, oh my, how I fell in love with this basket. There was so much space in there. I decided to fill it up with fruit, so that I'd remember to eat my five-a-day, and then on top of the fruit I put biscuits and chocolate and crisps because, you know, they're more exciting aren't they? And there was still room for a water bottle, a map, maybe my camera. It was the greatest addition to my bicycle that I'd ever made.

Our time in Denmark was drawing to a close, but it had been a wonderful time, and as we headed south for the German border we saw something that had us dreaming of returning. A plot of land that was for sale for a reasonable price. "We could buy some land like that and put some yurts on it," we mused. "Maybe we could live in one and rent others out."

"Like a yurt village!"

"Yeah. And we could grow our own vegetables."

"Have apple trees."

"Keep chickens."

"We could get our own wind turbine for energy."

"Yeah! We could make it sustainable."

"We could have a donkey to cut the grass!"

It felt like such a crazy idea, but it was a brilliant one that we both only grew more and more excited about. I'd loved visiting Denmark, and now, having spent some time cycling around the country, living in it, meeting Dea's friends and family, I really could see my future here with Dea. In a yurt. It was good, great, to have this idea, to have this reason to return someday.

"And what about making our own beach volleyball court?"

"Of course! And what about mini golf?"

"Well, let's not carried away now, Dea."

18

We weren't far into Germany when my attempt to circumnavigate the planet only by bicycle and boats ran into trouble again. This time it came in the form of the Kiel Canal, which we needed to cross using an underground pedestrian tunnel. There were escalators taking people down into the tunnel, but I couldn't use them due to their pesky electrical motors. In any case, trying to manoeuvre a fully loaded bicycle down an escalator seemed a pretty foolish thing to be doing. So instead we made our way over to some elevators. These were just about permitted by my rules, as they only moved up and down, and therefore contributed no horizontal movement to assist my progress around the world. We wheeled our bikes in and dropped down into the tunnel.

The tunnel looked surprisingly short once we rolled out of the elevator. We cycled through it and in no time came to another set of escalators and an elevator. It couldn't possibly be the other side of the canal already, and I guessed this elevator was going to take us to another level of tunnel, where we would continue to progress under the water. We rolled our bikes in. The doors closed. A few moments later they reopened, and daylight poured in. We were outside, on the far bank of the canal already.

"Oh no!!!" I cried. "How did we get here?! The elevator must have done it."

"What are you talking about?" Dea asked.

"That must have been one of those fancy elevators that move diagonally. That's a thing, isn't it? Oh no, oh no, no, no!" I was panicking. I'd been tricked by one of those fancy elevators that move diagonally. I'd been moved just a little bit horizontally, and everything was ruined. All of the progress I'd made since Mori was for nothing. I was going to have to start everything all over again.

"I don't think it was a fancy elevator. I think we just cycled through the tunnel, Chris."

"No, the tunnel wasn't long enough. Oh, this is bad, Dea, this is really bad."

"Well, how about we go back to the other side, then find another way to cross this canal? Would you like to do that?"

"Yes, I think I would."

But I knew even that wouldn't be enough as we returned to the elevator and descended back into the tunnel. My continuous line had been broken again, and backtracking wasn't going to change that. My mind was racing. I kept thinking about how very stupid and unfair it was that they didn't put warning signs on diagonal elevators for people who aren't allowed to be powered horizontally by things. It was so unbelievably inconsiderate of them.

The doors reopened and we were back down in the tunnel. It looked a little longer now. Maybe, just maybe, I'd been mistaken. "I really do think we just cycled through the tunnel," Dea repeated.

We cycled back through the tunnel and took the elevator up to the other side. Now back where we'd started I went over to look at the water. The canal wasn't quite as wide as I first thought. Maybe diagonal elevators weren't even a thing.

"Chris, come and look at this."

I made my way over to Dea. She was standing beside some information boards just near to the elevators. By chance they displayed information about the tunnel, including two diagrams of the layout of the tunnel, the escalators, and the very normal straight up-and-down elevators on each side.

"Phew! Wow, that was a close one," I said, with a big sigh of relief. "Shall we go back across then?"

"Yes, let's do that," Dea said, looking at me like I was just a tiny little bit crazy as we descended into the tunnel for a third time.

But I certainly wasn't the only crazy person travelling through Germany. Not far beyond Rendsburg we noticed a man out jogging who was pushing a pram that, in lieu of a baby, contained what looked like camping gear. He stopped in a bus shelter and we saw him lie back with his feet up, somehow simultaneously singing loudly and stuffing a bagel into his mouth. Dea and I stopped and looked at one another. "That guy is completely mad. Let's say hello."

Our initial assessment of the man was soon corroborated by his rapid, overexcited speech as he told us that his name was Aleks and that he was running from North Cape at the top of Norway all of the way down to Gibraltar. "You can find me online by searching for Barefoot Aleks," he added. "Because that is me, I'm Aleks, and I'm running barefoot."

We looked down at his feet. He was wearing a pair of sandals.

"Err, yeah. The ground turned out to be a bit hard for running barefoot."

Aleks was around our age and was a teacher from England who'd got a bit bored and decided to do something more exciting with his winter term. But the most extraordinary thing about our encounter here was that it reminded us that we'd seen something similar a few weeks earlier in Denmark. On our way to the reception following the wedding near Aarhus we had seen a man running with a pram who was singing loudly as he passed us. Dea now asked Aleks if he was in that area at that time. He said that he would have been, and not only that, but he remembered he'd seen a couple of cyclists with heavily loaded bicycles around that time too.

It was a funny coincidence that amused us all, adding a little bit of magic to our day. But actually our days were already becoming quite magical, just with the simple act of cycle touring in winter, a highly underrated activity. We left any bad weather behind us in Denmark and for the rest of our ride back to the U.K. had clear skies. It was cold of course, but riding our bikes kept us warm enough and we had sufficient sleeping bags to continue camping quite comfortably. We passed many Christmas markets in towns along the way and got into the spirit of things by decorating our bikes with tinsel. Catching leaves and playing The Spotting Things Game kept us entertained and my basket buffet kept us well fed as we followed the well-marked bicycle routes across Germany and back into the Netherlands.

The first Dutch town that we came to was Groningen and it gave us a great opportunity to catch up with an old friend. Robin, a young German man who Dea and I had both met in Luang Prabang, Laos back in 2014, was now living and studying in Groningen and had invited us to stay with him. When we first met he'd been on a cycle tour across Eurasia, but he'd had enough of cycling and had just bought himself a boat to paddle down the Mekong instead. Two weeks later I was reunited with him when his boat rather unfortunately ran aground. With Dea having returned home, Robin and I then hung out together for a while in Thailand and became friends. We were two long distance cyclists in far away lands who, unusually for two long distance cyclists in far away lands, didn't actually do any cycling together. But we did play a lot of games.

I was really looking forward to see Robin again and it was great to find him looking his usual cheerful self as we reunited outside his Groningen apartment. He welcomed us inside and we got straight down to the important business of playing more games. First up was a match of Fifa on his Playstation, which ended in considerable controversy when Germany claimed an undeserved victory over England after Jack Wilshere's 86th minute equaliser was ruled out by a dubious offside decision. Fairly livid, I suggested we head off to the pool hall, where I knew from experience I would have the upper hand. Sticking to our tradition of not cycling together, Robin and I walked across town to get there. We were pretty much the only ones not cycling, Groningen being a town of bicycles. I can't say as I've seen any place in the world with so many bicycles as Groningen, though this is easily explained by the fact that it is a university town, in the Netherlands.

We reached the pool hall and got down to business. So far as my memory goes, I was able to beat Robin very easily at pool in Thailand, so you can imagine my surprise and disappointment at losing three games to two. I next challenged him to darts, which I knew for sure I would beat him at, for I'd won every time we'd played in Thailand. Well, would you believe it, but he beat me at every game of this too. Some things, it seems, are just better left in the past.

Robin wasn't the only long distance cyclist that we stayed with in the Netherlands. In Rotterdam we were invited to visit Martin and Susanne, a young couple who had only just got back from a three year trip across Eurasia. They had actually been a few months behind me for much of 2014 as I made my own way through Central Asia, and, even though we had never met before, we had plenty of common ground to discuss. Joining the party were two Belgians, Marteen and Saar, who were themselves planning to begin a similar long bike ride in 2018. It was a great evening of cycle touring past, present, and future, that carried me back to the deserts and mountain passes of Central Asia as we compared notes on different routes and shared stories and advice over dinner. Best of all was the look on Dea's face throughout the evening. Her beaming smile at every tale of dodgy roads, every donkey-based anecdote, told me she was all in for this adventure. She couldn't wait to get started riding her own bike east, to start writing the story of our own Eurasian crossing.

The next day we returned once more to the Hook of Holland and the place where Dea and I had been reunited a few months earlier. Now we were boarding a ferry back to England together, and it was another emotional moment for Dea. Three months earlier this had been her limit, this had been as far as she could go before having to turn around and go back home to Denmark for more eye treatment. But now she had the all-clear, and there was nothing to hold her back any more. There was a tear in her eye as we sailed away from mainland Europe, but this time it was a tear of happiness, now that she was truly free to move forward with our adventure.

19

W
e sat and ate breakfast on a bench, watching the sun as it slowly rose over the sea. We'd arrived into Harwich late the night before and had no time for anything more than diving behind a hedge and making camp beside a rusting pram and broken bottles. But by daylight Harwich looked a lot nicer, a typical English seaside town with brightly coloured beach huts along the shoreline and seagulls circling overhead. Children walked past us in their matching school uniforms and gasped at our loaded bikes.

"I like England," Dea said, perhaps a little prematurely.

She sure seemed to like it a lot less as we began cycling on the narrow English roads, busy with the morning traffic of an overcrowded land. But as the day went on we got away from the worst of it, finding our way to smaller, more peaceful country lanes, where our bikes, so heavily laden with all our winter gear, continued to bring us plenty of attention.

"Picked a good day for it!" remarked one old man, as he took a brief break from his gardening, resting on a spade.

"Wrong time of year for that!" countered a passing cyclist, who had clearly failed to notice that he too was out cycling at the exact same time of year.

"Gosh, where are you going?" asked one woman out walking three dogs, who added, "Looks like you're doing a tour of Britain!"

and then hurried off without waiting for a reply.

Dea seemed to rather enjoy the slight eccentricity of the people, and she was certainly taken by the quaint English villages that we passed through, with their village greens and old stone churches. But most of all she was intrigued by the traditional pubs, and her wish to see inside was granted when we stopped at one to ask for water. Her face was alive with excitement as she looked around at the big wooden beams overhead, the old fireplace, the pictures on the wall, and the locals sitting nursing their pints while reading the newspaper or chatting to one another. It seemed like Dea really did like it in England, and had found in it a culture as interesting as any she'd come across in more exotic parts of the world.

It was good that Dea liked the little English villages so much, because after a couple of days it was time to introduce her to the little English village of Newton Blossomville, the village, and the house, where I had lived for the first nineteen years of my life. And then again when I was twenty-two. And briefly again when I was twenty-four.

It was an odd feeling to return to my parents' home now along with Dea, putting together pieces of my life that had never mingled before. It was all very civil, of course, and my parents made Dea feel welcome in much the same way as her parents had done for me. I encouraged my dad to show some photos of him as a young man, when he had built his own boat from scratch on his parents' lawn. There was something in this unusual project I found I could associate with, the outside-of-the-box ambitions of a younger Dad, and it helped to break the ice. Later on my aunt and uncle came around to join us for dinner, and the conversation became rather overrun by talk of television and internet packages and other things Dea and I knew little about. But at least it stayed clear of Brexit.

Dea and I only stopped over for one night, as we had already arranged living quarters further west in Malvern and needed to continue our progress there. We did, however, have time the next morning to stop off at the local primary school. A little over two and a half decades earlier this had been the place where I'd learnt how to read and write, and now I'd been invited back to talk to the children about my travels. The big, wide eyes and open mouths on their little faces revealed their surprise at seeing our overloaded bicycles. A brief talk about the places I'd been with the aid of the classroom globe only added to their amazement. It felt really nice to return here after twenty-five years, to the little playground where I'd once run around, so carefree and oblivious to the wider world that lay beyond the school gates, to see a new generation of youngsters enjoying their snotty-nosed utopia, and perhaps even to plant in their growing heads a seed of future adventure.

We waved goodbye to the little ones and two days of navigating more country lanes westwards brought us within sight of the Malvern Hills and the town we would call home, at least for a short while. We rode in with the sun setting behind the hills and made a stop at my sister, Angela's, house. Here I donned my Uncle Chris cap once more and Dea quickly adjusted to her new identity as Auntie Dea as she was introduced to more little ones, Summer and Finley, and we both met for the very first time their newborn and ever so adorable little sister Skye. It was good to be with family again.

But this was not our new home, there simply wasn't space, even if a house with three young children was a good place to write, which it isn't. Instead we'd been fortunate enough to find a room to rent in a little apartment where we would have our own big window that looked out over the hills. It was the home of Jane, her partner Lawrence, Jane's ten-year-old daughter Leela, and a gentle old dog by the name of Benji. A dish of pasta was waiting for us and and a warm, open-hearted atmosphere that immediately made us feel welcome into yet another new life.

The reason behind us living for a while in Malvern was two-fold. First, it gave us the chance to spend time with my sister and her three children, allowing us to enjoy Christmas with them and my parents for the first time in three years. And second, it provided me with the time to sit down and finish the book that I'd started in Copenhagen. On the first count things went well. Christmas was a success, with Auntie Dea fitting in well with my family, and in Summer and Finley I had my energetic playmates who could match my enthusiasm for games (one of their favourites being to pretend to be kangaroos knocking me off my bike). On the second, things didn't progress quite so positively. The writing was not going well.

I tried going for long walks in the Malvern Hills, the very same hills that once inspired J.R.R. Tolkien and C.S. Lewis to their own great literary feats. And while the hills were undoubtedly impressive, I returned from these walks not with inspiration, but with dread. As I'd approach our front door I'd be overcome with negative thoughts about returning to *that* chair, at *that* desk, to look at *that* computer. By the turn of the year the novelty of trying to write a book had long since worn off. It just wasn't fun any more, and it felt like I would never make it to the end.

A potential solution came one day with a sudden idea to up sticks and move to Edinburgh. I was in need of a change of scenery and the time it would take to cycle up to Scotland would give me a much needed break from the writing. We were also still low on funds, and I thought that a few weekends of working on the rickshaws (a job I'd already done in Edinburgh four years previously to save up for the start of my trip) would be perfect for topping up the travel points. Then there was the fact that J.K. Rowling had written Harry Potter in Edinburgh, and she'd done alright out of that. Maybe I'd find the inspiration I was looking for in the picturesque old city. Dea, who had just been out cycling on her own around Wales due to a growing restlessness, thought it was a great idea, and so a new plan was settled upon.

Dea and I left Malvern together on the 14th of January, waving sad farewells to my sister and her lovely children and wondering what they would be like when we saw them next. Dea had picked up some pain in her knee during her trip around Wales, so on our way out of town we stopped off and bought her a knee support, hoping that might help. As for me, I hadn't cycled at all for a whole month, the longest I'd gone without cycling in a five and a half years, and it felt really good to be back on the bike, even with the steep climb over the Malvern Hills. We'd decided on taking the more scenic route – west across Wales, ferry over to Ireland, cycle up to Northern Ireland, then another ferry to Scotland – but returning to the Welsh hills was not good for Dea's knee. By the time we set up camp in a small patch of woodland on the first night she was struggling a lot, and I was worried.

The following morning things got even worse. We had some more hills to climb, and Dea was clearly in a great deal of discomfort. She was forced to a stop by the pain.

"It feels like something is really wrong," she said, tears welling in her eyes. "I feel like I'm going to just damage it worse and worse by keeping on cycling on it."

Scotland seemed like a really long way off, and with our big trip to China starting soon it seemed like a really bad idea for Dea to keep damaging her knee like this. We discussed our options, and decided to first cycle on the flat main road to Hereford, which was only fifteen kilometres away, where we could figure out the best solution.

In Hereford we made ourselves at home in a leisure centre café (because of the free Wi-Fi) and came up with another new plan. Dea would not continue to cycle, our ride to China was simply too important to put at risk. Instead she would take a train from Hereford to Edinburgh. Having friends in the city, I made arrangements so that she would have someone to meet her off the train and give her a place to stay. There was, of course, no way that I could join her on that train, and I would have to cycle up alone.

Leaving my girlfriend behind at the station and biking off without her was a sad moment. I knew how much she wanted to travel the world by bicycle, and these things that were beyond her control – first with the eye infection, and now her knee – kept holding her back from it. I could see how frustrating it was for her, but I also saw in that frustration a deep determination to eventually succeed and that was one of the reasons why I loved her so much. I remained confident that she was my ideal cycling partner, that there was no one I would rather try and cycle around the world with than her.

Heading for the Brecon Beacons alone I struggled up steep hill after steep hill, thinking for the first time in a really long time that perhaps cycling everywhere wasn't such a brilliant idea after all. I was only doing this to get to Edinburgh, and suddenly a train seemed like such a nice, convenient, comfortable method of transportation. It would get me there so fast, with so little effort. But I could not give in to such temptations, and forced myself to suck it up and continue to grind away at the pedals. Taking small roads I was forced to climb up insanely steep gradients then whizz down the other side. These hills reminded me of waves on an ocean. I felt like a tiny boat, struggling up and then cresting each wave-hill, knowing that there were more to come, more and more, appearing to simply go on forever across an endless sea. But I told myself that if I only kept going I would have to make it to land eventually. Which, in this case, was the sea. But that was alright, because when I finally did make it to the sea, there was a great big ferry waiting to carry me to Ireland. It was the first sunny day in ages, and the cliffs of the Pembrokeshire coast looked amazing, glowing in the light of the low sun, as the ferry sailed me away from Britain.

I rolled off the boat in the dark winter evening, unsure of where to make camp. By luck I found right in front of me a large area of dunes and I pushed my bike into them, to my own private world. I fell asleep beneath a sky full of stars, the sound of the ocean in my ears. The fifty-first country of my travels had made a good start.

But cycling up the east coast of Ireland failed to live up to this early promise. Thankfully it was flatter than Wales, and the weather remained mild and dry, but the cycling was a bit on the boring side. I followed quiet country roads through repetitive farmland. There were no benches to sit on, no places for taking breaks, and nowhere to camp at night. Everywhere was privately owned land and it was not well set up for the wild camping cycle tourist. I made the best of things, sleeping in patches of trees right next to the road, and listening to my radio to keep me company as I rode.

Dublin arrived with a surprising number of impressive European-style bicycle lanes. In the cramped city centre I made time to meet up with a friend from Australia. Fernando, a young, stylish Italian who had recently moved to live and study in Dublin, had been my pedicabbing colleague, although taking a quite different path from me he now told me he hoped never to ride a bike again as long as he lived. It was good to see him again and we took a seat together in a little park to chat about old times. As we did so a young man approached and said to me in a thick Irish accent, "Excuse me, but are you homeless?"

"Well, no, actually I'm travelling," I said.

"Well you look like you're homeless with all that stuff there. Where do you sleep?"

"In a tent."

"Ya are, you're homeless so ya are!" he cried out with what appeared to be glee.

Fernando, well-dressed as ever, watched our conversation with interest.

"This doesn't usually happen," I told him, as the Irish fellow called over his friend to come and pose for a selfie with the homeless man he'd found.

One thing brightened up my time in Ireland considerably and that was hearing from Dea. She was having a good time in Edinburgh and her knee was getting better thanks to a regime of rest and daily stretches. She also wrote that she thought we should leave Edinburgh and start cycling to China on the 21st of March, as a symbolic nod to the fact that we had left Surfers Paradise exactly a year earlier than that. It was a date that was a little later than we had talked about, and while I knew she was so keen to get started I thought it was good that she recognised the need to give her knee time to recover. But best of all with this later start date I suddenly felt a surge of real belief that I could get my book finished before we left. I would now arrive in Edinburgh with a realistic chance to leave as an author.

Crossing into Northern Ireland I picked up a towpath alongside a canal that made for very pleasant cycling all of the way to Belfast. Another ferry ride and I was in Scotland, and it felt good to be in Scotland. Now finally it wasn't just all farmland, and I enjoyed cycling along the rugged coastline, where wild moors dotted with car-sized boulders and forests of oak and alder reminded me that there was still some nature in this part of the world. I saw a deer, for goodness sake, I saw a deer! But it couldn't last forever, and in the town of Ayr I was brought back to the human world by an interesting encounter with a young man by the name of Ross. He was walking along on the seafront path and stopped me as I went by to ask what I was doing. A slim guy with long hair, he said he was twenty-two, though he looked like he could have been even younger. He seemed like an odd guy, but a nice one, and as we were both going the same way we continued on together.

"Do you meditate?" he asked me suddenly.

"No," I said. "But sometimes I can feel like I'm meditating when I'm cycling a long way in some places."

"Wow, man, that's so cool what you're doing. I ought to do something like that. But I don't have any money. But I need to do something. I've done too many drugs!"

Ross had his problems, for sure, but with his frank and open nature, he came across as an extremely likeable young man.

"I'm living in a homeless shelter now. But I'm on my way to a job interview. It's as a dishwasher. Where are you going?"

"Oh, I was looking for the library."

"I'll take you there if you want."

And he did, going out of his way to show me where it was. We said goodbye and I wished him good luck, then I locked my bike up and went into the library to charge my laptop and check my e-mails. When I came out again my bike was where I'd left it, untouched, but Ross was back and he approached me as I went to leave.

"Hey, man," he said, walking closer to me, "can I show you some gemstones?"

"Erm, sure."

And so we walked together to a little shop, with Ross babbling on about how much he loved this shop and telling me about some of the things he'd bought there before.

"Here it is!"

We stepped inside. It was a tiny store, with shelves full of little stones of all colours as well as plenty of other trinkets. Ross looked like a kid in a sweet shop.

"Who needs money and girls when you've got stones?" he said, a line that I agreed with only out of politeness.

Then he found a stone that he really liked.

"Wow," he said, "look at this one. Isn't it amazing?"

"Sure is."

"I'm going to ask them to keep it safe for me behind the counter. I'll ask my mum for a pound so I can come back and buy it later."

"It only costs a pound?"

"Yeah, not bad is it?"

"Here, I've got a pound."

Ross stared at me like I'd just given him a thousand pounds.

"Really? Ah wow, really? That is so nice of you." And he bought his stone, announcing to the sales lady, "This guy just gave me a pound, he's a really nice guy!"

But the truth was that Ross was the nice guy. His friendly, innocent nature reminded me that good-hearted people exist in all walks of life. One of the things I loved most about bicycle touring was that it brought me in contact with so many different people and, so far as I could see, there was goodness in almost all of them.

This point was validated further after I passed through Glasgow and joined another canal towpath for the last few hundred kilometres to Edinburgh, when along the way I met a man walking eight dogs.

"You've got a lot of stuff!" he said at the sight of my bike.

"You've got a lot of dogs!" I replied.

Norry's wife ran a dog walking business and he was helping her out. He told me he liked to do walking trips himself, and he'd made a long motorcycle trip some years ago that he talked fondly of, and he took a keen interest in my own story also. We stood and chatted for a while on the towpath and he was such a nice guy that before going he thrust five pounds at me and said, "Please, buy yourself a coffee when you get to Edinburgh." Well, I probably was looking a little tired.

A few hours later and I was finally there, back in Edinburgh, making my way through the bustling crowds of people on Princes Street, pushing my bike and looking up at the castle on the hill that I'd last seen three and a half years earlier. I'd been in the city then to work hard, save up some money, and prepare myself to cycle around the world. Now I was back once more, back to be reunited with Dea, and to do the same thing, all over again.

Progress Report
Edinburgh, March 2017

1.   Circumnavigate the planet

Mission accomplished!

2.   Do so using only my bicycle and boats

Mori: 90.3° E. Edinburgh: 3.2° W.
13.5° out of 360° around the planet.
(74% of the way around.)

3.   Pass through antipodal points

...I would be cycling a distance greater than the
circumference of the planet at the equator (40,075
kilometres)...

4.   Visit all of the inhabited continents

Four out of six still, and starting to repeat myself.

5.   Cycle at least 100,000 kilometres

60,968 kilometres completed. 39,032 to go.

6.   Cycle in 100 countries

Cycled in fifty-one. Past halfway!

7.   Return with more money than I start with

Still up. One word: Matched Betting.

PART FOUR

EDINBURGH TO
ISTANBUL

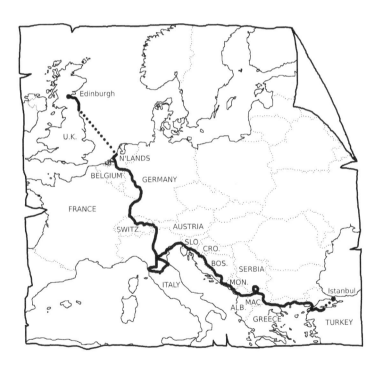

20

Edinburgh, United Kingdom
19th March 2017

We're cycling to China!" I informed the woman as I passed her my camera. Dea and I were standing together with our loaded bikes outside of the apartment of my friend, Jethro. He'd been good enough to put us up during our last few weeks in Edinburgh, but he was away for the weekend and, as there was no one else around to take our official leaving photo, I'd roped in a passer-by.

"Wow, that's a long way!" the woman said, shaking her head in disbelief and a snapping the picture for us.

She was right, it was a long way, yet it was somehow fitting that there was no one else there to wave us off. I had a few friends in Edinburgh from when I'd last lived in the city, and yet I'd been so busy over the previous six weeks I'd had barely enough time to catch up with them. Realising that it was my last chance to get the book done I'd dived into the process one hundred percent. There were days when I worked on it from seven in the morning until three in the morning and then when I did sleep all I did was dream about it. Dea looked after me so well those days, but she'd got herself a job selling hot dogs and wraps at a stall in town and sometimes she'd return home to find that I'd completely forgotten to eat. There was just so much to do with the writing, the editing, the formatting, the rewriting, the reformatting, the making a colourful cover. I learnt a lot about self-publishing but it was one hell of a lot of work. Who would have thought that writing a book about cycling around the world could be so much harder than actually cycling around the world? And then, just when I thought I was almost done, I realised I'd used the wrong type of apostrophe, and I had to go through and change them all. But eventually I made it through to the end, and just a few hours before we stood on Jethro's step, *No Wrong Turns* had gone live on Amazon. A couple of people even bought it. One chapter in my life was complete, just in time for a new one to begin.

We pedalled away excitedly, the first pedal strokes of what we dared to hope would be a continuous journey all of the way to Mori together. My bike, as it often did after a few weeks off, felt ridiculously heavy, and I struggled to find my balance. We wobbled our way down George Street under bright blue skies. I'd pedalled here many times before, usually on a rickshaw carrying drunks home at three in the morning. I hadn't had much chance to do that this time, however. My busy writing schedule, coupled with a worrying pain in my own knee, had limited the amount of work I could manage to a couple of weekends. But Dea had worked hard on the food stalls and I'd had a bit of luck on the horses, so we had enough money to set off with, and we hoped that sales of my book might provide the additional income we'd need.

We reached Princes Street and stopped to look up at the castle one last time. There was a wonderful atmosphere, a general feeling of goodwill in the air, perhaps as a result of the sunny skies hinting at the end of winter. Or maybe it was just coming from us. We were both in such a good mood, to have done what we needed to do, to have finished our work and earned our freedom. All we had ahead of us now were unwritten adventures and I had that feeling that always comes at the beginning of a long journey, that sense of anticipation of all that's ahead. And it was the start of a journey, not simply the continuation of my challenges, but the beginning of *our* world trip, me and Dea together, and that was really something very special. It was such an overwhelming sensation it almost made me dizzy with excitement. The first day is somehow always the best.

"Where you gonna go, where you gonna sleep tonight?"

Someone was playing music in the street nearby, and by some twist of fate it was the most appropriate song for us. A song that had always made me think of the road, of the wonderful uncertainty of bicycle travel, of not knowing where you were going to end the day. I looked over at Dea. There was a smile on her face bigger than I'd ever seen before. We didn't know where we were going to sleep tonight, and we loved it.

As it happened we ended up in a small patch of woodland just off the Sustrans cycle route that we'd followed all day. From Edinburgh's old town we'd veered around the city's iconic mountain, Arthur's Seat, alive with the first yellow flowers of the year, and out along the coastline through suburbs and fishing villages. It had been a lovely start to our trip, but now we were faced with the tricky task of putting up our new, and very inexpensive, tent for the first time. It was quite windy and after a long struggle to thread in the poles it took a frustratingly long time to assemble, with us starting to wonder if a tent that cost only forty pounds was really going to be good enough to house us all of the way to China. Or for that matter, to Newcastle. By the time it was finally standing it was already dark, so we cooked our dinner by the light of our one pound head torches.

"We've got a lot of really cheap stuff, haven't we?" I said, as the pot slipped off our five pound camping stove.

"And look at your shoes!" Dea laughed.

I looked down at them. The only thing stopping my toes from slipping out of the ends were a couple of carefully placed cable ties.

"Nothing wrong with my shoes, Dea."

The next day we had more good weather, feeling blessed by the blue skies and strong tailwind that were easing us gently into our journey. Following the well-signposted cycling route we rode on a mixture of cycle paths and quiet roads, playing The Spotting Things Game as we went. It felt so good to feel the freedom of real cycle touring again with Dea at my side, or at least it did until the route plummeted us down into a cove and then requested we cycle back up on an implausibly steep road. Suddenly things weren't quite so much fun, as I felt my whole body object to the tough workout. My heart raced and my lungs cried out as I gasped madly for more air, my muscles struggling to find the strength needed for the steep ascent. I was not at peak fitness after six weeks hunched over my laptop, and this climb was an early test of resolve.

Thankfully we were both able to pass the test, but as we neared the top and paused to admire the views out over the sea, we were surprised by the sight of another loaded cycle tourist powering up the hill behind us. And as if his speed wasn't enough to embarrass me about how tough I'd found the climb, he also appeared to be of pensionable age. He stopped to talk, barely out of breath, and asked us how far we were going.

"China," Dea said. It sounded so far away, so impressive. "And what about you?"

"Oh... New Zealand."

David had started a few days before us from Inverness, and he explained that his intention was to take eighteen months to reach New Zealand, cycling like us through Europe, Turkey, Central Asia and China. For a while we stood there at the side of the road talking of our respective plans and I was back in that travelling zone, of meeting with other long distance cyclists riding the Silk Route, of comparing notes and plans for the Pamir Highway. I'd told Dea we'd be sure to meet with plenty of other long distance cyclists making their way across Eurasia, but even I hadn't expected it to happen on day two.

Like all long distance cyclists (including those approaching seventy years of age) David was faster than me, so we wished him well, agreeing that we were sure to meet again somewhere along the way, and watched him disappear off ahead of us as we crested the hill through a man-made forest of wind turbines. The wind was continuing to blow us along too, and by the end of the day we were south of Berwick and over the border into England. We camped just off a trail on cliffs that overlooked the sea, making for a lovely place to spend the night (so long as we ignored the fact that on the other side of us there was a busy railway line).

England brought with it a change in the weather. The temperature plummeted as the wind started blowing in at us from the North Sea. It was a bitterly cold wind that numbed our cheeks and any other exposed skin. But it was spring, nevertheless, and the daffodils and newborn lambs that we passed were a heart-warming reminder of that. As the still-upbeat Dea pointed out to me, this season was really the ideal time to start our trip – the new life all around us and the reawakening of nature after a long winter felt like the perfect accompaniment to our own new beginnings. We celebrated with a game of Pine Cone Wars. With my face half covered to protect me from the wind I assumed a character by the name of the Masked Bandit and I felt confident this new persona would help me to a first ever Pine Cone War victory. But alas, it turned out that the Masked Bandit wasn't much of a throw, and Dea won easily.

We continued south on a mixture of quiet roads and coastal paths, passing numerous old castles along the way. Our final day of cycling in England brought even worse weather, with rain showers adding to the cold wind. But we had a *warmshowers* host in North Shields to look forward to staying with, and that spurred us on. We passed the long beach of Whitley Bay and struggled on up the hill to the castle at Tynemouth. Finally we looked down upon the Tyne river, from which a ferry would be carrying us to mainland Europe. We had made it. The first small task on our long journey had been accomplished.

Our host, Roy, welcomed us into his home, but after a quick shower it was time for me and Dea to hit the road again and cycle into Newcastle to get something to eat. And I should point out that it was not because we didn't want to eat dinner with Roy that we went back out in the rain, but because Dea's work colleagues in Edinburgh had been kind enough to give her a leaving gift of a voucher for a meal in a restaurant. They couldn't have anticipated when they'd chosen the restaurant that it would mean for us an additional seventeen wet kilometres, of course, and it was a very thoughtful thing of them to do, knowing that we would not often be able to treat ourselves to eat out during our frugal travels. We arrived in the centre of Newcastle freezing cold and soaking wet, and must have made for quite a sight as we walked into the tidy restaurant dripping all over the floor. Roy was waiting for us at a table, as we'd invited him to join us, and he'd been sensible enough to take the train. After a quick visit to the bathroom, Dea and I transformed into more respectable members of society, thanks in no small part to a shirt and trousers borrowed from Roy, and we took a seat. The location had been thoughtfully chosen, as the restaurant served Asian tapas, and we ordered a variety of little dishes that offered a glimpse of some of the cultures that Dea and I had to look forward to.

We were very happy to share our meal with Roy who, as with David, was an older man that reminded us that an active and adventurous life could still be enjoyed in one's later years. He had a passion for travelling, and at the age of sixty-five he'd just bought a camper van that he planned to take to Europe in the summer with his girlfriend. He was also learning to play the ukulele and it was refreshing to see his approach to life, still seeking out new things, new challenges and embracing it all head on. We liked Roy a lot, and the evening was full of laughter as the tapas slowly disappeared from the table.

The next morning Roy accompanied us to all of the second-hand shops in North Shields in a desperate hunt for some replacement footwear for me, but we found nothing. He even tried to give me a pair of his own as a last resort, but they were too small.

"I really think these shoes are going to be alright for a while longer," I insisted, as we said goodbye to Roy and headed down to the ferry dock.

I'd been looking forward to this particular ferry. It was an overnight journey to the Netherlands on a big ship that I hoped might make up for the disappointment of the last cruise that Dea and I had taken together. But alas, there were no swimming pools, no table-tennis tables, and most disappointing of all, no free food. Instead we sat in our cramped cabin and made ourselves sandwiches. We were too tired to do much more, but I ventured to the outside deck at one point. It was dark and cold and I was all alone. The lights of the northeast coast of England were just visible, fading into the night as a cold, salty wind whipped at my face. I knew that those lights would be my last glimpse of the island that I'd once called home for a good long while. It was not the first time I'd left her behind in search of adventure, of course, but I still felt the same excited buzz dreaming of all the things I might see before I laid eyes on her again.

21

Ijmuiden, Netherlands
24th March 2017

The next morning I woke up early and hurried back outside to get a first glimpse of continental Europe, but there was no sign of it, there was absolutely nothing around us except water. I suppose the Netherlands just isn't the kind of country to rise up out of the sea, but a couple of hours later we did bump into it. Dea and I went down to the car decks to retrieve our bikes and there we encountered David, the cycle tourist we'd met a couple of days earlier. It was a shame that we'd not found each other on board before (perhaps because Dea and I were in our cabin eating sandwiches), for David was planning a much more northerly route across Europe than us, and there would not be time for a long chat now. So we made do with a brief conversation as we waited for the cars to depart the ferry ahead of us, in which David revealed that he was indeed sixty-nine years old, and planned to reach China in time for his seventieth birthday. He said that he'd found the last days in England tough with the cold winds and the hills (but then so had I), although one thing was for sure, he was certainly more prepared than us. Not only did he already have many of the visas needed for the journey, he'd even got around to booking his accommodation in Dushanbe, Tajikistan for August 22nd. That's some good planning, David.

We lost David at the first roundabout, with him turning north and us south to head down the coast from Ijmuiden. It was such a lovely sunny day that it had me wondering just how long we'd been on that boat, the weather had improved so much. The cycling was easy of course, and the people were very friendly, with many stopping to ask us where we were going and wishing us luck. We were winding our way through the same dunes that we'd ridden through the previous summer on our way to Denmark, and there were plenty of similarities now, with us playing games and having fun as we rode. But the one big difference was that Dea was no longer constrained by her eye infection. Her left eye was almost entirely back to normal, with just a small scar left that had only a minimal effect upon her vision, and this time we were really free to go off where we wanted, and that was a great, great feeling.

At one of our little rest breaks we finished off the last of our supply of British biscuits, and I informed Dea that she had one last chance to correctly state the name of the biscuit she was most confused about. For some reason she got the name the wrong way around every single time. "This is your last chance now Dea. What are these biscuits called?"

She closed her eyes, the lines of her forehead furrowed with intense concentration, before she said, as she always did, "Cream Custards!"

"No, sorry Dea, they are called Custard Creams." We both laughed. A lot. It was about the one hundredth time she'd got it wrong.

"Oh, never mind," she said. "Do we have any Jammy Badgers left?"

"It's Jammy Dodgers, Dea."

For the third time in the past year we cycled into Holland's second largest city, Rotterdam. On our earlier visits we'd had neither the time nor the inclination to stop and really see the place, but now Martin and Susanne had offered us the chance to not only stay with them again, but also to get a guided tour. We had felt a good connection with this couple when we'd visited them the previous November, so it was not a difficult decision to accept their invitation. They had recently moved to a new apartment high up in a tower block with a great view over the city and we were welcomed in with smiles and hugs. It was a friendship that came easily, with our similar ages and the common bonds that tend to link all long distance cycle tourists. Martin and Susanne had set off from the Netherlands in 2014 with a goal of cycling all of the way to Nepal, and after a circuitous route that included visiting Mongolia (in winter), South Korea, and Myanmar, three years later they rode triumphantly into Kathmandu. Now they were back home and working on a new, more settled, way of life.

The next day Dea and I took a break from cycling and walked around Rotterdam with Martin and Susanne. As promised there was plenty to see. From the Markthal, where a large food market sat beneath an enormous arched roof, to the Kijk-Kubus (bizarre cube-shaped houses), to the array of tower blocks lining the Nieuwe Maas River, interesting and unique architectural experiments were a defining feature of the city. For lunch we stopped at the lively Fenix Food Factory, a big old warehouse housing food stalls from all over the world, where our hosts generously treated us to Moroccan bread with a variety of dips. But the real highlight of our day together was introducing Martin and Susanne to The Spotting Things Game, which we played in teams as we walked. It was the boys against the girls, and thanks to the girls totally misusing their bonus swap and Martin being not at all shy to walk up to several people to see if they were eating the right kind of ice cream, I was soon able to chalk up another victory.

Back at the flat with the light from the setting sun filling the apartment Dea and I made pizza, both to return the hospitality of our hosts and also to celebrate. For the result of The Spotting Things Game was not the only good news of the day; back in Denmark, Dea's sister Sara had just given birth to a healthy baby boy, to be named Laurids. It was wonderful news, and we toasted it with beer and pizza, more games, and an evening of conversation about our shared desires to travel and to live in a different way. Yet talk of the newborn baby and families led to some moments of apparent tension between our new friends.

"I feel like I'm ready to have babies now," Susanne said, "but Martin is not sure he's quite there yet."

And this was easy enough to laugh off in the moment, but it still felt like their hopes for the future were perhaps not quite aligned, with uncertain talk of Martin working in China, Susanne staying in Holland, and them buying land in Portugal all being a little vague and mixed up. It made me think for a moment, that, while Dea and I were still in the first days of our journey together, a journey that might prove as long as Martin and Susanne's, there undoubtedly would come a time when it was at an end. There would come a time when all of the excitement of setting out together on the road was but a distant memory, and the realities of life would confront us. So I felt comfort in the idea we shared of buying some land in Denmark and living in a yurt, an idea that we talked excitedly about almost as much as we did the cycling trip. We also both knew that we wanted to have kids, and it seemed to me that we were on the same page about our future, and that having a good sense of where we wanted to be in five or ten years' time meant that we could enjoy and appreciate our trip all the more while it lasted.

It was sunny again as we left Rotterdam behind, and with the temperatures rising by the day we were even able to cycle in shorts for the first time, exposing our ghostly white legs to the spring sunshine. By the afternoon it was even warm enough for me to remove my sweater, and realising what that meant I declared to Dea, "Look at me! I'm wearing shorts and T-shirt. We have made it through the winter!" It felt so good to be able to say that, and as a result we were both in a tremendous mood. "I could cycle here forever," I cried out, as we enjoyed the smooth, well-maintained network of cycle routes that led us peacefully along the Dutch dikes.

I couldn't really cycle in Holland forever, of course, it's not that big, and before we knew it we were at the Belgian border. But there wasn't just one Belgian border for us to cross. We'd actually chosen our route specifically after we'd spotted a bizarre-looking anomaly on the map that we wanted to investigate further. And what we found when we arrived in Baarle-Nassau/Baarle-Hertog was a very curious place indeed. It was essentially a town in the Netherlands, but with a great many Belgian enclaves within it. Parts of the town were Dutch, parts were Belgian, and there seemed to be no real logic behind the random organisation of the different pieces of the jigsaw. I got an introduction to how strange it all was when I stopped at a pharmacy to get some medicine for my worsening hayfever. The woman told me that sadly they didn't sell the drug I was after in the Netherlands, but that I might have better luck in Belgium. She then directed me to try asking a couple of streets away, like it was the most normal thing in the world.

We walked our bikes through the town and tried to understand how it worked. Along the way we several times crossed lines painted on the footpath with NL printed on one side and B on the other, indicating each border crossing as we moved about between each enclave. Then a nice man came up to us at a supermarket to ask about our trip, and we took the chance to ask him about his strange little town. He was Belgian, but was out shopping in Holland. He insisted that everyone got along alright with each other and explained to us how it all first came about, something about a deal that a Dutch duke made with a Belgian prince or something.

"But why is it so randomly arranged?"

"Well, he gave the Belgians all the worst bit, of course."

A couple of hours later we reached the proper Belgian border and celebrated with a penalty shoot-out in a football goal that was positioned right next to the bicycle path, where I claimed a rare victory thanks to a new technique I'd developed of lying down on the goal-line to put Dea off. This win indicated to me that we were going to have a tremendous time during our brief visit to Belgium, and we got the chance to put this hypothesis to the test when an older couple stopped to talk with us at a railway bridge just outside Turnhout.

"Where are you going?" gasped the man, with a look of curiosity and wonder on his face.

"China," we replied, and his curiosity turned to amazement.

More questions followed, and it wasn't long before the man asked, "Would you like to come and stay the night at our house? We would love to have you visit."

Even though it wasn't very long into the day, we'd not cycled much, and I'd spent a fair bit of it lying down, it was still an offer that we gratefully accepted, changing the expression on the man's face to one of excitement and joy.

We walked into Turnhout together as the man, Ludo, eagerly took photos and videos of us and constantly repeated how great it was that we had accepted his invitation. Apparently they had met a few cyclists like us over the years, but they'd always been too busy to stay. That seemed like a real shame, but I knew I too had often been like that, rushing somewhere to make a visa deadline or to catch a cruise and not always having enough time. Dea and I were certainly keen now to try and slow down enough to seize these kind of opportunities to meet people.

And Ludo and his wife Alda were certainly worth meeting. They first invited us to come for a drink in Turnhout's central square, where we sat outside of a café and chatted, casually sipping drinks like proper Europeans. They were both in their sixties, with Ludo's seventieth birthday fast approaching, and, while they were now retired, they kept themselves busy playing sports, riding their bikes, and volunteering doing cool things like offering cycle training for kids, and rickshaw rides to elderly people. Ludo especially had so much energy and enthusiasm for life and, like David and Roy before him, was once again proving to us that age need not be a barrier to making things happen. In fact Ludo and Alda were themselves planning a long bicycle trip through Europe following the Danube later in the year.

We walked with them back to their lovely home, where we were shown to our room. Ludo then looked at Dea with a mischievous glint in his eye and said, "Unless you would like to sleep with someone else, then you can go in here," which might well have made her a little uncomfortable, were it not for the fact that he was show-ing her to another spare room which was filled with cuddly toys. Ludo and Alda had spent much of their lives running a toy shop in town, and this room made us confess to them that we were carrying a few cuddly toys of our own, most of which we had picked up dur-ing our time in Australia.

"I gave Dea a cuddly toy kangaroo when she flew into Melbourne to meet me, you see. Then she bought me a platypus, and it sort of went on from there," I tried to explain, a little embarrassed. But Ludo and Alda were smiling. They thought it was wonderful.

We enjoyed a nice dinner together, although Ludo didn't eat too much of it. He was trying hard to keep fit and to get his weight down before his birthday which was just a few days away. He had a Fitbit to help him and he seemed to love how the technology enabled him to keep track of his health. He reminded me somehow of a child in a man's body, there was such enthusiasm and energy in him.

The next morning there was a gift waiting for us at the breakfast table. It was a cuddly toy clown. Dea and I had agreed that we'd probably got a bit carried away in Australia, and should try to avoid buying any more cuddly toys for a while, but we weren't going to say no to such a lovely present. Dea named the toy, and Connor the clown was soon joining Karen the kangaroo and Mr Plopples the platypus in our panniers. Along with Wilma the wombat, Kevin the koala, and Thomas the turtle, of course. And not forgetting the cuddly toy Santa Claus we'd rescued from a tree branch in England. I think that's all of them. I thought I'd done well not mentioning them before now. Ryan Gosling doesn't have cuddly toys, does he?

Then Ludo and Alda asked if they could buy my book, a copy of which was sitting in my basket with a tattered piece of paper for-lornly declaring that it was for sale. I was happy simply to give them the book as a present, but they insisted on paying as they wanted to contribute to our journey somehow, although they'd certainly done that already. But I was delighted to have finally found someone will-ing to buy my book, at least at first. Then suddenly I froze in something like horror, when I realised that the only thing I'd written about Belgium in the whole damn book was that it was a bit of a boring country.

We said goodbye to Alda, promising to come and visit in a few years on our way back home, while Ludo joined us cycling for the first twenty kilometres or so out of Turnhout alongside a very long and very straight canal lined with trees. When we stopped for a break at a bench he showed his child-like nature once again by pulling out of his pannier a plastic Fisher Price lunch box that he must have had since at least the eighties. We all laughed about it. "Well, it stills works," he said. He was so positive, so happy. It was a pleasure to have met him, to have taken the time to get to know him and Alda just a little bit, and as we hugged goodbye and rode away I was left with one thought to take with me into Germany: *'I guess Belgium's not so boring after all!'*

22

Northwest Germany
31st March 2017

We continued east into Germany and made our way towards the Rhine River, which we planned to join at Cologne and then follow south all of the way to Switzerland. Originally we had hoped to take a more westerly course via Luxembourg, but that would have meant a lot of hills, and we thought it a more sensible idea to start off with a few weeks of flat cycling in order to ease Dea's troublesome knees into the ride. But taking the Rhine also meant that I would be repeating some of the same route that I'd done during the first weeks of my trip out from Paris (albeit in the opposite direction), and this put a slight ripple of discontent into proceedings. For I had not cycled this section alone; I had been with Karin then, and that, I knew, made things a little uncomfortable for Dea. On our last night camping before Cologne there were tears running down Dea's cheeks about it. She explained that it had been hard for her to read about me and Karin (and one or two other girls) in my book. I knew that, it was not the first time this had come up, and I did my best to reassure her that it all happened long in the past, before I even knew that she existed, that it had only been a brief fling anyway, that no girl could compare with her. I could understand why it made Dea sad, but it also made me so sad and frustrated, as I struggled to ease her concerns, to convince her that she was the only girl I wanted to be with now.

But if Dea was still unhappy when we arrived in Cologne the following day she did a good job of concealing it. For some reason she had a bit of a thing about German cities, and she had a smile on her face again as we passed by the giant cathedral and arrived for the first time at the river bank. There were lots of people out enjoying the good weather, strolling or cycling along, or just sitting and chatting with friends on the promenade. But evening was approaching, so Dea and I soon pedalled down the riverside bike path to find a place to camp.

The next morning we were in another German city, Bonn, where we had arranged to meet an old university friend of mine. As we sat in one of the cobbled central squares waiting for him to arrive it was instead a woman that approached us. Her name was Monika, and she said that she just had to let us know that we had arrived in Bonn on a very special day, for the Japanese cherry trees that lined a couple of the streets in town were in full bloom, having only just sprung out the day before.

"Usually they have a big festival to celebrate," she told us, "but this year the local people protested, because there come too many people, the streets get crowded. I think it ruins the beauty of the thing, all those people. But this year the festival was cancelled, so I can ride my bicycle up and down the street beneath all those pink flowers. It is wonderful, you must go and see it."

Monika was such a friendly, enthusiastic woman, and just as she wished us well and went on her way my friend, Vivek, appeared in her place. He had driven all of the way from his home near Brussels to meet with us and join in with our journey briefly, a journey which I knew he had been following online via our blog for many years. In actual fact he was pretty much the only one of my old university friends to keep up to date with my travels like that, which was quite surprising, because to be honest we weren't exactly friends. Vivek was a few years older than me and had been the warden for my block of student halls during the first year of my studies, a year that had involved a lot more in the way of alcohol and silly pranks than it had studying. I fear I may have been something of a ringleader in a lot of the mischief, and Vivek had been the man with the unfortunate task of keeping us all in line.

"Good to see you again, Chris," Vivek said with a smile. "How long has it been? Ten years, I think? Last time I saw you was when you were on another madcap adventure."

Indeed I was. A year or so after somehow graduating university, on my first hitchhiking trip abroad, I'd stopped by in Brussels and stayed with Vivek, where he had just moved to work. He took me out to dinner that time, and I had repaid his kindness by accidentally breaking off his shower head.

"You must let me buy you a coffee or an ice cream," he now said as we stood reunited in Bonn. I thought maybe I was the one who owed him something, what with the broken shower, and that time when I orchestrated the stealing of all of second floor kitchen's furniture, but Vivek was quite insistent, and I thought maybe it was finally about time I started doing what he said.

Following Monika's advice, the three of us walked together to Heerstrasse, and there, as promised, was a little street lined with beautiful pink cherry trees in full bloom. They arched right over the street as far as the eye could see, making for what I can only reasonably describe as a pink corridor of loveliness. We found a seat outside of a café and sat down to look at the menu. There was cherry tea and sweet cherry tea and cherry juice and cherry smoothies. I saw what they were doing here, but how long was it that Monika said these trees were in bloom for? A few days of the year? It seemed a questionable business model to me. In any case, we ordered ourselves some cherry-based drinks and then got down to reminiscing about old times.

"Vivek was the warden for my halls at university," I explained to Dea. "And me and my friends weren't always the best behaved."

"Oh, you weren't that much trouble, really," he said.

"Vivek, I set fire to the kitchen!"

"Oh yes, I'd forgotten about that."

Vivek was supposed to have brought his bike with him in order to cycle for a little while with us along the Rhine, but it had apparently not turned out to be in working condition, and he'd left it at home. I wasn't about to let him off that easily, though, not after he'd driven such a long way to be part of our trip, and so I suggested he rent a bike from somewhere. To my surprise he agreed, and went off to get one from a rental place near the train station.

We cycled off together out of Bonn and along the first stretch of the 'Romantic Rhine'. And what could possibly be more romantic than cycling along with the girl that you love on the banks of the beautiful river, with your old university warden sandwiched between the two of you? Vivek was dressed in smart shoes and trousers, but was nevertheless perfectly capable of keeping up with our slow pace, at least for a little while. Along the way we talked more, about serious things like relationships and families, and about less serious things, like his Fitbit.

"You're not the first person we've met recently with one of those," I said.

"Yeah, well, it is quite clever," he replied, pointing at his wrist. "It can even tell automatically what it is that you're doing. It knows if you are running or cycling or whatever, so at the end it will tell you 'you have been running for half an hour.'"

"I suppose that's useful. But does it ever get it wrong sometimes?"

"Yes, it does. Actually... it seems to think I'm mowing the lawn at the moment."

After ten kilometres or so Vivek turned around to start on his journey home as we continued ours south. It had been great to catch up with him again, and I considered the whole thing to have been a resounding success, if only because I'd managed to avoid breaking any of his possessions this time.

Not long after saying goodbye to Vivek, Dea and I came to an area with a beach volleyball court and football goals and, as usual, we couldn't resist stopping to play. After Dea won an epic volleyball match, I gained my revenge in a penalty shoot-out. The goals were full size, real, big, proper football goals. "The goals are too big!" Dea complained, just before putting two of her kicks wide.

The Rhine was such a great place to cycle, with a flat path next to the river guiding us through the increasingly hilly and beautiful terrain. The weather remained warm and sunny, and we made life even more fun by competing in races with some of the barges that plied the waters, while simultaneously competing against each other in some truly epic rounds of The Spotting Things Game. When racing boats and looking for stuff got exhausting we'd stop for a refreshing dip in the river, then construct sand sculptures on the beaches. In the evenings, with nowhere to wild camp beside the river, we'd head away from it, up into the hills to look for some forest, where on one occasion we spotted two wild boar who came over to investigate us before scampering away into the darkness. It was fantastic to be sharing this all with Dea, who it seemed had got over her earlier reservations about coming here. I loved her all the more for it, and I loved that we were building our own memories to take away from this place.

And a very special memory was created as we looked for a place to sleep one night in the hills above the town of Boppard. Just as we stood at the roadside consulting over a turn-off that looked promising, a fast sports car drove over the hill and stopped near to us. An athletic, tanned, good-looking couple with bright white smiles jumped out and came over towards us. As they approached I wondered for a brief moment if these were the mythical 'Tent Police', the special agents that every wild camping cycle tourist fears might find them in their hiding place, or while they are in the process of looking for it. They didn't exactly look like they were Tent Police, but I couldn't be sure, because of course nobody has ever seen the Tent Police. But this couple, Hardy and Martina, seemed quite nice, and were just keen to ask about our trip. And then when Hardy said, "There's a good place to camp just up there. You go up there and set up your tent and wait for me, and I will come back with pizza for you," I was pretty sure we were safe.

Dea and I went up to the spot that Hardy had suggested and it certainly was a nice one, nestled behind blossoming orchards and with a nice view over Boppard, the Rhine, and the castles on the hillside beyond the river. We put up our tent at dusk and then sat on a wooden fence looking down at the lights of the town as the sky turned purple, our arms around each other, our cheeks gently touching. "This is pretty romantic, isn't it?" I whispered. And there was no denying that it was, and although the lights of Hardy's sports car returning rather altered the mood we were both pretty hungry, so it wasn't anything to complain about. Thankfully he hadn't gone for back-up, and instead had with him three very delicious pizzas and some drinks, and as we sat and ate together he explained how he loved to meet and help people like us, and how he himself was about to retire young in order to travel. Listening to him, I hoped he would find similar special moments as this one on his own travels, his small act of kindness having absolutely made our evening. The pizza soon disappeared and Hardy stood up, wished us the very best of luck, and drove off into the night, leaving us sitting there and asking ourselves if that had really all just happened.

§

We paused in the middle of the pedestrian bridge, not quite sure what country we were in. Behind us on the east side of the Rhine was Germany, the country we had been riding in for a week, ahead of us on the west side was the French city of Strasbourg. Someone had graffitied the words 'No Borders' on the ground. It was a slightly confusing protest, for this was a pedestrian bridge that people could walk freely back and forth across. In fact there was almost nothing to mark the border at all, other than that graffiti, and a clearly French sign that indicated that cycling was not permitted down their side of the bridge. I also noted that there were several empty beer cans strewn on the floor, on the French side of the sign. "There's more litter in France," I said.

"They are German cans, look. The Germans come over to France and leave their trash." It was Alex, our *warmshowers* host. He'd come out by bike to meet us, and we'd been cycling back with him on the

German side of the river for the past two hours. He seemed like a really nice guy, and we certainly had plenty in common, with him not long back from his own extended bicycle trip that took him from France to New Zealand. He was also very, very French. He moved to continue cycling across the bridge. "We're not supposed to cycle on this side," I said, pointing at the sign.

"Ah," he sighed, "f*ck the law!" and off he rode. We had arrived in France.

Dea and I followed along behind Alex, doing our best to keep up with him through the streets of Strasbourg. There were plenty of bicycle lanes, this being the most bike-friendly of French cities, and yet there were moments when Dea and I wondered what we should do when Alex suddenly veered across the road to make a turn, or skipped ahead of us through a red light. So quickly the orderliness of Germany had disappeared.

But it wasn't too long before we arrived at the home Alex shared with his Iranian wife, Sanaz. In what I thought a pretty unoriginal life story, Alex had met Sanaz during his bike trip, fell in love, and then persuaded her to come and cycle with him. She had been his *couchsurfing* host in Tehran, then later joined him cycling in Southeast Asia and Australia. I naturally thought back to my own time in Iran, the strict Islamic laws and the warnings I'd received of the danger of getting involved with local girls. I asked Alex if this wasn't a problem.

"Yes," he told me, "we could have got in a lot of trouble. Could have been executed, actually."

I was pleased that hadn't happened. We wouldn't have had anywhere to stay, for one thing. But I was also inspired to hear that they hadn't given up, that their love had been strong enough to conquer. That they had not given in to the restrictions the Iranian authorities had tried to place upon them, and that they had found this happy life together. And then, as Sanaz took up the story and told us how difficult it had been for her to get visas to visit Australia and other places, I was reminded even more of how extraordinarily fortunate I was to have been born where I was, allowing me to both live and travel so freely.

The next day Alex took us on a walking tour of Strasbourg, a vibrant old city famous for its cathedral that, for a staggering 227 years after its 1647 completion, had been the tallest building in the world. Alex did his best to be a good tour guide, reading to us from a guide book as we went and taking us to a gallery of modern art. But it was in little moments that Alex and Strasbourg showed us their true character, such as when he told us about a pillar that we might not have otherwise noticed. "It's a way to measure if you are in good health," he told us, half-serious and half-joking. "If you can make it through the gap between the pillar and the wall without touching, then you are healthy."

He then squeezed through, followed by Dea and myself. Thankfully it seemed like we were all in pretty good shape.

With grateful goodbyes to our hosts, Dea and I continued on our way, and the warm sun of France beat down on us as we followed a canal out of the city. For a little while we were away from the Rhine, taking in a little of the French countryside, but early the next morning it was time to head back over and rejoin the great river. We crossed a bridge and turned right on the far bank, and began following a trail south.

"I thought there would be a border sign," Dea said.

"Don't worry," I replied, "we are back on the German side. This path will take us all the way to Switzerland now."

The path was, however, mysteriously very quiet, and six kilometres later we found out why when it came to an abrupt end. We had foolishly only crossed half of the Rhine, and had been cycling on a big island, all the while, funnily enough, still in France. Now we had no choice other than to turn around and backtrack the six kilometres.

"Oops, sorry," I said, before, thinking on my feet, I quickly added: "But remember, Dea, there are no wrong turns, just different parts of everywhere." This was a philosophy I firmly believed in and on this occasion it applied well, as my error had led us to a nice secluded spot, perfect for a dip in the river, although I did recognise that there was probably a limit to how often I was going to get away with leading us the wrong way with this excuse.

We retreated and then crossed the rest of the Rhine, a great big sign welcoming us back to Germany. Now we really were able to follow a path beside it all of the way to Switzerland, and for me this represented something of a trip down memory lane. Some eight years earlier I'd walked this path, accidentally stumbling upon the Rhine during a hitchhiking adventure. I'd been having no luck thumbing a lift at a motorway service station and had walked out the back of it, where by mere chance I'd stumbled upon the very path we now pedalled along, and decided to just walk the twenty-five kilometres into Basel.

Now, eight years on, I made us stop at the same point and walk the other way, from the path into the service station. The noise of the traffic, the motorway, the hustle and the bustle, the petrol fumes in the air, it was truly horrible. We turned back around. Back to the riverbank we retreated, to the singing birds and the greenery and the peace of the river that was all ours to enjoy.

Bicycle touring is the best.

23

Swiss border
14th April 2017

Before leaving Germany for Switzerland we made what for me was a customary stop at Aldi to do some shopping. Lots of shopping, actually. We loaded up our trolley with enough bread, spreads, fruits, vegetables, peanuts, cookies, chips, pasta and beans to see us through to Italy. This, I hoped, was going to be my third successive visit to Switzerland without spending a franc. It was just too much of a hassle to change money, and too damn expensive to be buying things in Switzerland.

So our bikes were even heavier than normal as we entered Swiss territory. Arriving immediately in Basel we enjoyed sitting beside the river, where we saw lots of people riding bicycles, men playing boules, and everyone generally seeming to enjoy life. For a moment it seemed like everything was perfect in Switzerland, but then we tried to follow the signed cycle routes out of Basel, and they took us on some quite busy and not very nice city roads. They weren't as clearly marked as they had been in Germany, and somehow we went wrong, and ended up going around in a big circle, not realising it until we were practically back where we'd started. Sweaty and more than a little frustrated, I turned to Dea. "Don't worry, there are are no wrong turns..." I said, through gritted teeth.

Eventually we made our escape from the city and resumed following a cycle route slowly up a valley, through lush grassy meadows full of colourful wild flowers beneath forested hills, that calmed us both and promised that Switzerland was going to be alright after all. The sporadic Swiss homes that dotted the landscape were all so big, with brightly-coloured shutters on every window and great piles of firewood stacked outside. In every village we found fountains of fresh drinking water that flowed constantly. This was really a land of abundance. We made our own home at an outdoor recreation area, where we built a fire in a firepit and sang songs as Dea played her ukulele, while a full moon rose above us.

This idyllic natural bliss was rudely interrupted the following morning, however, when we found ourselves climbing uphill for the first time since England. We both struggled to adjust to the sudden physical challenge. After a while we reached a village and I reassured Dea that it was probably the top of the pass. But, as is so often the case, I was wrong, and we had to climb some more. We both found it very difficult, and as we inched our way towards the true summit I was left wondering if carrying a five-day supply of food was so smart after all. And perhaps taking the flattest route through Europe hadn't been the best training for the Alps. But this was not yet even the Alps, this was just a 400 metre climb, and with the 2,100 metre Gotthard Pass soon ahead of us, we both worried about our physical condition, as we stood gasping for breath at the top. Were we really up for the task that lay ahead?

Cycling in Switzerland swung back to idyllic bliss at Lake Lucerne. We cycled along one side of the vast lake, enjoying the view of snowy peaks visible beyond fields of yellow flowers. We stopped for a swim, rippling the surface of the mirror-like water as we jumped in. The sun was shining brightly once again, and it felt so good to be in the refreshing cold water, looking up at the snowy mountains we believed we would soon be pedalling up and over.

A little later we arrived at a small ferry that would take us across Lake Lucerne so that we could continue our journey on the other side. On board another passenger noticed our bikes and asked Dea where it was that we were going. She explained that we were now about to cycle over the Gotthard Pass. He looked back at her with concern. "I don't think you can cycle over the Gotthard Pass," he said.

"Yes, I think I can. We have small gears and we will just take our time. Many people do it every year. It is my first time cycling over a mountain pass, but I'm almost certain I can do it."

"But I think the pass is closed. They don't usually open the passes before the middle of May."

Oh, how foolish we had been, to look up at those snowy mountains and not notice the snow, that was sure to be blocking the road. Dea began to panic. She had been planning a short trip home to meet her newly born nephew, and she had a flight booked out of Bologna for ten days' time. Now she was worrying that she wasn't going to make it, as it seemed that there was an impenetrable barrier of high mountains in her way.

I remained calm. This type of situation had happened to me many times before. Things do tend to go wrong when you travel such long distances, particularly if, like me, you don't do enough research. I knew that it was all part of the journey, that we had to remain flexible to such obstacles, and I soon processed the information and came up with a new plan.

"Okay," I said. "Let's go to the Brenner Pass then. That'll be open."

"Where's the Brenner Pass?"

"It's in Austria. A bit of a detour, but we can do it."

"And it's definitely open?"

"Oh yes, I'm quite sure about that," I said, without having looked it up.

We got off the ferry and started cycling on the other side of the lake, our plans still up in the air but at least vaguely being to head east for Austria. Then another cyclist, a local man just out for a ride, pulled alongside me and asked me where it was that we were going. I explained that we were trying to get to Italy, but we'd just found out that we were going to have to go via Austria.

"No, you are very lucky," the man said. "There is in fact a pass from here in Switzerland that you can take, and it is just your luck, because they only opened the pass this morning."

"Oh, that is lucky."

"Yes. The only thing is that you have to take a train for three kilometres because the road is not safe for cyclists and you aren't allowed to cycle up."

"No, we can't do that I'm afraid. We'll have to go to Austria."

"But it is only three kilometres."

"No, no. No, no. Won't be doing that, sorry."

The man, Hubert, wanted to help us further, so he suggested that we all stop together in the next town and he would help us to make our plan. And as if this wasn't already nice enough of him, he also insisted on sitting us down in a restaurant and buying us lunch. It was another act of generosity from a complete stranger – following on from Ludo and Alda's hospitality in Belgium, and Hardy's pizza delivery in Germany – that was becoming a running theme of our trip through Europe. As we tucked into our pasta, sitting outside with a stunning view of the lake and mountains, it was time to get down to planning our route. Once Hubert had been thoroughly convinced that there was no way on earth that I was going to be getting on a train for three kilometres, a detour to Austria was confirmed as our only real option. The relatively easy 1,300 metre Brenner Pass was indeed open, according to the internet on Hubert's phone, but to get there we would have to first navigate the 1,800 metre Arlberg Pass.

"The Arlberg Pass is open," Hubert said, looking down at his phone. "Ah, but they are doing some construction work on the motorway tunnel, so all of the traffic will be on the smaller road and, oh no, it says here you are NOT allowed to cycle over this pass now, because of the traffic diversion. I'm sorry."

This was a serious blow to our chances. With the Arlberg Pass blocked, the only way we could get to the start of the Brenner Pass would be to make a massive detour back north through Germany. That was going to take a long time, and I began to worry as to whether we would be able to make it to Bologna for Dea's flight after all.

"Wait!" Hubert interrupted my thoughts. "The motorway tunnel isn't closed until the 22nd of April. You will make it just in time."

It was a lucky break at last, and now we had a clear route through the mountains, via the Arlberg and Brenner Passes. But then a gentleman at the next table entered the conversation. He was a kind-faced motorcyclist who'd overheard us talking, and he now suggested that instead of taking the Brenner Pass, we could turn south a little bit sooner and take the Reschen Pass. Apparently it was a little higher, at 1,500 metres, but was a lot quieter and much more bicycle-friendly.

"Yes," Hubert added, growing more excited. "That's a really good idea. There is a bicycle route that goes that way. The Via Claudia Augusta. I remember now. It goes all the way down to Verona. You should just follow that."

And so, thanks to the kindness of strangers, we had ourselves a great new plan.

We said our grateful goodbyes and took off over a 500 metre pass, a little warm-up for the challenges that now lay ahead, that certainly did warm us up. The descent down the far side then linked us up with a cycle route that was familiar to me. I'd ridden it in the opposite direction back in 2013, on my way to Zurich to meet my old university friend and living legend, Dr. Dave. On that day it had been raining, and Lake Walensee had looked miserable and grey. Now, in the bright sunshine, it looked like a completely different place. The water was as turquoise as the bay of a Caribbean island, while the mountains on the far side sparkled like diamonds in the sunlight. It certainly offered a striking demonstration of the difference that the weather could make to the feel of a place.

Soon the cycle route had led us all of the way back to the Rhine River, but such a long way from where we had first encountered it in Cologne. Here we crossed over a bridge and suddenly we were in a new country, and a very small one at that. It was Liechtenstein, once again, and it felt good to be back on the flat path beside the river with Alpine mountains all around us. Back in 2013 the landscape in this tiny country had made me feel like there was nowhere I'd rather be, nothing I'd rather be doing. In 2017 I looked around me once again, at the mountains, at the river, and particularly at Dea, cycling alongside me and smiling, and I realised that it was all still true, now more than ever. There was nowhere I'd rather be, nothing I'd rather be doing, and no one I'd rather be doing it with.

We were soon in Austria and following another river, a tributary of the Rhine, towards its source in the mountains. For a long time the ascent was a gradual one, so that it almost came as a surprise when we passed through a little village that bore indications of the skiing activities that took place in winter, with ski lifts and maps of the slopes. Further confirmation that we were getting higher came when we found a first patch of snow on the ground, one that inspired an impromptu snowball fight, that ended almost as soon as it began when Dea landed her first throw right in my face.

Until this point the going had been easy, but then suddenly a wall of mountains rose before us, the road zigzagging up the face of it in a series of switchbacks. It was an intimidating sight, especially for Dea who had never faced such a climb before, and we decided to take a break to build up a little courage before tackling it. As we sat there stuffing our faces with cookies a man came over to us. His name was Helmut and he lived in a nearby village. "Don't worry, you have only seven kilometres to the top, and it is not as bad as it looks," he reassured us. He was very interested in people making adventures such as ours, and he asked if we would send him a postcard from China when we made it there. We hoped we would be able to fulfil his wish, especially when, a few minutes after leaving, he returned carrying a handful of chocolate bars for us.

Filled with sugar and positive energy, we headed up the switch-backs, climbing slowly but steadily. It grew cold and before long we couldn't see more than fifty metres in front of us, for we literally were riding up through clouds. Yet Dea had in her eyes a look of determination, and I never felt in any doubt that we could make it, even when snow began to fall upon us. It was quite a contrast to the sunny valleys we'd been riding through in shorts and T-shirts for most of Europe, but in a way this was what our trip was really all about – moving towards the edges of our comfort zone, finding challenge and adventure in the wilder places. We paused briefly to munch on some of Helmut's chocolate, then pressed on for the summit. After a while a few buildings appeared out of the fog. There stood a restaurant and guest house, on which were the words 'Arlberg: 1,800 metres'. I looked over at Dea, wrapped up in her raincoat, hood pulled up over her head, as she looked up at those words. She looked so happy, as if climbing her first real mountain pass had made her believe that the rest of our journey was possible too. I was impressed again by Dea and how well she'd handled the climb, but I was not surprised. It was simply a testament to how badly she wanted to succeed at making this journey. But it was cold at the summit and getting late so we didn't stop to celebrate for long. We put on all of our clothes and began on an exhilarating descent. It was quite a rush to be flying along so fast, and within moments we were back below the snowline and heading rapidly for more green valleys. After finding a nice spot to camp behind some trees, the next day we took things steady, easing our way down the rest of the mountain to a place called Landeck, where we turned south, joined the Via Claudia Augusta, and started to follow another river that would lead us eventually to the Reschen Pass. We took our time, giving our bodies the chance to recover with another night of rest in a grassy field that offered views of the snowy peaks ahead. Refreshed, we continued along the bike route the next day, and I was seriously impressed by how far it continued up the pass. Almost the whole way up we had our own segregated bicycle path that was a pleasure to ride on. Only when we got to the business end of the climb, the final steep section, were we forced onto the road. Here, in a rather odd quirk of geography, we had to return briefly into Switzerland for the steep switchbacks. This time they posed us no great difficulties. Conquering the Arlberg Pass had given us the confidence that we could do this one too, and with the weather being much better it turned into quite an enjoyable climb. It was also quite enjoyable to reach the summit, of course, where we passed once again back into Austria, and celebrated for real. From here to Bologna it was all downhill. We had done it. We had taken on the Alps and we had won.

We crossed the border into Italy and paused to admire the church tower at Reschensee, a large man-made lake high up in the mountains. The tower was these days something of a tourist attraction, for it was positioned in an area of land that had been flooded by the creation of the lake, and now stood poking from the water, looking forlornly back to land as if to ask what it had done to deserve such a fate. And it was at Reschensee that we met two elderly gentlemen out for a walk. Having crossed into Italy it was initially a bit of a surprise to us that the men spoke in Austrian, but one of them, Ferdy, who also spoke a bit of English, explained to us that they lived here in this area known as South Tyrol. It was once a part of Austria, he told us, but had been given to Italy during the First World War and never returned. Despite Italy's efforts to make South Tyrol more Italian, the people had apparently done their best to maintain their Austrian heritage, and nowadays lived with a decent degree of self-autonomy.

Dea explained to them about our trip, having to shout a bit for the old fellows' hearing was not the best, and their eyebrows lifted in surprise. Ferdy's friend (who never replied when I asked him his name, so let's call him Marvin), asked in sign language whether we had suspension on our bikes. We shook our heads, and his eyebrows rose still further.

As we prepared to say goodbye and move on, Dea rather optimistically offered Ferdy one of our homemade contact cards with our website address on.

"This is our blog. You can follow us on our journey to China," she said.

"No, no, no, I don't want to go to China," Ferdy protested, refusing to take the card.

From the lake we began on the long downhill. It was such a long downhill, in fact, that it went on for three whole days. We were still able to follow the Via Claudia Augusta bicycle route, and it continued to lead us on secluded bike paths and tiny roads, down through a valley filled with an uncountable number of apple orchards, the white flowers of their trees in bloom, surrounded by sheer cliffs that looked down on us defiantly in the sunshine. With a tailwind at our back and clear blue skies it was yet more blissful cycling.

By the time we reached Verona and the end of the bicycle route the landscape had changed. Gone were the mountains and all around us in their stead was flat farmland, dotted with old stone farmhouses in various states of disrepair. Such ruins were not something to be seen further north in Europe, but here it didn't seem to matter so much. We were beyond South Tyrol by now, into the real Italy, and here it seemed there was less incentive to make everything look modern and nice, the pace of life was slower, there was no need, everything just looked old and nice, and that was fine.

We arrived into Bologna on the planned date and made our way to the home of Nicolò, our host. He helped us to carry all of our possessions up three flights of stairs to the apartment he shared with some friends, before welcoming us in the typical Italian way, by cooking us pasta.

The next morning Dea would be back home in Denmark to spend a couple of weeks with her growing family. The first stage of our trip to China had been completed, and it had been a resounding success, with us having been able to ride all of the way from Edinburgh to Bologna almost entirely on cycle paths. Dea's knee had given her no further trouble, and all in all it had been a most fantastic beginning to our long journey together, as good as we ever could have hoped. But there was still a very long way to go, and for the next little while I would be going it alone once again.

24

Bologna, Italy
23rd April 2017

The alarm rang and woke me at three thirty in the morning. If there's one thing I don't like, it's being woken by an alarm at three thirty in the morning. But Dea had an early flight to catch and, trying to prove myself a true gentleman, I'd offered to walk her to the bus station. I'd made the offer the previous evening, of course, when it was much easier to be chivalrous. Now I slightly regretted my own attempt to be a good boyfriend, but it was too late to reverse my decision. I dragged myself out of bed and pulled on some clothes, and Dea and I wandered out onto the streets of a sleepy Bologna.

"Would you like me to carry your bag?" I asked.

"Oh, yes. Thank you."

I took Dea's pannier and slung it over my shoulder. It was heavy. Really heavy.

When will I ever learn?!' I thought to myself.

We walked for twenty minutes beneath Bologna's covered walkways, where a few homeless people lay twitching under blankets. One such old woman sat up as we passed, rubbed the sleep from her eyes, and asked us the time by pointing at her wrist. "Quatro," I said, which may or may not be the Italian word for four. When I returned back past the same spot half an hour or so later, she had moved on.

Dea and I made it to the bus station just in time, where our goodbye was intruded upon by a faulty ticket scanner and a bus driver who eventually just threw his hands in the air as if to say, "Sod the ticket scanner, just get on the damn bus."

Dea waved to me from the window as her transport to the airport pulled away. It would be seventeen days before we would be re-united at this location to resume our trip. Seventeen days that I had all to myself. What was I going to do? Well, I started, funnily enough, by going back to bed.

I spent most of the first of my seventeen days hanging out with Nicolò and his housemate, Suzy. They were both young, just starting careers, but still with a passion for travelling and the outdoors, so we had plenty of common ground. The three of us cycled together to what had been described to me as a 'soup festival'. It sounded like something worth investing my time in, especially after Nicolò had used the phrase "there will be free soup." And he was right, there was a lot of free soup at the soup festival. It was a really fun social event, with hundreds of people there, each grasping their own bowl and spoon, wandering among a few dozen stalls each with its own vat of soup. There were also bands playing live music, people walking about on stilts, and an all round great atmosphere. I met a few of Nicolò and Suzy's friends, and it was fun to hang out with some people in their twenties, at an event like this. It was the sort of thing I'd done a lot more of when I was first travelling, and it was good to do it again, even if it did remind me that I was getting older. I was thirty-two now, seven years older than when I'd started my cycling nomad life, and my way of travelling had undoubtedly evolved slightly. In the early days I was content to sleep on concrete if I had to, spend whole days cycling around in circles, and hang out with twenty-somethings getting hideously drunk. Now I had two sleeping pads and three sleeping bags, I navigated using a smartphone GPS, and the only time I hung out with twenty-somethings was to eat soup.

But Nicolò and Suzy also showed me around Bologna's historic old town, which was all historic and old, and we then sat and ate piadina, a classic Italian wrap thing, at a quaint little restaurant.

"How would you describe piadina? To someone who never tried it?" Nicolò asked.

"Erm, well, I'd probably say it was a classic Italian wrap thing."

There was a slight pause.

"I'm not that much into food really," I added. "I mostly just eat peanut butter and jam sandwiches. But I do think this tastes really good."

Nicolò was a nice guy. A teacher, he was busy planning his own trip for the summer holidays, a tour of European cities. His plan was to travel by bus, train, or plane between cities, then take out his folding bike to ride around and explore them.

"I just got my folding bicycle recently, and I love it!" he said, with real passion. "Really. It changed my life!"

Once done eating we moved on to a bar to meet with some more friends of Nicolò and Suzy. One of them, whose name has escaped me (let's call him Luciano), was particularly taken by my cycling endeavours and asked lots of interested questions. Then he noticed my shoes, which by now had almost fully completed their evolution into open toe sandals, and his enthusiasm for my project extended to offering me a replacement pair. I had been on the lookout for a new pair of shoes for quite a while now, but the collective second-hand shops of Edinburgh, North Shields, the Netherlands, Belgium, Germany, France, Switzerland, Austria, and Liechtenstein had turned up nothing in my size. This was a problem, because if there is one thing I refuse to do in my life it is to buy new shoes new. Either you buy a cheap pair and they fall apart in a week, or you buy an expensive pair and you've got no money left for peanut butter. Much better, in my opinion, to get a good pair with plenty of life in them cheaply second-hand. So I was disappointed to have heard from Nicolò that Italy didn't really have second-hand shops, and even more disappointed when he revealed to everyone that I was leaving town in the morning, and the idea of Luciano's kind shoe donation was dropped as the conversation moved on.

So it was with my old shoes still clinging onto my feet the best that they could that I made my way out of Bologna the next day. In fact it took me most of the day to get out of the city, not because it was a particularly big city, but because I was being spectacularly lazy. My plan for the next sixteen days had by now been decided on. I'd first looked into the possibility of making a tour down to Rome and back. Never having been to Rome, I thought it a place I really should visit, especially as it's got its own country in the middle of it. But I put the idea to Google Maps and was told I'd need to average around a hundred kilometres per day to make it there and back, and I really didn't feel like cycling that much. Then I found out that Vatican City, while categorised by some criteria as a country, was not actually one of the 193 full members of the United Nations and therefore could not be counted towards my attempt at visiting a hundred of them, and I lost all interest in the idea. Instead I thought a tour of Tuscany at a relatively sedate fifty kilometres per day pace, taking in Florence, Pisa, and Siena, would be enough for me, when combined with a side trip eastwards to visit the Republic of San Marino. Yes, yes, the Vatican could keep the Sistine Chapel and the Pope and all that fancy stuff, San Marino was what I wanted to see, with its beautiful, beautiful, full United Nations membership.

But, as I said, getting out of Bologna was a bit of an adventure in itself. I wanted to leave to the south, but the nearest Lidl was to the north of town, so in the name of cheap groceries I had to make a detour there. Luckily there was a bike path all of the way, although it was only really some paint on the footpath beside a busy main road. As I was waiting for some lights to change so that I could cross, I was approached by a man who had been sitting with a girl on some grass nearby. The man was wearing three-quarter length khaki trousers and a waistcoat, and he had dreadlocked hair tied back beneath a brown hat, and a goatee beard that was somehow both neat and scruffy at the same time. He introduced himself with a big smile that seemed never to leave his face. He said his name was Milan. "It's just like the city, Milano, but without the 'o'."

Milan was travelling around Europe together with his girlfriend, Margo, and six other friends, who were riding bikes. "They are just like you, with their bikes, but Margo and me don't have bikes. So we hitchhike or take trains, and meet up with our friends in places. We are waiting for them here."

"But why here?" I asked, looking around at the nondescript road junction.

"Why are we here? Watch! I show you!" And Milan grabbed something from his bag, and leapt gleefully out into the road. The lights had just turned to red, and Milan positioned himself in front of the waiting traffic. He had two sticks in his hands and a third that he began tossing up between them. He juggled it, he flicked it, he dropped it to the floor, he picked it up again, he bounced it on his head, he tossed it, he turned it, he dropped it again. Then he did a big "ta-da!" and took a bow, before removing his hat and striding down the middle of the queueing cars. One driver wound down their window and dropped something in Milan's hat and, as the lights turned green, he ran back over to me brandishing his takings.

"How much did you get?" I asked.

"Twenty cents!" he beamed, his smile as big as ever.

The hills started immediately to the south of Bologna. With my relaxed schedule, I'd decided to use the smallest roads possible in order to distance myself from the 'everyone thinks they're a racing driver' Italian traffic, but these were incredibly steep. I found them awfully hard work and I even began to wonder what the point was in doing this. I felt lonely with Dea suddenly no longer at my side and I wondered how it was that I had managed to live this way for so many years. How was it I had coped without anyone to talk to, anyone to share the experiences with? But my spirits were lifted by the views as I got higher into the hills, and I found a sense of satisfaction in not giving up, in conquering each steep climb. And as if to prove that I was not exaggerating the severity of these hills, on one steep section a couple who had just passed me on road bikes with no luggage found that the going was just too tough, and got off to push.

In researching my little side trip I'd read of many people cycling from Bologna to Florence in a single day. It took me four. This was partly because I took the small roads, partly because I was in super-

-relaxed lazy mode, and partly because when I came out of the hills I got so excited by the sight of a library with good Wi-Fi that I spent a day and a half in it. But I did eventually reach Florence, cycling into it along the banks of the Arno River, on a nice route that took me through a large, green park that was destined to be my best memory of Florence. The thing about Florence is that it must be so very, very great if you appreciate art and culture and things like that. I'm just not that kind of person, preferring to find my own aesthetic joys in nature – in the mountains, rivers, and forests, in animals and clouds and butterflies, that kind of thing. So I don't know why I went to Florence really, and I didn't stay very long. I pushed my bike around among the mass crowds of tourists outside the Duomo, the city's magnificent old cathedral, which, to be fair, did take my breath away when I first saw it. Then I went and saw Michelangelo's David in some plaza. It was a statue of a big naked dude. I know that Michelangelo's David is the most famous sculpture in the world, but I wasn't overly impressed. The thing is, it was on one side of a door-way and there was another sculpture on the other side, and this sculpture had TWO naked dudes on it. So, in my opinion, Michelangelo's David wasn't even the most impressive sculpture in the doorway, never mind the world. But my opinion on such matters doesn't count for much, and as you may have already gathered, I don't really know what I'm talking about. But before you start writ-ing in, I know that what I was looking at was only a replica of Michelangelo's David. The real one, I know, is in a museum that you have to pay to enter, then queue for half the day to get to, and then probably get forced to shuffle past very quickly. I did that with the Mona Lisa once, and I wasn't about to make the same mistake again here. And while I'd been doing my research online, I'd read many people on blogs and forums insisting that you have to see the real one to really, truly appreciate Michelangelo's David. They said that seeing a replica just wasn't the same. I can only assume that these people don't understand the word 'replica'. Means the same, doesn't it?

From Florence I headed west towards Pisa and I was quite taken by the beauty of the Tuscan hills. Olive groves and vineyards and lines of poplar trees covered these rolling hills, dotted also with the orange tiled roofs of old farmhouses. In the villages old people shuffled along, in a way that suggested they had been there, old and shuffling along, since the dawn of time, while freshly laundered clothes flapped from every balcony. It was a fine part of the world for a bike ride, there was no doubt about that, and I felt like I was back in my stride, enjoying my little solo tour.

After a few days I arrived in Pisa, and there should be no prizes for guessing what I had gone to Pisa to see. That's right, crowds of people standing next to one another, all posing for photos with their hands up in the air turned sideways so that the image created might come out vaguely looking like they were holding up a big tower. Except of course, that if the illusion truly works, the big tower doesn't look that big, relative to the person holding it up. Anyway, due to the fact that every single photo I'd ever seen of it had someone holding it up, I was a bit surprised when I got to the Leaning Tower of Pisa to discover that it could actually stand up pretty well on its own. I was also quite interested to discover that the tower was not really a solo building, but that it stood right next to a vast and grandiose cathedral like some kind of extravagant, leany outhouse. I found it a funny thing that this magnificent cathedral was completely ignored by the tourists and left out of everyone's photos, presumably because of how boringly well it was able to stand up straight on its foundations, and if God really does exist, I'd say this probably pisses him off a little bit.

I was nevertheless glad that I'd gone to see the Leaning Tower. It's such an iconic landmark that to see it in real life gave me goosebumps, and I left Pisa happy, heading next in a southeasterly direction. I passed through more very pleasant Tuscan hills towards Siena and began to have some nice encounters with people. Not Italian people, however, for they mostly kept to themselves, but American people. Firstly I met a man from Las Vegas who was on holiday in a Lidl car park, who spotted my bike and wanted to know what I was up to (and I should just clarify, I do not mean that he was actually on holiday in a Lidl car park, but that he was on holiday in Italy, and we happened to meet in a Lidl car park). He was a very nice man named Bill, and he thought it terrific what I was doing, even if he did look a bit sceptical when I told him that I usually had a girlfriend. We chatted for a while and I think he must have noticed my shoes, because before leaving he forced twenty euros upon me. It was a kind gesture, but I never like to take money for nothing, so I forced him to take a copy of my book in exchange, which was a bit silly of me because it was the last copy I had, and I was supposed to be reading through it checking for errors.

Then after Siena (another old town, kind of interesting, kind of touristy, I bought some new underwear at a market), I met a really nice older man called Crispin up in the hills. He was leaning on a wall looking all friendly, so I said hello and then we had a jolly chat about things. He was another American, and he told me he came on holiday every year with his family to this little village in Tuscany, and it was a really nice village and a really nice chat too. It was good to talk to someone in English and it put me in high spirits, so later in the day when I reached a town called San Giovanni Valdarno I arrived in another Lidl car park once again in the mood for making new friends. Now more or less every Lidl car park in Italy (and I had some considerable experience of them by now) had an African man in it, and this one was no exception. The man was leaning back on the store window watching me as I pulled up on my bike, and he had a friendly face, so I asked him if he spoke English. He said that he did, very well, as he came from Nigeria where English is the official language. His name was Andrew and it was obvious to me that he was a nice guy as I listened sadly to his story. He'd had a good business importing car parts to Nigeria from Europe, but the exchange rate had apparently changed and there was no money in it any more. Now he was reduced to hustling in a supermarket car park for money, helping people with their shopping, taking their trolleys back for the fifty cents they'd release. With this he was getting by, trying to support a family with two kids. He was clearly an intelligent man, and when he spoke of the problems with his country, the corruption, the lack of opportunities in Nigeria, I felt sadness and anger at the injustices of the world. But I also saw hope in the way that many of the regular customers treated him in a friendly manner, saying hello to him as they passed or thanking him for his help, and in the way that he kept on smiling through it all.

At some point another man arrived, a friend of Andrew's from somewhere in Eastern Europe, called Ajie, which is a name I have almost certainly misspelt. Ajie couldn't speak English, but Andrew translated into Italian something about my travels, and Ajie nodded along, looking impressed. Then he noticed my shoes, and said something back to Andrew.

"He says that he wants to give you new shoes. Good ones. But there is a condition. You must agree to throw those ones away."

"Really? Okay, that sounds like a fair deal to me."

Ajie disappeared off on his bicycle, returning a few minutes later with a pair of blue trainers. He placed them down at my feet, then indicated with a fierce emotion that I think might have been bordering on anger, that I should remove my old ones and put them in the bin. I pulled off the offending items and slipped my feet into his blue ones. They obviously weren't new, for they both had a small hole in the toe, but they fitted quite well, and they each had a Nike swoosh down the side that made me hope they might hold up for a while. I looked up, ready to thank Ajie for his kindness, but he wasn't there, he was several metres away, slam dunking my old shoes into the trash.

I woke up the next morning at my campsite and pulled on my new shoes, hoping that they might be magic shoes, because I wanted to cycle to San Marino, and standing in my way were a lot of mountains, including three passes over 1,000 metres. Given how much I'd struggled on the hills south of Bologna I was feeling a little apprehensive about this task, and I hoped my brand new magic shoes might help me out, even if they weren't magic. Or brand new.

I made an early start and found the first pass surprisingly easy. It was on a quiet road that made for quite an enjoyable climb. I put on my radio and listened to a mixture of classic pop songs, and before I knew it I was at the top. I whizzed down the other side to a town in a valley where I'd planned to stop at a library and make use of the Wi-Fi, but the library turned out to be closed, so I decided to just carry on and do the second pass. This was a longer, tougher climb, but I still had my classic pop and I eventually conquered this peak too. Down, down, down I went from the forested hills and into another small town where I headed straight for the library. It was closed too. *'Ah, sod it,'* I thought, *'I'll just do the third pass too then.'*

The third pass was also very difficult, but I had magic shoes, and so I made it over that one as well, before making my way down for a third time and setting up camp beside a river. In the morning I woke with tired muscles, but made my way along to another town where I finally found a library that was open. The previous day I had cycled more than a hundred kilometres over three mountains, something which had surprised even me, and now at last I had my reward, free Wi-Fi.

"Sorry," the librarian told me, "but we don't have Wi-Fi here."

It didn't matter. I didn't *really* need Wi-Fi. Ahead of me now was country fifty-three, San Marino, also known as the Republic of San Marino, also known as The Most Serene Republic of San Marino, and I was eager to go and check it out. I didn't know much about this little nation, but I was keen to visit, and to try and discover why they were so spectacularly bad at football.

I was following a bike path near a river when the most serene of republics appeared up ahead. San Marino, it turned out, was built al-most exclusively upon the slopes of a steep mountain, and it rose up before me like a giant serene mountain republic.

I arrived at the border and took my first pedal strokes in San Marino. Almost immediately it began to rain quite hard, and I de-cided that I didn't really like San Marino, and almost turned around again. But it looked much wealthier here than in Italy, with freshly painted, well-maintained buildings, and a covered walkway where I could hide until the rain passed. When it did I decided to carry on with my mission to uncover the secrets of San Marino.

The one thing I soon knew for sure about San Marino was that it was very, very, very not flat. I climbed up on the very steep roads, with the idea to cycle up and visit the capital, also called San Marino, which was inconveniently situated at the very peak of the mountain. Along the way I had to pause several times to catch my breath, and on one such occasion a San Marinoian stopped his car to ask if I needed any help with anything, which I thought rather nice, as it was not something anyone in Italy had done. I told him that I was fine, but this was in fact a lie, because I was not fine, and after a while I gave up on the steep climb. This was not entirely down to my tired legs, but more because San Marino was such a densely populated mountain republic that the road was too busy and dangerous for me to ride on. So I locked my bike up and proceeded on foot, finding a nice walking path up to the town at the top of the mountain.

I liked what I found there. San Marino was an interesting place, with three forts standing guard along the ridge of the mountain, the old town hidden safely away behind. Italy was once divided into a great number of such republics, until one day they all decided to get together and form a country, all apart from one. The rugged location must surely have helped San Marino to defend its independence, and the views from the turreted city walls were staggering, absolutely amazing. Italy crowds around San Marino on all sides, and back west I could see the rows of mountains I'd climbed through, while to the east it was possible to see all the way out into the Adriatic Sea, but it was the flat plains to the north that made the most welcome sight for me, for they promised me an easy ride back to Bologna.

The one thing that I didn't like so much about San Marino was that, in amongst all of the gift shops catering to the tourists who provide fifty percent of the country's GDP, there were a great many shops selling guns and swords. I'd heard that San Marino was the gun capital of Europe, and I'd even heard gunshots as I'd been cycling up the hill (hopefully from a shooting range), and now I saw guns openly on sale everywhere. Not only that, but many of the souvenir shops had massive swords and knives in their windows. I suppose a tiny republic must defend itself somehow, but the whole thing made me a little uneasy, and I concluded that if San Marino were a person, then it would almost certainly be a psychopath. How else do you explain the name?

"Oh, nice to meet you, I'm San Marino, the Most Serene Republic of San Marino."

Yeah sure you are, 'most serene' San Marino, with your massive great big stockpile of weapons.

25

Northern Italy
12th May 2017

Dea and I, having been reunited at Bologna's bus station, continued on together out of the city, now on a northeastern course. After a couple of days of cycling across the north Italian plains (days that could only fairly be described as unremarkable) we arrived in Chioggia, the Adriatic port town that provided our gateway to Venice. It was a delightful little town of colourful buildings alongside canals that hinted at the Venetian wonders ahead of us. We'd eventually chosen to come this way after a bit of indecision. Our other possible route would have been to head around the Italian mainland and then to cycle to Venice across the causeway that tethers it to land. I'd done this once before, back in 2012, and I knew that it wasn't a particularly pleasant ride. So we'd opted to come to Chioggia and take a series of ferries across a string of islands to reach Venice instead, and it was a decision we would not regret, despite the sixty-six euros it cost for both of us to have two-day passes for all the Venetian ferries.

The first ferry took about twenty minutes to arrive on Pellestrina, a long, thin island that, along with another island, Lido, forms a natural barrier between the Adriatic Sea and the Venetian Lagoon. Within minutes of arriving on Pellestrina we knew that we had made the right choice. It was a wonderful place to ride a bike. We rode along on a series of little paths and streets, to the left of us was the blue-green waters of the Venetian Lagoon, to the right rows of brightly coloured old homes. There were green homes, red homes, yellow homes, white homes, blue homes, and pink homes, their bright paint peeling from the walls, shutters on every window, bicycles leaning against plant pots outside. Fishing boats sat in the water, while old women sat out on the promenade wall and gossiped, like old women have no doubt done for centuries before them. There were lots of people sitting around chatting, or casually wandering about, or leaning out of windows and watching. The atmosphere was easy, life was laid-back, and in the same mood we turned our pedals slowly and tried to soak it all in.

Further along Pellestrina the houses thinned out and we switched over to the Adriatic side to look for a beach. It took a little while to find a way past the large concrete flood defence that lined the island, but it was worth it when we did. A private beach and a refreshing swim ensured that we left Pellestrina with nothing but good memories.

A second ferry took us to Lido, another long, thin island protecting Venice. In the morning we would explore it, but we arrived late and our immediate priority was to find somewhere to camp. Our research (looking at Google Maps satellite view) suggested that we should find a forest to the south of the island and we were pleased to arrive and find this to be true. What we were less pleased about were the signs warning us that we were close to a military area. Still, it was only the Italian military, so how dangerous could it be? (Had it been the San Marino military, I'd have been much more concerned.) So we pedalled off down a trail into the forest until we arrived at a fence and a gate. There was nowhere to pitch the tent and we needed to turn back, but we couldn't help but stop and look at what was behind the gate first, particularly as there was another sign warning us that this was the military area. Within this fenced-off military area, you see, was a most extraordinary ensemble of animals. The most remarkable of these were the peacocks. There were three males and about eight or nine females, and the males were in the mood for showing off. They were fanning their tail feathers up above them in that impressive courtship display and making advances upon the females. Unfortunately for them, none of the females seemed to be in the mood for anything besides pecking the ground. It was all very entertaining to watch, and it got a whole lot more so when a family of goats arrived and began mingling with the peacocks (and the geese, who were also there, by the way). The goats were ever so cute and clumsy, and seemed to annoy the male peacocks who were, of course, getting rather sexually frustrated. Then suddenly a cat ran in from somewhere, and all hell broke loose.

The Italian military, as you can tell, is a force to be reckoned with.

Having found a better place to camp a little further along, we awoke the next morning excited to press on and see Venice. But first we had to cycle the length of Lido, and it was another nice island, if a bit more developed and a little less charming than Pellestrina. The best thing about Lido was actually at the beach where we swam. It wasn't the soft sand or clear water that we liked the most, though, it was the completely free hot shower that stood at the back of the beach. Oh, how we enjoyed that! "I think this is the best thing about Venice," I cried out to Dea, as she suggested we move on, and I pressed the button to get a few minutes more.

Eventually I was torn away from the shower and we headed for the main island of Venice. Bicycles are not allowed here, and would be impractical anyway with all of the stepped bridges, and so we locked them up securely on Lido and jumped on a passenger ferry. This took us to a leafy park on the southeast of the island. From there we wandered towards the centre, the unmistakable tower of Piazzo San Marco helping to guide us. As we neared it the crowds of tourists grew and we did our best not to be swept away by the Chinese and Indian tour groups as we paused to look at the Bridge of Sighs en route. The crowds were incredible, but I suppose a small price to pay for being in such a wonderful city (there are no cars in Venice, how could I not like it?) and reaching Saint Mark's Square made it all worthwhile. It was Dea's first time in Venice, and I could see from her face that looking up at the intricate design of Saint Mark's Basilica was a special moment. For me, being back in Venice was also special, for slightly different reasons. When I'd visited in 2012 I'd arrived very early in the morning and Saint Mark's Square had been almost completely empty, save for myself and a few pigeons. I sat on some steps and looked around and I felt unimpressed, uninspired. It was towards the end of my first long bike trip, I'd been travelling for two years at that point, and I was getting tired of it. I wondered to myself whether or not it was really what I still wanted to be doing. It was then that I decided to go home to Britain for a while, which ultimately led me to start on this new project. So that morning in Venice had been an important moment for me. It had somehow helped me to find my way, helped direct me to all the things I'd done over the past five years, and therefore led me somehow to Dea. So to return here in 2017, somehow not only still travelling, but still loving to travel, with Dea smiling next to me, was something really quite special.

From Saint Mark's Square we headed to Rialto Bridge and looked down on the Grand Canal. We were amazed by how busy the waterways of Venice were and wondered what it would be like to see the city from the water. We couldn't afford a ride on one of the hundreds of gondolas that navigated the canals, but our two-day travel cards gave us unlimited time on the ferries that plough up and down the Grand Canal, and so we hopped on one to try and get our money's worth out of our tickets. Unfortunately we got on the worst possible ferry, for it was heading for the train station at rush hour, and so we got a bit squashed. After escaping to wander on foot through the maze of little backstreets we tried our luck on a quieter ferry. This was much more enjoyable, especially for Dea when it gave her a view of Venice that was just exactly as she remembered from a jigsaw puzzle she had done as a child. It was lovely to see the way her face lit up as she recognised the scene, and in a way it felt symbolic of what travelling is all about. To find those places we dream about as children. To make them real, to bring our imaginations to life.

The only other thing of note that happened before we left Italy – besides Dea accidentally stabbing herself in the hand with a pair of scissors (it drew blood, but she survived) – occurred when we tried to find somewhere to camp in a small forest we had seen on the map. It was unusually easy to find a way into this forest, and it was full of tracks going all over the place, so we decided to leave our bikes and split up to look for a good place to pitch the tent. I walked off along one track, but as I searched the ground for the sort of flat, sheltered area we liked to make ourselves at home in, I noticed something else, and I began to wonder if this forest was really going to be a good place for us to spend the night. I turned back to look for Dea, and was relieved to find her back at the bikes.

"I don't think it's good here, Chris," she said. "I just saw two men. One walked past me with a big grin on his face, and the other one was going the other way with some tight leggings on."

"Haha. Have you noticed all of the condoms lying on the ground. I think something... ahem... happens in these woods. Shall we go somewhere else?"

"Let's!"

That incident aside, our last few days in Italy were a little boring, as we did our best to navigate through more populated areas via less busy roads. We were both eager to leave Italy behind and reach the Balkans, for neither of us had ever been to the region before and we anticipated finding plenty of interesting experiences there, given the fascinating diversity of cultures and the terribly troubled recent history. The break-up of Yugoslavia happened within my lifetime, and yet I had shamefully little knowledge of the area and its people. The weeks just ahead of us therefore promised much, and not just because they would be very good for my country-count.

We crossed into Slovenia full of anticipation and, even though we spent just one full day there, it didn't disappoint us. We rode on nice, quiet roads through natural green landscapes. It was a more developed country than I had anticipated, and people seemed to live good lives in nice houses, but at the same time the majority of the land was open and green and in its natural state. There was clean drinking water taps in all the villages and lots of different recycling bins and it seemed as if this was a place where humans had learnt to live in harmony with nature.

By chance our route through Slovenia led us to a place called Lipica, which got Dea very excited. This was apparently the place where Lipizzan horses had been bred in unbroken lines since the sixteenth century, and she knew them well from the Spanish Riding School (confusingly in Vienna), where they famously performed.

"The horses are all white and very beautiful," she said. "When I was little it was my dream to ride them at the Spanish Riding School."

We were able now to cycle into Lipica and to stand and watch some of the horses in a paddock. A kind stableman came over and spoke to Dea, telling her some facts about the horses, and saying she should keep watching, as they were soon rounding up some more horses. And sure enough a few moments later sixty-five bright white mares came galloping past us, running in towards their stables in an elegant blur. Dea's face was a picture. "That was more amazing than I ever imagined it would be!" she said. Once again our travels were turning childhood dreams into reality.

Our transition from Slovenia to Croatia was an easy one, for after crossing a remote border point where our passports were checked for the first time on the trip (despite Croatia being in the European Union) we continued on an excellent quiet road through more great nature. The road weaved through a landscape of rock and trees, where nobody seemed to live except for one deer that we stopped to watch as it frolicked about. "That must be one happy deer," remarked Dea, as we looked around at all of the great nature that it had to enjoy.

Our luck broke the next morning, when we awoke to heavy rain for the first time. We got our things packed up anyway, and were on our way out of the forest we'd camped in when Dea noticed that she had a flat tyre. Like a trooper she just got on with fixing it in the rain, and then we were on with our day. As chance should have it we now had to ride down a big hill, which meant we were soon extremely wet, and to make things even worse we had left behind the idyllic nature and now had to share the road with cars. The rain only got worse, and as soon as we could we escaped into the refuge of a café. Here we sat and made use of the Wi-Fi, all of a sudden feeling quite grateful to be out of all that soaking wet nature.

But it never rains forever, and we were soon back on our way again once the skies had cleared, doing our best to stick to small roads that took us up into the hills and gave us views down to the Adriatic and its islands. After another night in a forest, the following day we had some bigger, steeper climbs, and here Dea began to encounter problems with her knee. For the first time since leaving Edinburgh it was giving her a lot of pain, and it hurt me to see the anguish on her face, the fear of what it might mean. I knew how much this trip meant to her, and I could only admire the determination she showed to keep going, insisting on continuing even though she was soon forced to get off and walk up the hills. This must have been so incredibly frustrating for her, but it was also frustrating for me, because she was still bloody faster than me.

We stopped to take a break halfway up a particularly steep climb. We were just sat on the kerb at the side of the road, when I noticed a woman looking at us from the window of a nearby country house. She disappeared from the window almost immediately, but a few moments later she reappeared, now walking up the road towards us. She had with her a large slice of burek, a cheese pastry that Dea knew and loved from her time living in Istanbul, and a big bottle of cold water. She gave them to us, and we spoke with her a little. Her name was Andrea and, now a middle-aged woman, she said that she had lived here, in the same house, her whole life. As a child she had walked up and down the steep hill that we'd just struggled up, to go to school, every single day. It brought things back into perspective for us.

It was the first of several nice encounters we would have with Croatians. The next morning, tempted to stop and buy more burek from a town bakery, a man named Goran came over to greet us, and was so overexcited by the whole thing that he showed us the goose-bumps on his arms. Then later we were called over to join a family for coffee outside of their house. Actually it was two families, but nobody could speak any English. We found ways to communicate by sign language and by showing them maps, and as we did so I was reminded of my travels in poorer lands. Croatia seemed fairly well developed, but it was not really like Western Europe, and sitting there with these two families on their beaten-up porch I felt like our transition to a different way of life was well underway.

A beautiful, quiet road took us to Slunj, where we stayed for two nights with a *warmshowers* host named Frane. He was a very welcoming man, who talked to us for hours as he prepared dinner. He had suffered plenty of hardships in his life, but maintained an inspiringly positive attitude, and was planning to soon leave Croatia and make a multi-year bike journey around the world himself. He'd calculated that for the trip he wanted to do he would need to stay with hosts for about 300 nights, and so he'd decided some time ago to try and first host at least 300 guests in his apartment. He'd been at it for a while, and Dea and I brought the total number of guests he'd had up to an impressive 320.

Frane sure could talk, but listening to him all evening gave us a good insight into the history of Croatia and the difficulties of the region. For example, he'd asked himself what he would do if a Serb ever asked to come and stay with him. It wouldn't have been an easy decision, for the Serbs and the Croats were at war with each other within Frane's lifetime. But he told us that one Serb had asked to come and stay. Encouragingly, and commendably, Frane had said yes (although sadly the guy never showed up in the end).

From Slunj Dea and I headed for Plitvice Lakes, Croatia's star natural attraction. We made camp just before the lakes so as to try and get there early and avoid the crowds. Frane had told us that visiting the lakes cost a budget-busting fourteen euros a head, but we weren't even sure where the main entrance was, and by chance found ourselves looking down upon the lower lakes at a pull-out stop on a small road we'd taken. We left our bikes and followed a series of steps that led us down to the lakes with no sign of any ticket booths. There was a tremendous waterfall gushing down from the cliffs we'd walked down, and from there a narrow boardwalk allowed us to walk right out over the water of the lakes. And what a beautiful place it was to be, with several series of small waterfalls flowing between the calm turquoise lakes.

We enjoyed walking around the lower lakes for a while, at least until the tour groups started to arrive. Then the boardwalks suddenly became rather a dangerous place to be, with large groups of Chinese wandering around staring into their cameras and stopping suddenly to take photos. We wondered how often people got knocked into the water, and agreed that it must be quite often, and we'd soon had enough of the crowds and decided to move on.

26

Bosnian border
25th May 2017

As we approached Bosnia and Herzegovina across a plain surrounded by dark mountains it felt like we had reached somewhere different, somewhere far from home, somewhere that inspired a mixture of excitement and trepidation in me. Any nerves, however, were eased by the Bosnian border official, who was very friendly and laughed cheerfully as he welcomed us to his country. It wasn't until we were a kilometre down the road that I remembered something I'd read on the FCO British Government Travel Advice website, about it being very important to make sure we get our passports stamped when entering the country.

"He didn't stamp our passports, did he Dea?"

"No, I don't think so."

"We'd better go back."

"Are you sure? I don't think it can be that important."

Dea didn't really want to cycle back for nothing, but I knew what I'd read on the website, and I didn't want all that reading to have been for nothing, so back we went to get our stamps.

The cheerful man was happy to oblige, and we were soon on our way into Bosnia again, this time with correctly stamped passports. And we were immediately transported into a different world. There were mosques and headscarves, stray dogs and young boys riding motorcycles without wearing helmets. It felt like we had stepped through a magic door from Europe to Asia. Dea, a big fan of the chaos of Asia, was in her element. I'm a bit more ambivalent about the chaos of Asia myself, but even I felt a surge of excitement about being in Bosnia as we rode on a footpath alongside the busy main road towards Bihać. It was as we were cycling along on this that we encountered a girl in her twenties who was cycling the other way. She removed her headphones as she stopped to welcome us to her country with a big smile. We told her of our plans to cycle to Sarajevo and her smile dropped.

"This might be difficult," she said. "I don't know how you can do that, because there are no motorways, only these roads." She indicated the narrow road, choked with traffic. "So all of the traffic is on the same small road all the time. We have trouble moving on in Bosnia. People think that because there was war twenty years ago we can't do anything." She shook her head. "Of course there is corruption and... no money for building roads, sorry."

But thankfully the footpath continued the rest of the way to Bihać, a town with a name that is amusingly pronounced "Be-yatch," at least when I pronounce it. The girl had told us that it was trying hard to become a tourist town, tempting travellers to cross over the border from Plitvice, but that it wasn't doing too well. We thought it was quite nice. A turquoise river, the Una, ran through the town, and we crossed a wooden bridge to an island park where we could sit and watch the water. There were a few run-down buildings in town and we were surrounded by litter, but there was nevertheless a nice atmosphere in Bihać, and we would have stayed longer had we not already booked accommodation elsewhere. It was an unusual move for us to pay for accommodation, but I'd read on the FCO British Government Travel Advice website that it was necessary for all visitors to be registered within seventy-two hours of arriving in Bosnia – something that needed to be done through accommodation – so we'd pre-booked the cheapest place in Bihać, which of course wasn't actually in Bihać.

Avoiding the main road, we tried following a cycle path along the river, but this soon became a field. We carried on regardless, pretending we couldn't translate the sign saying 'Privata' and as luck would have it we found our way back to a road eventually. It was bumpy and pot-holed and a real mess. As we bumped along it in what we hoped was the right direction a young man on a motorcycle skidded to a halt next to me and asked, "Excuse me, but are you from Great Britain?"

I was staggered. How could he possibly have known that?

"Yes I am! How did-"

"You are staying with us. You booked our apartment."

Ah yes, of course. I'd entered my nationality during the booking process. I'd also entered our estimated time of arrival, which I think had turned out to be a bad estimate, some might say spectacularly so. I hoped this poor boy had not been riding up and down this road looking for us for the past three hours.

"Follow me, please."

Well, the least we could now do was cycle behind him as fast as we could to keep up, but then he turned up a hill. A very steep hill. A very long, very steep hill. Noticing our struggle, he puttered along as slow as he could, stopping often to wait for us as we sweated along behind. Then came a reprieve as the road started to go downhill. The boy continued at the same pace. "We can go faster now!" I shouted. He sped off, and almost immediately the road swung back uphill again. "Wait...!"

Somehow we all eventually made it up the hill to the entrance of our accommodation, but we were not done yet, for there was still a very steep driveway to overcome. The boy parked his motorcycle and helped Dea push her bike up the steep gravel and before I even had time to shout "Hey, what about me?" a man came running down the driveway to help me push mine. This was Mustafa, the owner of the building we'd be staying in. He was a thin man in his forties, with tidy black hair starting to grey at the temples, and small, kind eyes. After helping us up to the house he immediately invited us to join in with some family celebrations that were taking place on the back terrace. It was Mustafa's son's fourth birthday (not the son who came to meet us, mind you), and to celebrate in traditional Bosnian style there was a whole lamb roasting on the barbecue.

"Ah, but I'm vegetarian," I said.

"I thought so," the elder son quipped, an assumption that I could only imagine was based on my performance on the hill.

"Don't worry," Mustafa smiled, "there is cabbage."

Very delicious cabbage it was too, and a real pleasure to sit and converse with Mustafa and his family. It was all so very different from the Europe we knew and had so abruptly left behind. Mustafa was keen to stress that all of the food was local and organic. The goat had come from a neighbour, the cabbage was homegrown. In our apartment we would find our fridge freshly stocked with jar after jar of homemade jam, and duck eggs, laid by the very same ducks that Mustafa's four-year-old was presently chasing around the yard. A donkey strolled around, munching on the grass, more economical and efficient than any motorised lawn mower. It was a simple, wonderful place.

And it got even more wonderful when we were shown into our apartment. It was essentially the top floor of the family house, but just for us, and it was a spacious, three-bedroom affair with a big kitchen and a rooftop terrace, with a view out over the valley and the hills beyond. It was amazing.

"Oh, I think we could stay two nights here, don't you Dea?"

"Actually, I think it would be very good for my knee to have a little rest."

And so that is just exactly what we did. The next day we took a break from cycling, and I spent the whole morning trying to catch up with a long to-do list of things that needed to be completed online. Then in the early afternoon we had a visitor. It was Jacob, another cycle tourist who I knew of loosely through his blog, and who I had been in touch with about meeting up and cycling with at some point. I knew that he was close by, so I'd e-mailed him the previous night to say he should come and meet us here, and now he'd done just that.

It was a bit of a surprise when Jacob arrived, because I knew that he'd been on the road for well over a year, and yet he appeared to have a bike that was equipped for a day ride. He was astonishingly lightly packed compared to us, with most of his possessions squeezed into a triangular frame bag that he'd made himself, and a small backpack, with just a couple of things strapped on the front and back of the bike. I was also a bit surprised by his height, for he was a very tall man, who some people (not me) have said looks a bit like Dave Grohl. I must have mentioned his height, because in response he turned to Dea and said, "I was actually expecting you to be taller." He said this because he'd read in my book that Dea was very tall, which meant that he'd read my book, which meant that I already liked him very, very much.

We sat down and ate some lunch together. Jacob was a straight-talking American from Idaho, in his mid-twenties, who had been planning and saving up for his trip for a number of years. He'd begun from the United States a year or so ago, and had ridden down through the Americas before, maybe inspired by my tales, he'd taken a cruise ship from South America to Europe. Now he was on a circular tour of the continent, hoping to take in every country if possible.

"Then I want to go down one side of Africa, and back up the other, and then I'll ride across Asia," he added plainly, as if it really were a day ride. His goals were certainly ambitious, and, as I told him in response to his Africa plan, "Even I think you're crazy!"

Jacob had been following my travels for so long that there wasn't much we could tell him about ourselves, but our blog was a bit behind at the time, and he asked if much had happened since Bologna.

"Erm, well, Venice was nice..."

We stumbled around, looking for a good story. "Oh! Dea hurt her hand, didn't you Dea?"

"Oh yes..." And Dea told him the whole story about how she had reached into her bag without looking and stabbed herself with a pair of scissors, and how there had been a bit of blood, and how we'd had to go into a bar and sit her down with a glass of water because she'd got a bit dizzy, and about how the nice bar woman had got her a plaster. She told the story very well too, I thought.

A little later, after more homemade jam had been consumed, Jacob told us a story about his trip. Having reached South America, he'd left his bike to climb solo up a high mountain of the Andes. For several days he'd hiked up, staying alone in cabins each night, seeing no one else. On summit day the temperature grew very cold and at one point he ripped his glove, exposing one of his fingers. He made it to the peak, but at the cost of altitude sickness and severe frostbite. It sounded like he was lucky enough just to survive the ordeal, somehow staggering back down the mountain to his bike, and then riding it straight to the nearest hospital. By then his finger was in a really bad way. They did what they could, but soon there was no option left. "So, in the end, they had to amputate my finger," Jacob concluded, holding up his hand for us to observe the missing digit.

"Wow..." I said, trying to take it in. "Wow..." Dea was shaking her head in disbelief. It really was an incredible story. I looked over at her. "Hey Dea, I bet you wish you hadn't told that thing about the scissors now."

After lunch it was back to the Wi-Fi and the to-do list for me. On the bikes all day every day it was so easy to fall behind, and there was a lot for me to get on with. A blog to write, people to e-mail, a book to promote, it was all too much. I noticed Dea slip into the room and out again with her ukulele. She was going outside to play with Mustafa's eldest son. I thought I should go and join them, but I just had a little more to do online first. A little more Wi-Fi. A little more screen time. After a while I finally put down my laptop and wandered outside. Dea was playing the ukulele and singing. She finished up her song, then Mustafa's son told her that she sang very well, but it was now time for him to leave as he was going on a date.

"You missed it," Dea said to me. "He was just playing the guitar and singing. He sang a real Bosnian song. It was great."

I felt sad. I'd missed it. I'd missed out on this boy singing, this wonderful moment in time, all because I was staring at a stupid screen, lost in the world of Wi-Fi. I found it very frustrating. I hated the way the internet could steal my attention like that, distract me from the real world where such amazing things were happening.

Determined to spend the evening in the real world, Dea, Jacob and I headed out for a walk together up to a castle on the top of a nearby hill. This evening it was the beginning of Ramadan, and we had been told that there was going to be a party up at the castle to celebrate. We walked up through the village, past the mosque, then had to hike up a grassy track. At the top we found the castle, where there was a rather underwhelming party already underway. It essentially consisted of a bunch of men standing together under a big Bosnian flag, looking a bit glum.

"I should think the party at the end of Ramadan is a bit better," I said.

We bypassed the men and climbed up the old stone tower beyond them. A narrow spiral staircase led up three flights to the top, where we found magnificent views up and down the valley. We also found a man with a mixing deck and three giant speakers, placed precariously on the tower's turrets and facing out in the direction of the village. From these he soon started pumping out some extremely loud Arabic techno music, in a desperate attempt to get the party started. I quite enjoyed this unusual soundtrack, but peering over the edge at the solemn men below us, it didn't appear to have been enough to get them in the mood for forty days without food. They still just stood around looking a bit sullen, and we decided to head back.

At the apartment Mustafa asked us if we could do anything to help fix his bike. It had a couple of flat tyres and I was more than happy to assist him. And apart from keeping the donkey from nibbling the inner tubes as I checked them for holes in his water bowl, there was no trouble getting them patched up. It also gave me the chance to spend some more time with Mustafa, a man who I really liked very much. He seemed to have the right outlook on life. As we spoke, a loud cannon went off up at the castle to mark sunset, and the official start of Ramadan. Mustafa told me more about it all, and to my surprise, he said that he liked the experience of fasting.

"The first days you feel really hungry. But it reminds me to appreciate what I have. It makes me think of the poor people, those who don't have all that I have. It is good to be able to remember that sometimes."

The man spoke such sense. He also told about how he thought that television, the internet, all these screens, were the poison of the modern world, stealing people's attentions from what really mattered. These things really struck a chord with me, like he was putting into words my own thoughts. I felt a strong connection with him, and standing in his garden next to him and his pet donkey, his four-year-old once again running around chasing ducks for fun, the call to prayer from the mosque now blending with the Arabic music still coming from the castle, I felt so happy to be in Bosnia, to be travelling, and to be in the real world.

27

Bihać, Bosnia
27th May 2017

We planned to cycle together with Jacob for a few days through Bosnia, despite him usually cycling a bit faster than us, and when I say 'a bit' I mean 'a lot'. With him carrying so little weight, plus a history of bicycle racing in his youth, his typical average speed was approximately double ours, and he was used to putting in days of well over a hundred kilometres. But he'd read my book, so he was only too well aware of how slow I was, and he said he'd be happy to take things easy and ride at our pace for a while.

We left around ten, saying our goodbyes to the wonderful Mustafa. He seemed tired and a bit more irritable than before, but then he hadn't had any breakfast, and he couldn't eat until sundown, so he was bound to be a little grumpy. Still, I was going to miss him. He was a good man. But it was a beautiful day and the road called out to us once more. We'd been given some advice to forget Sarajevo, and head down the west of the country where it would be less busy, and we set out on a nice quiet road. It was well paved and would have been perfect were it not for the fact that it climbed up and over a big hill.

We tried to turn right off this road on a dirt road into Una National Park to visit some waterfalls that had been highly recommended to us. But blocking our way was a barrier and a very friendly official man with a very friendly dog. Neither of them spoke English, but we managed to understand that the man did not think the road suitable for us to attempt on our bikes, as he indicated that it was only passable by four-by-four. We all knew very well that anything a four-by-four could do, so could we, but I was put off by the fact that this dirt road went up and over another hill, which probably wasn't the best idea for Dea's bad knee, especially as there was an alternative route to the waterfall that was flat. Jacob was keen to go ahead and try this road anyway, but there was also a sign next to the barrier warning that there could be bears on the road, and that settled it for me. Bears steal food, Jacob, bears steal food.

So we all went the other way, which was quite alright because it led us past a little shop where we could buy ice cream, and then to another dirt road that ran alongside the Una. And it was a beautiful river now, as brilliantly turquoise as a robin's egg. Before we reached the waterfall, we saw a rope swing hanging from a big tree that leaned out over the water. Goodness, that looked like fun to me. We all stopped and I ran and got the rope and swung myself out over the river, making a dramatic leap and landing perfectly in the water – if a perfect landing is to land flat on your back, for that is what I did. The water was so startlingly cold that I found it a wonder there weren't blocks of ice in it. I got out as fast as I could. Goodness, it *had* been fun. I wanted to have another go, but I had to share, so I let Dea and Jacob take their turns. Jacob took us all by surprise by doing a weird flip thing, where his head actually went through his own legs, while still holding onto the rope, over a river. It was very impressive. On my next turn I decided to try and see if I could do the same. I almost broke my neck.

The water was too cold to make any more leaps, so we got back on our bikes and made our way along to the waterfall. Now this was really a sight. What a staggeringly beautiful waterfall it was. We stood and stared, stared a little more, then we sat down and stared, then we got out some food and ate it while sitting and staring, then we stared a bit more, then we left.

We got back to our bikes and were all surprised to see a fourth touring bike alongside them. It belonged to Rob, an Australian man who'd been cycling around for a while. He told us that he'd just come along on the four-by-four dirt road against the best advice of the man and his dog.

"How was it?"

"Fine. Not that difficult."

"No bears?"

"No bears."

Jacob looked upset. He must have forgotten about the rope swing.

We left Rob to stare at the waterfall, and retreated eight kilometres along our riverside dirt road, soon returning to tarmac and flying along. Well, Dea and I felt like we were flying along, I think Jacob might have felt like he was in a slow bicycle race. But the going was pretty flat now and progress was steady, until we stopped to take a break in a little town and sat down by the river. I noticed that there was a bar opposite us and, realising that the FA Cup Final between Arsenal and Chelsea was about to kick off, I put forth the idea that we might go and see if they had a telly. To my surprise my two companions, neither of whom had any great interest in football, said they thought it a fine idea.

Unfortunately the bar did not have a television, but they did have free Wi-Fi that was just about good enough to stream the match on my laptop. It took a little while to set it up, however, so I missed the first five minutes, and Arsenal's opening goal. It was alright after that though, and I enjoyed watching the first half with a pint of lager. The prices weren't too high, so Dea and I shared a giant pizza, while Jacob, who I'd already noticed could eat more food then anyone I'd ever met, had a giant pizza to himself, and then ordered a burek for dessert. Neither of them had any interest in the football, but I was engrossed by the second half as Chelsea looked to find a way back into the match. Then in the seventy-third minute, with Arsenal still ahead 1-0, the Wi-Fi connection cut out. I ran around after the barman, encouraging him to fix it if he possibly could. It came back on in the eightieth minute, by which point the score had somehow become 2-1 to Arsenal. It ended that way, and I'd managed to watch seventy-eight minutes of the ninety, and miss all three bloody goals.

Back in the real world we made camp just outside of the town at a riverside rest area, then continued along in the morning, making a visit to another set of (less spectacular) waterfalls, before beginning a long climb out of the valley on a very empty road. There were lots of rocks in the road that had fallen down from the cliffs above us, and it was unusual to be cycling somewhere where the biggest potential threat to life came not from being hit by a car, but by a landslide. To take our minds off the effort of the climb and the imminent threat of rockfall, we distracted ourselves by playing games. Twenty Questions was a big hit, and led to an interesting debate about whether lemon trees are really alive or not. But even Twenty Questions could not distract Dea from the pain which had returned once again to her knee.

"Looks like you should put your saddle a bit higher," Jacob said, in his casual, matter-of-fact manner. It was an inspired suggestion, a potential turning point. Dea raised her saddle and immediately felt more comfortable.

We descended the other side of the pass into a town called Drvar. Since arriving in Bosnia we'd only been travelling in Muslim areas, but suddenly in Drvar we found ourselves in a Serbian town. We stopped at a restaurant run by a friendly Serbian woman. She couldn't speak English, but the free Wi-Fi taught me that all of the Serbs had been completely displaced from Drvar by Croats during the nineties, but many had since now returned. It was the beginning of our introduction to the complicated history of Bosnia, with its three main ethnic groups – the Bosniaks, the Serbs, and the Croats – living in a tentative post-war union.

A German couple cycling in the opposite direction briefly joined us in the restaurant and warned us that we had a big climb ahead. They were right, and this time Jacob preferred not to crawl up at our pace, instead shooting off ahead and then periodically waiting for us. The pass was long and steep, but it took us through lots of natural forest and provided some great views. It also would have provided us with great camping, were it not for all the signs warning about land-mines. Another haunting reminder of the war, and one that had us waiting until we descended the pass and found a flowery meadow with car tracks in it before pitching our tents for the night.

The next day we decided to partake in our favourite game, The Spotting Things Game, with Jacob as a guest player. It only added an extra layer of excitement to have a third person throwing things into the hat, even if with his complete lack of experience he surely had no chance of beating us two. Well, wouldn't you just know it, he only went and spotted a cave from about two miles away, and won the game.

But while it was a lot of fun cycling with Jacob and playing games, the day was also quite sobering, for we were travelling through an area that had obviously been greatly affected by the war. It was a Serb area, and a large percentage of the houses that we saw had been left completely abandoned. They were mere stone shells of buildings, with caved-in roofs or no roofs at all, trees growing up out of them. We saw one whole village that had been entirely left to nature, and buildings riddled with bullet marks. In amongst all this we also saw some homes that were occupied, some Serbs who had moved back, returned to their land after the bombs had stopped falling to try and find a normal life again.

Around five thirty we arrived into a small village, the biggest set-tlement we had seen for hours. We were after a shop, but in our search found ourselves standing inside of a bar, empty except for the proprietor, a short man of about sixty. Bald and brown-eyed and sporting a neat little moustache, he was friendly and keen to talk with us, despite not being able to speak much English. I indicated to him that we were looking for food, as much to make conversation as anything else. It was obvious enough that this was not the kind of bar that usually served food, but the man was determined not to dis-appoint us, and said he would go and find us something to eat. I tried to tell him not to worry, but there was no stopping him now, and he ran off to his house across the road to talk to his wife. Two minutes later he returned with a bowl of goulash and a big plate of mashed potato for us to share. His wife was clearly a very fast cook. The man's grown-up daughter, who could speak some English, came out to see us as we, somewhat reluctantly, tucked in.

"Are we eating your dinner?" I asked.

"Yes!"

But there was nothing to do about it, they refused to take the food back. So we just enjoyed what was a tasty dinner and made sure to pay them well for it. The man, whose name we now found out was Yakov, sat with us and spoke the best that he could. He and his family were Croats, this village marking the end of the Serbian area and the beginning of the Croatian. We tried our best to understand how it must be to be Croatian, and yet live in Bosnia.

"I love Bosnia Herzegovina," Yakov explained, "but I love Croatia. I am Croatian. I love Croatia. But I love Bosnia Herzegovina."

He was clearly a good man, that was obvious. He showed us around his land, on which he grew a large variety of vegetables and kept chickens, and on which was also a small football pitch that he said we could camp on. But before camping on it, I proposed a match. Unfortunately Yakov was injured and couldn't play, though he dearly wanted to, and so his fourteen-year-old son, Ivan, was drafted in to make up the numbers. As you'll no doubt remember, neither Dea nor Jacob were much into football, so when Ivan and I were put on the same team (by me), I thought we were sure to win. Alas the game ended 1-1 after a rather miraculous punt up the pitch by Jacob somehow rolled into the goal. I was sure that Ivan and I would have gone on to find a winner, but before we could do so Dea and Jacob both sat down and said they'd had enough.

With our opponents seated, Ivan and I had to find a way to play without them, and this basically turned into him crossing the ball high in the air so that I could do spectacular scissor-kicks towards the goal. The first time he crossed it I did such a spectacular scissor-kick that it surprised everyone, including me, because I didn't actually know that I could do spectacular scissor-kicks. The ball missed the goal, of course, but that didn't really matter, it was still spectacular.

So we did a few more, and it was great fun, even if I did keep landing hard on the ground, banging my elbow into my ribs in a painful way. And it proved worth it, because one time Ivan crossed the ball and I scissor-kicked it into the top corner of the goal. It was a simply amazing goal, perhaps just exactly how Arsenal's winning goal was scored in the FA Cup Final, by whoever it was that scored it, but I don't know, because I bloody missed it, didn't I? Anyway, doing the scissor-kicks remained great, great fun, until I landed very hard on my ribs and it really hurt. Then I did one more, and it hurt really, really bad, so bad that I started to worry that something was seriously wrong. And then I only did a couple more after that.

We headed back to the bar, but it was not the end of the games, for next up was table-tennis, a sport that Yakov was fit enough to partake in. He was also fit enough to beat me in the first semi-final. In the second semi-final young Ivan defeated Dea by fourteen points to one, and that left the father and son to take part in a truly epic final (I sensed, not for the first time). The battle eventually got so intense that one table was no longer enough, and they moved two tables together to make one super-long table, and in the end somebody won.

As the evening drew on we got a round of beers in and sat around and chatted into the night. Despite a lack of common language, Yakov had a way about him that made him interesting to communicate with all the same, and it was lovely to spend the evening with him. He was such a warm, friendly man, and yet there was also a sadness to be sensed in him, a sadness that stemmed from the history of this land. He told us that he still thought often of the war. The very building we sat outside had been bombed three times. But he was not bitter. "I have Serb friends," he said. "Serb people," he pointed down the road from which we had arrived, "they come here, they drink. They are my friends. Good people are good people. No Serb. No Croat. Just people. Good people are good people."

28

Bosnia and Herzegovina
30th May 2017

Before saying goodbye to Yakov the next morning I suggested we all have a game of table-football. I'd noticed the table in the bar the night before. It was a proper table-football table, the kind with metal players with paint peeling off them, where the ball often got stuck in between the rows and someone had to reach in and give it a flick. Yakov's competitive nature was revealed once more, and the game was taken extremely seriously, at least by him, and me. It was Dea and me against Yakov and Jacob, and it turned into an exciting contest. As the game went on Dea and I edged ahead, much to Yakov's dismay, and in the end we claimed a narrow victory. Yakov was evidently frustrated by the loss, but he seemed to know where the game had gone wrong, as he then requested Jacob stand aside. Without the handicap of a tall American keeping goal he took control of all of his players and showed us what years of practise could do, as he easily beat Dea and me in the rematch.

Another nice day of cycling followed. We were now passing through Croat areas, and there was quite a contrast from the war-torn ruins we'd seen in the Serb areas. Now we passed many nice houses that were big, modern, freshly-painted, and completely lacking in bullet holes. The downside was that the road grew busier with the increased habitation, and a long, hot climb was made even less enjoyable by the trucks and cars we now had to share the road with. Jacob went on ahead again and sat at the top watching a couple of episodes of his favourite shows on his phone while he waited for us. He was really a very different sort of world cyclist from us, and the way he skipped up to the top made me think he maybe had a valid point about the advantages of travelling light.

Down from the pass we detoured around a town called Tomislav-grad and made camp in a field of yellow flowers a short while later. Jacob's tent was only a compact little one-man thing, and it looked comically tiny next to our oversized three-person gazebo. But Dea and I really appreciated having the extra space to store our things in the tent and to be able to move around, things that Jacob certainly couldn't do in his. In fact, I thought it a marvellous trick that such a tall man could even fit inside. He had his tent up in no time and, as Dea and I struggled with the daily construction project that was the assembly of ours, I happened to glance over at the wrong moment. Jacob's tent clearly wasn't spacious enough to act as a changing room, and he had decided to pull down his cycling shorts and reveal his backside to the world, and by 'the world' I mean 'me'. It brought back haunting memories of Andreas, the Austrian man I'd cycled with in Turkmenistan, who was similarly uninhibited.

"Do you remember in my book?" I asked Jacob, as he pulled on some underwear.

"The Austrian guy?" Jacob knew very well what I was talking about. I had to laugh.

"Jacob, I think you're trying a little *too* hard to get in the next book."

The next day we made an unusually early start, for we had a goal of reaching Mostar, a historic town where we had already booked accommodation, seventy-five kilometres away. We rode on the main road and for fifty kilometres everything went okay. The road was narrow enough that I worried about our safety, keeping a keen eye on my mirror to watch for close passes, but the traffic was not overly excessive and we made good progress. Then we reached a town called Široki Brijeg, and traffic became... well... overly excessive. It was bumper to bumper and there was absolutely no shoulder. There was at least a footpath that we could navigate the town on, but with twenty kilometres still to go to Mostar the main road just seemed too dangerous to me once the footpath ended. Jacob had no such concerns and, keen to get to his guest house, he headed off alone for the last stretch. Dea and I moved to a café to use the Wi-Fi there to look for an alternative, safer route, but the only possibility involved long detours over steep mountains. Dea was keen to get to Mostar, take a shower, and relax. "Let's just take the main road, Chris," she said, and I relented, and we headed out of town.

We didn't get far. We stopped and took a breather just out of town and as I looked at the road ahead and the traffic streaming past I really began to worry. There were so many big trucks and the road was narrow, with no shoulder and few places to dive out of the way in an emergency. It looked a very dangerous place to be on a bicycle. Dea still wanted to carry on and get it done, but I had such a bad feeling about this road that I actually began to cry. I wasn't crying because I was scared of the big, bad road myself (although I was scared of the big, bad road), I was crying because I didn't want Dea to be in danger. I couldn't stand the thought of something happening to her, and it occurred to me that she was only really here because of me. If anything did go wrong it would be my fault, I would blame myself. I thought of the promises I'd made to her family that I would look after her, do what I could to keep her safe. And this road was not safe. So I cried.

"Let's take the other way," Dea said, trying her best to soothe her blubbering thirty-two-year-old boyfriend. "It doesn't matter how long it takes."

It was good that she said that, because the other way ended up taking quite a long time. We later found out that it took Jacob only forty-five minutes to cycle from Široki Brijeg to Mostar. It took us five hours.

Nevertheless, it was one hell of an adventure. First we went north of the main road on a tiny little lane that went up a steep climb, and, while I use the term steep climb quite a lot, this really, really was a steep climb. It was such a steep climb that we really should have used climbing equipment, and carabinered ourselves to the cliff every now and again for safety reasons. But it was a nice road, even more so when it flattened out at the top, and even more so still when it went back downhill again.

We crossed over the main road and took some very small roads to the south of it that were marked on the map on my phone. It was a bit strange that they were marked on that map, though, because they weren't actually roads. They were just a place where someone had driven a car through a field. We kept following them anyway, agreeing that this was surely more interesting than the main road. Then we rejoined a proper gravel track, which was great until it crossed a stream, or more accurately the steam crossed it, or even more accurately the gravel track and the stream combined and merged into one wet, gravelly entity. We needed to ford this entity and to do so we walked our bikes through the fairly deep water. My front panniers floated up as if they might go off their own way at any moment, but the water felt cool and refreshing on my skin. It was so cool and refreshing, in fact, that once our bikes were safely across I left mine and waded back into the water, collapsing backwards and merging myself into the cool, refreshing, wet, gravelly, stream/track/cyclist entity. It was lovely.

Next we tried our luck on a road that was, we think, technically closed. It was completely empty, absolutely nothing on it but us. It seemed as if they'd been building a new road and then the money had ran out, so it was never quite finished. Consequently we were worried that we might not be able to make it all of the way through, and there was a certain level of apprehension that we may be forced to retreat. But luck was on our side, and it was finished just well enough for us to make it, and see down below us the town of Mostar. We had succeeded in our mission, and how we had enjoyed this side trip of ours. "It was the right decision to come this way," Dea smiled. We'd had five hours of exciting adventure instead of one hour of life-threatening danger, and it was proof in my mind that the old cliché about taking the road less travelled was worth the effort to follow.

We descended down into the valley and made our way along the river into the old town where we found our way to the Hajde Guesthouse. A man with frizzy hair welcomed us in a manner that was overwhelmingly friendly and also a little bit crazy. I noticed he had blue hands. "I've been eating mulberries from the tree all afternoon," he explained. "I've been waiting for you for hours."

Ah yes, the expected time of arrival thing. I'd got it a bit wrong again. I offered my apologies.

"Oh, don't worry, I fell asleep anyway. It was nice. I had a good sleep."

The man had a name that I could not pronounce, with letters that I didn't know, but Dea thought his name was Javar. He showed us inside, and once again our room was fantastic. There was a simple bed and seating area made from wooden pallets, but covered in cushions and decorated in a wonderful way. There was also a balcony that we could use, with a hammock and a view of the river and the old town, with all of the many minarets of all of the many mosques, for we were suddenly back in Muslim territory. It was almost too good to be true. Javar left us to it and Dea took a shower while I went out on the balcony by myself to lie in the hammock and read a book about Mostar that had been in our room. The hammock was one of those tight, flat ones. I laid down upon it, and it immediately spun me around and spat me out onto the hard floor with a thud, an a way that made me very glad that I was alone.

A little later on we were invited downstairs to share dinner with Javar and his sister, Nadia. They had only just begun this guest house project and we were only their second guests. They were really nice to us, the latest in a long line of good and kind-hearted people we'd met in Bosnia and Herzegovina (and we were apparently now in the Herzegovina part). The food was delicious, once again with a lot of homemade produce to enjoy. Despite the property only being small there was an extraordinary amount of food growing all around us, from the mulberry trees leaning over everything to the herbs and vegetables in the garden, and the vines that spiralled through the trellises above our heads.

Jacob came over and joined us. He was staying at a different guest house and would be going a different way from us after Mostar, but we'd arranged to meet up one last time. And after dinner Javar led all three of us off on foot, doing his best to act as our tour guide and telling us about the town as we went. When we got down to the old bridge which Mostar is most famous for, however, he bumped into some friends of his and went off to have a drink and a smoke with them. That left us three cyclists to sit and admire the bridge, all lit up in the darkness, and reflect on our ride together, before saying good-night and goodbye. It was the end of our time riding with Jacob and that was a shame, for he had been good company, and had added an extra something to our time in Bosnia, a country we were all sure to remember fondly for a long time to come.

The next day Dea and I returned into town to see it by daylight, but disappointingly all we found were streets crammed with tourists and shops selling tourist trinkets. Returning to the old bridge we saw the famous bridge jumpers. A few men stood on the bridge wearing nothing but tight red trunks, and eventually, when they'd collected enough money from the tourists who wanted to see them dive into the river below, they would jump. We saw only one guy jump once the whole time we were there, and, after all of the anticipation, I sus-pect some of the tourists might have regretted their donations. It was, after all, just a guy jumping into a river.

One thing did catch our eye and that was some photos of Mostar from the 1990's, before, during and after the war. This old bridge, supposedly built by the Ottomans way back when, was, it turned out, not that old. The original was tragically destroyed during the war, and the photos dated 1994 showed an empty space over the river where it should have stood. The bridge that we now saw was in fact an exact copy, built in 2004. Our interest in the photos caught the attention of a nearby stall holder, an older man, who came over to talk with us. He was an interesting fellow, who had lived for a time in Italy but had chosen to return here to his homeland. "In Italy they have everything, but the people go to work with sad faces. Here people talk to each other, they know their neighbours, they help each other. That's why I came back." And in so saying he had perfectly summed up one of the many reasons we liked this country so much.

Having long since abandoned our plans to head for Sarajevo we instead turned our wheels south towards Dubrovnik and the Croatian coast again. We'd found out from an article on *The Guardian* website about a new cycle route that had just opened, running from Mostar to the coast, and we wanted to check it out. Following an old railway route, the E.U. Funded Ciro Trail promised to be flat and light on traffic, so we decided to follow the advice of the article author, and give it a go ourselves.

At first the Ciro Trail followed paved roads, which took us alongside a modern railway line through a narrow river gorge. Almost all of the traffic was on a bigger highway on the other side of the river, but there was still enough coming our way to make it a pain having to stop and move over for them due to the very narrow nature of the road. So, when the option came for us to take a traffic-free section of old railway line, we jumped at it.

This gravel section was hard work. The trail climbed, albeit gradually, into the mountains, and the surface was made up of quite large rocks that were not easy to cycle on. And they were especially difficult for me, due to the pain I had in my ribs. It was no joke about the damage I'd done to them scoring Arsenal's spectacular scissor-kick FA Cup Final winning goal. They hurt like hell. I'd bruised them for sure, and bumping up and down on the rocks was very painful. For this reason I actually had to get off and walk much of the trail, but it still remained an adventure, taking us through a dozen unlit tunnels, where hundreds of bats nested, squealing incessantly above our heads as we passed.

It was an enjoyable experience to take on this off-road section, and we thought it fantastic that this cycle route had been created, even if we did wonder how well maintained it would be over the coming years in a country with plenty of other infrastructure to work on. After a while the trail ended and we rejoined a road, but it was quiet and for the rest of the route there was hardly any traffic on it at all. It was a real pleasure to cycle, and it was a fitting end to such a great country. We spent our last night camping next to one of the many abandoned railway stations along the old line, still cautious not to wander off the beaten track for fear of landmines. Bosnia's troubled recent history was there to see throughout the country, but it was a country that had nevertheless earned a special place in our hearts, and one that we hoped to return to one day.

The quiet road continued until just before the Croatian border, where it met with a bigger road to take us down to the coast. Even on this bigger road, however, the Bosnian side of the border was as primitive as any I'd seen anywhere in the world. It was nothing more than a portacabin at the side of the road, with stern-looking officials approaching each car, collecting the passports, and taking them away to be checked. *'Here we go,'* I thought, relieved that I'd had the sense to make us go back and get our passports stamped on entering, relieved that we'd stayed somewhere and got ourselves registered. All that reading on the FCO British Government Travel Advice website was about to prove itself worthwhile. We reached the front of the queue and one of the stern-looking officials walked over to us, looking all stern. We handed him our passports, confident that everything was in order. He looked at the front of each of them, saw what countries we were from, and then, without scanning them to check for our registrations, without so much as opening them to look for any stamps, he handed them back, and waved us on towards Croatia.

29

Dubrovnik, Croatia
3rd June 2017

A ctually, I think I've heard that the best thing about Dubrovnik is the view of it from a distance," I said to Dea, as we sat on a cliffside looking down on the round towers of the fortressed old coastal town, its medley of orange roofs contrasting with the green of the hillsides and the blue of the Adriatic. It had been our intention to go into it to experience it close up, but now we could see that the route we'd planned to take down was a narrow one-way road going the wrong way, and in any case it was sure to be swarming with tourists down there, so we agreed that we'd seen all we needed to of Dubrovnik, and continued south along the coast instead.

Many cycle tourists follow this coast road all of the way down from Slovenia but we couldn't understand why, for while the coastline did look scenic enough, there was no time to look around and enjoy any of it as all of our attention was taken up by the constant roar of traffic passing within inches of our left shoulders. It was not the sort of road for us, and as soon as we had crossed another international border into Montenegro we left it behind again to follow a smaller road around the magnificent Kotor Bay. This was a long and winding route through numerous old fishing villages now reinvented as vacation destinations, with countless holiday-makers out sunbathing or cooling off in the clear waters of the bay. We took a swim ourselves, of course, and then continued on around a corner where our breaths were fairly taken away by the sight of a sheer wall of granite cliffs at the far end of the bay. The grey cliffs rose up to a uniform height behind the old town of Kotor, towering above everything, and encircling half the bay, forming the most incredible natural barrier. *'How the hell are we going to get past that?'* I wondered.

We found out the next day, when we began on a series of switchbacks somehow carved out of the wall of rock. After five switchbacks we already had magnificent views down over the bay, and they were only destined to get more magnificent the higher that we climbed. By the fifteenth turn I was absolutely exhausted from the effort of the long climb in the intense heat, sweat irritating my eyes. But what a road it was! All afternoon we slogged ever higher, until the hotels lining the shore were nothing more than distant specks below us. It was evening before we navigated the last of the more than thirty switchbacks, and finally reached the summit, to be rewarded by being chased on the other side by a ferocious shepherd dog.

We followed a quiet road through the rest of the country, vaguely following the shore of a giant lake, though up in the hills so that we had to continue to work hard. Thankfully Jacob's advice appeared to have paid off, and with Dea's saddle higher her knee was able to stand up to all of this climbing without complaints. Unlike her boyfriend, I might add.

We both liked Montenegro. It was one of the more beautiful countries we'd ridden through, but it wasn't very big, so we were soon increasing my country-count further by crossing into Albania.

And what a contrast it was to cross into Albania. Gone suddenly was the relative peace and order of Montenegro, replaced by a form of chaotic life that I only really knew previously from certain corners of Asia. The land was suddenly flat farmland again, and the pot-holed road was busy with old cars, motor scooters, and tractors carrying trailers overflowing with giant loads of hay on top of which sat one or more farmhands, gripping on as best they could. The air was full of the smell of animals and trash and freshly cut hay, and everywhere donkeys and chickens nibbled at the roadside. We passed a man walking with his pigs, another waved to us from a horse-drawn cart. Then a cow crossed my path, sauntering across the road, dragging behind it a rope on the end of which clanged along a metal stake, that hadn't quite been enough to keep it where it was supposed to be. It was chaotic and alive and wonderful.

We stopped at a bakery just to buy some bread, and the old couple that owned it couldn't help but give us some salty homemade cheese to eat with the freshly baked loaf, and to force upon us a big bag of plums. We tried to pay this kindness forward later when, taking a break on a quieter section of road, an elderly shepherd came over to see us. He was a gaunt man in an oversized tweed suit, and he held in his hand a staff, though he appeared to have only one sheep with him. He sat himself down five metres away from us and simply stared. Conversation was a little slow, so we offered him some of our plums and peanuts, and he reluctantly came forward and took a handful of the peanuts, slipping most of them into his pocket for later.

"It has begun," I announced to Dea as we rode on from this odd encounter. "The staring, the lack of communication, the people inviting us to eat with them, giving us food. This is how it will be all through Asia, you know."

And I looked at Dea and saw her smile, daydreaming about all the adventures we still had ahead of us.

It was just before sunset when we arrived at the outskirts of a town called Lezhë. There had been no good places to wild camp in Albania and we were getting a little worried about where we were going to lay our heads for the night when, as we stopped at a junction to discuss the best course of action, we heard a female voice call down to us.

"Are you from England?"

The question came from a young woman in a garden just above us, in flawless English. How she had guessed that I was from England I'm not sure, for I had long since lost my accent somewhere along the road. The dark-haired girl, Rosina, explained that she lived in England herself, in Abingdon, a little town near Oxford that I'd cycled through once or twice. She had moved there to study, but now she was married and had a two-year-old daughter, and an Albanian husband who also lived and worked in England. She was now home in Albania for a month, spending time with her large family, who were at this moment beginning to congregate around her to see what all the fuss was about. She introduced us to her uncle, whose house we were standing in front of, her aunt and grandma, both short, stout women with white head coverings, and a young, female cousin who looked similar enough in features to be Rosina's sister, with her dark eyebrows and long, flowing black hair.

"My parents also live in the house next door. All of the family live together. Here it is the traditional way of living," Rosina explained. "Altogether there are about seventeen or eighteen people living together."

We explained that we were looking for a place to put up our tent, and after a brief discussion in Albanian with her uncle, Rosina announced that we were welcome to camp on their lawn if we liked. It was a very flat and grassy lawn, and we happily accepted the kind offer. But as we began the daily routine of assembling our home for the night, the whole family gathered around to watch, and a heated discussion began to take place. The grandma, dressed in a black skirt, white blouse and black cardigan, with a long shawl over her head that made her look not unlike Mother Teresa, was the most vocal participant. "She says she feels sorry for you sleeping there," Rosina translated. "If you prefer, you can sleep inside the house."

"It's okay, we don't mind sleeping in our tent. We do it every night," we replied, not wanting to take anyone's bed.

"Okay, if you like it that way then it's okay. But you are welcome to stay in the house."

"No, no, it's not necessary," we insisted, and the back-and-forth continued similarly for a while, with the grandma growing ever more frustrated, until I realised that she probably really would prefer to not have us on the lawn.

"Would you *like* us to stay inside?"

"YES!" Rosina gasped. "We have never had a guest sleeping outside. We want you to sleep in the house."

And with that we packed the tent away and were shown inside, to everyone's satisfaction. The house was big and well-furnished, and would not have looked out of place in Western Europe by any means. We were given our own room with a big bed, and invited to shower and wash clothes if we needed. And we were soon also well fed, with a whole table filled with dishes of bread, vegetables, cheese and meat laid out before us that we were encouraged to eat as much as we wanted from. It was all homegrown, homemade, and organic food; once again the close relationship people in this part of the world had with their food was on display, and it tasted delicious.

The family ate with us, for they were Roman Catholic, a religion making up a significant minority in the mainly-Muslim nation, and were therefore not observing Ramadan. Many more people came in to see us during the course of the evening, including a cousin who worked as a policeman and was proud to tell us that he had the job of controlling illegal marijuana production in the Albanian hills. We also met Rosina's grandfather, a wonderful eighty-two-year-old who looked like an Albanian Woody Allen, and for a moment he and his wife were stood in front of us, their faces gleaming and eyes shining, as they talked and talked to us in Albanian. It seemed they struggled to understand our lifestyle, why we would choose to live like poor people going about by bike and sleeping in a tent, but we did our best to explain that it was to bring us experiences like this one. Even Rosina's husband in England was introduced to us over the internet. "Please feel like you are at home," he insisted, "eat as much as you want!"

We felt very lucky to have had such a great experience to take with us from our short stay in Albania, and it was with some reluctance, and the whole family waving us off, that we continued on our journey the next morning. There was more for us to experience from this country before we left, though, as we rode on through the picturesque gorge of Ulza Regional Nature Park, where a turquoise river cut through the rugged mountainside. Beyond that we came out to more farmland, and were invited to come and visit another family home by a young blonde girl of about ten years of age. We followed her and were given watermelon slices and lemonade by her mother, a most welcome respite from the ongoing heatwave, before the girl excitedly showed us all of the animals that they kept on their little farm. There was such a good, welcoming vibe about Albania, with lots of people pausing their work to wave or shout hello to us as we continued on through the farmland that evening. Once again it was a country that we wished we could have devoted more time to, but the fact was that we were now into June, and still absolutely nowhere near the high mountains of Central Asia that we wanted to pass before winter set in, and so we had to keep making some form of steady progress east.

We entered Macedonia at the border town of Debar. As with many of the Balkan nations, it was necessary for us to register ourselves in the country within the first twenty-four hours, and this time we thought we'd try and do it directly at the police station, rather than having to cut our day short by stopping at paid accommodation. In order to locate the police station we stopped at a random junction and stared at a map, looking lost, until someone offered to help us. This strategy worked well, and within a matter of seconds a car had stopped and a young man spoke to us in English to ask if he could help. No sooner had we explained our predicament, than he told us to follow behind him and his cousin in their car. And so we did as we were told, even when the cousin launched the vehicle up onto a pedestrian footpath and sped down it in order to park as close as possible to the front doors of the police station.

Osman, the man who spoke good English, offered to come in and act as a translator for us. This was a kind offer on his part, but he wasn't entirely needed, as it was perfectly obvious to me from mere body language that the policeman we encountered in this particular police station had not the slightest interest in taking on the extra paperwork that registering us would require him to do. "Sorry,"

Osman confirmed, "he says he cannot register you here. You must go to a guest house and register through them."

But Osman's presence now came in very useful, as he next offered to show us to a place he knew of that cost only ten euros, and as we now had little option but to stay in town we were happy to follow him again. It was probably also lucky for Osman's cousin that the police had such a lax attitude, for he proceeded to put the car into reverse and then hit the accelerator so hard that the wheels spun noisily before it zoomed off backwards down the thankfully empty footpath. We then all made our way through the town, being delayed slightly by a flock of sheep that had overtaken an entire roundabout, before arriving at a gas station. There were some rooms to rent on the top floor of the building, and it was actually a very nice place to spend a night, with a decent shower and Wi-Fi that allowed us to sit and plan our onward route through Macedonia.

Osman and his cousin had suggested we meet up for the evening, and at eight thirty they returned, this time on foot, to take us into town. Osman was a really nice guy who had lived most of his life in Switzerland, but he was now back in Debar for a week to spend time with family. As such he was the ideal person to give us an insight into the differences between life here and in Western Europe. He first explained to us that Debar was not really a Macedonian town, that everyone in this whole area including him and his family were in fact Albanian and Muslim. And as it was still the month of Ramadan that meant that there was a special atmosphere in Debar.

"After fasting all day, everyone in the family comes together for a big meal," Osman explained. "And then they are so full, they need to go for a walk, and so everyone walks up and down the main street. Look!" And we looked, and saw that the main street in town really was absolutely full of people walking. "Some people will walk up and down this street ten times tonight," Osman smiled. "Just meeting friends and family, stopping to chat along the way. It's a social event really."

Osman took us to a popular bar called The London Lounge, with two big red phone boxes in the doorway and British flags all over the interior décor. It was a big place full of groups of young men and women, all drinking non-alcoholic drinks because of Ramadan, but nevertheless the place was buzzing. We took a seat and chatted more with Osman and he told us about how almost every family had at least one family member living somewhere 'outside', in Western Europe or the United States, providing a form of financial security for the family back home. In his case all of his immediate family had settled in Switzerland when he was young, but he said he still missed it here, that it was somehow where he belonged, and he had plans to soon invest in some property in the area.

We finished our drinks and returned to the street to take our turn in walking up and down. It was no surprise that the friendly and outgoing Osman stopped to talk with many people along the way, and we could see for ourselves how this strange custom really was a social event.

We were then invited to walk up to see an old mosque, one of several in the town. We arrived just as the evening prayer was ending, with groups of people streaming past us down the dark street, and the imam about to lock up for the night. But Osman explained the situation and the imam smiled warmly, happy to allow us in to see his mosque. And it was a sight worth seeing, with Arabic inscriptions on the walls and thick carpets on the floors, and best of all the passionate look on the devoted old imam's face as he told us all about it.

Osman and his cousin walked us back across town to our guest house and we said goodnight, although this was not the end of their night. They planned to now drive for an hour to Lake Ohrid, where there was apparently a party taking place. It seemed like there was a lot of life in this part of the world during the hours of darkness, at least during Ramadan, and waving goodbye to Osman we felt really lucky and honoured to have been given the chance to experience just a little bit of it.

30

Skopje, Macedonia
12th June 2017

The streets of Skopje were empty. Even the ginger cat that wouldn't leave us alone when we'd arrived at the hostel the previous afternoon was nowhere to be seen now. I clipped my rear pannier onto my bike. Just one of them, for I didn't need much today. Passport, check. Camera, check. Cookies, check. I was ready. I slung my leg over the frame and reset my cycle computer to zero. As I did so the time flashed up. 5:00 a.m. My day had begun.

It was fun to ride on the empty streets of the city, awake before the rest of the world, sneaking more out of my day. I followed a small road that climbed eastwards up out of the city towards a pink sky. I passed stray dogs digging in trash that barked at me and I think considered giving chase, until they saw my speed. I was taking a leaf out of Jacob's book today, travelling light and putting in some effort for once. As the sun appeared on the horizon the road started to grow busier, but only with traffic going into the capital. Macedonian commuters. My lane was empty. I was the only one going the other way.

My plan was to ride around in a big loop – northeast to the border, northwest across a corner of Serbia, west through Kosovo, then south back to Macedonia and our Skopje hostel. It was country-bagging at its finest, an idea born out of my insistence to visit every country in the Balkans, and Dea's insistence that she didn't want to go to a country for the sake of just going to a country. A compromise had been reached – she would take a rest day in Skopje, and I would cycle 160 kilometres in one day, alone.

For much of the Balkans, Dea and I had been only riding sixty kilometre days, and even though we'd been trying hard to improve on that we were still struggling to make eighty kilometres on a regular basis. I therefore had some doubts that I was going to be able to ride double that, hence my early start, and a determination to cycle faster than normal. I was also taking fewer breaks, keeping food in my basket and eating on the go. And all this worked, for I completed the forty-five kilometres to the Serbian border before I'd normally complete waking up. Crossing the border was easy enough, even though the man on customs looked very confused by my lack of personal belongings. I shrugged my shoulders, as if to say "what more does a man need than cookies?" and I was waved on into country number sixty.

Throughout much of our travels in the Balkans it seemed like the Serbs were painted as the bad guys, and so I would have appreciated giving them the chance to answer back, to show me what Serbia and being Serbian is really all about. Unfortunately, I wasn't going to give them that chance, as I was only cycling twenty-five kilometres in their country, and even then I was passing through the only area of their country populated almost entirely by Albanians. I rode on an empty highway for a while, then up through a busy town of mosques and Muslims, reminiscent of Albania, and the Albanian parts of Macedonia, that gave me no real impression of Serbia whatsoever. As I left the town and headed for the mountain pass that would lead me to Kosovo I felt a bit silly to think about claiming Serbia on my list of visited countries. It was the first time I'd made such a brief visit into a nation without getting to know it even a little bit. Sure, I'd only gone to Vietnam for the sake of going, but I gave it three days. Serbia was only getting a couple of hours. And true, Liechtenstein only got a couple of hours, but I went there twice, and I saw most of it.

But at least I would not pass through Serbia without one memorable experience to take with me. It happened as I started on up the pass and two boys of about ten said hello to me. One was on a bicycle and, as so often happens in such situations, he and I soon found ourselves in a race. Ordinarily when I have all of my bags it is difficult for me to triumph in such contests, but today of course I was going as fast as possible on an unloaded bike. So it was especially embarrassing when the kid pulled ahead of me, and to make my humiliation complete I noticed that the boy's rusty old bike had a flat tyre to boot. I told him to stop so that I could put some air in it for him. "If you're going to beat me, you could at least do it on a working bike," I told him.

The other boy was a little younger and carried a big stick in his hand. It took me a little while to realise this was because he was supposed to be in charge of the five cows that were heading up the hill with us, roaming about in the middle of the road and getting in the way of the army trucks that occasionally drove down from the sensitive border. He did seem to have a certain measure of control though, and here was certainly a wonderful way to cycle a pass, with a couple of smiling Albanian children and a smattering of cows. Yes, Serbia was alright with me.

The younger boy headed off into a field with his cows, but the other continued to ride with me a little longer, pointing out things and saying words I didn't understand like he was my tour guide. I wondered for a while if he might go all the way to the top and into Kosovo with me, but after a while he decided he'd had enough and turned back down the hill, leaving me to continue on with what was really quite a nice pass. There was lots of green forest, almost no traffic on the road, and the intriguing promise of Kosovo at the top.

The thing about Kosovo, of course, is that it is a country, but it is also not a country. For a while I considered whether or not to include it in my country-count, realising in the process that doing so either way could be seen as me making something of a political statement, something which in turn made my head hurt. But then I decided I could quite easily and fairly pass the buck over to the United Nations, for I said from the start that only full U.N. members would count, and so, even with its partial U.N. membership and ongoing battle for full admittance, I decided not to count Kosovo as a country in the end. But it certainly did look a lot like a country when I arrived to find that it had a proper border and, even though Serbia doesn't recognise Kosovo's independence and insists that Kosovo is Serbia, there was nevertheless a Serbian man to stamp me out of Serbia, and a Kosovan man to stamp me into Kosovo. There was also a Kosovan woman on customs, who asked me if I had anything to declare. "Just cookies," I said, and she smiled, and said, "Welcome to Kosovo.

I was really happy about being in Kosovo, and especially so when I rounded a corner and had a great view down over the land far below me. It was a peaceful spot, up on a forested hill, and down below I could see a flatter landscape of fields and villages, with little roads linking these villages, and it all looked thoroughly pleasant. So I whizzed on down the hill towards it, and then I arrived in the wide valley and started cycling on the small roads and what do you know? It *was* thoroughly pleasant. The roads were paved but had basically no traffic on them, and they were lined with wild-flowers, red poppies and purple something-or-others. There were golden fields and green hills and little houses and it all seemed a little too perfect. It was just a really, really nice place to ride a bike. Before I'd come here I hadn't known the first thing about Kosovo. It was a troubled place in my mind, a place of war and anger and darkness. And now here I was riding my bike in it, and it felt like a little piece of paradise, a really nice place cut straight from the pages of a children's picture book. I loved it.

I also discovered that Kosovo is, like many places outside of Albania, populated primarily by ethnic Albanians, essentially the reason for its determination to seek independence from Serbia. I passed through some villages where I saw mosques, and one children's playground that had flags all around it demonstrating Kosovo's allegiances. Two of the flags were the Kosovan national flag, and there was also one of the European Union and one of the United States (both of whom support Kosovo's claims for independence), and the other twenty-odd flags? All the red and black double-headed eagle of Albania.

Unfortunately I did have to join a busier road after a while that made me like Kosovo just a little bit less, and then I went on another road that was still under construction, and there were road workers and big dumper trucks everywhere. This would have made me like Kosovo a lot less, except for the fact that I spoke to some Kosovans here, almost all of them construction workers, and they were all really very nice. It seemed to me like a good country, a pleasant land filled with pleasant people, that I had greatly enjoyed my brief cycle through. It was somewhere I wished I could add to my country-count.

But I could not stay in Kosovo forever, and soon I reached the Macedonian border, where I was extremely grateful to be allowed back into the country, for it was where I had left all of my stuff, and my girlfriend. Time was getting along, and I still had a long ride back to Skopje. I did this on a main road that was in the mountains and might have been quite nice were it not for the possibility of being run over by a truck at any moment. It only got busier and busier as it neared the city and it was with great relief that I spotted a bicycle path down by the river. I was essentially up on a motorway at the time, and to get down to the river involved scrambling down a mountainside, but that was alright because I'd eaten all my cookies and my bike weighed almost nothing at all, so I threw it over my shoulder and carried it down.

The cycle path into Skopje was a great end to a great day. I rode along with the other cyclists, with joggers and roller bladers and walkers, enjoying the anonymity I'd benefited from all day. Without all my panniers I was just another guy on a bike, and I kind of liked that. And passing through the centre of Skopje was cool, for it was absolutely full of crazy statues, including one of a warrior on a horse which was surely the biggest statue I had ever seen. I stopped and stared at it, lit up as it was by the last of the day's sunlight. It felt like a long time since I'd watched the sun rise over the hills to the east of the city that morning. I'd seen a lot. I'd cycled a lot. 163 kilometres, to be precise, more than a hundred miles. And I'd added one more country to my country-count in the process. As a full member of the United Nations, Serbia would be the name going on the list, but, just between you and me, it was Kosovo that I had seen.

31

Macedonia
13th June 2017

Beyond Skopje we managed to find some nice dirt roads that took us east across Macedonia. They were not always of the best quality, varying from loose sand to thick gravel, muddy to rocky, but they allowed us to escape back into nature. We climbed up a long way undisturbed and eventually made it to a village that appeared to be completely deserted, save for a donkey that briefly blocked our onward path. Later we set up camp in an area of wilderness that felt a million miles from civilization, at least until a dog came barking up to us. The dog was followed by an old goatherd tending his flock, who came over to see us for a while before he and his animals moved on and left us to it.

The next morning we continued down our gravel tracks but unfortunately they led us to a main road. It seemed to be the only route for us into Bulgaria, where we planned to continue through the mountains to Turkey, but the traffic on this road was going so fast and there was so little space that I once again didn't feel safe riding on it. After a couple of kilometres we pulled over into a gas station to buy ice creams and think through our options. I checked the map on my phone and found a faint grey line running parallel to the main road.

"It must be up there in the hills," I said, causing Dea's face to drop. I knew she sometimes grew tired of the difficult back roads and could appreciate flat tarmac, but the main road here was so dangerous that I wanted to pursue this alternative if we possibly could. We asked the owner of the gas station about the other road, but his reaction was not so positive.

"There is no road there," he said. "Only path for shepherds. Not possible with bicycle."

To try and convince him we could do such roads, I told him about the gravel tracks we had come through the previous day.

"Those are bad roads. This is bad, bad road."

Dismissing his concerns, half an hour later we were clambering uphill through a field, the gas station and the dangerous highway far beneath us. Unusually for us I was ahead, leading the way, trying to show that this wasn't going to be so bad, that it was going to be as fun and adventurous as the day before. But I knew Dea was in a bad mood for it, that she didn't want to be working this hard for our kilometres, especially as we'd by now booked accommodation in Istanbul and had a bit of a deadline to stick to. But, in contrast to Dea, I was loving it. The man at the gas station had been right; it wasn't much of a road, more of a goat track. It was narrow and bumpy and overgrown, and kept dropping down into ravines and climbing out again. It took a bit of concentration to navigate and in my opinion was much more interesting and exciting than any tarmac road could be, but all the while I was aware that my thoughts in this matter were not being shared by my companion. We stopped to take a break and sat in silence for a moment until a crazy-looking old lady came past with a flock of sheep. "Wicky, wicky, wicky, wicky!" she shrieked, hurling stones at her animals to keep them moving. She stopped briefly to offer us a toothless smile, before moving on.

"Isn't this what this is all about?" I asked Dea. "Seeing the real country, meeting crazy women, instead of just rushing through on the highway?"

Dea said nothing. Tears began to roll down her cheeks.

"Oh baby, come here. What's wrong?"

"I just don't want to do this right now. This was supposed to be the easy part, but this is so hard. Maybe I'm not right for this, maybe you'd be happier by yourself. I've been feeling like going home."

I did my best to comfort Dea. She'd proven to me time and again how strong she was, how much she could do, and I had no doubt that she could handle this too, but I was sad to see her struggling like this.

We continued along on the same course, for we had gone too far to turn back and there was no way for us to return to the main road even if we wanted to. Conditions only got worse, however, and we lost the tracks as they petered out into a grassy field. Concerned for Dea's mental state, I didn't want to admit that we were lost, but we certainly were, and when a loud clap of thunder sounded overhead I knew it was time to call it a night.

"Let's get the tent up, shall we? We can figure the rest out later."

And we did just that, putting up the tent just in time to sit out the rainstorm. Once it had passed I went outside and walked around to figure out where we could find the right route again in the morning. Once that task was complete I returned to the tent and Dea and I sat and talked some more about what we wanted to do, and looked again at our maps, until we came up with a new plan. Going through the mountains of Bulgaria was scrapped in favour of a new route through Greece. I'd been against Greece because I'd heard only bad things about the standard of driving there and I preferred to stay on the small mountain roads, but Dea said that she'd read on Martin and Susanne's blog that it wasn't so bad, and I recognised now the need to compromise. By the time we were done talking things through Dea was in much better spirits, her brief desire to quit and go home replaced with a new sense of optimism.

The next morning we found our way back to tarmac and climbed up over a pass on a less busy main road, before a wonderful long descent brought us to the town of Negotino. Here we looked around for a restaurant where we could eat and use the Wi-Fi, and were tempted in by a hotel and restaurant complex that also had an outdoor swimming pool that we were allowed to use. It was just what we needed. I was so excited to find such a place after the stress of the past day and the continued heatwave that I ran to dive into the refreshing water as fast as I could. But before I got there I saw a sign asking people to shower before swimming, so I changed direction, and ran to the showers instead. After inadequately cleaning myself I stepped out of the shower ready to run back to the pool. That's when I felt my foot slip on the wet floor. Instinctively I put my other foot down as I fought to keep my balance, but unfortunately that slipped too. Then I had no feet helping me keep my balance, and in fact both of my feet were above my head, which was a bad sign, and a warning of the impending impact. I landed square on my back on the hard floor. I lay there for a moment in shock. A cleaning lady started shouting in Macedonian and Dea came over. "I'm okay," I said. And I was, but only just. My head had missed hitting the hard, sharp edge surrounding the shower cubicle by a matter of centimetres.

But that wasn't the only danger to my health. On our last night in Macedonia, unable to find anything better, we'd made camp behind some vineyards, and we awoke in the morning to the sound of tractors. The workers were already out spraying, and judging from the harsh taste in the air and the masks on their faces, they were spraying poison. Well, that's what you get for sleeping on someone else's land, I suppose. We packed up and moved on as fast as we could.

Greece, too, was somewhere I feared we might encounter trouble. I'd not done an awful lot of research into cycling in Greece, but most of what I'd heard about it was bad. Dangerous roads, dangerous drivers, dangerous dogs. I was really quite apprehensive about going there. But this could not have proved more wrong. We began Greece with a small road beside a lake, where there was nothing else in the road apart from the occasional turtle crossing. It was wonderful. Then we reached a sleepy little village, where some old men sat chatting in a café, as they do everywhere, but here there was a woman with them, more than holding her own in the conversation. I liked that a lot. We continued beyond the village and there were more quiet roads, little picnic areas with springs, fields of sunflowers, and storks nesting on electric pylons. There was no stress at all. Just easy, enjoyable cycling. To our left, above the flat plain we were now crossing, rose a giant range of formidable dark mountains.

"Is that where we would have cycled if we'd gone to Bulgaria?" Dea asked.

"Yes, I think so," I said, greatly relieved we'd changed our plans.

The people of Greece were nice without being intrusive. When we encountered some grey skies and a little rain a car stopped in front of me and a woman jumped out. She had in her hand a box of pastry treats, which she gave to me, saying nothing more than the word, "Umbrella?" and pointing to my stuff, as if to say, "Surely you have an umbrella in there somewhere?" Around the next corner I saw the same car stopped and the woman running over to give a similar box of pastry to Dea, just at the same moment that a man was calling her to come over and sit out of the rain. So we ended up sitting with this man and another woman in his garage eating delicious snacks until the worst of the weather had passed, grateful again for such acts of kindness.

Greece seemed so sleepy, so peaceful, so quiet. Even on the main roads we felt safe enough, for they were wide and not too busy. After a couple of days we found ourselves at the coast and we stopped on a private beach for a swim. It was a great place to cycle tour, and I felt so happy we'd changed our plans and come this way. We followed the coast eastwards towards the famous ancient town of Kavala, which we were excited to visit, obviously, to see the Lidl supermarket. The small shops in Greece were so expensive, and so this had become a necessary stop that we were greatly looking forward to. We arrived and spied the Lidl across the street, but our joy rapidly turned to despair. The car park was empty. The lights were off. It was closed.

So on the other side of Kavala it was with some relief that I saw a big billboard advertising all of the Lidl stores in the area and I noticed that there was still one more to come, out of the city to the east, in a town that I could neither pronounce nor remember, but I noted it began with an X. Looking at my map later I determined that it most probably was in a small village up a hill, because it was the only place I could see beginning with an X. So we cycled up there. It was the end of the day and we were both tired, and I could see Dea was getting frustrated about the steep hill, which was not even on our route. You can imagine how worried I became then, when we arrived to find that there was no Lidl in this tiny village, just a very smelly dog. It was then that I looked more closely at the map and saw that there was a bigger town, not up this hill but a bit further east, that also began with an X, which, now that I thought about it, was a much more likely destination for a Lidl. Dea took the news quite well. There are no wrong turns, after all. And our Lidl-hunting detour worked out quite well in the end, for on our way back down the hill we stumbled upon a huge abandoned marble mine. It was a pretty remarkable sight. It was a vast excavation of cleanly cut white terraces, formed by the big blocks of marble that had been systematically removed, that provided us with a flat location for us to put up our tent. After dinner Dea retired to bed and I sat alone in this great Greek amphitheatre and watched the moon rising over it. I got lost in my thoughts, reflecting back on our trip so far and realising that it had been really rather brilliant. Holland had been brilliant, Belgium had been brilliant, the Rhine was brilliant, Switzerland, the Alps, North Italy, all brilliant. Venice was brilliant, Bosnia brilliant, all of the Balkans were brilliant, actually everywhere had been brilliant. And now Greece, Greece was brilliant too.

The next day we reached the bigger town beginning with X and finally found our elusive open Lidl store. We went in very excited, but after all that effort, were disappointed to discover that it wasn't all that cheap here. We shopped anyway, it was still Lidl. Then we briefly mulled over whether it was really a good thing to visit Greece and give our money to Germany. "Oh, I'm sure they'll give it back to them eventually," I said.

Secretly, though, I was quite excited to leave Lidl behind, because it meant that Europe was drawing to a close, Turkey was just around the corner, and all of the excitement and chaos of Asia was right there ahead of us. It also meant that the European nations had been crossed, and my dream of a bikes-and-boats circumnavigation was one continent closer to being realised.

There was a positive atmosphere about us during our final couple of days in Greece, and we decided to play The Spotting Things Game one last time in Europe. I'd been doing very well since Edinburgh, and had a healthy lead in the overall standings, but on this particular day Dea made an outstanding start. We went through a village and she was spotting things left and right. By the end of it she had a formidable 6-0 lead.

"How are you feeling?" I asked her.

"Pretty confident. I think I can relax a bit now. How are you feeling?"

"Oh, I'm feeling great! I'm very excited, because the scene is now perfectly set for the greatest comeback ever in the history of The Spotting Things Game!"

I think Dea must have got a little bit nervous when I said this, and her face had practically gone white by the time we were through the next village.

"Shepherd!" I screamed. "Yellow car! Pigeon! CAT!!! CAT!!!"

The score was suddenly back to 6-5, and Dea was looking anything but relaxed.

I was determined now. I had to win this game. Unfortunately Dea saw another couple of things on her own list, and moved into an 8-5 lead. But as the day went on we headed out towards the coast again, and I still had to spot a fisherman and a topless man, so I thought I was in with a chance. I also needed a snake and a turtle, and I was scouring the road for them. This went on for a long time, until we passed over a pond of water and I glanced at it and saw what looked like a turtle diving. I went back to check and saw that there were actually lots of turtles, a whole pond of them. They all bobbed up to the surface to see what was going on, and what was going on was that I was back in the game. From then on, I knew I had to win it. A short while later we reached the sea and I saw a fisherman throwing in his line, and the score had been tied up at 8-8. Dea was fretting now, searching frantically for a blue and white tablecloth that just wasn't there. It remained 8-8 for a while, only adding to the anticipation, until, with the most dramatic swish a little snake danced across the road right in front of me. "SNAKE!" I cried. "SNAKE! DEA! It's a snake! It's 9-8! I can't believe it!" I was almost in tears. "I'm winning!" And we cycled on a few hundred metres into another little village, and I heard some girls sitting on a balcony, and just as I looked up at them, there emerged from behind them a topless man, his bronzed Greek torso looking down on me like a heroic God. "TOPLESS MAN! TOPLESS MAN! DEA! DEA! TOPLESS MAN!!! It's 10-8! I can't believe it! I've won! I've won! From 6-0 down! From 6-0 down! From 8-5 down! To win it 10-8! This is the greatest comeback ever! I've done it! I've done it!" The girls on the balcony started whistling. They must have known. Somehow, they must have known. It was truly an incredible, incredible moment. Absolutely incredible.

Dea didn't care too much for it though

32

Turkish border
22nd June 2017

Where is your e-visa?" the policeman demanded.
"I don't know. It's an e-visa. It's electronic. It's in the cyber world somewhere isn't it?" I said, wondering how this could possibly be happening. Turkey's very simple online e-visa system had been up and running for three years, and I'd assumed that when they scanned my passport at the border it would automatically come up on their system. No such luck. They wanted to physically see my electronic visa, and it took several frustrating trips back and forth between the border post and a nearby police station, with nobody quite sure what to do with me, and me muttering all that time that "surely this must have come up at some point in the last three years," before I fired up my laptop and showed them a confirmation e-mail I'd received. Finally we were allowed into the country. We had arrived in Turkey.

We were both very excited to be back. I'd enjoyed my ride here in 2014, while Dea had spent a semester studying in Istanbul in 2015, and she was now very keen to see what the rest of the country was like beyond the confines of the big city. It started with a long stint on the wide shoulder of a main highway. The country seemed to stretch out forever in front of us, everything suddenly enlarged and expanded by the vast open vistas that surrounded us.

After twenty-five kilometres we reached a big town, Keşan, and needed to go into it to look for an ATM and a supermarket. The streets were chaotic and stressful to cycle on, choked with traffic and people, honking horns, shouting, and dust.

"This is just how it's going to be from now on, isn't it?" Dea said, pragmatically alright with the disorderliness of Asia.

"No, I hope not," I replied. I was hoping we would continue to take smaller roads and avoid these bigger towns as much as possible, but this was a necessary stop. We withdrew some lira and did some shopping, and being reacquainted with the fantastic variety of biscuits on offer in Turkey certainly raised my spirits as we headed back towards the highway.

We cycled on across the sparse open landscape, then climbed gradually up into a forest through the afternoon. Dark clouds formed overhead, warning of an impending rainstorm. We noticed a rare building close to the road and headed towards it, hoping for shelter. Before we even got to it a group of men appeared, urging us on, with their cries of "chai, chai" rolling back the years for me. Once we got closer we saw that it was a fire station, and I was encouraged to put my bike in the garage beside the fire engine, where it would stay dry. It was also blocking the fire engine in a bit, so I hoped that there wasn't going to be a fire during the heavy rainstorm. Inside we were handed glasses of tea and given seats opposite the firemen as the rain began to lash down outside. We were very grateful to have been saved from a soaking but the Turkish hospitality didn't end there, and a spread of tomato, cucumber, cheese, olives and bread was laid out on the table in front of us. We ate it somewhat awkwardly, for it was still Ramadan, and none of the hungry men staring at us could eat, though they all insisted we do so. On the wall beside us was a map of the whole of Turkey, and after we'd done eating we studied it, making a rough plan for our route in the process.

"It really is a big country, isn't it?" Dea said. I could tell that she was feeling a little apprehensive about the task ahead. "I've never cycled across such a big country before."

"It'll be okay. We'll just take it one day at a time, and enjoy all the tea," I said, as a fireman approached with more for us.

The skies cleared and on we went, setting up camp on a hill over-looking the sea where we watched a pink sunset and agreed that it felt really great to be in Turkey. The next morning, however, our campsite felt momentarily less secure when three men in army fatigues holding machine guns appeared over the hill striding towards us. *'So, this is what the Tent Police look like,'* I worried for a moment. But then the soldiers changed direction and, without appearing to have any actual interest in us or what we were doing, they left again. Yet it had somehow been an appropriate sight, for it came as we began our brief cycle on the Gallipoli peninsular, the location of the Gallipoli landings and sight of the great First World War battles that, in victory, helped lead to the formation of the modern-day nation of Turkey.

We continued to follow the highway until the town of Gallipoli, where we hopped on a ferry that took us quickly across to Anatolia, the Asian part of Turkey. We had reached a new continent, but not permanently. We wanted to return to Europe by visiting the great city of Istanbul, and had come up with an ingenious plan to get there without having to trouble ourselves with the hassle of cycling through a city of eighteen million people. Instead we rode through Anatolia until we reached the town of Bandirma on the southern shores of the Marmara Sea, where we got on another ferry. This whisked us quickly and effortlessly across the waters, and directly to the heart of Istanbul's old town.

Taking the boat into Istanbul proved to be the correct decision, as we disembarked right beside the historic centre, and on a bicycle path no less. We followed this path as it circled around the coastline within sight of the iconic Blue Mosque and Hagia Sophia, then made our way over a bridge where hundreds of locals still stood with their fishing lines dangling down into the Bosphorus, past the point where three years earlier I'd met with Suzy and Dino for the first time, and then up along the narrow hilly backstreets. Things were strangely quiet here, the result apparently of many people having left the city to celebrate the end of Ramadan, but the peacefulness soon evaporated when we arrived on Istiklal, the famous main street in the modern part of town. There were police everywhere among the crowds, and all of the side roads joining the street were blocked by armoured vehicles. I wondered if this police presence was to try and prevent another terrorist attack against this country that had suffered so many over recent years, or simply a show of force in light of the previous year's attempted coup. Either way it was an unsettling sight.

We had rented a studio apartment just off Istiklal for four nights through AirBnb, and we were welcomed by Erdin, the owner. After helping us to move in he of course invited us to drink tea with him, and as we did so he explained to us that the police presence was actually only because of a Gay Pride parade that was due to take place down Istiklal on this day. It had been banned by the government, and the police were there to make absolutely sure that it couldn't go ahead. I had thought that the hundreds of armed officers and armoured vehicles had been there to protect everyone from the twenty-first century threat posed by murderous terrorists, but no, it turned out they were just there to keep out the homosexuals.

It was nice to have our own place to relax for a few days and recuperate before the next stage of our journey. We had a few things to get done, including applying for a Letter of Introduction for Uzbekistan (a prerequisite for applying for a visa) which stated that we'd be entering the country on the 15th of August. This meant we would have to pick up our pace a little bit in order to make it on time, but I knew that Dea was getting worried about making it through the high mountains of Tajikistan and Kyrgyzstan before it got too cold, so it was time to get a move on anyway. With this in mind we had to make the most of our little Istanbul break, and it gave us a good chance to keep in touch with our families. I knew that back home Summer and Finley were suffering with chicken pox, so before video calling with them I covered my own face in dots of ink with a marker pen. They were quite amused by this show of moral support, although I'm not quite sure what Erdin thought of it when he knocked on our door a little later on and I opened it having quite forgotten about my spotty face.

But our best experiences in Istanbul came when we left the apartment and ventured out into one of the world's great cities, and especially so when we met up with a friend of both of ours. Özgür had been my saviour three years earlier, welcoming me into his home after one of the hardest cycling days of my entire trip, and he and his mother had done a great job of looking after me as I immediately fell ill. But I wasn't the only one enjoying a reunion with Özgür as we sat down to dinner at a cosy little café on one of the backstreets. Dea also knew him from her time in Istanbul as, after I'd put them in touch, they'd realised that he worked in an office right next to the university Dea was studying at, so they'd met up a few times for coffee. It was great to see the kind, gentle Özgür again, and to hear that both he and his mother were doing well, and I loved that returning this way was giving me the opportunity to reconnect with people I'd met the first time around. But there was also some slight cause for concern when, even though the heavy police presence around Istiklal was gone by now, Özgür told us that he no longer really felt safe in Istanbul. While it wasn't obvious at first glance, there was surely no doubt that times had changed for the people here.

One thing we absolutely had to do while we were in Istanbul was to visit the place where Dea had lived during the four months she'd spent studying here. It was on the Asian side of the Bosphorus, and so one day we took a ferry over there. It was nice to do this together with her, getting off in Asia and walking up through a lively local neighbourhood, just as she had once done on a daily basis on her commute to university. She led me up a steep hill and showed me her old apartment building, the place where she'd been while I'd been cycling through Southeast Asia, the place where she'd sat and set her heart on coming to join me in Australia. From outside this apartment there was a beautiful view back over the Bosphorus and Istanbul, so we took a seat on a bench and held hands and thought about how amazing it was to be back here together.

"The first time I sat here I'd just come back from being with you in Laos," Dea reminded me. "I was so excited about cycling with you again. I was only half present in my life as a student here, all I thought about was going on a bicycle and travelling the world. Sometimes I saw a cycle tourist in the city and I longed to be like them."

"And now you are!"

"I know, it's incredible!"

Progress Report
Istanbul, June 2017

1. Circumnavigate the planet

Completed.

2. Do so using only my bicycle and boats

Mori: 90.3° E. Istanbul: 28.9° E.
298.6° out of 360° around the planet.
(82.9% of the way around.)

3. Pass through antipodal points

...total distance travelled (by bicycle and boat combined)
would be close to *double* the circumference of the planet
at the equator...

4. Visit all of the inhabited continents

Still four out of six.

5. Cycle at least 100,000 kilometres

67,016 kilometres completed (67.016%).

6. Cycle in 100 countries

The Balkans and Greece brought it up to sixty-one.

7. Return with more money than I start with

Initial sales of the book were a bit disappointing, but I
found three euros.

PART FIVE

ISTANBUL TO ALMATY

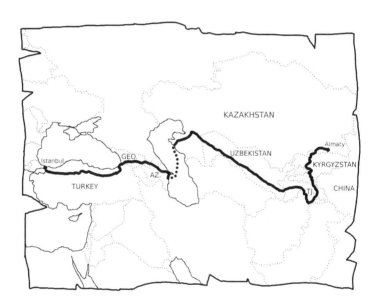

33

Istanbul, Turkey
29th June 2017

"Would you like to play a game?" Dea asked as we rode along on the waterfront cycle path. "We could spot cats?"

Obviously I did want to play a game spotting cats, it would be a very odd situation indeed for me to refuse that kind of challenge, but truth be told my heart wasn't quite in it. This was how I came to explain Dea's early 5-0 lead, anyway.

"Cat, cat, cat!" she went on.

'Yeah, whatever,' I thought. I was in a melancholy mood. It was a bit strange, because we were following a fantastic cycle path through the Asian part of Istanbul, from Kadıköy to Pendik. I knew it was a great place for us to cycle, because I'd ridden it before, three years earlier, the first time around. But that was the problem. For the first time on our trip together I was literally retracing my wheelturns, and it naturally brought back memories and encouraged comparisons. This excellent cycle path had been my first introduction to Asia (and quite a misleading one, at that). I had been so excited about all that was ahead, but now I kind of knew what was ahead, and I was a bit anxious about it. Asia. Again. Really? Was I up for the challenge? And was it still going to be as exciting as it had been the first time around?

"Cat, cat!"

Dea was 12-6 ahead by this stage. Even Istanbul's famous stray cats were against me. I needed to snap out of this, pull myself together.

"Ah, but Dea, the scene is now perfectly set for the greatest comeback in the hist-"

"Cat, cat!"she interrupted, as she brought the score to 14-6. Dammit. I was going to need a miracle to come back. But then I happened to peer over some rocks by the water near to Dea's last cat spot, and there I saw a litter of kittens.

"Cat, cat, cat, cat!" and the score was 14-10.

On we went, Dea pushing ahead, scouring the parks we went through for felines with such intensity that she failed to look inside the open door of a little café. I looked in, and saw five cats lounging around on the floor. Maybe Asia wasn't going to be so bad after all.

With Dea still smarting from becoming the victim of the greatest cat-spotting comeback ever seen we took the ferry from Pendik to Yalova, escaping the busy roads east out of Istanbul by returning to the southern shore of the Marmara Sea. In Yalova we happened upon a bike shop where I asked after a new gel seat cover to put over my ridiculously misshapen Brooks saddle. The shop owner looked at my saddle, what was left of the last chewed-up gel cover clinging to it in a mess of electrical tape, and sighed. He told me via very impressive sign language that what I needed there was not a new saddle cover, but a new saddle.

"Do you know how much that saddle cost? It's only done 120,000 kilometres. Got to get my money's worth," I said, before adding, "and I can't get the damn thing off anyway."

He threw his arms up in despair, and we left. A few minutes later he came panting after us on his own bike. He'd found a gel seat cover from somewhere, good man that he was. I bought it from him and he left again, still shaking his head.

With me sitting slightly more comfortably we made our way up the hill out of Yalova and had a nice camping place in some trees, before continuing the next morning towards Iznik on a road that took us through olive groves and past men selling freshly picked fruit from rickety wooden stalls. At Iznik we found a beach where we bathed and ate ice creams surrounded by Turkish families, then rode the narrow backstreets across town. We made a stop at a grocers to buy some fruit, and soon found ourselves invited to sit and drink tea with the kind old owner. Everything seemed to be going very nicely in Asia, but unfortunately then came the road east out of Iznik. It was a narrow, two-lane road, very busy with lots of trucks powering along blasting their horns. There was nothing in the way of a shoulder and it was simply too dangerous for us to cycle on. We needed a plan, and the opportunity to think of one came when we were invited to sit and drink tea by one of the roadside fruit sellers. He was a very friendly man who gave us a bag of fruit to enjoy with our tea, and then went off on his scooter and came back with ice creams too. Turkish people, as I well remembered, were proving themselves extremely hospitable.

"You just wait, Dea, we'll soon be meeting Mehmet."

"I know, I can't wait."

Mehmet was a man that I'd met when I cycled this route three years before who had invited me in for tea, then when I left had followed me and made me go to another tea house and drink more. I had the feeling he would have followed me all across Turkey drinking tea with me if he could, and he'd earned himself a place in my first book as an example of how generous Turkish people were with their glasses of tea.

"Oh, we're going to get plenty of tea when we find Mehmet, don't worry about that Dea."

"Great!"

The nice man who'd given us tea in the present situation suggested to us that we could sleep on some sofas that were set up beside his stall, but seeing as they were also right beside the busy road we declined. Instead we rode off and made camp behind an old olive grove.

A few hours later we were awake and ready to implement the cunning plan we'd come up with. It was not yet four in the morning and still very dark. We packed up by the light of our head torches, then, as we pushed our bikes out of the olive grove, the sky began to lighten and the call to prayer echoed around the hillsides. It was a special moment, that reminded me instantly why I was doing this. We were on an exciting adventure, far from home, no doubt about that.

The previously busy road was now almost empty, and we cycled quickly onwards, feeling excited to be awake before most of the world. In a small town a few dogs barked at us and a handful of the more dedicated followers of Allah traipsed along the road, returning home after their morning prayers, but otherwise we were the only ones enjoying the sunrise. The skies lightened, the sun climbed up over the hills in front of us, and we made it to a wider, safer road just in time before the rest of the world awoke and the morning traffic began.

We stopped in another town for a burek breakfast before continuing on some really nice small roads. We were even more of an unusual sight on these, and before the morning was out we had accepted two further invitations to stop and drink tea with insisting men.

"They really want us to drink tea with them, don't they?"

"This is nothing. You just wait until we see Mehmet!" I said. "We may never be allowed to stop drinking tea!"

We climbed up for some time, often steeply, into a landscape of pine forests. It was very, very hot and very hard work, but it was worth it, because at the top we found my old friend Mehmet.

He was outside of the little tea-house/restaurant/home that he'd invited me into before, standing at the roadside next to a wooden stall laden with fresh fruit. Dea and I stopped and looked over at him. He started shouting across the road at us, thinking that we might want to buy some of his fruit. We went over to him.

"Mehmet?" I asked.

There was not the slightest hint of recognition in his face. He had not the faintest idea who I was.

"No, Mehmish," he said.

Oh no, I'd got his name wrong all these years! It was probably best not to show him the book then. Having told me his correct name and showing not the least interest in how it was that I had almost known it, Mehmish went back to trying to sell us his fruit, talking rapidly in

Turkish in his familiar way.

"No, no. We don't want fruit, we already have loads. Wait a minute," I said. And I pulled my laptop out of my bag, and found the photos I had from my first visit, of him standing proudly with his son and wife. He looked at it, momentarily confused as to how I had a photo of him on my laptop, and then it dawned on him what was going on. The bemused look on his face was instantly wiped away by a broad smile. He remembered me now, and seemed pleased. Dea and I were invited to take a seat in the shade, and we were given yet more fruit, now for free. He explained that his son was away, studying at a university in Ankara. His wife was still around though, wearing the exact same headscarf she'd sported three years earlier, in fact. I'd not had a chance to talk with her then, as with most women in Turkey she had been in the background, but this time she came up to Dea and spoke with her. It was nice. We were welcome to stay a little while, and Dea even took a brief nap she was so exhausted by the hills and the heat and getting up at four in the morning. Before we moved on, Mehmet (he'll always be Mehmet to me) gave me a gift of a white baseball cap with 'Evet' written on it, the Turkish word for yes. "Evet, evet!" he said enthusiastically, as he put it on my head. He sure was an odd man. A kind one, though, and it had been great to see him again, but one thing puzzled me as we waved goodbye and cycled onwards.

"I can't understand it Dea. I really thought he would've offered us some tea."

We camped in a pine forest and then continued the next day over more big hills in more extreme heat. A moment of reprieve came when we stopped at a little shop and met a man and wife. The woman was sitting outside making gözleme, a traditional food. We were curious, and so she invited us to sit and watch her work. She rolled out balls of dough with great skill, until they were unbelievably thin circles. Then she added in fillings, sometimes spinach, sometimes cheese or mashed potato, then folded them over and fried them. It was fascinating to watch her hands work so rapidly, so automatically knowing the right movements. We got to try the end product, and of course they were delicious.

We descended from the pine forests in the direction of an other-world-type landscape that I remembered so well from my first visit. But first we had to get through the bigger town of Nallihan, and we stopped in the centre to stock up on supplies. After getting what we needed we took a seat in the busy town square to rest and watch the people. Of course they also noticed us, and we had quite a few visitors. The best of these was undoubtedly a young man called Deniz. He told us that he was a geologist who lived in Ankara and was here visiting relatives. He seemed kind and he could speak English, a considerable rarity for such encounters, so we invited him to sit down so that we could have a talk that extended beyond the usual few sentences we could manage in Turkish. And it seemed to be extending into the field of politics when he asked me, "Do you like Erdoğan?"

I wondered how I should respond on such a controversial subject, but before I could formulate any kind of response Deniz continued, "It's just because, your cap, it means that you support him, it means to vote yes in the referendum."

Dammit Mehmet! Forcing your political opinions on me. I took the cap off and threw it in the bin.

We had a really nice long chat with Deniz. As a geologist he was able to tell us more about the incredible rock formations of the area, and the other-planet landscape that was ahead of us. I told him that I'd seen it before, and took out a copy of my book to show him what I'd written about it. He seemed to like the book and what Dea and I were doing, and maybe it even gave him some inspiration for his own life too. "This is, how do you say, a lightbulb moment for me!" he beamed, and hearing this I decided to give him the book as a gift. He thanked us profusely. "I just wish there was something I could give you. Oh wait, I have." And he dug a scarf out of his backpack, a scarf that would soon become one of Dea's most prized possessions.

Dea and I rode happily on and set up camp soon after, on a cliff that looked down over the start of that incredible other-planet landscape of pink and yellow stripey rocks. As I sat there, looking down towards it, I thought back over the previous few days, cycling this same road I'd been on before, and yet how different, and how amazing it had been. We'd met so many people, enjoyed so much generous hospitality, been made to feel so welcome by everybody. I smiled and looked over my shoulder. Dea was walking around our campsite. She was wearing her baggy traveller trousers and a sports bra, her blonde hair tied up by her new scarf. She looked radiant in the light of the setting sun. I thought back on when I'd last passed this way, all alone, dreaming of finding someone to join me. How could I ever dare to believe I could get this lucky? My initial apprehension about returning to Asia was gone. We had such a great adventure ahead of us, we really did, the two of us, together.

34

Central Turkey
4th July 2017

We skirted around Ankara to the north, seeing no reason to go into Turkey's sprawling capital. Last time around I'd spent close to two weeks in the city organising visas for Central Asia, but in just three years things had become significantly less complicated on that front. The benefits of increased levels of tourism must have hit home to the majority of the Stan countries, and they almost all now offered either visa-free travel or at least simple online e-visa applications. The only exception on our route was Uzbekistan, but we'd heard that we could get that visa without too much trouble in Baku, Azerbaijan, so there was no need for us to go into Ankara.

Instead we made our way by the smallest roads that we could, in farmed valleys and over small mountain ranges, through empty villages and past colourful mosques that five times a day would blare out the call to prayer. Our life fell into a routine of cycling by day, camping by night, of washing in and filling our water bottles from the natural springs all over the country, and of stopping at every gas station to eat ice cream. Turkey was its usual hospitable self. Everywhere we went we were met with smiles and greetings and waves, and many, many times we were invited to stop, to share food and tea with some of the most welcoming people in the world. One such occasion, in a town in the middle of Turkey called Çubuk, was particularly memorable for me. This was because the invitation to stop and drink tea came not from a man as it usually did, but from a middle-aged woman who, like all such women, had a shawl wrapped around her head and was covered in more clothes than I would have liked to wear in such heat. She led both Dea and I into a part of Turkey I had never seen before. It was a sewing workshop, where several women of different ages were sitting around, one or two working at machines in the shop, the others just there for the gossip. I had, for the first time, entered into the women's world. And soon there was tea poured and given out to everyone in little glasses, and it was just like in all of the tea houses across Turkey, except instead of Dea feeling out of place as the only female, now it was my turn to be seeing across the gender divide. And the women smiled and laughed and gossiped and I saw that it wasn't so very different from what the men did. Except the women got a bit of work done.

At a place called Turhal we joined a main highway and planned to follow it for a few days as there were no alternative roads through this section of the country. The highways in Turkey were generally quite safe as they had wide shoulders, and they allowed us to make ground faster than on the back roads. We preferred to be on the quieter roads, as they gave us the chance to really be in Turkey instead of the isolated experience we got on the highways, but the main roads did at least have more gas stations, and therefore more ice cream breaks.

It wasn't always easy to find places to camp. One night, seventeen kilometres before the city of Tokat, we left the highway and found an orchard that seemed quiet enough to camp at the back of. Before we could put up our tent, however, the owner of the orchard turned up in his car, but that was alright because he was Turkish, and therefore very friendly. He asked us if there was anything we needed, and then left us to it.

We put up the tent and cooked some dinner on our little camping stove, our happy little evening routine, and then lay down in the tent. The temperature was hot, as always, and before long I started to feel quite uncomfortable. I felt very sick, actually, and had to make a sudden bolt out of the tent. I didn't get very far before throwing up my dinner in the poor man's orchard. Unfortunately this didn't make me feel any better at all, and a short while later I was at it again. And again. My stomach was empty but I kept on retching up nothing. It was all very reminiscent of one night long ago in Turkmenistan. Dea comforted me for a while, but there was really nothing she could do. I dragged my sleeping mat outside and lay there in the cooler air. Every twenty or thirty minutes a horrible hot feeling would wash over me and I'd have to vomit, a horrible new routine that continued for the whole long, miserable night.

By morning I felt truly horrendous. I had not slept and I had no food or water in my system. The most worrying part was that I could not hold down any liquids at all, meaning that, not only did I not have any energy left, but I was also seriously dehydrated. I honestly felt like I needed to be in a hospital. I needed to be on a drip.

The owner of the orchard returned to see how we were getting on. He chose a rather inopportune moment, for it coincided with one of my more spectacular vomiting episodes. He looked very concerned. I looked at his car. I knew that the only sensible thing to do in my condition was to ask him for a lift to hospital.

But of course I'm not really known for being sensible, and there was no chance I was going to be getting in a car so long as I was still capable of movement. Sure, I was dangerously dehydrated, with no food or water in my system, and I hadn't slept all night, but if there was one thing I was confident my body knew how to do on autopilot in any circumstances, it was to ride a bike. In fact I was pretty sure my body could go on riding a bike even if I was unconscious, which was a theory I was getting perilously close to testing as we returned to the highway and turned our wheels in the direction of Tokat. My whole body ached, my mind drifted, and it took everything I had just to keep turning the pedals. After a long two kilometres we came to a gas station and I simply had to stop. Dea looked concerned, and bought me some cold water and a can of sugary orange juice to try and revive me before the day grew too hot for me to stand any chance. I sipped at the drinks cautiously. There was still fifteen kilometres to go to Tokat, and it felt like my hopes of making it under my own power before I was disabled by complete dehydration rested on holding these drinks down. While I tried to mentally talk my stomach muscles into not turning themselves inside out again, Dea ran off to ask the gas station attendants about where we might be able to find hotels and hospitals in Tokat.

I didn't really want to get up again, but I knew we had better continue before the sun got too high in the sky. I wobbled my way back to the road and focused on just turning the pedals to Tokat, counting the kilometres constantly. I was expecting to be back on my knees vomiting at any moment, but somehow the water and juice stayed down, and my confidence grew. Slowly but surely we made our way into Tokat, but the city was big and busy and there were no hotels on the main road as we'd been promised. Instead we diverted in towards the city centre, but none of the many people that we asked were able to direct us towards a bed. It was a nightmare. All I wanted was for somewhere to lie down, but I had to go through this agonising process of hunting all over town for it. Finally we sat down at a café to ask to use the Wi-Fi, and spotted a cheap hotel behind it at just about the same moment that the owner came over and, seeing my weak, fraught, unable-to-stand condition, told us that there was a hospital just across the street. Somehow I'd made it.

We moved into a small room at the hotel and I fell instantly asleep. When I awoke in the afternoon I was feeling a bit better and, now able to eat and drink again, the hospital was thankfully not required in the end. But it had been a warning for sure; I knew that my goal of a continuous circumnavigation without motor vehicles was still very far from assured, and things could go wrong at any moment. I actually felt lucky that this had happened where it had, so close to a city and not out in the middle of nowhere, far from water, sugary orange juice, and beds.

That night Dea also got sick, although not as badly as me, and we took the next day off in order for us both to recover. Unfortunately this delay only made Dea more worried about our lack of progress. Her concerns were perfectly logical. She had never done anything like the Pamir Highway before – cycling on very remote gravel roads at altitudes in excess of 4,000 metres – and I could well understand why she would not want to make things harder by attempting to do so in the middle of winter. I was a bit more laid-back about it myself, having had the experience of riding the Pamir Highway before, and having cycled in some pretty cold places, and because I believed in Dea completely. She continually impressed me with her perseverance and resilience and physical capabilities, and I had no doubt that we could handle whatever obstacles came our way. But I also understood her point that there was no sense in making a hard challenge that much harder, and getting to Central Asia before winter was surely the best thing to do. So in order to keep up our progress we worked out a schedule that would get us to Baku in twenty-four days, which was roughly what we needed to do to stay on track for arriving in Uzbekistan on the date we'd applied for. This actually only required us to cycle eighty kilometres per day, and I went so far as to make a spreadsheet, entitling it the '24-day Tokat-to-Baku challenge'. It made us both feel better to have this target written down, at least briefly.

The next morning I did not feel so good about our new challenge. I was still feeling rotten and I did not want to get out of bed and cycle again. Had I been on my own I would have stayed another day to recover, but I knew I had to consider Dea and our promise to start moving forward faster. I was irritable and frustrated and not very good company, just turning the pedals and trying to get through the day.

Gradually over the next few days I returned to normal, but the atmosphere of our trip seemed to have changed. Up until Tokat it had all been so good, but for these days neither of us enjoyed ourselves. The 24-day Tokat-to-Baku challenge, far from making things easier, had only added extra pressure, and cycling on the highway being constantly beeped at all day, every day, brought few moments of joy to our lives. This was not the way that either of us wanted to experience this trip, just rushing along on a highway, cycling only to get somewhere else.

We decided that we needed to get off the highway, and taking some smaller roads again made us both feel better about things. They led us off down a picturesque river valley, through some small villages, and back into the real Turkey. Then we hit an even more dramatic river valley that was almost entirely unpopulated, and it felt great to be somewhere so remote, cycling on a little traffic-free road through scenery that was often truly breathtaking. Smiles had returned to our faces.

We dared to believe that this perfect cycling might continue for several hundred kilometres, but unfortunately the road grew much busier further east. The valley continued, but there was also a drastic change to its appearance and atmosphere, brought about by the hand of man. In a series of places the valley had been blocked by hydroelectric dams, and instead of a peaceful little river, all there was to look at now was a series of giant reservoirs. It was sad to think that the people who once called this valley home were long gone, their homes now underwater, and the new road that we cycled on clung high up on the cliffsides. It was a horrible, lifeless place. The reservoir waters filled the whole valley from one steep grey cliff to the other, and it felt almost surreal, all of the plants and creatures and life of the valley washed away.

Further east the flooded valley became narrower, the cliffs steeper, and the only way that the road could continue was through a series of tunnels. Thankfully they were never more than two kilometres long, but when one ended there was usually only a short reprieve before the next began. It became quite ridiculous in the end, these never--ending tunnels, and over the course of a day and a half we passed though no less than fifty of them. They were at least well-lit, and had footpaths we could cycle on, but these paths were not without obstacles. Usually there would be a big kerb to get up onto them, there were often random slabs missing which would be difficult to navigate around, occasionally a road sign or sharp metal pole stuck out from the wall threatening to decapitate us for not paying attention, and every so often a truck would beep loudly at us... in a f*cking tunnel.

Eventually we made it through to the big town of Artvin, a welcome sight for it indicated that the end of the hydroelectric dams was

near. We stopped in town to buy groceries and bumped into two foreigners. Simon from Sweden and his American girlfriend Ann were
long time travellers who'd been in Georgia trekking up in the mountains and had just crossed over into Turkey to do the same, indicating
to us how close we were now getting to the border. They were both
very nice people and Simon had done a lot of bike travelling too, but
I had a bit of an odd feeling talking to them. Then I realised why this
was – they were the first non-Turkish people we'd encountered in
over a month in the country.

The next morning – our last in Turkey – was spent cycling up a
pass on a narrow road, through lush green forest and tea plantations
that covered hillsides shrouded in mist and cloud. It reminded me of
Costa Rica, and was in complete contrast to the hot, dry, sunny, and
quite yellow environment we'd experienced through most of the
country. The explanation for the sudden change was the climactic
effects of the vast Black Sea on the north of Turkey, and it was this
that we descended down towards on the other side of the pass. Here
we joined the coast road, the big highway that we could have cycled
on all the way from Istanbul had we wanted to, and we realised we'd
made the right choice in cycling further south, away from all the
heavy traffic that plied this route.

About fifteen kilometres from the border with Georgia we
stopped to spend the last of our Turkish lira, not surprisingly on ice
cream. As we sat there beside the busy highway we agreed that we'd
had a good time of it in Turkey. It seemed to have gone by so fast, yet
there had been so many good experiences crammed in. At times it had
been brilliant and at times it had been very hard work. The people
had been wonderful, some of the hills and intense heat had been challenging, but we certainly felt a sense of achievement to have made it
through, and we were probably leaving stronger than we'd been at
the start.

Just as we finished up our ice creams and prepared to move on, a
touring cyclist pulled up alongside us. He was a man in his fifties,
dressed from head to toe in layers of clothing that made him look
more like he was riding in mid-winter than mid-summer. He pulled

down his neck-warmer and greeted us. "Hello," he said, "I'm from Greece. Well, actually I live in New York, but there's plenty of time to talk about that. Which way are you going? To Georgia? Me too!"

We had just met Vassili.

35

Eastern Turkey
23rd July 2017

I immediately thought Vassili to be a most intriguing character, as he began explaining to us the logic behind his excess of clothing. "I was in the Sahara desert and I almost died from dehydration," he said. "And I was saved by the Bedouins there. And I looked at how they dressed, they're all covered up aren't they? So then I thought, ah yes, that's the way to do it, that's the way to survive in the heat. It's the same reason I drink a lot of hot tea when it's hot. Do you know why? It makes the body cool itself down."

Vassili pulled his neck warmer up and the three of us cycled on together, passing by long queues of trucks as we closed in on the Georgian border, that forced us to ride out in the fast lane of the dual carriageway. Almost unbelievably when the road passed through more tunnels the queue of stationary trucks continued, an unbroken line of lorries in the gloom. To get around this obstacle Dea and I hopped up onto the footpath on the other side of the tunnel, while Vassili simply continued down the middle of the roadway, completely without lights.

It was a relief to reach the border all of us intact. Having cycled this way before I knew that we would find no tunnels on the Georgian side. Had I thought about it a little more I might have remembered the utter chaos we would find instead, but I was too distracted by the sight of Vassili merrily snapping photographs of the border area while standing right in front of a serious-looking official. He wasn't the most streetwise of travellers, perhaps, but he was an endearing fellow nonetheless. A Greek national in his late-fifties, Vassili had told us he worked as a Professor of Economics at a New York university and was making his bicycle ride along the Silk Road a multi-year project. Each season he returned to ride for a few weeks and further his progress which had originally begun from Greece. This latest section of the journey had started in the Black Sea city of Trabzon just a few days earlier and was destined to end in Baku, which meant our routes and schedules now aligned in a way that made it almost inevitable we would be riding together, at least for a little while.

Once the border official had concluded that Vassili was not a Bedouin spy but merely a bit naïve we were all allowed out of Turkey. Getting into Georgia was a bit more tricky. We weren't allowed through with the other vehicles, and instead had to walk our bikes on an unnecessarily long, circuitous walk through the border building, and then wait in a crowd of impatient, aggressive people, where our bikes got in everyone's way and almost caused a fight to break out. This was our introduction to Georgia. A new country. A new culture. And a new companion.

It did not take long for my memories of cycling into Georgia to be rekindled. The wide dual carriageway shrank to a narrow two-lane road, busy with chaotic drivers. Dea and I retreated to the shoulder, which in this case was not a shoulder, but rather the hard mud and dirt and grass and gravel and whatever else happened to be beside the road. We watched on as Vassili continued on the limited tarmac, with cars swerving around him, swerving around each other making risky overtakes, and swerving around the cows, which were wandering aimlessly about everywhere. It was simply madness. Ah yes, it was Georgia alright.

With an enormous sense of relief we arrived at the edge of the coastal town of Batumi and switched over to a cycle path along the promenade. Oh, what bliss this was! It felt good to be back in Batumi. I remembered it as an extremely odd place, full of weird and wonderful buildings and sculptures that made no real sense at all. Now it made slightly more sense, for unlike on my previous visit it was now summer, and there were lots of holiday-makers around that these things pandered to. Tourists from Russia, from Saudi Arabia, from all sorts of places, were here to relax and, presumably, escape the real world for a bit. As we cycled on towards the centre of town the cycle path grew busy with vacationers pedalling rented four-person sit-down bikes, or whizzing along on rented electric scooters. It reminded me of our time in Surfers Paradise. It was the same kind of random place. The kind of place where you can pass a giant pair of sandals resting on a dozen giant eggs and not look twice.

Dea and I had booked a hotel room and we made our way towards it. We'd been looking forward to a night of relaxation, a bit of privacy from the world before continuing on. Vassili tagged along with us, of course. I'd told him that when we'd made the booking it had said we were taking the last available room, but he wanted to come along just to be sure. We'd booked the cheapest available hotel, of course, and as a result it was situated several kilometres away from the town centre, on a pot-holed backstreet. It took quite a bit of locating, for there were no signs, and once we got inside we realised it was really just somebody's house. The three of us were shown to our room and my heart sank a little when I saw that there were two double beds in it. Vassili asked the owners if there were any other rooms available, but there were not. He sat down on one of the beds, looking up at us forlornly with puppy-dog eyes. "I'll just go somewhere else," he said sadly.

I slept very badly. The double bed was just a fold-out sofa-bed and was extremely uncomfortable, and there were also mosquitoes in the room. The biggest problem, however, was the very loud snoring that bore right through my ear plugs and into my skull. For once it wasn't coming from the lovely Dea, whose melancholic nightly exhalations I'd become accustomed to. No, this unbearable noise was coming from the nostrils of our new Greek friend, who we had of course let share the room. And I think in his defence he must have been very tired, for we'd just spent the evening walking some distance into town and back to see what must surely be one of Batumi's great highlights – the dancing fountains. Dea had never seen a dancing fountain before, and she found the bright lights and rhythmic watery movements quite enchanting. I daresay it would have made for quite a romantic evening, were it not for the Greek man sitting beside us, occasionally making bizarre random comments. And on the walk back to the hotel, poor Vassili had started limping very badly. He said he had something wrong with one of his hips, but he refused our suggestion to take a taxi, proudly stating that he would make it on foot, even as he dragged one leg behind him in a motion that made me hope Kevin Spacey might be persuaded to revive his best Kaiser Sose act for the sequel. And I suppose he'd be glad of the work these days.

The thing about Batumi is, while it is absolutely wonderful in a weird way, it bears not the slightest resemblance whatsoever to the rest of Georgia. And the real Georgia was what we returned to the following morning when we found ourselves heading out of town once again on a terrifyingly dangerous road. It was very stressful and a relief when the traffic eventually started to thin out to give us a fighting chance of survival. Vassili decided to celebrate by buying us a giant watermelon from a roadside vendor. The three of us then tried valiantly to consume the whole thing in a single sitting, without success. Vassili had also insisted on paying for the hotel room the night before. He was alright, was Vassili. A little eccentric, perhaps, but a good man, and we were glad of his company.

We were cycling in the direction of Akhaltsikhe, on a road that would climb from sea level up and over a 2,000 metre high pass. This was a daunting prospect for all three of us, and we made little progress this first day. That was because I had been a little way on this road before; back in 2014 I'd reached a small village, where I'd been invited in by a family. I'd stayed a couple of nights and got to know the people of the village, sat around singing songs with them and watched them plant potatoes in the fields. It had been a special insight into Georgian life and now, three years on, I wanted to see the friends I'd made back then. I wanted to return, to tell them all of my travels and to proudly show them the beautiful girlfriend I'd found in Mongolia, and the slightly-odd Greek man I'd found the day before.

It wasn't more than twenty kilometres beyond the chaos of Batumi that we found the village again, situated in a lush green valley beside a partially dammed river. We stopped at the point that I had first met Gio, the young man who had invited me to stay with his family over a glass of chacha (homemade liquor). I had imagined that somehow arriving back here everyone would be sat in the same spot waiting for my return, but it wasn't quite that simple. The benches were vacant and there was nobody in sight that I recognised. I knew, having kept in touch online, that Gio was away working in Turkey, coincidentally in Trabzon, but I had the phone number of his sister, Irina. What I didn't have was a working phone, but luckily a car stopped and offered to help, and it wasn't long before Irina had been contacted and was on her way to meet us.

Ten minutes later Irina arrived with her cousin, Shorena, who I also knew, and another friend, Diana. It was really nice to see them again, and we sat down at a little café to catch up. I got out my laptop and showed everyone the photos I'd taken three years earlier, and they all got out their phones and took photos for Instagram. They loved meeting Dea and it was all just thoroughly nice. Then Irina invited us to come and stay with her, in the same place that I'd stayed before, up on the hillside.

It was a slightly awkward moment. Of course we wanted to stay, but we were still clinging to this pressing schedule of getting to Baku in twenty-four days, so we apologised and declined the offer. We tried our best to explain that this was because we were meant to be in Uzbekistan on the 15th of August, that we needed to keep moving, that winter was coming. But it was still July and none of this made any sense to the Georgian girls. It didn't really make sense to us any more either. After a while it dawned on us how silly it was to pass up on the chance to stay here in this amazing Georgian home just in the interest of making distance, getting somewhere else. What were we even doing this for? When Irina asked a second time, we accepted.

We followed the girls down the street and turned away from the road and the river. The house, as I well remembered, was up an extremely steep hill. The last time I had needed help from Gio just to push my bike up, although in my defence I had been under the influence of several glasses of chacha. This time I managed to push my bike up all by myself, but I was still very much upstaged by Dea, who pedalled away ahead of us all. Irina looked at her in awe. "She is cool girl," she said, "very cool girl."

"Yes... she... is..." I agreed, panting and gasping for each breath alongside Vassili, who was in much the same state of exhaustion pushing his own bike.

We arrived at the house and I felt confused, for it was nothing like I remembered. I was sure it had been built of stone, but now it was concrete. "This is new," Irina explained. "The house... replaced." In fact it had been rebuilt on exactly the same spot, bigger than before, but still with the same rustic charm, food growing in the garden, magnificent views down to the valley and the mountains opposite. Irina and Shorena sat us down on the porch and turned into hosts, in the typically hospitable Georgian way. They first placed before us a huge plate of watermelon, which we poked at cautiously, unsure of how much watermelon it was safe to consume in one day, and then they cooked us up a feast of a dinner, including, I think, the best potatoes I've ever eaten. As before, various people came to see us and say hello. Unfortunately absent were Irina and Gio's parents, who were both away working, and Luka, who I remembered so fondly from three years earlier. He'd been a cheeky twelve-year-old who had told me that when he grew up he wanted to be a singer, and had at my request belted out the most fantastic traditional Georgian melody. He was no longer in town, but his mother came to see me again. She explained that Luka was now living in Batumi, where he had just started to work, as a singer. His dream had already come true. The boy had become a man.

Another visitor who was new to me was a young man named Merab. He could speak English fairly well and we were invited to walk with him up to his house, higher on the hill. Vassili stayed back, perhaps wisely deciding to rest his legs for the huge climb we still had to cycle, but Dea and I went along. It was really nice to walk up there in the cool evening, occasionally passing homes where people would wave and say hello. Everyone knew everyone else here, it was a real community. At Merab's place we were invited inside the simple home and given a delicious homemade strawberry drink. The people here didn't have very much, but they were so welcoming, and so generous with what they did have. This was really a special place.

We said goodbye to Merab and his family, but our adventures were not over, for on our walk back with Irina and Shorena we were invited into another yard, where half a dozen children ran around playing and half a dozen adults sat around a table eating and drinking. One man, sitting at the table with his big belly exposed, was the most vocal, the alpha male of the group, and it was he who insisted that we take a drink with him. This was the side of Georgia that I'd not been too keen on last time, the drinking culture. But we could hardly come back here and not have at least one glass of chacha, the homemade spirit that was somewhere in the region of sixty or seventy percent alcohol. The man showed us how it was done. First down the shot, then take a big gulp of ayran, a watery, salty sort of yoghurt drink. We did as we were instructed. "Wow!" I coughed. "That is quite a combination!"

We escaped again without having to drink any more, thanks mostly to Irina's forcefulness. She was really an admirable character, a lovely human being, and I felt lucky to have got to meet her again and to introduce Dea to her. And how amazing it had been to have this evening back here in this community, to meet the people and see how they lived and to share it all with Dea. As we staggered back down the hill in the darkness I felt giddy with the feeling of happiness and/or chacha, and it occurred to me how very stupid it was that we had almost missed out on all of this just to make a few more kilometres of distance. What were we thinking? This, right here, was what this journey was all about. These experiences were what made the ride worth doing in the first place. We had to remember that. We simply had to make the time for this sort of thing.

36

Acharistskali, Georgia
25th July 2017

A very nice surprise awaited me in the morning. I was still in the house, rubbing the sleep from my eyes, when I heard Dea out on the porch saying, "Nice to meet you, I heard a lot about you," and I realised immediately who it was she must be talking to. I rushed outside and sure enough, there he was. It was Gio. I couldn't believe it was really him. He'd travelled all the way back from Trabzon on a late-night bus, arriving here at two in the morning, just to see me. I gave him a big hug and told him how great it was to see him again.

We all sat down and reminisced over a breakfast spread that included, I think, the best potatoes I'd had since the day before. And as we sat down to this meal, Gio pulled out a bottle of white wine and placed it on the table, grinning. *'Oh, Georgia,'* I thought. But this was a moment of celebration, and there was nothing else for it but to have a nine a.m. drink and enjoy the moment. And the potatoes.

We still had a lot of climbing ahead of us but we could not very well rush off now, so we spent the morning hanging out with Gio, Irina, and Shorena. Dea got out her ukulele and played some very beautiful songs. It was a funny thing, but the reaction of all three of our young Georgian counterparts was, at the beginning of each and every song, to lift up their smartphones in order to record the whole thing, something that made us wonder whether the concept of just 'appreciating the moment' was something that was being lost to future generations. I decided to test the theory by taking the instrument from Dea and belting out a passionate rendition of Eddie Vedder's *Society* that was so painful on the ears that nobody in their right mind would wish to record it. Their phones dropped to their sides in unison, and the three of them just stood there, open-mouthed, at the cat-strangling-esque noise being made before them. Oh, they appreciated that moment alright, they appreciated that moment.

Our departure was much more easy to leverage after that, and we really did have to do a bit of cycling in the afternoon. Gio gave each of us a bottle of local wine as a parting gift, one further act of generosity from this wonderful family. "We love you," the girls said to Dea, hugging her tightly as we prepared to pedal away. We would not forget this place.

With spirits soaring we set about conquering the 2,000 metre pass. This was always going to be a gradual task, for we climbed only very gently alongside the river for most of the afternoon. The road was narrow and twisted and turned, and was too busy for relaxing, but the pleasant scenery offered some measure of compensation. There were many little villages set among the hilly terrain, and consequently not many options for wild camping. We therefore planned to try and get to the town of Khulo, where we should be able to find a cheap guest house, but we made the mistake of relying on Vassili's GPS to tell us how far it was to Khulo. Either Vassili, his GPS, or most likely a combination of the two got the distance to Khulo quite wrong, and by the time the last of the day's light was fading, we were struggling up a steep section of remote road with no sign of Khulo or anywhere to camp. To make matters worse, Vassili was physically struggling. He'd never done much in the way of climbing before and he was off and pushing on this steep section, hobbling along with his bad leg and all the while insisting that he was fine despite all visible evidence to the contrary. It was almost a desperate situation for us, but fortune shone upon us when a man who looked quite a lot like Santa Claus in a hi-vis vest found us and told us we could camp next to a construction project. He showed us in through a gate, where we found a patch of grass, benches, even clean flowing water for drinking and washing. Under the circumstances, it felt like a miracle. We returned the favour by sharing our bottles of wine with the construction workers, before they went home and left us to our excellent campsite.

The next day was a really tough one. The road became very bad, mostly just bumpy gravel, and it climbed relentlessly all day. We made slow progress and only covered thirty kilometres. Dea was looking strong and wanted to go faster, and I could tell she was getting frustrated. There was no doubt that having Vassili with us was holding her back a bit, but I wanted us to stick together with him. There is something of a bond that exists between long distance cyclists, and it would have felt wrong to abandon him on such a tough road. Plus, you know, I wasn't really up for going much faster myself. In any case, we did eventually ascend out of the valley, and ended the day camping on some grassy plains not too far from the summit. It was an example of the best of Georgia – an open landscape of green grass, blue skies and fantastically fresh air.

In the morning we struggled up the final few kilometres to the top of the pass. There was a real sense of achievement for all of us in succeeding at such a long climb, but I was especially impressed by Vassili. He'd never done a pass like this before, hadn't cycled much at all since his last trip a year earlier, and he must have been sweltering under all his layers, and yet he had persevered and, despite looking like he might pass out for much of the climb, he had made it! We'd all made it! And as we sat eating a celebratory burek at the top, another touring bike came up behind us. This, we soon found out, belonged to Alex, a young man from Guernsey who was also going the same way as us. He'd made it too! "Actually I just took a lift for the last bit. I got bored," he said.

Alex had ridden from his home island and was going, in a vague sense, to Japan, although you would never have thought so to look at his bike. He had only one half-full pannier, a tent rolled up on the back, and a sleeping bag tucked under the handlebars. He was taking travelling light to new levels. He explained that he had tried riding a bike with lots of stuff as we did and found that he didn't enjoy cycling like that, he found more freedom in being on a light bike, unencumbered by material possessions in more ways than one. "I'm still trying to cut down on the stuff I'm carrying actually," he said, to raised eyebrows.

So our peloton had grown to four as we started down the other side of the pass. But we hadn't gone more than a few hundred metres when Alex realised that he had a puncture and we all had to stop. He did at least time this well, as we were beside an interesting-looking mosque, and Dea and I went inside to take a look. With Georgia being a predominantly Christian country we'd been surprised by how many mosques there had been along this road. The imam of this one was a very friendly little man who, having shown us around, followed us outside again to see what all the fuss was about with regards to Alex's tyre. It turned out that Alex was not experienced with fixing punctures, which meant that Vassili was trying to help him, which in turn made me think that I should probably now help as well. With all three of us crowding around, it made the imam think perhaps he should lend a hand too, and then just when we thought we had it all under control, what should happen but two more touring cyclists arrive up the hill heading the other way, and they stopped to see what they could do too, and within an hour or so the puncture was fixed and we could all get back on our way.

This side of the pass went down through unpopulated forest, but the road remained bumpy gravel that made much of the descent not entirely pleasant. At least there was plenty of conversation to keep things interesting, with Alex being a nice, laid-back young fellow who was good to chat with. But then I made the mistake of asking if anyone knew of any good jokes, and Vassili started on a long story about Sigmund Freud, and the rest of the descent was ruined.

Eventually we reached a tarmac road that grew increasingly busy as we proceeded towards Akhaltsikhe. We had the idea to spend a night at some cheap accommodation here, but Alex and Vassili were ahead as we entered town and cycled past plenty of cheap accommodation without stopping, and we ended up outside of the Royal Palace Hotel.

"Well, we might as well just go in and ask the price," I said, and Alex, Vassili, and I, all three of us coated in filth, sweat dripping off us, wandered into the giant foyer. The many receptionists looked at each other nervously, and were probably pressing the button for security as we approached their desk. We were soon informed that this hotel was not within our price range, and a big man, no doubt the security, arrived to escort us out the back door. But good man that he was, he led us all of the way from the premises, and to a much cheaper guest house around the corner.

That evening Dea and I went out for a meal with Alex. The odd Vassili said he'd prefer to stay in the guest house. He very rarely seemed to eat, claiming that the ideal scenario would be to not eat at all. "The best would be to be a breath-atarian," he said with apparent seriousness, "If you can live on just air, then you can live forever." But the three of us were of quite the opposite opinion, and we soon found ourselves enjoying a veritable feast. Georgian food is some of my favourite in the world, with a good selection of vegetarian options, and on this particular evening I enjoyed the best potatoes I'd had since a couple of day's earlier. Alex had come out for the evening wearing the same grey T-shirt and little shorts he'd had on all day. He was a very relaxed character, who seemed like he'd just decided to get up and ride his bike around the world one day. He didn't have any silly challenges like me, he could take a lift if he wanted to, his only goal was to have a good time. There were no time pressures, no deadlines, and he said he would often stop in cities and stay in hostels for a while to meet other young people and go out clubbing.

"But what do you wear?" I asked.

"This," he said, looking down at his one outfit. "I just go out with my cycling shoes on."

We continued on a busy, narrow road through a valley which might have been pretty and tranquil were it not for the exhaust fumes and horn beeping. Vassili and Alex, both wearing dull colours, cycled in the road, while Dea and I bumped along on the shoulder hoping no one was going to get run over, and not very much happened. The next day we escaped onto some smaller roads as the valley widened out into a broad plain, and a big tailwind carried us on towards Tbilisi. There were few options to escape this wind for camping, and we ended up all four of us sleeping together in a ditch. Luckily it was quite a spacious ditch, especially after Vassili had spent half an hour trimming the weeds with a pair of scissors. It was our last night camping together, and the effects of our arduous journey coupled perhaps with severe malnutrition seemed to be getting to poor Vassili, who spent much of the evening insisting to us that aliens were real, and already here on Earth, living among us. I wondered for a while if this was Vassili trying to tell us something, and I thought that if there were aliens living on Earth there would be a decent chance one of them was in this ditch, but before I could push the issue the ever--so-laid-back Alex suggested we make origami paper swans, so we did that.

The next day we rode into Tbilisi. Having ridden in on the main road three years earlier I knew what an absolute nightmare it was to do so, and so I wanted to take a route through the suburbs on the smaller roads. Alex and Vassili, with no previous experience of the main road into Tbilisi, preferred to just crack on, so we split up, agreeing to meet up later for dinner. Dea and I watched them go and then made our own way via the back roads. This took a long, long time, because the roads went up and down the hillsides that Tbilisi is built around and were not all paved, or existing, but it was another tremendous adventure, and we got where we were going eventually.

We had pre-booked our hostel in a moment of silliness, for it was called Alcatraz, and the dormitories were all made to look like jail cells. Oh, what fun this had seemed when we'd made the booking, yet how appropriate it came to feel. Our own journey had become a bit like a prison. We were somehow still clinging to the idea that we could make it to Baku within the twenty-four days if we just spent one night here and then hurried across the flat southern parts of Azerbaijan in several hundred-kilometre-plus days. But that morning Alex had told us that he was going to spend five nights in Tbilisi, and then take the more interesting northern route to Baku, and it made both Dea and myself feel extremely jealous of him for having the freedom to do that. We really were doing something wrong here, and something had to change, we both knew that. Dea and I sat and talked it through.

"We need to let this Baku challenge thing go," I said. "It's ruining our trip a bit, isn't it? I think we can change our dates for the Uzbek visa if we need to."

"I know Chris, I feel the same, I hate having this time pressure. But what about doing the Pamirs before it gets too cold?"

"A week or two isn't going to make much difference now. People do it in the middle of winter, we can do it in October. It's not going to be that bad."

We agreed that we needed to slow down, we needed to just enjoy the ride there first. Winter was going to catch up to us somewhere before Mori anyway, that much now seemed certain. I remained confident we could handle it.

37

Tbilisi, Georgia
31st July 2017

We ended up spending three nights in Tbilisi, a city too interesting to pass too quickly. One advantage our hostel did have was that it was situated right in the old town, the historic heartland of Tbilisi, a maze of narrow streets, crumbling buildings, ramshackle wooden balconies and mysterious piles of rubble. Beyond it, down by the river, modern buildings and a futuristic bridge brought a 21st century edge to Tbilisi, all of it lit up each evening by bright neon lights.

One night we went out to sample more Georgian cuisine with Alex and Vassili, as well as a German cyclist named Chris they'd found in their own hostel. Chris, a big man in his forties, was taking a quite different approach to us, and going along very slowly. He'd been in Georgia for a month already, and had just given up hope of making it to the Pamir Highway before it got too cold. He said he'd go south instead, to Iran, maybe to India somehow. His way of travel was unhurried, unplanned. It was a fun evening, and it highlighted how differently people can travel by bike. There was Dea and me moving slowly towards a goal, Alex moving fast but lacking a goal, Chris moving slowly without a goal, and Vassili, well, it was just a relief to see Vassili eating a good meal.

After dinner we all went outside and sat on a park wall beside the road to eat ice cream for dessert. We watched on with interest as policemen came and blocked off the traffic. Soon the street was empty of all motor vehicles, until a large police escort came through. There were at least a dozen blacked-out vehicles rushing right past us, many with the American flag on them, sirens flashing everywhere, and even a helicopter swirling overhead. It wasn't until later that we discovered that the Vice-President of the United States, Mike Pence, was passing through town.

From Tbilisi Dea and I cycled on alone, for Vassili had opted to take the southern route to Baku across the flat plains, while Alex was hanging around in town for a bit longer, presumably to go clubbing in his cycling clothes. We'd had fun riding in our little group, but were happy now to settle into our own rhythm and routines again. But our options for getting out of the city were limited, and we had to start on the horribly busy main road east. We suffered it for thirty kilometres until a turn northeast that we'd read would take us on a quiet road up into the mountains. It did no such thing. It took us on a busy road up into the mountains. Escaping the traffic in Georgia was no easy task, but with cars beeping us at every turn we made surprisingly light work of the climbs, and made our way on towards yet another new country.

Crossing into Azerbaijan brought no relief from the traffic. There were almost exactly the same narrow, overcrowded roads we'd experienced in Georgia, but the overall feel of the country was instantly quite different. There were more people, more Ladas, and a lot more pictures of the President of Azerbaijan, Heydar Aliyev. His face beamed down on us from billboards everywhere that we went and evidently he was a real cultural icon, no mean feat for someone who'd been dead almost fourteen years. But the biggest difference came with the shift in religious beliefs, and the return to the Islamic world meant we were once again being offered tea and fruits from men in skullcaps and women in headscarves. We were always grateful for such offerings, for temperatures continued to rise and, having chosen the more scenic route to Baku, we had to suffer up many long climbs. On one day the temperature reached forty-two degrees Celsius, and it was horrible cycling along drenched in sweat. But when we passed dozens of people in one village standing at the side of the road, each of them holding out a bag of nuts desperate to flag down passing cars and make a few pennies from the sale, themselves standing unprotected in the full force of the sun, I remembered how lucky we really were. I had heard that Azerbaijan was growing wealthy from oil, yet these riches didn't appear to be being shared to all members of the community, and I was surprised by the level of rural poverty we saw. There were houses made of wood or stone in various states of disrepair, sheep and goats being led by skinny herders, people queuing at village water taps, and Ladas and clapped-out buses on the roads. It was not the poorest country I had ever seen, but it looked to me a very long way from one growing rich on oil.

On our last evening before Baku there was nowhere for us to put up our tent. The landscape was too hilly and too open, there were no good hiding places. We rode on and on, hoping that something appropriate would appear as it usually did, but this time there really were no options. It grew darker and darker and we were left cycling using our lights in a country where roads were dangerous enough in broad daylight.

"We really have to get off the road," I said, as we came to a little side road that ran up to a village not far away. I scoured the land between us and the village, hoping to see somewhere that would at least be flat enough for our tent, but there wasn't anywhere good. Then a shepherd, who had been leading his flock away in the direction of the village, some few hundred metres ahead of us, turned and saw us, and began walking back. *'Oh, great!'* I thought, fearing that this was going to turn into a typically awkward semi-conversation when we didn't really have time for it, because there was not the slightest hope of any common language.

"Do you need a place to sleep?" the shepherd asked in perfect English as he reached us. As I picked my jaw up off the floor Dea said that yes, we did, and the man, Merdan, told us we were welcome to stay at his home in the village. An English speaking shepherd in Azerbaijan, I couldn't believe it.

Merdan led us in through a creaky gate, half falling off its hinges, to a big open yard that was bordered by a high wall. There were some stables and sheds at the far end for the animals, and a breeze-block building in one corner that looked like it might pass for a house. Outside of this were two women, who Merdan introduced as his sister and mother. He then left us in their hands and went off to try and recover his sheep, that had unfortunately wandered off into the fields when we'd distracted him. The two women sat us down at a wooden table and served us bread, cheese, watermelon and tea, despite us insisting that we'd already eaten. We were their guests and the hospitality was simply unstoppable. The generosity was particularly kind, for they appeared to have so little here. The toilets were a hole in the ground, their water supply collected rainwater. Merdan's mum was clearly very old, and had trouble walking, yet she was still working, chasing the chickens away from the house and carrying heavy buckets of water to the animals in the stables. Their lives, like so many in this world, seemed occupied primarily with just doing what needed to be done.

At some point a cow and then a goat came in through the gate, apparently of their own accord, and a little later Merdan followed. A man of about forty or forty-five, he was balding but had a healthy grey beard, and a pensive, quite serious look about him. He sat down with us and it was interesting, for once, to be able to have a full conversation with someone. Merdan told us that he had studied at a university in Baku and had a masters degree, and this explained when and how he had learnt to speak English. It also went some way to explain, as our conversation meandered through a variety of topics, how it was that he understood so much about the world. What it didn't explain, however, was how this intelligent, educated man, who appeared to have been so ambitious and driven in his younger days, now struggled to get by in this simple rural lifestyle.

"It is the system," he explained. "It is not the person who is educated who gets the job. Not the person with the skill. It is the person who knows the right person. It is all about power and money. Your family has money, you get job. No money, no job."

And he went on with this theme, telling us many tales of the corrupt politics of his country, of the oil money remaining in the hands of the few, and of the difficulties faced by the majority of people in his country as a result. As he spoke I sensed in him a great frustration, a helplessness. Maybe in his youth he had tried to rise above it and make something more of his life, but now he just seemed lonely and lost. There was a sense of sadness in him that was heartbreaking. It reminded me again of my own great fortune in life, the freedom and opportunity conferred to me only by my place of birth. I felt humbled once again, as Merdan and his family fed and housed us for the night, and then wished us well, before we continued on our blessed journey the next morning.

We finally reached Baku after a long, hard day battling against one of the fiercest winds I'd ever cycled in. The wind swirled around and battered us from all sides, occasionally whipping up sand and dust into a frenzy all about us. So it was with some relief when we fought our way through to the outskirts of the city and found some shelter from this wind. Our joy was short-lived, however, for we soon discovered Baku to be one hell of a tough city to navigate by bicycle. Big expressways criss-crossed the city and there seemed to be little consideration for travelling without using them. At times the only way to cross them involved bumping our bikes down pedestrian underpasses and carrying our bags up the other side, rather a frustrating thing to be doing towards the end of a long day. But perhaps the most galling thing of all about Baku was how developed it was. Tall skyscrapers and fast cars finally revealed the oil wealth that the city seemed so keen not to share with the rest of the nation.

We found a hostel and settled in for a few days with two major tasks on our to-do list. Firstly we needed to get visas for Uzbekistan, and secondly we needed to figure out how we were going to get across the Caspian Sea. In the three years since I'd been to Iran they had changed their rules for British guests and that country was longer a route open to us, leaving a Caspian Sea crossing as our only viable means of forward progress (short of getting a difficult-to-get Russian visa). I knew that for years cycle tourists had been crossing the Caspian on a cargo ship that accepted passengers, but there was one absurd quirk that might make things difficult for me. The boat actually sailed from the port of Alat, seventy kilometres south of Baku, but tickets for the boat were only sold at an office in Baku, and only on the day of sailing, something that made it essentially impossible to buy a ticket and then pedal to the boat in time. It provided another potential stumbling block we would have to overcome.

Getting our Uzbek visas was a fairly simple process, and thanks to the good-humoured consulate we were even permitted to change from the dates we had requested when applying for the Letter of Introduction, meaning that our slightly late arrival in Baku wouldn't cost us. We needed to pay for the visas at a bank five kilometres away though, so Dea headed off on a bus and left me waiting in the street outside the embassy. This was not destined to be a complete waste of time, however, for it enabled me to to meet Roman and Tomas, two young guys travelling across Eurasia on motorcycles and themselves collecting their Uzbek visas. We fell into conversation about our trips, and in particular how we were all going to complete the Caspian crossing. They then made a phone call to the company running the ship, who told them that tickets were now available directly in Alat. If that was true it would solve a problem for us, and I exchanged contact details with them so that they could keep me up to date with the situation.

With Uzbek visas in our passports Dea and I spent the next day walking around Baku looking for bike shops as we needed a couple of parts, and then I briefly caught up with Vassili one last time. He'd made it to Baku by bike on the southern route despite some nasty headwinds and I only just caught him before he headed off to the airport for his return flight to New York. He still planned to return the following year and pick up where he left off again. And he wasn't the only cyclist in Baku. Alex had arrived not long after us too, and so we met up with him for dinner and then wandered down to the waterfront together. He was planning to hang around in Baku for a while so we wouldn't be continuing with him, but he was a faster cyclist than us and we figured he'd catch us up again before too long.

Our success at the Uzbekistan embassy meant that our route through Central Asia to the Chinese border was clear in terms of visas. All we had to do now was to get across the Caspian Sea, and a message from Roman confirmed that they had been issued tickets in Alat and were just waiting for the boat to leave. It was great news, and we would ride down to Alat ourselves in the morning. Everything seemed to be coming together nicely for us, as we enjoyed one last evening in the company of Alex wandering along the promenade beneath the bright lights of Baku. It was an extraordinary city of flashy lighting and sky-scraping architecture in the mode of Dubai. Most spectacular of all were the three iconic Flame Towers. Shaped like three giant shark fins, these looked impressive by day, but at night took on a whole new level of look-at-this showiness. Thousands of LED lights all over the towers constantly changed colour, creating moving images, of waves, then of flickering flames, then of people waving the Azerbaijan flag. I'd never seen anything like it before, and there was no doubt it was an impressive display, a sign of just what modern Azerbaijan is capable of. But as I stared up at the extravagant light show, I couldn't help but think of poor Merdan, rounding up his sheep in the dark.

38

Baku, Azerbaijan
13th August 2017

R iding down to Alat I was nervous about the upcoming crossing of the Caspian Sea. Until now travelling on cargo ships had been off-limits for my various ocean crossings because I knew that it was not usually considered safe to walk or cycle through port areas where containers were being hoisted around, and other transport is almost always required to get to the actual boat. I had not been able to confirm with anyone who had come this way in the past whether this would be the case here, and this was undoubtedly my biggest fear about the Caspian Sea. If I could not walk or cycle onto the ship my onward route would be blocked, and the only possible plan B – retreating to Tbilisi, sending my passport home for a Russian visa, then cycling up through politically unstable parts of Russia – was itself fraught with risks, especially given my previous bad luck with Russian borders and bureaucracy. This ship therefore offered us our best option for getting to Central Asia, but it was far from guaranteed to be plain sailing.

We arrived at the port in Alat late afternoon and found a large number of trucks waiting in a big parking lot. Beyond them, in the far corner, there were also many old cars with stickers and logos on them. These were all participants in the Mongol Rally, a yearly event where teams of people drive clapped-out old cars from London to Mongolia. Dozens of young adventurers were in and around these cars, some sitting chatting, others tossing a football around. Out of this little party appeared two motorcycles riding towards us. Roman and Tomas were still here.

"Hey guys, we've been waiting here a couple of days, nobody knows when the ship will leave but they said it should be tonight. You can get tickets over there."

And thankfully we could. The old, archaic system of having to buy tickets seventy kilometres away from the ship appeared to be a thing of the past (which probably saved Dea from a 140 kilometre round trip in a taxi). The only slight downside was that the ship leaving this evening was sold out, and we would have to wait for the next one, apparently sailing the following night. The man selling the tickets gave us a choice between beds in a four-bed dorm for seventy dollars each, or a two-bed dorm for eighty. We chose to save the twenty bucks and pray that we landed ourselves some non-snoring truckers. And there were sure to be plenty of truckers on board our ship, for there really were a lot of their vehicles lined up in the car park. But I was overjoyed with that. This was not a cargo ship after all, but actually more of a transport ferry. The trucks could roll on and off the boat, there would be no hoisting of anything, and hopefully therefore no need for us to take any lifts in motor vehicles. Things were looking good.

We spent the night camping away from everyone and returned in the morning to the small, shaded corner where the travellers gathered to wait. It had been overcrowded the previous evening, but almost all of the Mongol Rally teams had left during the night bound for Kazakhstan, and now only one of their fleet remained. This was a little annoying for me, as it left me with few chances of making sales of my book. I'd had some copies sent to me in Italy, thinking I might find some people eager to buy them along the way, and, well, I hadn't. Now I felt under pressure to get rid of them before we reached Uzbekistan, where we were likely to be searched thoroughly. I remembered from my last visit that Uzbek border officials were particularly interested in what books I had with me, and I was a bit concerned as to how they might react to me having four copies of the same book, all with my name on the cover, containing a chapter on Uzbekistan that was not entirely praiseworthy of the country.

So I laid out a bit of cardboard with 'For Sale' scribbled on it, put a pile of books on top, and called it a shop. I had to wait a while for anyone to get up and see it, though, because they were all a little hungover and bleary-eyed. The first of them to rise was a tall, sensible fellow named Angus who appeared to be the natural leader of the group. He explained that he and his three friends were recent graduates of Lancaster University and that they had driven from England to here in just three weeks. I was shocked again by the speed at which it is possible to get places when you manipulate combustion engines to your advantage, and even more so when Angus said that they were one of the last teams, almost everyone else had been even faster. They had also been travelling in convoy with friends of theirs in another car who had, perhaps a little rudely, just got on the last boat without them. But there was no shame in being in last place. It was clear that the Mongol Rally was more about the adventure than the race for these guys, more about the experience and the challenge of driving a car that is on its last legs to some far-flung corner of the globe. And then back again. In the past, all of the Mongol Rally teams would donate the cars to Mongolia and then fly home satisfied with their charitable work, but Mongolia had now introduced a large import tax on motor vehicles, essentially saying 'stop dumping your crappy old cars here would you please!' in the process. As a result, Angus was planning to drive his old green Skoda all of the way home again.

After a while Angus wandered away and another of the four came over to introduce himself. This was Benji, a young Norwegian with a much more convincing British accent than me. I decided that the reason I hadn't clinched any sales with Angus was because he couldn't have noticed my little shop, so with Benji I decided to be a whole lot more forward in my marketing approach.

"Do you want to buy my book?" I said, about thirty seconds into the conversation.

"Erm... what's it about?"

"Cycling around the world."

"Sure, okay."

"What?! Really?!"

I rushed up and shook his hand furiously before he could change his mind.

"Yeah, sure, I like travelling books. How much is it?"

"How much do you want to pay? I mean, it should be eleven pounds, but-"

"Sure, I'll pay eleven pounds."

Oh, I liked Benji, I liked Benji a lot. He gave me a twenty dollar note.

"This is too much. Let me find you some change."

"Don't worry about it. But it better be good!"

"Thanks. Well, it does have 4.8 stars on Amazon reviews."

"Nice. How many reviews does it have?"

"Six or seven. Mostly friends and people I know, to be honest."

"Some of your friends only gave it four stars?"

"Erm... yeah."

I sat and chatted with Benji for quite a while. He seemed genuinely very interested in my trip, firing questions at me and encouraging me to tell him all about it. So I explained to him about how, having cycled all of the way from Paris to Siberia, I'd been forced into a car at the Russia-Mongolia border by some irritating bureaucracy, about how I'd restarted the bike-and-boat circumnavigation in Mori, then cycled across China, Southeast Asia, Australia, Canada and Europe, about how I was getting really quite close to completing my goal now, and how very imperative it was that I not use motor vehicles. I told him about how Dea and I had met in Mongolia, how she had joined me at various stages, and was now my permanent and perfect cycling companion. He asked me more and more questions and I answered all of them and before very long there really was no need for him to read the book any more.

Mid-morning all of the Mongol Rally team piled into their Skoda and departed. We had been told that we'd be boarding the boat at six p.m. for an eleven o'clock sailing, so they had plenty of time to "nip to Baku to do some shopping" as they put it. Having spent the whole of the previous day cycling from Baku the idea of nipping back there seemed very alien to me and Dea, but the young travellers had a combustion engine they weren't afraid to use, especially in this land of cheap oil. So Dea and I were alone, and had to make do with the shop at the port for our groceries. It was just an old container, one of several in a line that between them also housed the ticket office and a bank, but it had a fair selection of food and water on offer, including some delicious fresh peaches. Altogether this car park wasn't the worst place to hang out for a while, although the toilet block was not the nicest old-container-full-of-squat-toilets-for-use-by-truckers I'd ever seen.

We spent the afternoon tinkering with our bikes and just enjoying not having to do much. After my early success the book shop began to stagnate. Only one other traveller came by all day, a French motorcyclist with a sidecar full of stuff. Sadly for him our ship was now sold out and he'd have to come back another day.

"Do you want to buy my book?" I asked desperately before he left.

"No," he said, looking horrified, "I don't like books."

The Mongol Rally team returned and once the sun had dropped low enough in the sky we commenced a tremendous game of three-a-side football in the shade of one of the trucks. It was me, Dea, and Claire against the boys, Angus, Benji, and Adam. Claire seemed like a competent girl, while the bespectacled Adam gave the impression of being more comfortable in academic fields than sports ones, so I was happy enough with the teams. And so it proved, as Dea put in an incredible goalkeeping display, constantly thwarting the boys' attacks with her long legs, and allowing me to score a hat-trick at the other end for a 3-1 victory. After that we all sat down together to play cards and eat dinner. It was really nice to enjoy some good company, and very relaxing that, just for once, we didn't have to worry about moving anywhere. Then, just as I was thinking this, a man came and told us that it was time for us to go through customs and board the boat, so we had better get moving. All of our stuff was lying around, strewn about the place. Knowing how these things worked we had anticipated a longer wait, and now we had to rush around scooping things up and getting ourselves ready in a hurry. But it was happening, we were boarding!

Well, that's not true. We weren't exactly boarding. First we had to cycle around the car park and go through passport control, officially exiting Azerbaijan in what one might have reasonably thought was a prelude to boarding. But beyond border control there was just more waiting. All of the trucks lined up on one side, with us and the Mongol Rally team on the other. Eleven in the evening, the time we had been told the ship would set sail, came and went with no more action. It was dark, everyone was tired, but nothing else happened for a long while. Dea pulled out her sleeping bag and dozed on the tarmac, while some members of the Mongol Rally team fell asleep in their car. I thought I'd better stay awake for a while. It still felt like we might board soon, and I certainly didn't want us to miss that, so I sat down on the kerb and just waited. After a while Benji came and sat with me. He'd made a good start on reading the book, and had even more questions for me now. I asked him a few of my own and we had a good long chat about things. With him being twenty-two years old and having just graduated from university his position in life made me curious and a bit jealous. He told me that he wasn't really sure what he was going to do next, and I was reminded of my own feelings coming out of university.

"I didn't know what to do either, but I knew for sure that I never wanted to have a career, I didn't want to go down that path," I told him. Benji nodded.

"This is basically the first time I've ever considered that it's even possible to *not* have a career," he said. With those words I realised that maybe me and my book might be able to help Benji somehow. Maybe not in the way his parents might thank me for, but at least to open his eyes to the idea that this conventional idea of working all the time to pay for things you don't really need was not the only path in life, and perhaps not the one most likely to end in happiness.

I don't know how much I really affected Benji, but there was something special about meeting him that definitely affected me. It was a timely reminder of why it was that I'd started to travel, and why

I loved to travel. It took me back to another boat journey I'd taken, to Iceland in 2010 at the start of my first big bike trip. I'd made so many friends on that boat, spoken to so many travellers in my enthusiasm and excitement. Meeting Benji and his friends now was similar in many ways, created the same sort of connections, but now they were the young ones, they were the ones trying to decide what to do with the world of endless possibilities before them.

Benji went off to sleep and I lay back alone on the tarmac, looking up at the stars until I too drifted off. It wasn't long before I was awoken again by the sun rising over the trucks opposite us, and still there was no hint of us actually boarding the ship. Dea and I moved our bikes over to a nearby building to get some shade, and from there we had a view out to sea, which gave us a good vantage point for finally seeing our boat. It was just coming into the harbour. It hadn't even been here! So now we had to wait for the ship to dock, unload, and for all the waiting trucks to drive on. It was around one o'clock in the afternoon before all that was done, and we could finally get on board ourselves. The boat eventually set sail at four, some seventeen hours behind schedule.

But at least we had been allowed to cycle our bikes aboard, in the style of a European ferry, and the voyage itself proved to be a good one. Despite having only paid for a four-bed room, Dea and I were given our own private two-bed cabin. It was even en-suite, and had a porthole window for watching the many oil rigs of the Caspian Sea drift by. The boat was not noisy, and we would be lulled to sleep by the sound of the sea drifting in through the window.

The boat took twenty-six hours to reach Aktau on the Kazakh side, and I think both Dea and I would have been very happy if it had taken longer, for it was a very relaxing time for us. We didn't have to cycle anywhere and there was no Wi-Fi, which meant there was no stress to do anything. So we just spent time hanging out with our new friends, playing cards and other games, although during one of these games I got another reminder of how old I was getting, when no member of the Mongol Rally team appeared to know who Justin Timberlake was. He's like the cool singer, top of the charts, who all the young people like, isn't he? ISN'T HE? Oh God, I'm so old.

The boat arrived at a port just south of Aktau in the early evening. From first sight Kazakhstan looked extremely flat, which was kind of promising. But we were well aware of the next challenge that was facing us. Thousands of kilometres of empty desert lay ahead, and if the wind should be blowing the wrong way, flat land wasn't going to be quite so good. But it was still an exciting moment as the boat came to rest against the dock. A new adventure lay ahead of us. The Caspian Sea had been conquered.

As we stood there waiting to depart the ship I fell into conversation once more with Benji.

"I've got as far as Russia in your book," he told me.

"Wow, You're most of the way through it already. Not much to do on board, I guess?"

"Yeah. I forgot though. Why are you cycling back to China now?"

"Oh, well, you're about to get to it in the book, but they made me get in a car at the Mongolian border, so then I decided to start all over again in China."

"Oh yeah, that's right. That must have been horrible when they made you take a car."

"Yeah, it was pretty bad."

Just then we were interrupted as some serious-looking Kazakh officials burst onto the ship. They took all of us, travellers and truckers alike, into a room and searched through our hand luggage. They seemed like they were taking their jobs seriously, they weren't messing about. Once the searching was over, they marched all of us off the boat down some outside steps. Below us I could see something that turned my stomach. There was a minibus waiting on the dock. I felt sick. I knew just what was going to happen. I was suddenly back in Russia. I was back at that bleak Siberian border post. My head span. Some of the truckers ahead of us were already climbing into the bus, ready to be driven away. One of the officials, dressed in army clothing, gun on his hip, pointed me to the minibus.

"Get in," he ordered. "Passport Control. Get in."

39

Aktau, Kazakhstan
16th August 2017

I tried to my best to remain calm. There wasn't space in the minibus for everyone to go at the same time anyway, so I walked away from it, to the back of the queue. It filled up with some of the truckers and drove off, giving me a little time to think before it would return for more passengers. But what was I supposed to think? My head ached. I couldn't believe that this was happening again. Not now, not so close to the end. After everything it had taken to get this far. I knew there would be no more starting all over again. I had to find a way out of this, or my dream was over.

I thought back to Siberia, to the last time this had happened. Flashing money around, trying to bribe my way through, had been a mistake then. I wasn't going to do that this time. I needed to make friends, plead my case more sincerely. The young guards in army fatigues were now standing in formation opposite us, so I approached them, asking if any of them spoke English. They waved me away dismissively, indicating that I should rejoin the queue for the minibus, not step out of line again. But when a more official-looking woman strode past us I had to take my chance. She probably held more sway in matters, and there seemed a good chance she might speak English, so I stepped towards her and tried to grab her attention. She simply ignored me, striding off to deal with more important matters, and the guards ushered me back to my place. Things were not looking good.

By now the bus was already on its way back. It could not be more than 200 metres to the building housing Passport Control. It was absurd that we should have to take this vehicle. It parked up next to us again and more truckers climbed in, as well as the Mongol Rally team, Benji looking at me with concern in his eyes. There was one young guard who was in charge of loading up the bus, and he beckoned for me and Dea to join our friends.

"No, no," I said, "I cannot use vehicles. Only bicycles."

"Bus," he said, pointing us over to it again.

"No, I can't. I really can't. Can I please walk?"

"Bus!"

He pointed at the bus. I made walking motions with my fingers. He pointed at the bus. I made walking motions with my fingers. This stand off went on for quite a while, but I stood firm. I needed to make it clear to him that short of him raising his gun to my head I was not going to be getting in that minibus, and very likely not even then.

The bus departed, but our back-and-forth continued. He actually seemed like a friendly chap, this guard. I could sense something in him that gave me hope, that he was a good person, that I could win him around. He became curious as to why it was that I wouldn't get in the bus, and so I did my best to explain the premise of my journey, that I was trying to go all of the way around the world without using motor vehicles. He could understand a little bit of English, and, even though I think he thought I was crazy, he also looked like he grasped how important this was to me. When the minibus returned he loaded it up with truckers and then jumped in it himself. "Wait," he said to us, before he slid the door closed and the bus drove off.

Dea and I looked at each other with a little bit of optimism. We hoped he was going off to ask his superiors over at Passport Control if we could walk there, good man that he was. But even so, the trip was still hanging precariously in the balance. Either he was going to return and tell us that we could walk, and everything would be fine, or he was going to return with his boss, who was going to tell us to get in the bus or be arrested. I took a deep breath and waited for my fate, thinking back over everything that had happened since I'd last been forced in a motor vehicle. Crossing China, crossing Australia, crossing Canada, crossing Europe. All those kilometres, all that time, pursuing this goal to make a lap of the planet without ever using motors on land, a goal which had grown more and more important to me with every passing day. A dream which I knew could at any moment be about to slip from my grasp all over again.

The minibus returned and the same guard jumped out. Initially he ignored us, and began shepherding the last of the truckers aboard. There were only a handful of them left, this was to be the last bus-load. I watched as the last man climbed in, praying that the guard would slide the door shut behind him, that he wouldn't turn to us and say he was sorry, but we had to get in too. I watched on, every second feeling like a minute, willing him to slide that door shut. *'Please, please, please...'* And then, slam, the door slid shut. The bus pulled away as the guard turned towards us.

"Okay," he smiled, "let's walk!"

The sense of relief was overwhelming. The guard accompanied us, walking together for the three minutes it took to get to Passport Control. He was even more friendly and happy now, as if pleased that he had played an important role in helping me towards my goal.

"Record... World... Guinness?" he asked, showing a remarkable ability now not only to speak English, but to speak it backwards.

"Yeah, maybe," I replied, knowing full well that the people at Guinness had not the slightest interest in what I was doing, but not wanting to dampen the enthusiasm of this man, who had, after all, just earned himself a special place in my heart as the great Kazakh hero-guard and ultimate saviour of everything.

After spending our first night in Kazakhstan in our tent concealed by a convenient bend in an oil pipe, we rode into the city of Aktau the following morning and found ourselves a hostel. And blow me down and call me Sally if you want, but what a magnificent hostel it was too. We had a big room to ourselves, air-con, good Wi-Fi, good showers, even a big world map on the wall for looking at and saying

"We've come a long way, haven't we?" to each other.

Dea spent the day rebuilding her rear wheel from scratch with a new hub she'd picked up in Baku, her old one having recently given up on functioning properly. She went at this challenge with a level of determination I'd come to expect from her, setting herself up on the floor of our room with no one to help her but an online video tutorial. She disassembled the old wheel, then methodically laced each spoke with the new hub, gradually building up her new wheel and truing it herself. Once again I was left seriously impressed by this girl.

As for me, I was feeling on top of the world to have come through the near miss at the border and to be in Kazakhstan again, and I was in a tremendous mood as I went about my own tasks, writing blog posts, washing laundry, and buying our food supplies. And there were quite many food supplies to be bought, for beyond this developed city built on oil, lay the vast emptiness of the Kazakh steppe. 475 kilometres of nothingness lay between Aktau and the next big town of Beyneu, and I couldn't wait to get out there and experience it.

We were not even out of Aktau before we encountered our first problems. The roads were busy, so we'd been bumping along on a dirt shoulder, but when our wheels hit tarmac again they made a gritty noise, as if the tyres were covered in stones. I ignored it for a bit, thinking it would sort itself out, but when I stopped and looked down I realised it wasn't going to be doing that. All of our tyres had scores of goathead thorns stuck in them. It was an absolute nightmare, and for the next half an hour we were stooped over our wheels pulling them out. Luckily most of our tyres hadn't punctured, but my rear tyre, which was the most worn, had in several places, and I decided to just put our spare tyre on the back. This was a pretty new Schwalbe Marathon Plus Tour that I'd been carrying as a spare for quite a while, but it simply would not fit correctly in the rim, and as a consequence when I resumed cycling it felt like it was making me somehow very unstable.

During all this faffing about a pair of touring cyclists had appeared, fresh off the latest boat from Alat. They were two short and cheerful middle-aged women named Jack and Barbara. They had cycled from London and were, like us, heading for the Pamirs. They seemed really nice and we'd have liked to have cycled with them, but we hadn't quite sorted out our tyres, so they went on ahead, thinking we might catch them up.

When we did get moving again, however, it was only a few minutes before we were stopped by some workers at the side of the road who wanted to take photos with us. I remembered well from my last visit to Kazakhstan how much the locals enjoyed such photoshoots, and we were happy to pose with them. Then before we could get moving again a car pulled over and man got out to ask if he could take a photo of us with his boys, and I began to wonder if we were ever going to make it anywhere across this country. But the man was nice and could speak a little bit of English. He asked us about our professions and I told him that I wrote books, which would have been true if I hadn't put the s on the end. I still had a couple of copies of *No Wrong Turns*, so I showed one to him and he asked me how much it cost.

"Erm... about 4,000 tenge," I said.

"How about 2,000?"

"You want to buy it?!"

"Yes, why not?"

I couldn't believe it. I'd given up hope of selling any of these books before the Uzbek border, but here I was flogging one at the side of the road to a random Kazakh man. Alright, he was getting it half price, but considering he probably couldn't read it, I thought that a fair deal.

Unfortunately the book sale did not mark a complete turnaround in fortunes for us, and almost as soon as we started moving again we had to stop for me to fix another puncture. Once again the new rear tyre just would not sit right. It was a pain to cycle on, but it was three thirty in the afternoon and we'd gone eight kilometres, so I had to cycle on something. And things did improve after that as we headed out into the steppe, occasionally passing herds of camels and horses, and making decent progress through the rest of the afternoon. But then, with the sun dipping towards the horizon and us on the lookout for a place to camp, my rear tyre suddenly deflated again. I sighed and set to work. But this time I noticed the real problem with this tyre. The wire bead that circled it had somehow deformed and bent itself over into a U-shape, and it had now burst through the tyre wall and speared the tube. This explained why it had felt so weird, and I could only guess it had occurred as a result of the way I'd been carrying it squeezed under the bungee cords on the back of the bike for so long. Either way, it was certainly now useless. I got the last of the thorns out of the old worn tyre and put that back on, but now we had a real potential problem. We were heading across Central Asia, destined for the remote Pamir Highway, and we had no spare tyre, and little hope of finding a decent bike shop for a very, very long time.

Despite these early setbacks we soon settled into the rhythm of life cycling across the Kazakh steppe. For the first few days it was actually quite interesting, for there were many buttes and rock formations reminiscent of America's Wild West to dramatise the landscape, with lots of camels and horses roaming through the big empty spaces. We both enjoyed these days away from civilization, and loved the evenings, spent setting up camp wherever we wanted to the backdrop of long red sunsets.

More good news came with another roadside book sale. A nice local man with a bit of English stopped his car to say hello, and asked if he could buy my book when I told him about it. The name of this man was Berdibay, he worked in the oil industry, and he was driving home to Aktau after attending an expo in Astana. He told us that on the way he'd seen two other cyclists not far ahead of us on the road. From his description it seemed like it was Jack and Barbara, and we pedalled hard to try and catch them up. We finally did so at one of the few chaikhanas that were sporadically positioned along the road. Chaikhana literally means teahouse, but out here they generally served food and a variety of drinks, and most importantly provided an opportunity for us to escape the heat and wind for a while. For Jack and Barbara the heat and wind seemed to be especially taxing.

They both looked exhausted and said that they were hoping to catch a lift on from here. We encouraged them to ride with us instead, suggesting that cycling as a peloton would negate the worst effects of the wind, but they couldn't be tempted out of the haven of the chaikhana. So Dea and I continued on alone, and the next morning as I was cycling a big truck beeped at me and someone leaned out of the passenger window shouting, "Hello, hello!" This was not particularly unusual, a high percentage of the vehicles here would beep at us all day long, but this one was different, for I looked up and saw Jack's face, beaming with joy.

Later on another car stopped, and I was surprised when Berdibay stepped out.

"Do you remember me?" he said. "I bought your book."

Oh dear, I hoped he wasn't after a refund.

"Yes, I remember. Hello Berdibay. Have you read any of it yet?"

"Just the first page. It's good. I read 'Some names have been changed.'"

"Yes, that's right."

"Based on a true story, yes"

"Yes, that's right. Did you read any more?"

"No, that's all."

Halfway to Beyneu the interesting scenery ended and we found ourselves cycling across an unbelievably featureless landscape. There was nothing besides dry yellow grass and sand for hundreds of very flat kilometres. The monotony of such a barren place could have brought us down, especially as we had an increasingly tough headwind to deal with, but actually both Dea and I rather enjoyed it. The remoteness and the emptiness and the endless horizons left me feeling humbled and inspired. These sorts of places were the ones where the process of turning the pedals could become almost meditative, an act of simple, stubborn defiance against the harsh environment, where patience and perseverance were our most valuable weapons.

And sure enough, eventually the brightly coloured roofs of Beyneu did appear on the horizon ahead of us. It was a moment of pleasure after six days in the desert to cycle into the simple town of dusty streets and find our way to a hotel, a shower, and a bed. And it was another pleasant surprise to see three touring bikes already parked up outside the hotel. We recognised two of them, and found Jack and Barbara relaxing in the hotel restaurant, tucking into a big pizza along with the owner of the third bike, a young Australian named Mark.

"Wow, well done guys," Jack said to us as we walked in. "We didn't expect to see you for days! The wind out there is awful!"

Jack revealed that they hadn't got too far with that first truck, and they'd been forced to cycle again, until another lift came along. Now the prospect of more desert had lost its appeal, and from here they would be leaving on a train that would carry them halfway across Uzbekistan. As for Mark, he'd left Perth a year and a half earlier and had ridden through Southeast Asia, India, Pakistan, and Central Asia. Having cycled all of the way across Uzbekistan he warned us that we had a lot more desert to come ahead of us. The road would also be in bad shape from here to the border, something that had cost Mark dearly, as the head of one of the screws holding his rear rack on had sheared off, leaving the rest of it stuck in the frame.

Mark's tale made me think it might not be a bad time for me to get my own front rack welded up. It had been cracked in a couple of places since England, but I hadn't wanted to pay high prices to get it fixed in Europe. I'd noticed it had cracked in the same two places on the other side now, and when I unwound the electrical tape that had been holding it all together, it literally fell apart into three separate pieces. Yes, it was probably about time to get it seen to.

Mark and I went off together to search for a welder, chatting more as we walked around the small town. He was a nice guy, in his early twenties. After graduating he'd worked for a while as an ecologist in Western Australia, but his passion for nature and curiosity about the world had led him to embark on this bike trip, generally bound for Europe, but with no set time-frame or deadlines.

It didn't take us too long to find a place, thanks to the directions of some locals, but it seemed a dubious location. We were allowed to enter through a big, solid gate by a man wearing a white cloth mask over his face, with sunglasses and dungarees completing the Texas Chainsaw look. As he pulled the gate closed behind us, enclosing us in a work yard full of men who were all looking us up and down suspiciously, I must admit I did slightly fear for my life. To try and lighten the atmosphere I held up all of the parts of my broken rack, and one of the men took it and welded it back together for me. It was a very long way from a tidy job, but it looked like a proper Kazakh industrial-strength weld, and that was certainly good enough for me.

Then it was Mark's turn. He had his bike with him, and he was rather hoping that the same man would be able to weld a new screw onto the old bit of screw that was stuck in his frame, in order to provide a means by which to unscrew the offending piece.

"I really don't think he can weld precisely enough for that," I ventured, but Mark was short on options and decided to take his chances. The man went to work and we both winced as the blowtorch licked at Mark's expensive frame. The welder continued, until the screw was glowing red hot, along with much of the frame around it. Then, much to Mark's alarm, the frame caught fire quite a bit.

"WHAT ARE YOU DOING?" the young Aussie screamed, desperate to make it stop. The welder did stop his torching at this point, and tried his best to twist the welded-on screw, which of course snapped off immediately. "Ah she-et!" Mark wailed, examining his poor frame, which had not been relieved of the offending screw, and was now, ever so slightly, a different shape.

We left the work yard and walked back to the hotel in silence. We hadn't been killed, at least, but I think that place will nevertheless always be remembered as a scene of horror by poor Mark. It worked out alright for me though, because the men all disappeared very quickly after the welding fiasco, and so I got my work done for free, so every cloud, Mark, every cloud...

From Beyneu, Dea and I had another 500 kilometres of empty desert to cycle through before the first Uzbek city of Nukus. As promised, the final road in Kazakhstan was of poor quality. For long sections it was unpaved and rutted to the point of being unusable, and a selection of other tracks had been carved in the desert that often made for better cycling conditions. It reminded me a bit of Mongolia. It was quite good fun trying to pick the best track, and concentrating on not hitting the big bumps or skidding in patches of thick sand took our minds away from the monotony of the desert completely. As we neared the border with Uzbekistan, Dea and I agreed that Kazakhstan had been a great, great adventure. The emptiness of the steppe was crazy, but it was also humbling, and it gave us great satisfaction to survive it, to pass through it. On our last night in Kazakhstan we sat outside of our tent in this vast desert, under a purple sky growing crowded with stars. Three camels wandered over towards us, then stood watching, curious, silent silhouettes in the twilight.

"This is pretty good out here, isn't it?"

"Yeah, yeah it is."

40

Kazakh steppe
26th August 2017

"hh, scorpions!"

Not the ideal thing to hear your girlfriend shriek when she's in the middle of packing away the tent, but at least preferable to, "Oh my God, Chris, there is a scorpion on your cap now!"

This was how our last morning in Kazakhstan began. The first two scorpions had burrowed under the tent overnight and were revealed as Dea folded up the tent. They weren't really very big, but their tails curled menacingly, ready to strike if needed, as they each scurried around looking for a new hiding place. They found it beneath our panniers, and there was much faffing about before we eventually managed to escape away to a nearby electric pylon where we leaned our bikes up and sat and ate some breakfast. That was when Dea's second exclamation occurred, although my cap was thankfully not on my head at the time, but hanging from my handlebars. Like us, this scorpion seemed to be enjoying breakfast, as an unfortunate grey moth was trapped in its grasp. I flicked them both off the cap with a stick, and we decided it was about time to hit the road.

We were soon at the Uzbekistan border, where we'd heard we could be in for a long wait, with officials going through all of our bags and possessions with a fine toothcomb. I'd not been looking forward to that at all, but after the events of the morning such an intrusion of privacy suddenly seemed like a great idea. Up we rolled to customs, hoping for a thorough scorpion check, where we were met by a young Uzbek man who tried his very best to speak to us in English, addressing me first as "Mister," before nodding at Dea and saying, "and sister." We were then waved straight through, our bags sadly untouched.

Uzbekistan began with several hundred kilometres of barren desert on a road that was very long, very straight, and very full of potholes. It was more desolate here than it had been in Kazakhstan, and in places there was more then a hundred kilometres between chaikhanas. It was also insanely hot and dry, and so we had to carry large amounts of water with us. This water would rapidly become unpleasantly warm under the scorching sun, so I devised a clever way of keeping it cool. I did this using nothing more than a spare pannier that I had with me (the one that the bear had been good enough to not steal from me in Canada), and an insulation mat that we sometimes slept on. I wrapped this mat all around the pannier and taped it on, and this simple construction worked remarkably well at keeping drinks cool inside. I put it on the back of my bike and from that moment on it was referred to simply as 'the fridge'.

Many cyclists we knew of that were heading across Eurasia had decided to skip the section between Beyneu and Nukus, preferring a day on a train to several days of inhospitable desert. I could certainly understand why they did that; given the oppressive heat and the monotony of the unchanging empty landscape there wasn't much to recommend this place for cycling holidays. But once again Dea and I both loved it somehow, for the challenge of it, and for the sense of awe that came from being in such a vast empty space. Crossing the desert was tough, of course, but it was something we were destined to look back on as one of the highlights of our journey.

Indeed, returning to more populated regions near Nukus came as a bit of a shock to the system. Irrigation had turned the desert here green, and suddenly there were people everywhere. And whether they were selling watermelons at the side of the road, riding their bicycles home from the fields, or driving past us at high speed, they would shout "Atkuda?" at us if they possibly could. The old Uzbek desire to know where we were from had not changed much in the three years since I was last here, and neither had the desire for drivers to give a loud toot of their horn as they passed us. It didn't take very long for Dea and I to agree that we both missed the peace and quiet of the desert.

But there was a good reason to stop in the small city of Nukus, aside from the fact that we both needed a good shower, for Alex from Guernsey was waiting there for us. We'd last seen him when he'd chosen to stay behind for a bit in Baku, but he'd now caught us up, or rather we'd caught him up, as he'd taken the train from Beyneu, leapfrogging ahead of us in the process. Now reunited, we planned to cycle together through another 500 kilometres of desert that stood between us and the ancient silk road city of Bukhara. But before leaving, Dea expressed a desire to visit the museum of Soviet-era art that Nukus is (almost) famous for. Fortunately just before we went inside she suggested that if Alex and I weren't that interested in the museum we could wait in a café while she went to look around. And by some small miracle the café that we found was trying very hard to be Western, and we could indulge in pizza, fries and milkshakes. Oh, it was a glorious alternative to a museum, to be sure, and good to catch up with Alex again. He was, of course, still wearing his one grey outfit.

Before leaving Nukus for the great unknown the three of us went to a supermarket (of sorts) and stocked up. Dea and I took half an hour to do our shopping, loading up our bikes with fifteen litres of water, six litres of chocolate milk, five litres of juice, three types of bread, jam, chocolate spread, pasta, chocolate, dried fruit, and a handful of Snickers. Well, we wanted to be ready for the desert. Alex popped in and took two minutes, coming out with a couple of bottles of water, a loaf of bread, and a packet of nuts. It was all a part of his laid-back, travelling light, mentality.

"Are you not worried about running out of food and water?" I asked.

"Nah," he said, in a way that suggested worrying wasn't something he ever really did. "It'll be alright."

We finally got out of Nukus around three in the afternoon, returning to the desert and straight into a strong headwind. There was nothing to do about that, so we battled on as best we could on what was an unusual road system. It appeared to have been designed with the intention that it would be a divided dual carriageway, but this was something that had not been made clear to the drivers, and so rather absurdly both sides of it were being used by traffic heading in both directions. All we could do was laugh and go along with it, but after just thirty-five kilometres we'd had enough of the wind and stopped to make camp. It was nice to have a new face to talk to, and we had a fun evening together, chatting away and electing to call ourselves 'Team Spirit' for the rest of our time cycling together. In other news, Alex also revealed that he'd like to be played by Ben Affleck should the movie series ever take off, and I drank far too much chocolate milk.

The next day our start was delayed by the inaugural Team Spirit Desert Long Jump Competition, which I won with a leap of two and a half metres, that everyone agreed wasn't even worth trying to beat. We were then further delayed by Alex suffering a couple of punctures, and by a wind that seemed determined to hold up our progress, but we did begin to slowly inch our way towards Bukhara. After a while we stumbled upon a café, where the kind owners gave us big plates of free food after being impressed by Alex's ability to solve a Rubik's cube in under a minute.

Finding the café so soon seemed to provide some justification for Alex's laid-back approach to carrying desert supplies, and sure enough there were plenty more chaikhanas to be found along this stretch. Appearing every forty or fifty kilometres, these were the most amazing refuges for us, where we could sit or lie on big flat tables covered in colourful rugs, shaded from the sun. Food would be served to us on a smaller wooden table in the middle. There was no variety to the food, we would always end up with round, chewy bread, a few fried eggs, and, if we were lucky, a salad of tomato and cucumber. But if the food was a little on the bland side, the wide variety of fruit juice that was on offer more than made up for it. When we didn't feel like eating much because of the heat, we turned to the juice for energy as well as fluid, and each new carton became the most delicious, refreshing, wonderful thing in the world to us when we pulled it out of 'the fridge'.

On our third day out from Nukus the wind turned, and we suddenly had the benefit of a massive tailwind. We were also on a brand new dual carriageway, a perfectly smooth surface that almost everyone managed to drive on the right side of. We now had such good cycling conditions, and for two whole days the wind carried us forward, blowing us across the hot desert. Only one thing blighted our progress. It happened as we neared a chaikhana. I think I must have been distracted by the sight of it on the horizon, for I failed to notice a big stone in the road and I hit it, causing my rear tyre to deflate instantly. I didn't want to have to change it under the hot sun, so I pushed my bike the rest of the way to the shade of the chaikhana. But then, as I went about my work, I discovered that the sidewall of the tyre had a big gash in it. It was perilously close to making the tyre unusable, a very worrying development when we had no spare. I wondered if I'd just caused that damage myself by pushing the bike along while the tyre was deflated. If so, then I was an idiot, because there was almost no hope of us finding a decent new tyre in Central Asia.

I put the damaged tyre back on with a new tube, hoping that it would at least hold until Bukhara. The next morning, our last of this desert crossing, I found myself stopping to fix punctures more than once. I put a patch on the inside of the tyre where the cut was, but I knew that was only a temporary solution. And this last day turned into even more of a test as the road shrank to a narrow two-lane road heavy with beeping traffic. So it was with a sense of triumphant exhaustion that Team Spirit finally sighted the famous Kalyan Minaret tower of Bukhara, and with just a little feeling of what it might have been like for the great caravans of the past to reach this oasis, we rode into town, our final long desert crossing complete.

We'd already pre-booked a hostel in Bukhara for four nights. It was cheap and it had good reviews online, so we thought it was going to be the ideal place for us to relax and recuperate. How wrong we were. As soon as we arrived we had to sit down with the frumpy owner lady so that she could take down all our details for the registration process. She spoke no English, but it was clear enough that she was unhappy that we hadn't registered anywhere since Nukus (Uzbekistan has a silly law about foreigners needing to register frequently in hotels, difficult to do in the desert), but she took our money all the same. Her husband, with some reluctance, then stood up and showed us to our room. We'd booked beds in an eight-bed dormitory, because it was cheap and came with a free breakfast, so we were a bit surprised to see there were only four beds, and horrible camping beds at that. The other four occupants would have to sleep on blankets on the floor. I sat down on one of the beds, quite exhausted from our desert trials. The man motioned frantically at me to get up, then handed me some bed sheets. Oh, I had to make the bed before I could sit on it. "You know, in some establishments I believe they do that for you," I said, growing more frustrated about the attitude of the hostel owners. Dea and I had been so looking forward to a place where we could relax for a few days, and this certainly wasn't it. The final straw came when we asked what time breakfast was and were told that it would cost an extra two dollars each. The booking we'd made clearly stated that breakfast was included in the price. We tried showing our booking confirmation to the frumpy lady, but she wasn't interested in looking at it, she just grew angry at us, insisting that breakfast most certainly was not included. Her attitude was horrible, and this was not a place where we wanted to stay. We wanted out. I told her that if she refunded us for the other three nights, we'd be happy to leave in the morning.

We went back up to our dormitory, where Alex was resting on one bed and a recently-arrived Russian girl was sitting on another. After a while the owner woman came up to the room and started making angry noises. The Russian girl translated for us. "Erm, she wants you to leave now."

It seemed like we were being kicked out. But we weren't going anywhere until we got our money back. "She says she will call the police if you don't go," the Russian girl added.

The frumpy woman nodded her head, a hideously smug look on her face. "Registration," she said, "registration problem. Police."

"Call the police then," I said. "We're not going anywhere until we get our money back."

"She says she will give you everything back except half the money for tonight," the Russian girl said.

That was good enough for us. We just wanted to get out of this place. Well, Dea and I did. Alex still laid on his bed, looking like he wanted nothing at all to do with any of this. "I think I'll just stay," he said.

So that is how Dea and I found ourselves kicked out on the streets at eleven o'clock at night. We gathered ourselves and walked our bikes towards Bukhara's old town, feeling a tremendous sense of freedom and adventure to be doing so. We walked past the massive Ark Fortress, and on along empty streets, until we turned a corner and suddenly stopped and stared, mouths gaping, at the sight of the Kalyan Minaret and the two madrassahs that flank it. A big moon floated behind the spectacular giant buildings in the silence of the night. It was a special, surreal moment.

On we walked, down a street suddenly busy with life. A hundred men kneeled before us, laying the paving bricks of a new pedestrian road. They worked with mallets and chisels much as they would have done centuries ago, taking advantage of the cool evening temperatures. We were stopped in our tracks and there was some debate about whether or not we would be able to navigate our heavy bikes through the chaos of bricks and piles of sand, but eventually it was decided, as so often is the case in Asia, that it must be possible, and we were led through. Just as we reached the other side of the worksite a man asked us if we needed a hotel, and offered to show us to a cheap one. He led us down a dark street, but we now trusted that fate was holding our hand, leading us somewhere good on this crazy night. And we were soon being welcomed in at a new hotel by the young owner, Akbar, who showed us a welcome much warmer than we had any right to expect from a man we'd just woken up.

The next day our decision to move felt even more like it was the right one. We were now at the Moxinur Bukhara, and for basically the same price as we'd been paying before we now had our own private room, in a peaceful, homely place with a big open courtyard. Akbar lived here with his young wife, their two children, his parents, and his sisters. All of them made us feel welcome, sometimes inviting us to eat dinner with them and showing us a little of Uzbek life. We felt so welcome, and it was absolutely the perfect place to relax for a while. Oh, and breakfast was also included.

One thing I needed to do was to make enquiries about bike shops. I knew that my latest tyre woes meant I was in real trouble, because Central Asia was no place to be finding good quality replacements, and the Pamir Highway was no place to be cycling on cheap alternatives. I looked into the possibility of getting something shipped in, but the cost of sending anything into this region was extortionate, and would take too long anyway. But Alex had heard of some bike shops, and we headed there together to see what they had. A lot of people do ride bikes in Uzbekistan, but they mostly use very cheap old bikes and parts, and the first shop I went in reflected this. The man in there had a tyre the right size, but like everything else here it was cheap and Chinese. It only cost three pound fifty, and I doubted very much it would last a week on my bike. I was contemplating how many spare tyres I would need to carry of this quality to get me through the Pamirs, when Dea, who had been talking to a man at another little bike store, interrupted my thoughts. "He says he has a Schwalbe tyre," Dea said excitedly. Frankly, I didn't believe it, but the young guy seemed quite insistent. He didn't have it there in the shop, but he promised he'd bring it in the next day for me. I left, feeling like I would believe it only when I saw it.

The following day Dea left early in the morning on a train bound for the magnificent old city of Samarkand. I'd seen Samarkand on my last visit to Uzbekistan, and we'd decided it didn't make a lot of sense for us to both cycle there again as it would add a lot of stressful cycling to our route. Instead Dea would go there for a couple of days by train, then return to Bukhara so that we could continue more directly to Tajikistan. So I was all alone as I walked back to the bike shops, still not daring to believe my tyre problems were about to be solved. When I got there the young man smiled and went to the back of his shop, where he pulled out a Schwalbe Marathon Original. I took it from him and examined it, and saw that it had been used a bit, and had some scratches, but it was the right size and looked in good enough shape to get me through the Pamirs. I couldn't believe my luck, it was surely the only Schwalbe tyre for sale in the whole of Uzbekistan, a country so lacking in quality bicycle parts, and somehow I'd stumbled upon it. It felt like a miracle.

I skipped merrily back to the guest house. I was in a fantastic mood. It was great to be in Bukhara, great to be relaxing, great to have the Pamir Highway ahead of us, and great to have a bike that now had a chance of making it through to the other side, where China was waiting for me. I put my new tyre on the back wheel and it fitted perfectly. I knew that a mechanical failure was one of the few things that could possibly stop me from reaching my goal, and having two good tyres on my bike again was a huge relief.

The next task on my to-do list was to clean and repaint my bike. This was something I did every so often to try and protect the bike from rusting, but it had been a couple of years since I'd last found the time. I'd picked up some black spray paint at the bike shop, and so I set myself up in the courtyard of the hotel and washed away all the dirt from the frame in preparation for repainting the areas where the old paint had been stripped off. I found a few small patches on the top tube that needed touching up, a bit on the chainstays, a lot on the racks where the panniers rubbed. Then I flipped my bike over and checked it from underneath. I came to my front fork and I froze. I stopped and stared for a while, trying to process what I was seeing. Three little holes, actual holes, formed from rust, linked by a crack that spread almost halfway around the fork on the underside of one of the top bends.

'Oh dear,' I thought, 'I probably should have done this a bit sooner.'

My fork was toast.

41

Bukhara, Uzbekistan
8th September 2017

*G*uess you're done then, hitch a ride, and make arrangements *to fly home.'*

Not exactly the inspired solution I'd been hoping to receive when I'd posted the details of my predicament to an online bike forum. To be fair, my fork did not look good. Actually, it looked as if it might collapse at any moment, and it surely wasn't safe enough to risk on the rough and remote roads of the Pamir Highway. And there was little hope of finding a replacement fork in Bukhara either, but I wasn't ready to quit just yet, what with the miracle of the Schwalbe tyre still fresh in my mind.

'If you know the dimensions and angles on you bike, you might see if you can get a first-world shop to DHL you a replacement fork.'

I appreciated this second reply much more than the first, as it had a lot less going on in the way of mass pessimism, but it still wasn't that useful. I'd already looked into this idea, and there was no possibility of getting a new fork to Bukhara before our visas expired. There also seemed scant hope of getting a new fork shipped to the next country of Tajikistan, because when I looked into it I found the headline, *'Tajikistan, a country with an atrocious state postal service, has shut down several international courier firms such as DHL, UPS and TNT,'* dated a couple of months earlier.

I left my laptop and went outside to look again at the damage, hoping that my bike might have somehow fixed itself. It hadn't. The fork looked a real mess. As I stood there staring at the damage, I heard a voice that I hadn't heard for quite a while.

"See what happens when you don't look after me?"

"Erm..."

"Spending all your time with that girl, that's the problem. Don't have time to take care of me any more, do you?"

"Talking bicycle! I thought..."

"You thought what? Where is she now anyway? Now we've got a real crisis, and she's nowhere to be seen, eh? Abandoned us, hasn't she?"

"She's in Samarkand. She'll be back tomorrow."

"Whatever. Are you going to weld me back together or what?"

Ah yes, of course, welding. This was a solution put forward not only by my talking bicycle, but also by several new contributors on the forum. It seemed to be a logical enough solution, at least temporarily, and even with the disaster of Mark's frame repair in Beyneu in the back of my mind I knew that getting it welded up would give me the best chance of at least making it the 500 kilometres to Tajikistan's capital, Dushanbe. So I removed the fork from my bike and walked with it back to the bike shop area. From there I was pointed around the corner, to a backstreet of makeshift metal shops, where I found myself a welder. He was an old man with a flat cap, something that I found strangely reassuring. He had just finished up reattaching a saucepan handle for a little old lady and it looked like he'd done a good job of that, so I saw no reason not to trust him. I showed him the fork and he nodded, placing it before him on his welding desk and giving it a good tap with a bit of metal. What he didn't bother to do before setting to work was to put on a welding mask or tuck in his shirt, which more than once in the minutes that followed almost caught fire. But it was too late for me to do more than stand back and put my faith in this man as he lit up my fork with his welding stick. After a while he seemed to be indicating that he was done, and he handed me back my fork. His weld looked rather ugly, but worse than that I saw that he hadn't even welded it all. One of the holes remained. "What about this bit?" I asked. He looked at it, as if noticing the glaring hole for the first time, and went back to working his magic.

With my fork fully welded up for less than a pound I wandered back to the bike shop where I'd got the tyre from. I couldn't say I was entirely keen on staking my trip and possibly my life on this ninety pence weld, so I stopped by and asked around, hoping for another miracle to fall my way in the shape of a new fork. But the shops here stocked only cheap Chinese bikes, with threaded forks that would never fit with my frame. However, there was a man outside the shop who could speak English. Rustam was his name, and he told me that the Schwalbe tyre I'd bought the other day had been brought back from Germany by his friend who had gone there for an operation. The friend was now right there beside him, and he said something, which Rustam translated for me. "He says he has some forks like yours, if you want one."

Well, yes, I did want one actually, more than anything. The man, Rustam, then told me that we could walk back to the historic old town to see them. And a very pleasant walk it was too, taking in the gigantic old bazaar along the way, where Rustam tried and failed to find a ball of wool for his mother. "Oh, she's going to be so mad at me," he said, as we gave up the search. Then we went on past the Kalyan Minaret again, now buzzing with tourists, and on into a labyrinth of narrow old streets. Eventually we found our way to the home of Rustam's friend, where we sat and waited for him to arrive by bicycle. "He's gone to see 'The Master' to get some forks," Rustam told me. I wondered for a moment who this Master could be; he sounded fantastic, some sort of bicycle parts God perhaps. But then Rustam's friend reappeared and threw down a pile of rusty old Chinese-made forks, none of which had the slightest chance of fitting my frame.

"Thanks, but no thanks," I sighed.

I went back to the hostel and put my welded fork back on my bike, who may or may not have thanked me. Then I checked the internet again and saw that the forum had gone a bit crazy, with people suggesting I should use wire or glue or adhesive tape, and somebody else telling me that *'some problems just don't have solutions'* which I thought highly unconstructive. I decided to appease everyone with a photo of the hideous weld I'd just had done. *'Can you get the guy who welded it to do a test ride?'* one of them quipped.

But then I checked my Facebook and found what promised to be a real solution. I'd posted a plea for help on a Pamir Highway cycling group and now saw that I had a reply from a man in Dushanbe. He was something of a local bike dealer, and he said he had a fork that could work for me. He'd even sent me a photo, and there it was, one brand new fork, the right size, the right brake type, the right length steerer tube. It was a suspension fork, but that was alright, my bike was going to love looking so seriously bad-ass. It felt good to have an actual solution for the Pamir Highway, and I just had to pray that Mr Flat Cap's weld was going to survive the 500 kilometre ride to Tajikistan's capital.

Dea returned from Samarkand and we spent another couple of days relaxing and appreciating the blue domes and mosaic-covered facades of this wonderful old town, before reuniting with Alex for the ride onwards. As it happened, the rest of Uzbekistan proved fairly uneventful, my welded fork holding up fine on the paved roads, and not much of note happened. Now that we were in more populated regions, the level of traffic and the constant attention we got brought all of our stress levels up just a little, but it was easier for me to handle with company than it had been alone, and, as before, seeing poor women working so hard in the fields reminded me that nothing about my life was truly difficult.

Late one afternoon we arrived in Tajikistan to be greeted by a bill-board with the face of a suited man bearing down on us. I assumed him to be an important man, for he was standing in front of a very grand building, and also quite an unconscientious one, for he was trampling on some flowers.

Beyond the billboard of this important but unconscientious man we found another billboard of the same man, and then another one, and another, and then somewhere beyond that we found Tajikistan.

But it was worth waiting for, as it was a lovely place for an evening ride. People were out working in the fields, picking cotton as they had been in much of the last part of Uzbekistan, but they had time for a hello or a wave for us, without being as aggressive about it. Mountains were suddenly on the horizons in all directions, and there was a lovely atmosphere as the temperatures dropped with the sun. It felt so good to be in Tajikistan, beyond the deserts at last, and looking ahead to the challenge of the high mountains.

We camped on a rare strip of unused land behind a graveyard before riding on towards Dushanbe the next morning. It was a good ride, and along the way we stopped to buy fruit at some of the many stalls set up along the roadside. We had come in the right season, and the colourful vibrancy of the fruits on offer was matched only by the bright floral dresses and headscarves of the women behind the stalls. They flashed their gold teeth at us and shook their heads and refused to take our money. And they were not the only ones being generous. People stopped their cars to give us handfuls of fruit, and at one point some men ran out of their field to hand me freshly picked cucumbers. The people of Tajikistan could hardly have been more generous or welcoming, yet there was one thing we loved more than anything about this country. "Listen," Alex said, "no one is beeping their horn!"

There was one more extraordinary thing about this ride that I must mention, and that was the ridiculous number of billboards with that important but unconscientious fellow's face on them. I assumed he must be some sort of god to these people, because according to the heavily photoshopped images he was responsible for the abundance of fruit, and flowers, and for the mountains and the waterfalls, and just about everything good in Tajikistan, including judo lessons. In reality, of course, he was no god, just a dictatorial president with insecurity issues. I decided that I should count how many times I saw his face beaming down on his people, and this was a task that took some paying attention, for he was literally everywhere. It took just thirty-two kilometres of Tajikistan for me to reach a hundred sightings.

Dushanbe was much bigger than I remembered. No Véronique to stay with this time either, sadly, for she'd just moved back to France. That had us heading for the new cyclist hangout, the Green House Hostel, and we arrived a little tired from the city traffic and ready for another good break. Dushanbe is an ideal resting point before starting on the long and difficult climbs of the Pamir Highway, but we were going to need an extra long stop, for we now had a to-do list as long as, well, the small piece of paper Dea wrote it on, but she does have very small writing. Most urgently I needed a new fork, but Dea also needed a new front hub and bottom bracket as both were failing her, and even though we had a full complement of tyres, some of them were getting old and we had no spares. And in addition to bike parts we were also both in need of new shoes and warm clothes, for we had arrived here very late in the season, with rumours of minus twenty degrees Celsius at night up on the 4,000 metre high Pamir plateau we were soon to be camping on.

There were a few other cyclists in town, though nothing compared to the numbers that we'd have seen had we come in the high season. Jack and Barbara were around, and another Alex, this one from Somerset, who we'd already met a few times on our ride from Bukhara. And there was also a French cyclist named Marion. She'd had some real bad luck, having cycled from Europe only to suffer a bad foot injury as she started the Pamir Highway, and she'd had to catch a lift back here to try and recover.

The first thing that Dea and I did was to cycle back across town to meet with Dilshod, the local man who had the fork that I so badly needed, as well as an array of tyres, hubs, and bottom brackets. He was just a young guy who sourced these parts somehow from Almaty and traded in the courtyard outside of his Soviet-era apartment. I was really looking forward to getting my hands on the fork he'd sent me a photo of, so I was a bit surprised when he pulled out a different one. I could see right away that the steerer tube was too short to fit in my frame.

"This isn't the one you sent me the photo of," I said.

"No. I sold that one to another touring cyclist a few days ago."

This was terrible, terrifying news. My best chance of replacing my old welded-up fork was gone. And there was more bad news. Dilshod's tyre options were no good, the hubs were worse, and the bottom bracket was too wide. We fitted it to Dea's bike anyway, mostly I think because we didn't want all this to be for nothing, and she'd just have to get along without her big chainring, which, with all the climbing ahead of us, we reckoned she wouldn't be needing for a while anyway.

Over the next few days we scoured Dushanbe, following every lead we could find in search of our desired bicycle parts. We tried a bike repair place, which turned out to be a man with a shed, we tried the bicycle section of the crowded bazaar, we even tried the one and only actual bike shop, but the man there didn't have any of our desired parts either. The problem was that all the bikes we saw in Dushanbe were mountain bikes with disc brakes. I looked at literally every bicycle I saw, and they all had forks for disc brakes, with steerer tubes far too short for my needs.

But our misfortune was nothing compared to Marion's. Back at the Green House we found her with her leg in a cast, a doctor having told her it was a serious ligament injury that would take time to heal. She was going to have to fly home now, her trip over for the time being. It was a terrible blow for the poor girl, and I sympathised with her by asking for her tyres. I think I said something along the lines of, "Oh no, that is awful bad luck. Are they Schwalbe Mondials? They are, aren't they? Can I have them please? I'll give you lots of money!"

Luckily Marion was a nice girl, and she agreed to sell me her tyres. I stopped short of asking if I could also purchase her fork and front hub, though I would have dearly loved to. She was planning to resume her journey before too long, and it seemed a bit too much to ask her to dismantle her bicycle, and in any case I'd come up with a new plan, one of my more cunning ones. Alex from Somerset was flying to Dubai for a few days to meet with his girlfriend for a little holiday, and then flying back to Dushanbe to pick up his cycling trip. A little research showed that there was a decent bike shop in Dubai, so I asked him if he wouldn't mind picking up some bike parts for us while he was there. Alex from Somerset was one of those very friendly and laid-back sort of cyclists, not quite as laid-back as Alex from Guernsey, perhaps, but very laid-back nonetheless, and he said that he was more than happy to help.

So I spent the next few days e-mailing back and forth with a man from Wolfi's Bike Shop in Dubai about a new fork. At first he seemed to think they would have one that would fit, but with the cycling scene in Dubai being very much centred around expensive road bicycles, in the end there wasn't anything they had in stock that would work with my touring bike. At least Alex was going to be able to bring back a hub for Dea's wobbly front wheel, but as for me, this was the last throw of the dice. I wasn't going to be getting a new fork, and it was now painfully obvious that I was going to have to try to cycle the rough, remote, 1,500 kilometre Pamir Highway on a cracked fork that had been welded back together in five minutes by an Uzbek man in a flat cap who may or may not have known what he was doing. If I was going to do that, then I thought I'd better have a back-up plan in case of a catastrophic failure of the weld. In this case, my back-up plan involved a bit of metal that once held Dea's mirror, a screw, another piece of folded metal, and a lot of electrical tape. I fashioned this into something of a brace around the affected area, and hoped that, in the case of a catastrophic failure, this might at least hold the fork together well enough for me to not die. I also bought the bazaar's entire stock of electrical tape to take with me in reserve, just in case.

By this stage Jack and Barbara were long gone, Marion had flown home, and even Alex from Guernsey had got bored of waiting for us and left to cycle the Pamirs without us. Team Spirit was no more, and I was a little worried how Alex was going to get on alone with so few possessions, but a photo he sent back of him cycling in the snow with a pair of socks on his hands in lieu of gloves relieved my concerns. Other cyclists took their place at the hostel, including an excitable young Brit named Henry, who opened up his conversation with us by asking if we could cycle the Pamirs together. "I hope you don't mind, I promised my mum I wouldn't cycle on my own," he informed us. But after a little more conversation we realised he was a lot faster than us, and, as he'd already cycled with Alex from Somerset earlier in his trip, it made more sense for them to ride together. To complete the ensemble of cyclists, two more women of about thirty, Liz and Miranda, arrived. Liz was a sprightly English woman with short hair and a big smile, who we instantly clicked with. She worked as a journalist writing articles for some major newspapers, and funnily enough had been responsible for writing the *Guardian* article that had led us to ride the Ciro Trail back in Bosnia. She'd started her trip alone and had cycled all of the way from England to Istanbul, where her former housemate and friend, Miranda had joined her. Miranda, a quieter Irish woman who had not done much cycling before, had struggled a little bit through injury and illness, and they'd consequently covered a fair bit of the distance from Istanbul by other means. They were, however, both looking forward to the challenge of riding the Pamir Highway together.

The days passed and still there were more things for Dea and me to get done. I did my best to fix our broken tent, and ordered a new fork to be shipped to Almaty, Kazakhstan. We also managed to locate an outdoor/hunting store that had brand name quality gear to set us up for the cold nights ahead. Dea got a down vest and a down sleeping bag and a new pair of Gore-Tex Merrell shoes. I needed new shoes too, but unfortunately there was nothing in the store that would fit my big feet, so I ended up with a pair of fake Adidas from the bazaar, that I teemed up with a roll of bin liners to keep me warm at night.

But just as we thought we were getting on top of everything, more things went wrong. Our crank-removal tool broke, I noticed my own bottom bracket was loose, then I broke my brakes. Our bikes were now kind of in a worse state than when we'd arrived. But by some miracle the bike shop selling only disc brake mountain bikes had some Shimano v-brakes, and Alex from Somerset returned from Dubai carrying with him a bag of bicycle parts and tools for us, including Dea's new hub. Her old one was ridiculously wonky and it would have made great sense to change it before we left, but building up a new wheel again would take time, and Dea was going crazy with all our delays. The Pamir Highway was something she'd been looking forward to so much, it was pretty much the highlight of the trip, and the long wait in Dushanbe had cranked the suspense level up to maximum. So she declared that her wonky hub would surely last a bit longer, and suddenly there was nothing left for us to do but start cycling. Dea had her new hub, which wasn't on her bike, and a bottom bracket that was too big, my own bottom bracket was broken, my new shoes caused me blisters, and my fork was basically being held together with electrical tape. We were finally ready to take on the Pamir Highway.

42

Dushanbe, Tajikistan
28th September 2017

When we finally left Dushanbe it was alongside Liz and Miranda, but it wasn't long before we went our separate ways. There were two route options for the first section of the Pamir Highway, and they preferred to take the slightly easier, better paved one. Had I been thinking only of my cracked fork I would have followed them, but both Dea and I had been so looking forward to cycling the more challenging and remote alternative that I decided I would just have to avoid carrying weight on the front of my bike and be as careful as possible.

Our road did at least start off being paved, and we found ourselves climbing steadily uphill for a couple of days. Along the way we passed a rock that I recognised. Three years earlier I'd sat on it, having pedalled out of Dushanbe alone in a bad mood. I'd felt then like I didn't want to be cycling any more, a rare moment of doubt about my lifestyle brought about by the constant solitude. How nice it was to return now and think about how far I'd come since that moment, all of the way around the world in fact, and to now have with me the company of the most beautiful girl in the world to share the experience.

Near to the top of this first pass we were ushered to a stop by a local man in a suit. His name was Ishmael, he was a mature twenty-seven years old, and he spoke good English. He asked us where we were from and where we were going, and told us that we were very welcome in his country. As we spoke a bit of a crowd gathered, including one of Ishmael's cousins, who said something for him to translate.

"He asks if you would like to marry a Tajik girl?" Ishmael said.

"Oh, no, it's okay," I said, "I have a girl already."

"Yes, but that is not a problem, because you can have two wives here."

That sounded pretty good! I looked at Dea's face. No, no, it didn't sound good.

"No, I'm okay with one, thank you."

"In England, very beautiful girls," Ishmael said, almost changing the topic, "I have seen them on the internet."

"Have you really?"

"Yes, yes. Would you like to come for food, drink, to stay at our house?"

Dea and I looked at one another. The opportunity to visit a Tajik home seemed like a good one, but maybe these weren't our ideal hosts. But the decision was soon out of our hands, because before we could respond Ishmael had got in a car and begun to drive off. "Bye, bye," he screamed.

Not long after that we were caught up by two cyclists. Alex (from Somerset) and Henry had left Dushanbe the day after us, but were predictably moving a lot faster, and had ridden in a few hours what had taken us a day and a half. We stopped and chatted for a few minutes, before they continued on ahead, keen to make it to a guest house in a nearby town. We had no such ambitions, and ended up camping on a ledge overlooking a narrow gorge. It was a picturesque location, but it got a whole lot less pleasant when I was awoken in the middle of the night by a wet tent in my face. A storm was raging outside, and our cheap tent was struggling to hold up to the strong wind and rain, largely because we'd lost or bent almost all of the original pegs. As I ran outside in the gale trying to force the few pegs we had left back into the ground, I vowed that we really must try and get some new ones before trying to make camp on the exposed Pamir plateau.

By morning things had calmed down and we descended to the town of Obi Garm through dramatic scenery and light drizzle. In the town we found Alex and Henry at their guest house, put off from making their usual early start by the weather. Before leaving, we all went shopping together for supplies. Of course none of the little corner shops had any tent pegs for sale, but I found an acceptable substitute – one little store had several pairs of scissors on a back shelf. I indicated to the owner that I would like to buy them. He indicated, with a great display of honesty, that they didn't really work as scissors and I shouldn't waste my money. But I then indicated that for my needs this was not an issue, and the transaction was completed.

It seemed like a nice idea for us to cycle together as a group of four, and we set out from Obi Garm in that style. The rain had now stopped, and freewheeling down through a spectacular narrow gorge was tremendous fun. But immediately we hit upon a problem, for Dea and I liked to take it slow and stop to take photos, whereas Alex and Henry were the kind of cyclists who liked to cycle. After just a few kilometres and with the road turning uphill we decided that it wasn't going to work. They both had deadlines and needed to press on, so we wished them good luck, especially when they said they would like to get up and over the 3,250 metre pass ahead of us in a single day.

I knew from my previous experience here that such a climb was not to be taken lightly, and Dea and I continued with our slow and steady progress for the rest of the day. At some point the road turned from tarmac to gravel, and this put a great deal of fear into me. My fork felt so fragile as it bumped and jarred on the rocky surface, and the hundreds of kilometres of similar conditions that lay ahead of us seemed an impossible proposition.

"If your fork breaks you can take mine, and I'll just take a lift," Dea told me, demonstrating her unwavering commitment to help me see my challenge through to the end.

"I can't do that Dea, maybe I can just walk," I said. I didn't want to take her bike and deprive her the experience of cycling here, that was for sure. We both hoped it wouldn't come to that.

We managed only thirty-nine kilometres that day, but this didn't seem like such a bad total after the next day, when we rode a mere twenty-two. There were reasons for such a dismal total, however, beyond the road conditions and our general relaxed attitude. First thing in the morning I found that my chocolate milk had spilt in my pannier, which took a while to clean up, and get over, and just when I thought we were ready to go, I was stung by a wasp on my ear, and we had to delay our start a little longer for me to get the required amount of sympathy. When we did eventually do a bit of cycling we kept being held up by flocks of sheep or goats that were being herded everywhere along the road, and then by Dea's front derailleur, which didn't want to shift properly on account of her bottom bracket being about two inches too wide. Then in the afternoon, just when we'd got a bit of a head of steam up, Dea's troublesome knee started to hurt a bit, and we thought it a good idea to stop.

We decided it was better to take the rest of the afternoon off so that Dea's knee might get a little rest. There was an understandable look of concern on her face. Her knee problems were something we hoped we'd left behind, and for them to be returning now, at the start of the longest, toughest climb of the trip, seemed really quite unfair. But we made the best of it, sitting in the shade of some trees and playing a truly epic game of Yatzy (I needed to roll a six with the last throw of the dice to win, and I did! What are the odds?! Must be a million to one!). And it was as we were sitting in the shade of those trees that a puppy came over to see what all the fuss was about. He looked a little lost and hungry, so we threw him some bread and he grabbed it and took it a little way away to eat nervously. He was an adorable little thing, this black and white puppy, and he spent the afternoon lounging around in the grass near us. He looked like he'd been left here by someone. We weren't near any villages, there wasn't much food around, and we wondered how long he'd survive out here by himself.

"What's his name?" Dea asked.

"Harry," I said, without really knowing why.

We thought it might be nice to give Harry some more food, so we were pleased when he followed us to our campsite overlooking a nearby river. He was still nervous about getting too close to us, and didn't want to lie in the pile of clothes we put out for him as a makeshift basked, but he ate a little bit of plain pasta. We cooked more pasta than we needed and mixed it with beans and tomato sauce, our regional speciality, then ate what we could and offered the rest to Harry. He licked at it, then turned away. "Don't like tomato sauce, huh?" I said. Poor Harry. He was quite thin and looked like he needed looking after. I fired up the stove again, and cooked up some more plain pasta for him.

We awoke in the morning to see Harry curled up asleep in his basket. "Aww," we said. He woke up and seemed pleased to see us. Up until this point we hadn't touched him, for that wasn't a very sensible thing to do with stray dogs, yet now I couldn't resist seeing how he might react to a pat on the head and a little stroke. Well, he loved it, and we were soon both stroking him and rubbing his belly and falling in love with this cute little puppy.

"You know we can't keep him, don't you?" Dea said. "We should probably leave him here."

"I don't think it's up to us," I said, and sure enough, little Harry ran along behind us as we returned to the road and began to cycle. Whether we wanted it or not, we'd got ourselves a dog. I tried to encourage Harry to run on the inside of me, away from the traffic, but that wasn't something he was very good at, so it was a relief when we soon arrived at the junction where we would leave most of the traffic behind and head for the mountains. There was a checkpoint at the turn, where Dea and I had to go inside and add our names to a big book of them. When we stepped back outside Harry was sitting there waiting patiently beside our bikes. As we resumed cycling he resumed running along behind, trusting us that we were going to look after him, trusting that we were leading him somewhere good. A shame then, that we were leading him on a narrow, winding, pot-holed track up into inhospitable high mountains.

Harry was such a good dog. He would occasionally bark at cows or consider chasing chickens, but he stopped this and behaved himself when we told him to. There were not many cars here, and when one did come along we would stop and call Harry over, and he would sit patiently beside us until the danger passed. Then one time when this happened the car stopped, and a familiar face leaned out of the passenger window. It was young Henry. "I got really sick," he said. "Almost as soon as we left you, actually. I had to take a day off yesterday. Now I'm taking a lift over the mountain to Kalaikhum to recover. Alex should be along soon."

Dea and I were in shock. We'd been cycling so little, plodding along like tortoises, yet somehow we'd got ourselves ahead of the hares. Well, until one of them got in a car anyway.

Dea and I soon stopped to take a break, admire the views, and wait for Alex. And sure enough, it wasn't long before he pedalled up towards us. It was good to see him again, and to introduce him to our little friend, and for the next couple of hours we went along together as a group of four, through mountain scenery that was so spectacular that it was difficult to make any progress at all without stopping every few moments to take pictures. Harry seemed quite pleased about this, and took to lying down and resting every time that we stopped. I started to think that maybe he wasn't going to be able to run behind us all of the way to China, and a plan began to formulate in my mind. The last time that I'd cycled this way I'd been invited to stay with a family in Tavildara, the last town before the really big climb began, by a man who could speak English. If we could find him again maybe we could convince him to look after Harry, or at least to help us find someone in town who would do so. We knew deep down that it was impossible for us to keep Harry, and our mission now was to find him a good home.

We stopped for lunch when a rare café appeared, and ordered the soup, which I think was the only thing on the menu. For once I was delighted to see that it came with a large chunk of unspecified meat floating in it. When the owner of the café wasn't looking I dropped this meat on the floor for Harry. But Harry was lying exhausted over by the bikes and didn't realise. I tried calling out to him but he didn't come. I whistled, but still nothing. "Quick, Harry, the owner is coming back!" I ran over and scooped him up and plonked him down by the meat, which he gobbled up. Dea then gave him her meat as well. Alex looked at us a bit strange, with a 'he's not getting my meat' expression on his face.

After lunch Alex pushed on alone, wanting to make up time, leaving Dea and me to work out what to do with our little puppy. It was obvious that he was getting tired, so as we prepared to go on I picked him up and put him in my basket. He only just squeezed in, but he seemed quite happy sitting there, and it was there that he spent most of the afternoon, bobbing along, watching the world go by. *'So much for keeping the weight on the front down,'* I thought, as we navigated the winding cliffsides and crossed streams together. It really must have been quite an adventure for the little guy, and whatever else happened, I was sure he was going to remember this experience for the rest of his life.

We made camp, having clocked up another thirty-two kilometres for the day, and Harry spent the night curled up in the porch area of the tent. In the morning he was so happy to see us, a joy matched only by how happy we were to see him. He jumped up in excitement and tried to get in the tent with us, but instead we came outside to run around with him, his tail wagging and his eyes shining with joy. He was such a lovely little thing and he had won such a special place in our hearts in such a short time. We loved him so, and only wished we could keep him, could fast forward somehow a couple of years to a time when we would be more settled, more able to care for a dog. But the truth was we couldn't look after him properly on our bikes, and this was most likely going to be the day we would have to say goodbye.

It was another twenty-five kilometres to Tavildara. The road was still bad, but Harry had his energy back and ran along behind us again, at least for a little while. We passed through a couple of smaller villages, where Harry was picked up and stroked by some kids, offering us hope that he might find some loving owners in this country. I knew that dogs are not kept as pets in the Islamic world in the same way as back home, and we had our doubts as to whether we were really going to find Harry a good home, or if we would be leaving him to try and survive on the streets of Tavildara. We were both filled with such sadness and anxiety throughout the morning, worried by what fate we were going to be leaving Harry to.

Just before the bridge into Tavildara there was a police checkpoint, and as we rode up to it two puppies ran out from behind it. "Ah, look Harry, new friends for you, maybe you can just live right here," was what I was about to say, but my words were drowned out by the vicious, angry barks being directed at him by these mean little dogs. "Okay, let's try going a bit further."

We crossed the bridge and some young boys ran to greet us, asking us if we needed a hotel, and showing some interest in our dog. We were not looking for a hotel, but rather a row of shops that I remembered. It was here that three years earlier I'd met Muhammad, the English-speaking man, and his shopkeeper uncle, who had invited me and four other cyclists to stay the night at his house. And sure enough, there were the shops, just as I remembered them, and inside one of them was indeed this uncle. I approached him and showed him a photo that I'd taken in 2014 of him and Muhammad in order to help explain who I was. It was a bit awkward, because his hair was all grey in the photo, and black now, but luckily he understood that I was not trying to say, "You dye your hair, I see," but in fact, "I slept in your house once." He smiled and shook my hand in recognition. I asked if Muhammad was around, for with his English skills he really was the key to finding Harry a good home. But the uncle shook his head. Muhammad was not here. He lived in Dushanbe now, and the uncle was unable even to reach him by phone.

Unable to communicate further with the uncle about the situation, I went back outside and sat with Dea on the steps of the shop. We'd left Harry to run around, hoping he might find his way to a new home by himself. He certainly seemed quite excited at being in a town, full of people and life and interesting smells. But there was an atmosphere about the place that was unsettling. People didn't seem very friendly, a group of boys were teasing Harry in a not very nice way, and one man even appeared to aim a kick at him. Were we really going to leave him to live on these harsh streets? Would he like it here? Would he survive?

I felt terribly sad and I did not know what to do. I didn't feel comfortable leaving Harry here, but I knew we couldn't carry him with us up to 4,000 metres, either. Then Muhammad's sister came out of the shop, so I showed her Harry. I tried my best to ask her if she could look after him. But she just shook her head and indicated that dogs belonged on the street, not in the house.

Oh, how sad this was. How we had failed Harry. We had brought him to this place, we had led him on this journey with promises to find him a better life, and now we saw this place and it looked mean and unfriendly and no place for such a good dog. But there was nothing else for it, no more towns before the first high pass. It was here or it was nothing.

We stocked up on some food. I bought some uninspiring groceries from the uncle, and then Dea said she thought it a good idea to check another shop to see what they had. While she was in there, I stood in the street with the bikes and watched as one of the boys we'd met when we first crossed the bridge into town came along. He picked up Harry, looked at me, and pointed at himself, as if asking me for permission to keep the puppy. I was unsure of this boy's intentions, but with so few options I decided to just take a chance on him being a good kid. I nodded my approval.

The boy's face lit up in delight, and he began to walk up the street with Harry in his arms. Another boy ran alongside, poking at him. I recognised him as one of the boys who had been teasing Harry before and I was struck with fear. What exactly were they planning to do with little Harry? Were they going to look after him? Were they going to torture him? Were they going to love him until they got bored and then start kicking him? It felt wrong. I wanted to run after them and grab Harry back. Where was Dea? I needed her opinion. I needed her to tell me to go and get Harry back from those evil kids. But she was still in the shop. I felt so sad. The boys rounded a corner at the top of a hill, and Harry was gone.

Finally Dea came out of the shop. She had a beaming smile on her face.

"Chris, I've found a nice man. He can speak English, he has a dog already, and he says he will take Harry! Isn't it amazing?!"

"Oh crap, Dea, I've just given him away to some kids!"

I didn't wait to see her reaction, I was already bounding up the street as fast as my legs would carry me, desperate to get Harry back before it was too late. I rounded the corner and saw the boy up ahead, Harry still cradled in his arms. "Sorry, but there has been a mistake," I said, taking the cute little puppy out of the stunned child's arms.

I walked back down to the shop and showed Harry to the man, whose name was Tohir. He looked at Harry and said, "You want to give this dog to me as a gift? I accept!" And he said it in a way that made it obvious that he was a good and kind man who would take good care of Harry. It felt like a miracle, it really did. He brought out a biscuit for the puppy and asked what his name was, and Dea and I were so overwhelmed with relief to have found a good owner for Harry. But then I looked up and saw the boy standing nearby, the boy who a few moments ago had had a new puppy and now looked on sadly. "Do you know this boy?" I asked.

Tohir looked up and smiled, "Yes, that is my brother, he likes dogs too, he has two dogs. He loves dogs."

And the miracle was complete.

I felt overcome by emotion. It was relief and joy and love and happiness at what had just occurred. Tohir and Tohir's little brother were going to look after Harry together, they were going to love him and play with him and give him the good home he deserved. As Tohir's brother picked Harry up again and carried him once more up the street (moving quite a bit faster this time, I might add), we knew that we had done the right thing. Harry was a great, great dog, who had, just for a little while, brought us so much joy. He'd been on one hell of an adventure, had this little puppy, and now at last he'd found his happy ending.

43

Tajik mountains
4th October 2017

"Yep, this is definitely the same place," I said. Dea looked at the trickle of water running through the rocky river bed with a sceptical look on her face. "There was a lot more water last time," I added.

We were crossing the same river that three years earlier had almost stolen my bike away from me, and probably would have done were it not for the intervention of Gábor and John, two of the cyclists I'd been cycling with back then. But it was hard even for me to recognise it now; the little stream looked so pathetic compared to my memories of the raging torrent of that day. Interestingly, this was one of the few times when I was exactly retracing my wheelturns. Crossing the Caspian Sea instead of going through Iran and Turkmenistan meant that I'd not repeated too many roads until now, less than twenty percent of all our kilometres in fact, but the Pamir Highway was unquestionably an experience worth revisiting. And as we climbed up and away from the river, gradually inching our way towards the 3,252 metre high summit, memories were frequently rekindled. The corner where Rob and I had huddled out of a sudden hailstorm, the puddle where Gábor had inexplicably stopped to clean his bike with a toothbrush. It was all still here, but it was also surprisingly different. Travelling in October instead of May meant that it was a lot drier everywhere, and not only were the rivers much less formidable, but the dirt road was also easier, as muddy sections where I remembered Rob and I struggling to push our bikes through were now bone dry. As we got higher up through the valley we came up upon the hills that I had so brilliantly likened to mint chocolate chip ice cream covered in white sauce in my first book because of their green grass and white drizzling of snow. Now, however, there was no snow at all, and the hills were a dusty dry yellow, that, if I had to push myself for another dessert-based simile, was more reminiscent of a sultana sponge.

We stopped and made camp before the top, as it was too much of a climb for us to make it all the way up in one day. Dea said she could feel the altitude, but thankfully her knee was behaving itself after some more slight adjustments to her saddle, and she looked strong. We had a long way to go before we'd be through with the Pamirs, but I knew that this first climb was as difficult as anything ahead of us, and Dea had tackled it with great gusto. Her positive attitude continued in the morning, and we made relatively light work of the remaining kilometres to the summit.

"Was that it?" Dea said, taking a seat in the world's most unlikely bus shelter. "That wasn't so bad, was it?"

A gloriously long descent through the mountains brought us to Kalaikhum. Despite having a population of less than 2,000 permanent residents, this was one of the bigger settlements we'd come across in this remote region, and we decided to take advantage of the opportunity for a night in a guest house. By coincidence, two Danish women who were cycling in the opposite direction were also there. Dea already knew about Marianne and Heidi, for the community of Danish cycle tourists is relatively small, and it was great to have the chance to hang out with them for a bit. Dea also took the time to rebuild her front wheel with the new hub Alex had delivered from Dubai, and her bike was soon looking in good shape. The same could not really be said for mine, but underneath all the electrical tape the weld at least seemed to be holding firm, and that gave me hope that we might just make it all the way through without disaster striking. And that was a good thing, because we could not rely on Kalaikhum to bail us out this time if something did go wrong, for the little kiosk where I'd once miraculously found a replacement for my snapped rear derailleur was sadly no longer anywhere to be seen.

In the evening Liz and Miranda arrived, having successfully cycled from Dushanbe via the other road. It had taken them longer than planned, partly because Miranda had come down with a chest infection which was clearly still troubling her. As a result they needed to rest a little longer in Kalaikhum, and so Dea and I were once again riding by ourselves when we continued the following day. And it was a particularly interesting day, for we were now following the Panj River, on the other side of which was the country of Afghanistan. We stared over at men in robes and women in burkas and children in bare feet, all travelling between adobe houses by way of motorcycle, donkey, or, more often than not, simply on foot.

For five days we followed this valley towards Khorog, on a gravel road that was the right mix of adventurous and challenging, yet possible. At times we passed through narrow canyons, where clifftops rose above us and rocks threatened to fall down on us and the river raged in rapids beneath us. At other times the valley was a little wider, and there was space for trees, many of which were turning yellow with the season. When these brightly coloured trees were set alongside the blue skies, the giant mountains, and the impossibly turquoise river, it was not hard to see how this area got its reputation. It was not just a naturally beautiful place, but the kind of place that takes natural beauty and redefines it to levels you could never have imagined possible. But the beauty of this region was not confined to its looks. One day we heard singing coming from the other side of the river. We looked over to see a young boy walking along the track on the far bank and, presumably with a long way to walk given the infrequent Afghan villages, he was keeping himself entertained. He had an angelic voice, and we couldn't help ourselves but to stop and stare, to listen to his melody and wonder about his life, taking place a hundred metres and a whole world away from our own. Then it seemed that he spotted us, and he stopped walking too, and his singing continued in what had now become a private concert just for us. He belted out the words with all his heart, this little Afghan boy, words that silenced the river between us and echoed through the valley. When his song reached its final note we broke into rapturous applause and shouted "bravo" to him across the river, so appreciative of this special moment, when our worlds dared to connect just for a moment.

And the locals on our side of the river were adding special memories to our journey too. The Tajik children constantly waved and said hello to us, sometimes people would stop to give us handfuls of fruits or walnuts, and a few times we were invited inside family homes to drink tea or eat salty yoghurt. The only frustrating thing about these interactions came with the limitations placed by the language barrier, but on our last morning before Khorog we were stopped by a woman who could speak English. She didn't appear at first glance to be the ideal candidate for such advanced language skills, for she was out walking her cow, but as we were soon to discover there was much more to this woman than that.

"Are you not cold?" were her first words to us, as we came up to her on our bikes. Actually the daytime temperatures were still well above freezing, but it was true that we were here late in the year, and she herself had a thick fur vest over her long black and white dress. We told her we were not doing too badly with the cold, but nevertheless we did not refuse when she suggested we come inside and have some hot tea.

The lady's name was Maya, and she showed us into her home, where her grown-up son was sitting watching television. The main room of the house was similar to the others we'd seen in this part of the world, with a raised platform covering three sides of the large room. This platform was covered in carpet, and had piles of rugs and cushions on it and seemed like it could at various times act as tables, chairs, sofas, or beds for all the family. But Maya's home was better furnished than most we'd seen, with a modern Western-style kitchen in one corner of the room, and the television hanging on the wall, which was currently transfixing Maya's forty-year-old son with an episode of the American reality show *Fear Factor* dubbed into Russian.

"It's a terrible programme," Maya said, shaking her head but flashing her gold teeth at us at the same time. She poured us some tea and set out a plate of butter next to it, explaining that it was quite normal to put butter in tea here. "If you want to put butter in your tea, that's your problem," she said, in what may or may not have been a rare mistake with her English. "And if you don't want to, that's your problem too."

It was great to have the chance to talk properly with someone, especially this charismatic old lady who seemed like she had a lot of things worth saying, and I only wished I didn't find the young Americans jumping into shark tanks on the screen above us so distracting. It can be frustrating the way moving images can steal your attention, and I did my best to focus on what Maya was saying as she told us about life here. "For a lot of people here life is very hard," she said. "People don't have a lot of things, it is just about trying to get enough to eat, get clean water. Here people only wait for tomorrow."

I knew from my last visit to the region that the people here felt hard done by the president, who was from a different ethnic group and preferred to look after his own people first. Curious to know more, I asked her if life here was better before him, when Tajikistan was a part of the Soviet Union.

"In Soviet times it was better, yes. But then came the civil war, and it was a terrible time. People from different valleys, you know all these valleys you've come through, people from different valleys fighting each other. Everyone just trying to kill each other. A terrible thing. And everything was closed off. The road was closed. We had to survive with just the food we could grow here. For many months, maybe a year, we had no help at all, except sometimes a little rice from Afghanistan. So many people died, it was very sad."

It was sobering to listen to this woman, to hear her tell us what real fear is all about, so very far removed from the 'reality' television going on behind her.

But it wasn't long before our conversation returned to happier topics. Maya seemed to know so much about the world, and we asked her if she had ever travelled outside of Tajikistan. I thought she might have been to some other countries in the region perhaps, but I certainly wasn't expecting her to say, "Yes, I have been to Italy!" but it was true. Three years earlier she'd been invited to go to Turin to represent Tajikistan at an international conference about 'slow food'.

"Oh, it was wonderful," she said. "We were there to tell people about the way we grow food here, how we cook with natural ingredients. Oh, it was such an experience for me to see Europe!"

Maya's eyes were all lit up, a big gold-toothed grin all over her face as she remembered those days. But talk of Europe moved to Spain, where Maya told us they had recently approved gay marriage, and she wanted to know what we thought about that. For a moment there was silence, for it seemed unlikely to be something anyone in Tajikistan would publicly approve of. But we wanted to be honest, and Dea told Maya that she thought it okay for a man to marry a man or a woman to marry a woman if that was what they wanted.

Maya shook her head, but instead of disagreeing all she said was, "The world is changing!" and her wonderful mischievous smile returned.

The Pamir Lodge is almost legendary among touring cyclists as *the* place to stop for a few days in the town of Khorog, before or after the great challenge of the Pamir plateau. In the height of the season it is packed with travellers, relaxing, recovering, exchanging tips, and sharing tales from the road. It seemed strange, then, to arrive and stand in the empty courtyard, the only sound being a slight breeze rustling through the yellowing leaves, and look over at a row of unoccupied rooms. It was now mid-October, and if we had not known for sure that Liz and Miranda were still behind us we would have believed we were the last cyclists foolish enough to be heading up to 4,000 metres this year. We had left it very late, that was for sure, but Maya had told us that October and November were actually the dry months, and the heavy snows would not come until the end of the year. That meant that the roads should at least still be open, but which one would we be taking? Once again we had a choice. We could either continue to follow the 'main' road, the M41, which I knew was a decent paved road as I had taken it the last time, or we could take a slightly longer scenic detour through the Wakhan Valley, on a road which we had been told was pretty much guaranteed to break our bikes. It was apparently all gravel and washboard and sand, and everyone we'd met this late in the season had avoided it. Alex from Guernsey, Jack and Barbara, Alex from Somerset, Henry, they'd all taken the M41. It made me wonder what was wrong with the class of 2017. Were cycle tourists getting softer? Almost everyone I'd ridden with back in 2014 had gone for the Wakhan Valley, and they'd absolutely loved it (the only reason I'd gone the other way was because I had so little time left on my visa). It was supposed to be a beautiful ride, and I didn't want to miss out on it again. I knew it was absolute madness to take my welded fork on a road that was notorious for breaking bikes, the only sensible option was to take the paved road. But the more Dea and I discussed it, the more times we told ourselves it was crazy, the more convinced we became that we had to cycle the Wakhan Valley. It was something we both wanted to do so much, and the call of adventure, that overwhelming temptation to test ourselves against this challenge settled it for us. It had to be the Wakhan.

We set out from Khorog with apprehension, excitement, and lots and lots of food. The Wakhan route continued to follow the Panj River and the Afghan border, and for the first 200 kilometres the road was not too bad, passing through a surprising number of small villages along the way. The local people continued to be friendly to us, and we were also greatly amused by many of their animals. It was the mating season, and several times we watched horny male donkeys chasing females around the fields, braying madly in a frenzy of hor-mones, while kids ran after them hopelessly trying to get them under control. On one occasion two giant male bulls held up our progress by staging a testosterone-fuelled fight in the middle of the road, while a few goats provided us with more light-hearted entertainment by climbing up in trees to get at the tastiest foliage.

But there wasn't much green left. Almost all of the trees were now glowing in red, orange, or most often yellow, and it really was the most spectacular of autumns, making us glad that we had come so late in the year. The scenery became even more spectacular, with the snow-covered Hindu Khush mountain range that marks the border between Afghanistan and Pakistan now a dominant feature of the skyline on the other side of the river, and other 6,000 metre high peaks rising up on ours. But every day was warm and sunny, we more often than not were cycling in shorts and T-shirts, and even though the temperatures would plummet below freezing at night, we had six sleeping bags between us and we coped just fine. It seemed like we had made the right decision in coming this way.

But then we got to the last of the villages, a place that felt like the end of the world, and the road suddenly became much worse, climbing away from the river in a series of extremely steep switchbacks. We struggled to pedal up, and with the road now an uneven combination of rocks and sand it took a monumental effort. Soon we were forced to get off and push, but this was barely any easier, and we stopped every few metres to catch our breath.

"Wow, I didn't know it would be this hard," I said.

"No, but we can do it," Dea replied, not allowing in a hint of negativity. And she was right, we could do it. We had to do it, actually; there was no turning back, not now.

After a few hours the road levelled out and we were able to ride our bikes again, and take in the magnitude of where we were. We'd climbed up onto the cliffsides of another valley, following a tributary of the Panj, and Afghanistan was still on the other side, but now we were somewhere truly remote, beyond all the villages and homes, where no shepherds or horny donkeys roamed. The mountains on both sides of the valley stood over us, gigantic, formidable, humbling, as we pedalled pathetically in their shadows. This was truly an epic adventure, in a landscape that belonged to another world, another time, a place where it felt like we did not really belong, and yet there was nowhere we'd rather be.

For three days we moved on up through this hidden world. We would be passed maybe five or six times per day by four-wheel-drive pick-ups carrying passengers up to the plateau, and once or twice we spotted caravans of Afghans travelling on the far side with camels in a scene that really did belong to another era, but for the vast majority of the time it was just us. The road was bad, sometimes just sand that we had to push through, other times rocks or washboard that rattled my fork and had me wondering just what our exit strategy would be if it failed out here. But my fork continued to stand heroically up to its task, and towards the end of the third day we reached a military checkpoint that we knew marked the end of our time alongside Afghanistan. We had heard that other cyclists had had trouble with corrupt and no doubt quite bored young soldiers holding up their progress at this checkpoint in the past, but we were allowed through without trouble.

From the checkpoint the road climbed more steeply upwards, one final challenging ascent as we at last neared the Pamir plateau. We set ourselves the task of getting to a lake that, at about 4,300 metres, was pretty much the top of the pass, the end of this long climb that we had been on since leaving Kalaikhum two weeks and 3,100 vertical metres earlier. We hoped that the lake would make for a good place to camp, and that motivated us to press on strongly up the climb despite the gravel road and thin atmosphere. And just before sunset we arrived triumphantly at our destination. Unfortunately the lake was quite dry and not as scenic as we might have hoped, and we were in quite an exposed spot, but we now had no choice but to stop. We hurried to put on all of our clothes and get the tent up quickly, fixing it to the ground with rocks and scissors, and then dived inside. At 4,300 metres this was going to be the highest that I had ever camped at and Dea was complaining of an altitude-induced headache, but my main concern was the cold, as we huddled together in all of our sleeping bags in an attempt to keep ourselves from freezing, even utilising my brilliant secret bin liner technique for added warmth (it involves stuffing bin liners down inside your clothes, not so secret any more, or brilliant really).

It was a bitterly cold night, but we made it through until morning, and there was good news as Dea's headache had apparently gone. I, on the other hand, felt truly awful. A very odd feeling washed over me as I climbed out of the tent and tried to stand up. My head simply wasn't right. I couldn't think straight, it was almost as if I were drunk, and the synapses in my brain just weren't quite connecting right. My body also felt incredibly weak, and, drained of all energy, I collapsed into the sand.

Dea was naturally very worried about me as I lay there motionless. I was conscious of the fact that I most likely had altitude sickness, but I couldn't find the energy to move. I was aware that it was very cold. I was aware that the only real cure for altitude sickness was to descend. I was aware that doing nothing wasn't really an option, but I couldn't move. I couldn't clear the fog in my brain and the malaise in my body enough to stand, or even to respond to the look of anguish on my poor girlfriend's face.

44

Tajik mountains
22nd October 2017

"Chris, you need to pack up your things. It's important."
Dea's words cut through the haze and struck a chord somewhere inside my mind. She was right. It *was* important. I needed to descend to a lower altitude to feel better, and to do that I needed to move myself. I could not rely on a car to come along and get me out of this mess. It would ruin my whole challenge, and in any case, there weren't any.

I packed my things into my panniers and loaded up my bike, a task which seemed monumentally more difficult than it ever had before. Every pannier felt like a lead weight and I was left gasping for oxygen just lifting them onto the frame.

"I'll pack up the tent," Dea said. "You just get going." The concern in her voice confirmed what a serious situation I was in. I felt so lucky to have her with me.

I left Dea to deal with the tent, confident she would easily catch me up, and began to pedal. As difficult as this was, I knew I had to do it, and my legs began moving on autopilot mode, muscle memory guiding me even as my brain failed me. I was aware that my fingers and toes were completely frozen but this did not bother me in the slightest. The only thought I had was that I needed to descend. I needed to get down to a lower altitude. Unfortunately this was not easy, as we had not quite reached the summit of the pass the night before, and so before I could go down I first had to go up. With the road being bad and my body being weak this was not an easy thing to do. I struggled on up, not daring to stop because I did not believe I would be able to start again. Slowly I edged on up the pass.

Eventually I made it to the top and a long descent loomed in front of me. I felt a sense of relief, but also one of concern, for my companion was still not yet at my side. As much as I needed to go down, I could not do so without Dea, I could not leave her on this harsh frozen mountain pass. So I sat down on a rock and ate half a Snickers, all that I could stomach, and waited for her. Before too long she appeared, and we could descend together.

Initially the road dropped quickly and I felt like I was on my way to safety, but sadly this steep descent lasted only a few kilometres. The road then flattened out and to my dismay even started to go up again in places. I knew parts of the plateau ahead of us were at 3,800 metres, which I hoped would be low enough to facilitate my recovery, but here we were still well above 4,000 metres and I wasn't feeling any better. In fact I was getting worse. The climbs were steep and just incredibly difficult for me. At times I had to walk, and even then I could walk only a few paces before needing to stop and catch my breath. Dea stayed alongside me, comforting me, promising me that it would all be okay. This was one of the hardest days of my life. All I felt like doing was lying down. I couldn't stomach any food. When I did force some down it was only a little time before it came back up again, and I was growing weaker and weaker.

Dea kept me motivated. "I think it's the last uphill," she said, as we stood looking at another climb, a statement which couldn't have been based on anything more than her sense of optimism. Ignoring the protests of every fibre of my being I walked up it, step by painful step, until I reached the top and saw that Dea was right. There was a long descent ahead of us. We freewheeled down that and arrived at a flatter section, where I announced that we were surely low enough now, and I could go no further. I collapsed on the ground. Dea put up the tent, and I crawled inside. We had gone seventeen kilometres.

I slept all afternoon, woke up briefly to eat some pasta and beans that Dea had cooked, then slept all evening and all night. It was almost certainly the best sleep I had ever had. It was a glorious, glorious sleep, it really was, and the following morning I awoke feeling so much better. My own mind was back in my head again, and I felt strong enough to ride onwards. We cycled the last few kilometres of the bumpy, uninhabited road that we'd been on for so long, and then felt the strange sensation of tarmac under our wheels. It was the M41. We had made it to the Pamir plateau.

This road was still very quiet, and the sense of remoteness remained as we began to make much faster progress eastwards through the wide open rocky landscape flanked on either side by mountain peaks. It wasn't long before we arrived in Alichur, a village of squat white homes that sits in the middle of all this nothingness. It felt truly bizarre to be back in civilization again. Just seeing people felt like a tremendous novelty. We found a shop, though the lady who owned it had to unlock it just for us. Inside she pointed to a handwritten note on the wall which stated in English, 'Come in and choose whatever you want', which was a nice touch, but not really all that appropriate given that her shop sold basically nothing other than sweets. Seeing as this wasn't really going to fill us up, we made our way to a café for lunch. Having not been inside a building for over a week it felt so unbelievably good to step in out of the cold for a little while and consume some warm eggs and sweet tea.

The discomfort of returning outside to the cold road was eased by the tremendous tailwind that blew us along for the rest of the day, and for much of the next morning. I put on some music and felt so happy to be back here. It was an almost perfect place to cycle – this great empty road, through such beautiful scenery, under a big blue sky, with my girl at my side. It was really only the fact that it felt so freezing cold every time that we paused to take a break that stopped it reaching perfection. But the cold of late October at 4,000 metres was beginning to take its toll. Dea was sometimes finding the long, cold nights camping to be a challenge, and so we decided a stop at a guest house in Murghab would be a good idea. This town of 6,000 souls appeared a hundred kilometres or so after Alichur, and consisted of more simple white homes inexplicably situated in this harsh world. When I'd last come through here in the summertime I'd been amazed at how people could live in such a remote place, but in our current season I was even more astonished at the thought of the freezing winter ahead that these people would have to endure. At the guest house we were each given a bucket of hot water to pour over ourselves, for there were no showers, but we were at least given a heated room to sleep in, and lots of fried potatoes. Overall our stay here provided the desired morale boost, my mood only slightly dampened by having to replace one of the Schwalbe Mondial tyres with our last spare due to an infuriating failure of the sidewall.

In the morning we restocked our dwindling food supplies at Murghab's bazaar, a collection of small shops housed in old shipping containers. We found a number of good things, including such surprising treats as cheese, cakes, grapes and apples, and stocked up with enough of it to see us through the rest of Tajikistan. With our bikes once again loaded down we wheeled out of town on the empty road. Ahead of us, beyond the first row of mountains, we could see two white triangles of cloud.

"Those are in China," Dea said, pointing excitedly at them.

"What are you talking about?" I said, confused. "They're just clouds, aren't they?"

"No, Chris, they are mountains in China, look." And she pulled out a map we had of the region to prove it to me. Sure enough, there were two peaks across the border in China, a fair distance away, but each standing more than 7,500 metres tall.

"Oh yeah, wow. You're right Dea."

And then I realised what that meant. I could see China. Three years after I'd left it behind, I could see it again. My dream of going all the way around by bike and boats was now so close to becoming a reality. I could see China. I could actually, really, actually see China.

It wasn't over yet, of course. There was still a long way to go through the rest of Tajikistan, all of Kyrgyzstan, and still more of Kazakhstan before I'd even get to the Chinese border, never mind Mori, but spotting those white peaks encouraged me to daydream.

For days after I was trying to imagine how it might feel to cycle back into Mori, to ride up to the sculpture I'd made the official start line when I'd recommenced my challenge. I fantasised about it over and over, but the truth was I had no idea how it would really feel to be there, to complete this goal after so many years. All I could do was pretend. I watched myself in my mind's eye punching the air in celebration, screaming with joy, throwing my arms around the great sculpture of Mori like a lunatic. But there was one thing missing from these fantasies: Dea. She did not have a Chinese visa, and it had become impossible for her to get one anywhere in Central Asia. I'd got mine in Edinburgh, thanks to a miraculous arrangement my country had with the Chinese granting us Brits visas with two year validities. Danish people, like most others, had to enter China within three months of the visa being issued, meaning that even if Dea had got one when we were back in Europe it would be worthless by now. We had desperately hoped that some of the embassies on our route would start issuing Chinese visas again, but that hadn't happened, and now we had to make a new plan. Dea would go with me only as far as Kazakhstan, perhaps up to the border with China, before I would have to leave her to cycle the final stretch to Mori alone. At first I had been quite alright with this idea. I knew that it was going to be incredibly tough going, riding through such a difficult country as China in the middle of winter, and I reasoned that one person instead of two equalled half the chance of something going wrong at the crucial stage. This was a project that I'd started alone, and it was one that I thought I could finish alone. But then I saw how upset Dea was about the idea, and I realised that, even though the bike and boat circumnavigation was my project, it had come to be just as important to her. From the start we had said that we were cycling to China, and I could tell it broke her heart a little bit that she wasn't going to be cycling into Mori with me. But, short of her flying home to get a visa, it was impossible now. It wasn't going to happen. And in the midst of this sad realisation was also the question of what we were going to do next, once my journey back to Mori was resolved. From our first plans we had said we would go to Nepal and India after China, and so we now decided that while I pedalled through China alone Dea would catch a flight to Kathmandu and wait for me there. With no cycling route possible between China and Nepal I would hop on a plane myself as soon as my mission was complete in order to join her there. I felt quite uncomfortable with the idea of voluntarily using motorised transportation again, it went against something that had become rooted deep inside me, but it was a compromise that needed to be made. It was the only way to get to Nepal and India, and that was where we had decided to continue travelling. Secretly I was extremely unsettled by the idea of getting on that plane, but I felt like I owed it to Dea to do so. She had made so many sacrifices for me, I would surely make this one for her.

Before leaving Tajikistan we had two more passes to climb. The first required us to go to the highest point of our trip, at 4,655 metres above sea level, and was an awful struggle. The lack of oxygen in the air became painfully obvious to our poor lungs, and we had to keep pausing every few moments to catch our breath. I found it much tougher than I remembered it being before, and even the superstar with me remarked that it was the hardest thing she had ever done. But one way or another we did eventually make it to the summit, and I found the energy to climb up onto a rock, so that I should be the highest that I had ever been (just beating the last time I was here, when I didn't climb up onto a rock).

Another cold, cold night had us waking up to ice on our sleeping bags and hopes of getting to Sary Tash, the first village in Kyrgyzstan, in order to find ourselves a guest house. But it was once again a clear, sunny day and there was no wind, perfect conditions for the final 4,300 metre pass that marked the end of Tajikistan. The conditions were in complete contrast to my first visit, when I'd had a mighty headwind and been pummelled by a blizzard. In my book I'd described it as one of the toughest climbs of my life, where I'd risked being blown off steep precipices. But now that the visibility was better I could see that the drop-offs at the side of the road were only a couple of feet high. "Are they the steep precipices?" Dea asked, unimpressed.

But it was really nice to be able to see things this time, to appreciate the phenomenal scenery of Tajikistan one last time. It had been an amazing country, and cycling through it this late in the year was an experience neither of us was going to forget. Dea made the climb look easy and, while I made it look very hard, it wasn't too long before we were celebrating at the top and then tumbling down into Kyrgyzstan.

The very long descent didn't just take us into a new country, but into a different landscape. The valley on the way down felt alive with colour in comparison to the yellow and grey we'd had on the plateau, with hints of reds and purples in the snow-topped mountains and a sudden reappearance of green grass. It seemed unlikely that anywhere could top the scenery of Tajikistan, but Kyrgyzstan had certainly made a good start, and this descent carried us down a tremendously long way, until we eventually emerged from the mountains and crossed a broad plain towards Sary Tash. Behind us a chain of mountains stretched as far as the eye could see in both directions, as white as if it were made of paper. It was impossibly beautiful. I had been here before too, of course, and I'd not been alone then either. We were now into the area I'd cycled with Ana, and I had been worried about coming back here for a while, unsure of how Dea would react. I knew it couldn't be easy for her, but she seemed to be handling it well; she was in a good mood and just enjoying the incredible cycling. Even during our night in Sary Tash, spent in a relatively warm guest house, there was no mention of it. The next morning we climbed up another pass, and made pretty light work of that too, and then arrived at the top of a series of switchbacks.

"This is a pretty special place," Dea said, as we took a seat and admired what was a truly spectacular view. The road snaked down the mountain below us, down to the place where years before I had needed the help of a motorcyclist named Wilko to navigate down around a landslide. But I wasn't thinking of the past now, my only concern was how Dea felt about being here.

I knew that it had been difficult for Dea to read about the girls I'd met before her in my first book. And it certainly could not have been easy for her to come back to those same places with me. But in each case – revisiting the Rhine River where I'd cycled with Karin, central Turkey where I'd been briefly with Hanna, and now the part of Kyrgyzstan where I'd met with Ana – it felt like Dea and I were over-writing the past, and stamping our own memories on those places. But the really amazing thing was not that Dea and I were together in such places, but that we were together in all of the places in between them as well, not just sharing some fleeting moment, but building something bigger, something truly special, a relationship, a love for each other that extended to all places.

Dea looked up and smiled at me. "Let's go down!" she said, and down we most certainly went, swishing around the hairpins and lov-ing every minute of the exhilarating descent.

45

Osh, Kyrgyzstan
2nd November 2017

"Maybe I'm just not meant to fly," I said to Dea.
We were sitting in the little courtyard of our guest house
in Osh, the big town which marked the end of the Pamir
Highway, and savouring every minute of an unseasonal heatwave
now that we were at lower elevations. I was on my laptop trying to
book my flight from China to Nepal, but every time I put in my payment details and hit 'confirm' I would get an error message. Had I
thought about it for just a moment I would have realised that my
bank in England was blocking the payment, just like it had when I'd
tried to book Dea's flight out of Hawaii, but the only thing that
crossed my mind was that this was a sign; maybe I really wasn't meant
to fly. The last time I had done so was five and a half years earlier, on
a plane that had taken me rather rudely from a hot and sunny
Bahamas to a freezing cold Toronto in a matter of hours. The unnatural sensation of being transported so quickly between such locations
had hit me hard, and it was as a direct result of that flight that I'd
decided to abandon aeroplanes in the same way I'd abandoned cars,
vowing from that moment on to travel the world using only my
bicycle and boats. And sure, by the time I'd pedalled the last couple
of thousand kilometres to Mori I would have achieved my aim of
making a full circumnavigation only by those methods, but did I
really want to abandon my principles so immediately thereafter? I

knew that if I was being honest with myself in my heart of hearts I didn't, and with the reprieve offered by my bank I decided to share that fact with Dea.

"I know, Chris. I don't think you're meant to fly either. It doesn't seem right somehow, the idea of you on a plane."

"But there is no other way to get to Nepal and India, we've been through all our options."

"Well, maybe we don't have to go there. I also really don't like the idea of interrupting our trip by flying."

"But I thought you wanted to go there."

"Yeah, but I've been there before, Chris. I don't need to go back."

And with this I felt a little relief. I'd never been to India myself, but I knew enough about it to conclude that with its crowded and crazy roads it would probably not make for the best cycling in the world. But if we weren't going to fly, the only other possibility would be to continue on across China, and Dea still didn't have a visa.

"If we're going to go all of the way across China, I'll fly home to get the visa. I don't mind doing that and then coming back and carrying on where I left off."

Things were getting interesting now, but this new idea would only work if we were able to find a boat across the Pacific, and so I returned to my laptop and one of my most visited websites, cruisetimetables.com. I knew that there were ferry connections from the east coast of China to South Korea and Japan, but where could we go from there? We began searching for cruises heading out of Japan, and almost immediately found one that was sailing from Yokohama to Vancouver on the 26th of April 2018. It was perfect timing.

And there was something even more perfect about this idea; it would mean we would be sailing into Vancouver on a cruise ship, together, almost exactly two years after Dea's eye infection had robbed her of the experience. We both grew even more excited, realising that our whole trip could be about to change, to take on a whole new crazy direction. From Vancouver we could cycle south down through the Americas, exactly like we'd intended to back in 2016. India would have to be scrapped from our route completely, but it turned out that neither of us was that bothered about that. But one thing we did not want to miss out on was Africa.

"Maybe we can fly to Africa from South America?"

"But then we're still flying!"

There were no cruise connections between the continents and we'd have to be extremely lucky to find a sailing boat that wouldn't sink under the weight of our overloaded bikes. But I was too keen on our new idea to give up on it now, and I kept searching until I found a potential answer. A company that rented out rooms on cargo ships had a route that ran from Brazil to Senegal. I sent them an e-mail, and they replied quickly to tell me that the ship sailed every week, and it should be no problem to get us aboard. It was the final piece of the jigsaw. From Senegal we could cycle up through West Africa and back to Europe by ferry across the Strait of Gibraltar. A whole new route around the world and all the way home had come together, one that would mean by the end I would have gone all of the way around the world twice, but more importantly it would mean that Dea and I would have completed our own full circumnavigation without flying, all of it cycled together. It was a new plan that made so much sense to both of us, that opened up the possibility for so much more land-based travel and adventures, and that would hopefully even provide enough drama to stretch the movie franchise out into a trilogy (if you're reading this Mr. Spielberg, maybe this is the time to start returning my calls).

We put our world map on the wall of our room at the guest house. It still had the coloured string on it that marked out our original plan, that we'd made way back in Copenhagen. Now we carefully peeled off that string and rearranged it to form our new plan. Our cuddly toys on the bed sat and looked up at this new map, unblinking, silent, looking like they were deep in thought. Dea and I did much the same, until one of us broke the silence with, "Are we really going to do this?!" but we both already knew the answer.

Dea would need to spend at least a month back in Denmark to organise the Chinese visa, but it would give her the chance to spend Christmas with her family, and she was very happy with the idea. It wouldn't be all bad for me either. I'd get a month off in Kyrgyzstan's capital city, Bishkek, waiting for her to return, and given that I'd now been cycling (either on a bicycle or a pedicab) almost non-stop for seven and a half years, that sounded alright to me too. Our new plan was settled, the rest of our trip changed overnight, and instead of a flight to Nepal, I found myself booking a cruise to Canada (and calling my bank to make sure the payment would go through).

We had only intended to stay in Osh for three days, but our peaceful guest house made for such a nice environment to relax and recover after the Pamir Highway that we ended up staying for a week. We also had the company of Liz and Miranda, who arrived a couple of days after us in the back of a taxi. Their Pamir adventure had not gone too smoothly, with Miranda suffering from quite severe altitude sickness, and she'd consequently had to use other transport most of the way. It seemed like Liz was growing a little frustrated at constantly being held up by her friend, and we told her that she was welcome to cycle with us the rest of the way to Bishkek if Miranda wasn't up to it. As it turned out, however, Liz also fell ill in Osh, and so she wasn't able to join Dea and me as we set off for our final ten days of cycling together before our winter break.

It began with a difficult three days of riding through populated regions on the edge of a busy highway, where the Mercedes of the wealthy few and the Ladas of the common man competed to force us off the road. We resorted to the gravel shoulder, shared with men herding cows, kids walking home from school, stray horses, stray dogs, stray chickens, and all the hustle and bustle of Kyrgyz life. And our memories of this part of the country were enhanced by one especially generous grandmother, who invited us into her simple home and lavished us with tea, bread and halva, followed by potatoes and eggs. Adina lived here with her husband, Adil, and one of their granddaughters. She told us that their children had all moved away, and now lived in Moscow, Ankara, and Bishkek, all of them seeking opportunities for a life better than that offered by rural Kyrgyzstan.

Towards the end of our third day a car beeped and pulled over in front of us, and out jumped Liz and Miranda. The latter was still not feeling up to cycling, and would be taking this lift all the way to Bishkek, but Liz pulled her bike out of the back, and for the next week she would be joining us. We were delighted; we got on very well with Liz, and she would prove a valuable third player for our nightly whist tournaments.

Liz had also timed things just right, for from pretty much the exact point she joined us the habitation ceased and the road grew less busy (although there were still a large number of oil tankers plying the route, leaving me for the first time seeing the great benefit a new pipeline might bring). The road ran alongside a narrow reservoir that was squeezed into a valley, reminding us of our similar experience in Turkey. At least there were fewer tunnels here, and while the man-made reservoir created a fairly unnatural scene, it was unquestionably a dramatic landscape that made for a spectacular ride along the rugged cliffsides.

Liz made for great company. She had a positive attitude, an enthusiasm for life that was infectious. In her early thirties, she worked as a freelance journalist, and was funding her travels by occasionally writing articles for some major British newspapers. She suggested I might try to do the same, but I didn't believe my travel writing would be up to scratch, what with my over-reliance on dessert-based similes. And then there was my name. "You have a great name for being a writer," I said.

"Liz Dodd? Yes I suppose it fits quite well under the title."

"Yeah, and people know how to pronounce it. Nobody knows how to pronounce my name."

"Hmm, really?" Liz said, stopping short of trying to pronounce Pountney herself, lest she get it wrong.

"Yeah, and it drives me mad. I don't get it, people know how to pronounce the word count, and mount, and fountain and bounty..."

"And pound too I suppose," Liz said, getting the hang of it.

"Yes and pound. And then these same people will look at my name, and look all confused, and say, Mr. Pootney is it?!"

"Well, there's no need to get all stressed about it."

"No, no," I said, calming down, "I'll just put this conversation in my next book, and then everyone will know."

We left the reservoir behind and circled around a giant lake, before beginning on a long climb up, the first of two 3,000 metre high passes that still stood between us and Bishkek. Liz had warned us that she was a very slow cyclist, but that worked out great for us, and we went along together quite happily, playing The Spotting Things Game to add a little interest. Liz was a big fan, embracing the game with an overwhelming enthusiasm. It was a close contest between the girls, and Liz might even have won had it not been so difficult for her to spot a fish, and with Dea just needing to see some discarded vegetables it was destined to be her day in the end. Rarely could the sight of some rotten onions on a grass verge have brought about such scenes of celebration as we witnessed that evening.

We camped that night in a big meadow beside the river we were following up through the valley. The padlocked trailers nearby and the large amount of dried horse manure everywhere revealed that in summertime this grassland would be filled with nomadic yurt-dwellers and their animals, but this late in the year we had it to ourselves. It was a shame we'd come too late in the year to experience Kyrgyzstan's yurts given our own future plans, but a bitterly cold night reminded us why we were alone. As Liz came to our tent to share the morning coffee she'd just boiled up, she looked at her smartphone and warned us that, "It's going to snow today," and no sooner had the words left her lips than a snowflake landed upon her shoulder. This pass was not going to be easy.

The steep climbing began straight away, and I was struggling with it. The effort of the climb at least meant I didn't feel cold, but I couldn't work out why it was that I found it so hard. I was sure cycling uphill never used to be this difficult. Dea and Liz were making it look so easy in comparison to me, going on ahead and then waiting patiently for me to catch them up. In the end, however, I was just too slow, and they went on further, all the way to the summit, leaving me to battle on alone on a road now lined with heavy snow. I found the going so tough that I began to think that there must be something wrong with me, some physical ailment that was slowing me down. Perhaps I had a collapsed lung without knowing it, or some such thing, for cycling had never been this hard before.

Eventually I made it to the top, and saw Dea and Liz, obviously sympathetic to my plight, gathering up snowballs to throw at me. What they hadn't reckoned on was that I was also capable of making snowballs, and what was more I had a basket to store them in, and approaching them on my bicycle I was a moving target, difficult to hit as I came towards them aggressively. They soon regretted making those snowballs, I can tell you.

There was a terrible irony to our descent, for having spent the entire morning dreaming of reaching it, as soon as it began we all wished it would be over. It was unbelievably cold. My fingers and toes felt so painfully frozen, and there was no respite so long as I was on the bike. Every so often I had to stop and warm my hands and feet by rubbing them, jumping up and down to try and encourage my circulation. Dea and I looked at one another and knew we were going to have to get a bit better at protecting ourselves from the cold if we were going to survive China in January, where the average temperatures were absurdly cold. Liz too looked absolutely frozen, her hands protected only by a pair of light woollen gloves. But there wasn't much to do about all this except to keep on moving down the hill, dreaming ironically for a little bit of uphill to warm us up.

Our salvation finally arrived with a little row of buildings, one of which was a café. We hurried inside, and basked in the sudden warmth, sipping hot tea and eating fried eggs until the feeling returned to our extremities. Then, just as we were considering moving on again, Liz spotted another touring cyclist coming down the hill. He burst into the café, shivering and looking for sugar. It was Ross, one of a trio of cyclists who had been staying at another guest house in Osh that we'd met briefly there. They'd all been well ahead of us cycling the Pamir Highway, but had taken such a long break in Osh that we had now gotten ahead of them. Ross, a British man of about my age, sat down with us and drank tea and ate fried eggs until the feeling returned to his extremities. After a while the door burst open again, and another European face staggered in out of the cold. This one was a French cyclist who sat down with us, and drank tea and ate eggs until the feeling returned to his extremities. A little while later, and the door burst open again. The lady running the café already had the eggs in the pan, ready to go.

Liz, Dea, and I took our leave and went to find somewhere to camp out in the grasslands, now that we were below the snowline. "Isn't this just what we dreamed about when we wanted to come here," I said, looking around at the wide plains and the rows of snowy mountains on every horizon. What none of us had dreamt about, of course, was spending the night here in minus twelve degrees, but we all survived to ride another day.

We were reunited with the boys in the morning. They had managed to wrangle a night in one of the buildings, and caught us up as we were packing away our camp. For a little while we then rode on as a group of six, although our differing speeds meant we were soon spread out quite a bit. The road was at least a great one, now being only a very gentle downhill across the plains, and we were further aided by a fantastic tailwind. I cycled along with the third (i.e. slowest) of the cyclists to arrive at the café, a young Italian named Daniele. He was a really friendly and nice guy, and we had a good chat all morning. He'd cycled all the way here from Italy, but was going to fly back to Europe from Bishkek, his trip nearing its end. And he wasn't the only one; almost all the cyclists left in Central Asia were going to fly out from Bishkek or Almaty, due to the Chinese visa situation and the cold weather. Dea and I would be two of the few to be continuing.

It had been a perfect morning, but it couldn't last. Ahead of us we could see the road leaving the valley and climbing up the side of a mountain in the most ridiculously intimidating fashion. We could see the whole mountain, and the entirety of the the road ahead, zigzagging up so high that it hurt my neck to look for the top. I gulped. Having found the previous pass so tough, this promised to be one almighty final mountain challenge.

The boys all went on ahead, taking Liz with them, and leaving slow old me behind. Luckily Dea, knowing how I'd struggled on the last pass, stuck with me this time. Just as I feared, the going was tough for me, but we knew that it was only about twelve kilometres to the top, so we just took it three at a time. I put on some music and ground out the first three kilometres. We then took a break to eat and enjoy the view, before continuing on for another three. It was hard work, on a road that was not only steep, but also busy with trucks trundling past, but Dea rode just behind me and her presence there helped me so much. We were going ever so slowly; the boys were surely already over the top by the time we were halfway up. But we needed to get to the top before dark, as there was nowhere to camp on the steep slopes. The day was already starting to get away from us when to make matters worse I got a puncture. I stopped to fix it, removing all the bags and turning the bike upside down to get the rear wheel off. It took an age to remove the offending piece of metal from the tyre with my cold fingers, but eventually I succeeded and put in a new tube. I put the wheel back on the bike and turned the pedals around by hand to get the chain in the right gear. I couldn't believe what I felt when I did this. It was so difficult. There was so much resistance from my bottom bracket, which I'd known had been wobbly since Dushanbe, but I had not known until this moment was by now almost completely seized up. I broke into a big smile. "I thought there was something wrong with me Dea! Oh my God! This explains everything! Look, it's just my f*cking bike!"

Now that it turned out that I was not, as I'd suspected, a weak and pathetic hill climber, but in actual fact a complete bad-ass who could cycle up mountains with a seized bottom bracket, I felt much better about the rest of the climb. What did not make me feel better was when a car stopped and a Kyrgyz man who could speak English told us that we would not be able to cycle through the tunnel at the top. We knew about this tunnel, it had a scary reputation, and we had come up with a plan as to how we could get through it safely. But we knew that there would be security personal up there, and that they might object to us riding through. Our research suggested that some cyclists had been permitted to ride through the tunnel before, others had been forced to take a lift, and with no alternative way to the other side of the mountain (any trail over the top would be buried by snow) the words of this man came as something of a concern. "I really don't think you can cycle through it," he insisted.

A short time later another car stopped. In this one was Liz, who, having fallen behind the boys, had for quite a long time been standing shivering and waiting for us higher up the mountain. Concerned as to what had become of us, she had hitchhiked down to find us. Satisfied we were okay, she then hitched back to her bike to wait some more. Eventually we reached her, and with the day almost at an end, the three of us pedalled the final couple of kilometres together. Rounding a corner we found at last what we had been seeking all day – a dark, narrow, unventilated, smoke-filled tunnel.

Warnings about this tunnel were not unwarranted. Two and a half kilometres long and without ventilation, a number of people had died in it from carbon monoxide poisoning in the past. Not too keen on adding to those numbers, we'd come up with a plan to camp at the top of the pass, and then go through the tunnel first thing in the morning when traffic would be light and pollution at its lowest. It was a plan that looked like it might just come together perfectly, having arrived at the very end of the day to find a little shack selling hot coffee and a big salt shed in which the tunnel security guard told us we could pitch our tents for the night. This offered us a little extra protection from the wind and the cold of camping at three and a half thousand metres above sea level, while I hoped that a makeshift barrier I constructed from string and paper would be enough to protect us from the many truckers who used the nearby area as a toilet. We sat in our salt shed, drinking coffee and beer, toasting our success at reaching this summit, and talking anxiously of the new challenge that faced us in the morning.

We slept fine and awoke before dawn, ready to implement our plan. We put on all of our clothes, took down our tents, and headed for the tunnel. Thankfully the man on security offered no objections to us proceeding on our bikes, and it looked a lot less intimidating now than it had the night before. The road surface inside the tunnel was not great, but it was all downhill and only a few vehicles passed us at such an hour. It was also much better lit than we'd feared, and the air inside perfectly survivable. Bursting outside at the end of the tunnel we whooped with delight, overjoyed that our plan had worked so well.

Now we had ourselves an extraordinarily long downhill, starting with lots of switchbacks through the snowy peaks. It was such a fantastic moment to coast down on the almost empty road. A buzz ran through me, a thrill about being awake so early to enjoy such an amazing bit of cycling surrounded by the peaks of Central Asia for the final time.

It was very cold of course, our extremities once again frozen solid, and with no prospect of finding a café this time we simply had to keep descending, at least until we could get out of the shadow of the mountains and find some sunlight. Along the way we saw the boys again. They were just waking up in a little valley, and we passed them by in our continued quest for sunshine. We eventually found it, and at the same moment opening up in front of us and extending all the way to the horizon was a broad, flat plain. It was the start once again of the Kazakh steppe. This was it, the end, the mountains of Central Asia were all behind us, we had made it through. There was much rejoicing, but also a little sadness too. "I'm going to miss it," Dea said. "It was such an amazing place." And no one could disagree about that.

The boys caught us up again, and overtook us, but the girls and I kept plodding away together, slowly and steadily on flat roads that grew increasingly busy as we neared Kyrgyzstan's capital. But we left the highway when we could, and our final ride into the city took place on small backstreets that were in a fairly terrible condition but almost completely traffic-free. It had been a long final day, begun at six a.m. on a frozen mountain pass, and ending 120 kilometres later in the dark, walking the final kilometre on the footpath beside a busy street, where almost being hit by a red-light-running car and having to pull my girlfriend away from a drunk alcoholic made me wonder if the city life was really going to be for me. But for better or worse, this was going to be my new 'hood', as Liz put it, for the next month or so. We had made it to Bishkek.

46

Bishkek, Kyrgyzstan
21st November 2017

The sports car was blasting along the straight coastal highway past an endless row of bright palm trees. It looked like Miami or L.A. or somewhere, and I was in the back seat, enjoying the thrill of the ride.

"Oh, hey Rio! How's it going?" I said. I'd only just noticed that it was the former England footballer Rio Ferdinand sitting in the passenger seat in front of me. He was reaching over to change the music, but the driver batted his hand away from the dial. I craned my neck forward to see who it was at the wheel. Only Sir David Attenborough, wasn't it? What a crazy car ride this was! I tried to remember when it was I'd got in, or why, and as I did so I suddenly remembered that I wasn't supposed to use cars. I was instantly struck by a mad sense of panic, screaming at Sir David to stop, but knowing that it didn't matter now, it was too late. Everything was ruined. I'd got in a car. Why? Why had I got in this car? What was I thinking? What was I doing? It was too late... too late... everything was ruined... everything... ruined.

I woke up in a sweat in my bed and tried to remember where I was. I looked around at the dark room and could make out the outline of Dea sleeping peacefully beside me. We were still in Bishkek, Kyrgyzstan, and nothing was ruined. Relief washed over me. It wasn't the first time I'd had this nightmare. It wasn't always a car, sometimes it was a plane or even an escalator that I was on without knowing how I'd got there, but always there was that sudden sense of panic, that realisation that my goal of going around the world without motorised transport had gone, a nightmare born from the reality of how easily all could be lost with one misstep.

A few hours later Dea departed Bishkek along with Liz and a French cyclist named Léo, all three of them bound for Almaty, a couple of hundred kilometres over the border in Kazakhstan. Dea would be flying back to Denmark from there and not returning until the turn of the year. I could only stay one month without a visa in Kazakhstan, compared with two months in Kyrgyzstan, so I needed to stay behind in Bishkek for a while. It was a little sad saying good-bye and waving them off down the street. It was the longest period of time Dea and I would be spending apart since our reunion at the Hook of Holland, and also the last time I would see Liz for a long time, for she would be flying on to Southeast Asia from Almaty to continue her ride in more favourable weather.

With their departure I was suddenly all alone at the Friend's Guest-house, ironically enough without any friends, and I was left wondering what to do with myself for the next six weeks. I had planned to start by moving from our private room into the cheaper dormitory, but it was small and cramped and had a Kyrgyz man living in it who seemed harmless enough but apparently had a habit of staying up all night drinking beer. He even had one in his hand at nine in the morning when Dea *et al* cycled away from me. So I spoke to the manager of the guest house, a nice man named Nurik, and negotiated a good discount to stay in a private room for the next month. It was still more than the price of a dorm bed, but I justified it to myself with the logic that having my own space would afford me the opportunity to write, and it was therefore a worthwhile investment.

With so much time to write, I made a start on my second book, the one you are reading right now, without yet knowing how it was going to end. I started off by thinking of a title, then I made a brightly coloured cover, then I did the maps, then I relaxed for a bit, then I watched some television shows, went for a walk, watched the football, watched some more television shows, and then at some point after that I started writing.

For the next two weeks almost nobody else came to stay at the guest house. The weather turned exceptionally cold and heavy snowfalls coated the city. The footpaths became frozen and slippery. I watched the street from behind the safety of my second floor window as people walked back and forth outside, their shoulders hunched up against the cold under their many layers. To join them was a risky activity. Never once did I walk any significant distance in the city without seeing at least one person slip and land upon their backside on the icy ground. A harsh winter had completely enveloped the city, and I preferred as much as possible to hide from it in my room and pretend it wasn't there.

But there was no getting away from the fact that to achieve my goal of getting back to Mori I was going to have to face winter head-on. We would be cycling in January, and my research told me that this was the coldest month of the year in Xinjiang, the province of China we'd be crossing. The average nightly low was a depressing minus twenty degrees Celsius (minus four Fahrenheit) but even worse than that was the average daily highs, of minus ten Celsius (fourteen Fahrenheit). We had survived the freezing nights on the Pamir plateau, but it was the relatively warm daytime temperatures that had kept our spirits up while cycling. How could we possibly live outdoors in a world that never even approached zero degrees? It was a scary thought, and one that had me visiting the local bazaar to pick up some big winter boots lined with fake fur, a down jacket, and matching balaclavas for me and Dea.

But my research wasn't just weather-related. I also took the time to plan the route we should take, and to find out as much as I could about the borders between Kazakhstan and China. I knew from personal experience that this was something that could very well derail my ambitions, so I wanted to be prepared. Indeed, it seemed that most of the border crossings would not allow cyclists to cross, but the most logical one for us, situated at a place called Khorgas, did. Or at least sometimes it did. There had been cyclists who had been made to get in a vehicle to cross it in the past, but apparently now it was okay to cycle. There was certainly potential for disaster there, and then once we were in China we would have to spend at least some of the time cycling on the expressway, as it was the only possible route in some places. Stories of other cyclists having been forcibly removed from the expressway by police reinforced the fact that there was still a great many things that could go wrong. Anywhere else in the world and with less then 2,000 kilometres to go I would be feeling confident about making it to the finish line, but this was China, and I had a sinking feeling that China was going to make things very difficult for me.

After two weeks another touring cyclist arrived at the guest house. It was Thomas, an exceedingly laid-back Frenchman of my age. He'd cycled from his homeland and had spent the last month riding around Kyrgyzstan with an English girl, but she'd just flown home and he was now unsure of his future plans. What he was sure of was that he planned to stay for a while at this guest house, which was a tremendous boost for my sanity, if not my book progress. The next week or so turned into one almighty long marathon of table-tennis, ended only when I accidentally knelt on the ball, ruining everything.

On the 20th of December I left Friend's Guesthouse for the 250 kilometre ride to Almaty, pleased that I had at least made one friend. Unfortunately he wasn't with me. Thomas was going to cycle to Almaty, but he wanted to wait a little longer in Bishkek first, whereas I had to press on to get a number of things done in Kazakhstan before Dea's return. The weather had warmed up slightly, and the ride was pretty uneventful, other than me getting some excruciating pain in my knees. It was something that always tended to happen when I resumed cycling after a long break, and, in a move that the sixty-year-old me probably won't thank me for, I did my best to ignore it and just kept on cycling.

I arrived in Almaty in time for Christmas, which I spent alone in a hostel, skyping with my family from the floor of a laundry room but otherwise barely noticing the festive season. On Boxing Day I had to make an expedition across the city to retrieve Dea's bike from a man named Nurseit, a *warmshowers* host who had been good enough to store it for us. Thankfully my knees held up okay to the fifteen kilometre walk, and the fifteen kilometre cycle back again, and in between I got to meet Nurseit. He was a friendly and interesting man, who owned a nice house that he lived in with his wife and kids. He had a good job in the city, but he said he sometimes wished he could leave it behind. He owned a motorbike that he was planning to ride the Pamir Highway on with his wife in the summer, and it was obvious that a part of him yearned for a life of adventure. But he said that wasn't the way he'd been brought up. That having a family, and providing for that family, was what mattered the most in Kazakhstan.

Nurseit had also been good enough to accept delivery of my new fork. My old fork had held up so well through the Pamirs, it was a miracle that it had made it through really. I certainly owed a good deal of thanks to an old man in a flat cap for his contribution to my progress, but it was finally time to say goodbye to his handiwork. I fitted the new fork with the help of Alexander, the 'Crankmaster', not only the finest bike mechanic in all of Almaty, but quite possibly the world. He told me as he went to work cutting my steerer tube that he had been the bike mechanic for the Kazakhstan national cycling squad, which I thought very impressive.

"Really?" I said. "That's very impressive."

"Mmm," he mumbled, before adding under his breath, "ladies squad."

"Well, that's still very impressive."

And even more impressive was the way that he managed to remove my defunct bottom bracket, with the most creative use of a chain whip I'd ever seen. Once it was removed I tried to turn the bottom bracket around by hand. It was quite impossible. No wonder my knees had protested so much.

A new fork and a new bottom bracket meant my bike was in the best shape it had been in for quite a while, but there were more adjustments needed before we'd be ready for the challenge ahead. One important alteration was to remove all four of our tyres and replace them with Nokian studded winter tyres that we hoped would be good enough to grip the icy roads. Dea had somehow managed to find four of these quality Finnish tyres in a shop in Almaty when she'd been in town a month earlier, and I collected them and installed them on our bikes. A less professional but equally important winter adaptation for our bikes came in the form of some homemade pogies that I fashioned. Traditional pogies are giant mitts that are attached to the handlebars, so that you can slide your hands in and keep warm. But making something myself that would fit around our drop bars was a challenge, and Dea's bike ended up with two big cardboard boxes wrapped in bin liners and lined inside with fake fur on each end of the handlebars. They didn't look all that great, but they sure were warm inside, and that was certainly going to be the most important thing.

New Year's Eve was another one to remember. Thomas had arrived in Almaty a few days earlier, with a plan to take trains all of the way across Kazakhstan and Siberia in order to resume his cycling odyssey in South Korea and Japan. He wasn't leaving until the middle of January though, and on the last evening of 2017 we went out on the town to look for a place to eat and drink and welcome in the new year in style. We wandered the cold snowy streets, thinking that we would have no trouble finding an establishment serving food and drink in this developed city. But the streets were quiet, all of the cafés and bars closed. On and on we walked, trudging through the snow, until eventually we spotted an Indian restaurant that was packed with people having a good time.

"That's more like it, Thomas. Looks like our new year could be about to pick up."

We went inside and asked if we might have a little something to eat. "Sorry," came the response, "but we don't have any tables free."

"Really? Nothing?" My stomach was getting desperate. "Do you know anywhere else that we can get some food?"

The waiter looked at our tattered cycling jackets and said, "There's a supermarket down the street."

So Thomas and I found ourselves buying a cabbage and egg pastry from the supermarket and wandering back to the hostel to put it in the microwave. And there we sat in the kitchen, trying pathetically to create an atmosphere via youtube videos, craning our necks to catch sight of some fireworks out the window, and thus ringing in 2018 in style.

I had enjoyed my time in Bishkek and Almaty, recharging my batteries and preparing for the final assault. It had been good to have some time alone, and it had been good to have some time with Thomas, but there was no doubt I was a happy man when on the 3rd of January Dea returned, a Chinese visa in her passport. It was great to see her again, and we spent a couple of days in the hostel together, savouring being warm as much as we could. But on the 6th of January it was time to get back on the bikes. The temperature was fourteen below and the roads were slick with ice, but this was it, this had to be it. There were fewer than 1,500 kilometres between us and Mori, and it was time, at long, long last, for us to go there.

Progress Report
Almaty, January 2018

1. Circumnavigate the planet

Completed.

2. Do so using only my bicycle and boats

Mori: 90.3° E. Almaty: 76.9° E.
346.6° out of 360° around the planet.
(96.3% of the way around. Holy moly!)

3. Pass through antipodal points

...time was spent in both the northern and southern
hemisphere, with the equator crossed twice...

4. Visit all of the inhabited continents

Still four out of six.

5. Cycle at least 100,000 kilometres

74,298 kilometres completed, 25,702 more needed.

6. Cycle in 100 countries

Stuck on sixty-one.

7. Return with more money than I start with

 Book sales picked up massively around Christmas.
Hurrah!

PART SIX

ALMATY TO MORI

47

Almaty, Kazakhstan
6th January 2018

I pulled my buff up over my mouth and nose as we left our hostel, leaving only a narrow slit of skin around my eyes exposed to the frigid air, and started rolling down the quiet street. It wasn't quiet for long; our winter tyres made an almighty racket as the metal studs connected with the solid tarmac. But in places the tarmac was coated with sheets of ice, and we were so glad to have these tyres, gripping on firmly. We would not have lasted two minutes on regular tyres, and before we were even at the end of the first street it was obvious that the Nokians had been a worthwhile investment.

We were soon following a main highway out of the city. The road was thawed out but it was far too busy with fast moving vehicles to risk cycling in. The shoulder was coated in ice and snow that in place had solidified into deep ruts, but with our tyres we felt confident we could handle that, and so it proved. Progress was slow, however, and after a while we turned off on a smaller road that we could follow parallel to the highway for a long distance east. It had not been completely cleared of snow and ice, but that was alright because there was not much traffic, and what there was had to move slowly. We weren't long on this road before a van stopped and two men came over to us. They wanted to take a photo with us, and were friendly and curious about what the hell we were doing. It was one of many little incidents we had connecting with people, who waved or said hello to us in a way they might not have done in the the summertime. Simply cycling here in mid-winter was already breaking down barriers and warming people to us.

We cycled until sundown, which wasn't particularly late. But it had been a great first day, with a great ending, riding on an empty road with a red sun low in the sky behind us. Empty white fields surrounded us, and we made camp in one of them, kicking away the snow with our boots to find some solid ground for the tent.

I woke up a few times in the night feeling cold, with Dea snoring beside me. I had my three sleeping bags around me and I was wearing a T-shirt, two hoodies, a down jacket and two regular jackets, but I hadn't used my bin liner technique, so I only had myself to blame really. We had no way to measure the temperature, but I was sure it must have been getting close to minus twenty. It was therefore great to hear Dea tell me that she had not felt the cold, despite not really having slept so well (I was surprised to hear that, what with all the snoring). Despite our troubles we made the effort to get up at first light, for the days were short and we did not want to waste them. There was a great view of mountains ahead of us on the horizon, with an orange sky behind them, as we breakfasted on frozen-bread sandwiches and cake. We then resumed cycling on our lovely road, the crunch of our tyres the only sound.

Again the few people that we saw were nice to us. One even stopped his Jeep and handed us some apples. We ate them as we stood talking with the man, for we knew they would only freeze solid if we tried to save them for later. The man, Alexander, had a grey moustache and kind eyes, and he looked even more prepared for winter than us, with a fur hat, thick coat, and huge winter boots. After hearing what we were doing he reached into his car and pulled out some thick mittens, and gave them to Dea as a gift. It was a nice moment, and it felt so uplifting to know that the people of Kazakhstan were on our side here.

On we went. Now there was no traffic at all, and we found out why that was when we came to a dead end. A bridge over a river had collapsed, and there appeared to be no way through. We stopped to inspect our options. I was not keen to retreat, and the river was frozen, so I went down to see if it might be possible to cross it. Dea watched me nervously, fearful that I might fall through the ice and be swept away. "It seems pretty solid," I said, as I stamped my foot on the frozen water. Then suddenly I heard a loud crack and felt myself falling into the ice cold water. In an instant I was completely submerged, fighting for my life in a blind panic, and not really, none of that happened. The ice was several inches thick and held fine, but beyond it there were two more streams to cross, it would be difficult to get back up to the road on the far side, and I could see that Dea wasn't at all keen on the idea, so we made another plan. We could see there was a small road leading north to the highway, where we could find a bridge. We took this route and then cycled back south on another small road, before finding ourselves looking back at the broken bridge again, now safely on the other side of it. In all we'd cycled ten kilometres to make ten metres of progress, but it had been the right choice.

In the evening we had to make a slight detour through a village to find something to drink. We were carrying plenty, but with the daytime temperatures well below zero it would freeze faster than we could drink it. We had not yet figured out a way to stop that happening, and we were consequently now carrying several blocks of ice with us. But the village was worth a detour anyway, for there were lots of people about. Kids were sledding down hills, men stood around trying to fix a frozen Lada, a mother pulled her young child along on a sled, while some older kids were playing ice hockey with curved wooden sticks and a rock for a puck. Life didn't stop here in winter. As we stood at the shop Dea looked around and said, "I'm so glad we can see Kazakhstan in winter," and I felt just the same. It was really quite wonderful. We camped that night on a ledge overlooking the steppe below us, mountains behind, everything painted in white, both of us enjoying this experience so much more than we believed we would.

I spent the night sharing my sleeping bags with several blocks of ice, a loaf of bread, and a jar of peanut butter. It was not such a cold night as the one before, so I didn't mind sharing too much, but, while my efforts meant that we could have a proper breakfast, not much of the ice returned to water. I was feeling very thirsty, and getting enough fluids into us before they froze was proving a challenge.

The morning was again beautiful, but the going was made more tough by a few hills and a frustrating headwind, and to make matters worse Dea was experiencing a bit of pain in her knee. I was relieved that the pain in my knees I'd experienced on the cycle between Bishkek and Almaty had not returned, but Dea having trouble was just as bad. So when we reached the village of Taukaraturyk we decided to leave our quieter road and head down to the highway where the going would be flatter. We also bought more water in the village, and stuffed it inside our jackets so that our body heat would keep it liquid for longer.

We were both feeling fatigued by the time we started back into the headwind on the main highway. The town of Shelek was ahead of us, and it didn't take long for us to agree that looking for a hotel there for the night was a pretty good idea. Dea could rest her knee, I could rest my everything, and the ten blocks of ice we'd accumulated could thaw out.

Finding a hotel in town wasn't the easiest thing to do. We asked a woman where we might find one, and she confidently pointed us across town. Once there we asked another woman, and were pointed right back again, eventually finding the hotel about twenty metres away from where we'd started. After all our exertions the warmth and comfort of the basic room felt so good, and we decided we'd better stay two nights to give Dea's knee time to recover. This decision was made easier by the weather forecast, which showed two days of big headwind followed by one of big tailwind. So we decided to rest the first day, cycle a little bit the next, and then hopefully take full advantage of the wind the day after that.

With a whole day to spend in Shelek we had a look online to see what there was to do in the small town. There was one local sight listed on Google, a museum that seemed like it might be worth checking out, if the Google reviews were anything to go by. The first review, translated from Russian, began:

'The museum is absolutely small.'

And this had us intrigued at once, but the review did not end there.

'But there is something to see. And stuffed animals, and the form of a soldier of the times of the Great Patriotic War, and coins of different years. In a word, you can visit.'

Yes, in a word, we could, and we would, we decided. So we left our room and walked a block to where Google said the museum should be. There was no sign of any museum. Perhaps it was too small, but we never found it. So we went to a park instead, which was closed, but we climbed over a fence and trespassed on a bench. Then we went to a shop and bought a Thermos flask to try and stop our water from freezing, and all-in-all it had been a great day out.

The rest day turned out to be a great idea, as the next day we awoke feeling revitalised and raring to go again. It took us a while to get out of Shelek, however, as we hunted for a supermarket and failed miserably. In the end we gave up and left town without enough food for the long stretch of empty steppe ahead of us. There was only one village along the way, Nurly, and we gambled on finding something to eat there.

We didn't know too much about the next section of our route. I'd tried to research it by looking at other cyclists' blogs, but every single one of them took the longer, more southern route to visit some canyons. We didn't much care for canyons, especially as they'd be buried by snow, and wanted to take the quickest, most direct way. All we'd heard about it came from the owner of our Shelek guest house, who we had no common language with, but we think he'd told us it was a new highway built by Italians. Who built it was not something we were ever able to ascertain for sure, but it was certainly a new highway, and a very good one at that, for it was a dual carriageway clear of snow, with a shoulder and hardly any traffic. It was kind of ideal, apart from the fierce headwind that we had to battle against.

It took more than two hours to cover the twenty kilometres to Nurly, which we then detoured to across the snow. I was not optimistic. It was not a big place, and most of the houses looked abandoned. But there were a few people around, and they pointed us in the direction of a small shop. It was locked up. We knocked on the door, and felt great relief when it was opened up by a sprightly young man. He gave us a big smile, the first of many, and invited us inside. We bought bread and eggs and chocolate, and everything we said or did was met with enthusiasm and laughs from the young fellow. He told us that his name was Zangar and that he was twenty years old, and he put an extra bar of chocolate in our bag as a present, or a "Surprise!" as he called it.

We went outside and sat on a wall to eat something. Zangar soon came out with two packets of crisps and gave them to us. "Surprise!" he beamed. Then he went back inside, and came out with two little chocolate bars. "Surprise!" Off he went again, returning this time with two little pens. "Surprise!" But these pens really did have a surprise, for they wrote in invisible ink. The other end of the pen was an ultraviolet torch, which when shone on the invisible writing made it visible. This was a very, very cool surprise.

But that wasn't the end of this wonderful meeting, for Zangar's grandmother then came out with a "What are you doing out here in the cold?!" expression on her face, and invited us into the family home for some tea. We didn't need too much persuading. It was great to get out of the cold wind and sit in the simple home, with Zangar and his large family. The hot tea was as welcome as any I'd ever had, and before we knew it we were being served dinner as well. A most generous surprise, to be sure.

We managed another twenty kilometres beyond Nurly before calling it a night. All around us was bare steppe. We found a big area that had been partly excavated and cycled down into that, hoping to get out of the wind. Unfortunately the sides sloped gradually down and we got no protection from the wind whatsoever. But it wasn't just the wind I was concerned about. A few people had warned us about wolves and I'd taken the time to do a little research on the subject while we were stopped in Shelek. I'd been sceptical about the stories, but it turned out that actually Kazakhstan could boast being the country with the most wolves in all of the world, and in winter they all come down from the hills to the steppe, hungry and occasionally even attacking humans. It was enough to make me nervous, and I put a pile of rocks at the entrance to our tent, just in case we should need to fight back. Dea came up with her own more passive form of defence by writing 'No wolves' on the tent, in invisible ink.

The wind battering the tent caused us both a little trouble sleeping, but it was not a particularly cold night (minus six we no longer considered cold) and Dea's sign must have worked, because the wolves stayed away. And climbing out of the tent in the morning I was delighted to feel the wind coming at us from the opposite direction. We had our tailwind!

We got on our bikes and barely needed to pedal, our average speed more than doubled from the day before. The wind was phenomenal. I put on some music and just enjoyed the ride on the wide highway that just went on and on across the empty landscape. The road had been well ploughed, but powdered snow would drift onto it sometimes, being blown along as fast as we were, and it was an immensely cool experience to fly along with it as it swirled and danced across the road surface.

By early afternoon we realised that with this wind at our backs it was going to be possible for us to reach Zharkent, the town that we'd intended to arrive at the day after. We put ourselves to the task, motivated by the thought of a warm hotel room, and sure enough we made it to the town in the last of the day's light, after a scarcely believable 124 kilometres.

The hotel room felt almost unbearably hot to us, perhaps because of our bodies adjusting to spending so much time in the cold. We were now just thirty-five kilometres from the Chinese border, and I awoke early feeling nervous. This was a big day, the day when we would hopefully finally make it back to China.

Hopes of getting there quickly were dashed by a heavy overnight snowfall. The streets of Zharkent were a pure white as we cycled through them. It all looked very pretty, but I knew that it was the effect the snow had on the main road that was going to prove our biggest challenge.

But before we got out of Zharkent we had one last happy memory of Central Asia to take with us. It happened when I went into a shop to spend the last of our Kazakh tenge, mostly on cheese (which we knew would be hard to find in China). The female owner of the shop was really nice, and gave me a couple of hot potato pastry things to wish us well. I took them outside, and Dea and I sat on a wall to eat them. But it wasn't long before the woman came out and invited us both back into the shop, where we were given proper chairs and hot drinks as well. We were sure going to miss the people of Kazakhstan, they had been so good to us.

Then our troubles really began. The road had by now shrunk to two-lanes and it was very busy with traffic, leaving us nowhere decent to cycle as the shoulder was buried under half a foot of soft snow. It was just about possible to cycle through this snow, but it was awfully hard work and the bike would occasionally slip and slide around. Whenever there was a gap in traffic we would move out into the road where the wheels of the passing vehicles had cleared a track, but we could never stay there long before the next vehicle came along. It made for painfully slow progress and our frustrations grew, as the novelty of cycling in the middle of winter began to wear off.

We passed through several villages, where lots of kids waved at us and to their great credit resisted throwing snowballs our way. We stopped for a break next to a mosque that was alive with the sound of the call to prayer. A Lada drove up next to it and the owner got out and headed inside the mosque. It was funny to think that these varied cultural icons, which had become so familiar to us over the past few months, were about to come to an end. China was certain to be a different world entirely, we already knew that.

As the day went on it started to snow on us as we cycled, and the road conditions only got worse. We persevered with it though, driven on by the thought of finally making it to China after so long. Ten months had gone by since we'd stood on a doorstep in Edinburgh and told a woman we didn't know that we were cycling to China. "That's a long way," she'd said, and she'd been right. But it wasn't a long way any more, and it was getting closer by the minute.

I grew increasingly anxious. This was it, the final border before Mori. The last chance for someone to hold their hand up in front of me and say, "Sorry, this is a car-only border," and shatter my dreams all over again. I knew China well enough to understand that this was something that really could happen here. Deep down, I think I'd always been expecting it to. I'd thought so very many times about this border over the previous weeks, months, years, building it up in my mind as the place where it could easily all go wrong. But there would be no more of that. The moment had arrived. We were at the border.

48

The Kazakh side of the border was a lot of work, with a total of seven people checking our passports at various times, and all of our bags having to come off the bikes and through an x-ray machine. It was a tedious process, but crucially nobody instructed us to get into a motor vehicle, and we managed to get onto the seven kilometre stretch of no-man's land on our bikes. We did, however, slightly sneak through the entrance to it in the shadow of a truck, and I remained worried. This long section of road through no-man's land existed for no particularly obvious reason, as it went around in a big loop for seven kilometres and then ended up at the Chinese border post only a few hundred metres from the Kazakh one. Fenced in on this snow-covered road I cycled quickly, looking up at the security cameras that were on almost every fence post with fear, terrified that at any moment a car was going to come along with someone jumping out and telling us that we weren't supposed to be cycling here.

It felt like such a long seven kilometres, but thankfully nobody came to stop us, and we made it to the Chinese side, where there was still the challenge of actually getting into China to be overcome. First all of our bags had to come off again and through another x-ray machine at the entrance to the building. *'I really hope they aren't going to ask us to do that again,'* I thought, as I loaded everything back onto my bike, knowing full well that they were.

It was a big modern airport-style building that was completely empty apart from us and the Chinese staff. One of them ushered us over to a passport control desk. The serious-faced woman there stared for a long time at my passport photo, then looked up at me, then back down at the photo, then up at me again.

"Why does this not look like you?" she asked me in a very sincere manner.

"Erm... because we're cycling," I said, although what I really meant was, "Because I hadn't just spent a week cycling in sub-zero temperatures when I had my passport photo taken."

The woman wasn't impressed by my explanation and continued to study my flushed, weather-beaten, heavily-bearded features for any likeness to the photo in front of her. She asked me to write down my signature to see if it matched the one on my passport, then consulted the woman next to her, then a more-senior looking male official, for their opinions on my face.

The woman's over-the-top scrutiny was interesting, because in front of me, on the outside of her desk, were four buttons below a question asking me for my opinion of her service. The options were 'Greatly Satisfied', 'Satisfied', 'Checking Time Too Long', and 'Poor Customer Service'. I was tempted to press the last one based on her not recognising me, or perhaps the penultimate one given how long all this was taking. She still hadn't decided whether or not to let me into China.

"Evaluate my service!" came a sudden electronic demand, and the buttons in front of me lit up. What was I to do? Was this a test? I couldn't very well say I was satisfied could I? She still hadn't given me my entry stamp. Would hovering my hand over the 'Checking Time Too Long' button perhaps speed things up? I wasn't sure, so I just stood there with my best passport photo face on. The lights went out again, and then some considerable time later, and with some apparent reluctance, the woman stamped my passport at last.

Dea had been in another line and had had a similar experience, but she too had now been stamped in. Alas, this was not yet the end of our border ordeal. A man now stood next to us demanding our phones. What he wanted with them we were not sure, but playing dumb didn't work, and we weren't going to be allowed into China without giving them to him, so we reluctantly handed them over. He then plugged them into a machine that seemed to be pulling all of the photos and files off for them to analyse, but I'm not sure because I wasn't allowed to watch. We were both naturally very put out by this gross invasion of privacy, but there wasn't much we could do about it.

"Well, it is China," I said as I slumped in my chair. Normal boundaries of privacy and consideration were going to be tested in this country, that was for sure. Eventually we were given our phones back and allowed to continue through the building. We were filed through to another area where we were met, inevitably, by another x-ray machine. "Breathe, Dea, just breathe," I said, seeing the look on her face.

All of this was worth it, of course, when we finally got out of the building and were permitted to cycle out of the gate. We'd been stuck in the building so long that it was now dark out, and the snow-covered wide boulevard in front of us was lined with ridiculous neon lights. It was China alright. We had done it, we had made it through the border, we had cycled to China. "We're in China!" we both cried out, unable to quite believe it was true as we hugged in celebration.

The hug didn't last long before being interrupted by a couple of money-changers. We didn't want to change any money, but I think we did show a tremendous amount of patience by agreeing to their request for photos with us, especially as they were rather like the Chinese Chuckle Brothers. The first one, who we'll call Barry, gave his phone to the second, Paul, and then stood and posed with us. But Paul couldn't work Barry's phone, which caused Barry to get rather annoyed with his friend's haplessness. They then swapped places, Paul standing with us and Barry taking his phone, and now the tables were turned, and Barry couldn't work Paul's phone either.

Eventually they figured themselves out and got some pictures, and then we asked if they wouldn't mind taking a photo of us with our own camera (which was not a phone), and you would not believe the trouble they had with that.

We rode on into a very weird town. Neon lights were everywhere, and a female voice addressed the street from speakers placed on lampposts. There was a strange, twilight-zone feel to the place, as a few people wandered about aimlessly, and a police car drove up and down the main street very slowly, constantly circling back around over and over again.

We looked around for a hotel, and rejected the first one mostly because it had an x-ray machine in the doorway. The second one was better and we stayed. It also had an x-ray machine and several security personnel, but crucially they let us push our bikes around it without having to scan everything. Checking in was a slightly difficult process with the language barrier, but we were expecting that, and with enough patience we eventually had ourselves a bed for the night.

We were both feeling exhausted and would have liked to have taken a rest day here in Khorgas, but there was heavy snow forecast for later in the week, and we had a mountain pass ahead of us that we hoped to get over before that hit. But the warm night in the hotel did us good, and we were on our way early the next morning. Actually it was noon, but now that we were on Beijing time we'd skipped ahead two hours from Kazakhstan, so our bodies were quite sure it was still morning really. The first thing we did was go into the shop next to our hotel and delight in the wide array of interesting snack foods we could now buy (tomato-flavoured crisps would become a firm favourite, the vacuum-packed chicken feet less so). Then we cycled back to the main road, which looked a lot less crazy in the daylight, and stopped at a mobile phone shop where Dea got a SIM card so that we would have a Chinese number. In most countries we didn't bother doing this, but in China having our own number would prove an invaluable help.

We left town and soon found ourselves cycling on the G30, the big expressway that from here headed east for unbelievable distances right across the country. The shoulder only had a little snow on it and was fine to cycle on. However, we knew that cycling on the expressway was strictly forbidden when there was an alternative road, and there soon appeared a service road running alongside the expressway, so we switched over. There was quite a bit more snow here which made it more difficult to cycle, and there was a fair amount of traffic on it too. The expressway right next to us would have been easier and safer, but there were an extraordinary number of police cars driving about everywhere, and we just couldn't take any chances.

There were some advantages to the small road, such as when it veered off into a little town, where we noticed lots of round bread for sale at a little shop. It was being baked on the walls of a big round oven by a group of smiling women, and with the addition of onion and herbs it was much tastier than the plain breads of Central Asia. The women wore headscarves as they were Muslim, like the majority of people in this region of China, and it wasn't long before they invited us inside to drink tea. We took a seat and the tea was brought over to us, although it was unlike any tea I'd ever seen before. We each received a giant bowl, easily three times as big as any normal tea vestibule, in which resided a splodgy pale liquid. But the ladies generosity did not end there, for they then placed in the middle of the table a salad of thinly grated vegetables for us to enjoy.

Consuming the salty liquid was a challenge, and likewise the salad, for the only utensils provided for eating it with were chopsticks. It had been a while since I'd used chopsticks, and my track record with them was not great. Picking up grated carrot and trying to carry it all of the way from the middle of the table to my mouth was never going to go very well, but it was a pleasure to just sit there and watch the women as they worked. They were rolling out the dough, shaping it into large circles by hand and kneading it down, adding in the pieces of onion, and preparing them for the oven, which was like a stone well with a fire at the bottom. The sticky dough was slapped onto the walls where it would remain fixed in place as it baked. The women didn't talk to us much, but it was a great pleasure to sit there out of the cold and watch them go about their daily work. Mostly thanks to Dea we finished the salad and did our best with the tea, although consuming it all was never going to happen (and in any case would have only exposed all the salad I'd dropped in it), before we said our thanks and returned to the road.

Our progress was slow all day, thanks to the snow on the ground and the fact that we were climbing gradually up. Ahead of us was a big test, the last mountain pass before Mori, a climb to over 2,100 metres. So it was not good news when, late in the day, I tried to get my bike restarted through some deep snow and as I pushed down on my right pedal I felt an intense pain shoot through my knee. It was different from the pain I'd had before, and more serious. It felt like a sprain and was very painful. I did the only thing I knew, and kept on cycling.

Finding a camping place was difficult. In the end we took a quiet side road to get away from the traffic, but this road had not been cleared of snow at all, and so we had to get off and push our bikes all the way through it. After a few hundred metres we found our way into a field with a small concrete building that we could at least partly hide behind. I knew that wild camping here was illegal, and being found by the police could mean us being forced into a motor vehicle and driven to a hotel. It was not an ideal location, and the tyre tracks we'd left in the snow could easily give us away, but with no better options, it would have to do. With enough excavating of the two-feet deep snow we had space for the tent and dived inside, but to our further dismay as soon as we did that we heard the sound of snow falling on the flysheet. I knew that a heavy overnight snowfall might make the pass almost impossible, and I was worried.

It snowed pretty much the whole night long, but it was not cold, and with considerable relief we found that come morning the volume of snow on the ground had not greatly increased. We had to push the bikes back along the side road, but from there we could cycle again. My knee was also feeling better, and we had hopes that we could make it up to the summit of the pass before the end of the day.

We could only follow the service road for a further nine kilometres before it ended and the G30 was the only possible onward option. At the end of the service road there was a little restaurant where we stopped to fill our bottles with boiling water (we'd by now developed a system of filling the flask and our water bottles with boiling water whenever we could to avoid carrying lumps of ice around with us), and to eat a meal. The female chef cooked us up a dish with eggs, tomatoes and peppers, served with steamed doughballs, that was genuinely one of the most delicious things I'd eaten in a very long time. It even came with tea that was actually tea, and it was just exactly what we needed to set ourselves up for the challenge ahead.

As we left the restaurant a man pointed at the expressway ahead of us, then shook his head and wagged his finger as if to tell us we weren't allowed to go that way. It only made me more nervous, as we approached the tollbooth that marked the expressway entrance. Taking no chances, we slipped through hidden by a truck in order to avoid any unwanted questions. Soon we were out of sight and pedalling away on the G30. The shoulder was wide and mostly just had a light covering of snow, although big mounds of it lay piled up against the right-side crash barrier. In any case, the road was surprisingly quiet, and often we could cycle out on the smooth tarmac of the inside lane, just moving over onto the shoulder when something would come past.

Big mountains began to appear all around us as we made our way steadily up a valley. There were evergreen trees all over the slopes, but they were not living up to that name today, covered as they were in a generous coating of snow. Our world was made up of various shades of white and grey, but it was staggeringly beautiful. As we took a break sitting on a mound of snow on the shoulder of the expressway we looked around and agreed that despite all the difficulties we were both pleased to be here at this time, because to see this place looking as it did in winter was so very special. We felt very lucky.

More snow started to fall and the winds picked up, but thankfully they were blowing the right way, up the valley, and we made steady progress through the afternoon. Then the valley opened up a bit and we saw what we had been waiting for. A massive bridge appeared high above us, crossing from one mountain to another. It was one of the most impressive construction feats I'd ever seen, and we were going to cycle on it. China had probably considered building a series of switchbacks up the mountainside a little too easy, so they'd done things a bit differently. The road we were on was soon to enter the mountain to our right and then spiral upwards in a tunnel to the start of the bridge high above us. It was an incredible spectacle, but I think my bike must have been intimidated by the sight of it all, because my gears began to skip terribly. "Not now, please," I said, but the deterioration continued rapidly, and soon my lowest gears became impossible to use, just when I needed them most. That meant I had to ride in a higher gear, which put more pressure on my knee, which in turn began to hurt like hell. It was intense, excruciating pain every time that I turned my right leg around. I knew that removing a few links from my chain might give me back my lower gears again, at least temporarily, but Dea was off ahead and I didn't want to stop and do that without letting her know what was happening, so I kept on riding, simply saying, "Ow!" with every rotation of my right pedal.

I caught up to Dea at the start of the spiral tunnel and stopped to remove some chain links. Thankfully the SRAM Powerlink came off quickly and it was only a two minute job, for the day was getting on and there was still some way to go. We headed into the tunnel, deciding to cycle in the roadway rather than the footpath to save time as there wasn't much traffic. I regretted this decision almost immediately. The tunnel was 1.4 kilometres long and with its constant right curve we would be almost invisible to the traffic coming up behind us. We cycled as fast as we could, and we were lucky, for almost as soon as we escaped out of the end of the tunnel a convoy of trucks came along, something that would have made for a very uncomfortable experience had they arrived a couple of minutes earlier.

Beyond the tunnel we were now crossing the bridge over the valley and it was a funny feeling to be up so high. We'd been worried about the strong winds on the bridge, so it was a relief that they weren't really a problem, and we cycled onwards confidently across the sky. On the other side of the bridge the road curved around to the right again and then up to one final tunnel that would lead us to the summit plateau that we had been dreaming about all day. We were almost at the tunnel when we heard a lot of noise and saw flashing lights coming up behind us. It was a team of giant snowploughs. We'd seen them before and knew how it worked. The first one would be in the outside lane, pushing the snow to its right, then the second one would follow, sweeping the inside lane, and then a final plough would come along in the shoulder and throw everything off the side of the road, or into the outer crash barrier. The thing we needed to do was to get well out of the way, but on this occasion it was quite impossible, for on the other side of the crash barrier there was a steep drop down a cliff. All we could do was stand there and hold our ground. The first two ploughs passed us, their drivers waving furiously at us to get out of the way, despite the fact that we couldn't. Then came the third plough, a great yellow monster going really quite fast along the shoulder towards us. The driver saw us and lent on the horn, but showed no indication that he was going to move out for us. The distance between him and us diminished rapidly and as he drew close Dea squealed, "He's not going to move!" and it really did look that way.

"He has to," I said, with more confidence than I felt, for the only alternative involved our certain demise. I could see the sparks flying out from where the plough scraped tarmac as it got closer and closer until, at the very last second, the driver veered to his left, covering us with snow as he avoided us by the finest of margins.

We gathered ourselves and rode on to the tunnel, electing to cycle on the footpath this time. By Chinese standards it was a pretty good tunnel footpath, and it brought us out upon the summit plateau, to our screams of relief and delight. To our left was the large Sayram Lake, although it was impossible to distinguish, for it was frozen solid and covered in snow, just like the rest of our surroundings. It was also late, just starting to get dark, and finding a place to sleep became an urgent priority. I had told Dea with some confidence that we would surely find a place to camp up on this flat plateau, but now I saw that it was not going to be at all easy. The expressway was not only lined with a crash barrier, but also a sturdy layer of fencing, and finding a way off it was difficult under normal circumstances. But these were not normal circumstance, for now we also had to deal with everything being covered in deep snow. In the end, however, that was what helped us. There was a culvert passing under the road at the same moment that there was a rare gap in the crash barrier. There was still a high fence to get over and a big drop down on the other side, but luckily the snow here was so deep that it rose most of the way up the fence, offering us an unlikely method for getting over it. The snow was so compact that we could even roll the bikes over it to get down to the fence. On the other side the snow was less stable, but I built some steps into it, and it was good enough to hold our weight as we ferried our bags and bikes down to the bare concrete below. The only disadvantage to our camping spot was the frigid wind that blew right through the culvert, but we quickly put on all the clothes we had, stuffed bin liners in them, got the tent up, and settled into our many sleeping bags. It had been a good day, we had succeeded in reaching our goal of the summit plateau, and even found a place to sleep. On the other hand we were now camping at 2,100 metres above sea level, in the middle of winter, and we were surely in for the coldest night of our lives.

49

Xinjiang, China
15th January 2018

Somehow the night didn't feel that cold. Maybe it was because the clouds in the sky kept the temperature from dropping too far, maybe it was because we'd by now adapted to the cold well enough not to feel it, or maybe, and this is my preferred theory, it was because of the bin liners.

Whatever it was, we made it through to morning and carried our bikes and bags back up the snow steps, over the top of the fence, and back up to the road. What we found there was not so encouraging. It had snowed in the night, and the expressway had not yet been ploughed. It looked like it was going to make cycling very difficult.

"Maybe we should just wait until the ploughs come through," I said

"No Chris, it's too cold. Let's just give it a go."

And Dea was right to say this, because it was actually easier than it looked to ride through the soft snow. It was also an experience in itself to cycle through this world of white, the road surface now matching the land and the sky around us.

After a while we reached the end of the summit plateau, where ahead of us lay a fifty-five kilometre descent. This was in some ways an even more daunting prospect than the long climb up had been. Freewheeling down, our bodies would not be generating any heat, and memories of how painfully cold we'd gotten coming down from the passes in Kyrgyzstan were still fresh in our minds. Here the temperature was easily ten degrees colder than it had been there, and this was going to be a real test of our equipment and our resolve. We stopped in the shoulder, leant our bikes against the crash barrier, and got to work putting on clothes. Every stitch of clothing we had went on. On my top half I was wearing four or five T-shirts, two hoodies, two sweaters, and three jackets, while on the lower half I had two pairs of regular trousers, one pair of ski trousers, and a pair of waterproof rain trousers. I had a pair of thick woollen socks and a couple of pairs of regular socks inside my big winter boots. Around my neck a buff was permanently positioned, and over my head I for the first time pulled the balaclava I'd bought back in Almaty. I put my helmet on top and fastened it down tight. By now my hands were freezing cold, so I stuffed them down the front of my trousers and rubbed furiously (on my thighs) to warm them up. I then pulled my thick winter gloves out from under my clothes (I kept them against my body when I wasn't wearing them to keep them warm) and slipped them on. I looked over at my girlfriend who had been undergoing a similar process. She looked almost unrecognisable beneath her own balaclava. We nodded to one another and, looking like two overweight bank robbers, we began our descent.

It was, as predicted, unbelievably cold. My fingers soon went numb despite the double protection of gloves and pogies, and my eyeballs stung as I zipped down through the cold air. My balaclava worked reasonably well at keeping most of my face warm, but the mouth hole was a little too high and icicles formed on my moustache. To alleviate this problem, I pulled my buff up over the balaclava, almost up to my eyes, which were now the only thing exposed to the world, watching on eagerly as we descended from the mountains for the final time. Ahead of us I could see the land flattening out, and knowing that it would remain that way all of the way to Mori I felt really good. The last great topographical challenge was behind us.

We stopped at a service station to warm up, where the Chinese staff looked at us with wide-eyed amazement as we staggered in. These service stations were a blessing for us, a place where we could get out of the cold and eat some hot food, top up our water bottles, and regroup before continuing. The staff in this one came up to us and presumably tried to ask us what on earth it was that we thought we were playing at cycling in this weather, but it would have been difficult for us to explain, even if we could understand each other.

Beyond the services we were out into the open, travelling through a vast unpopulated area that I probably would have described as a desert had it not been covered in snow. We had to wild camp as there were no options for accommodation anywhere. The snow was at least not so deep here and it would be easy to find somewhere for the tent, but there was still the challenge of getting off the expressway, and doing it unseen. We found a gap in the fence, but with no corresponding break in the crash barrier we decided to lift our bikes over it to save time. We helped each other to lift each bike, Dea at the front and me at the back, though our bikes were so heavy I almost put my back out. It was worth it though, for I wanted this process to be a fast one. I knew that if a police car should come along at the wrong moment we would be in big trouble, as they would surely stop and tell us we were not allowed to wild camp, insist that we make our way to a hotel that was out of cycling range. With this in mind I constantly looked back at the road as we pushed our bikes across the snow, fearing the sight of the blue and red flashing lights that could ruin everything. But they never came, and we made it far enough from the road not to be seen and set up the tent once again.

It was a cold night, somehow colder than the night before at higher elevation had been, but we woke up to clear skies and a determination to make it to the town of Jinghe, where we planned to rest up in a hotel for a few days. With this as our motivation we set out early, cycling once more into the sunrise.

The expressway was completely free of snow here and we made fast progress on the good, flat surface, listening to podcasts and music to pass the time. It was an uneventful day, which was all I really wanted now, and late in the afternoon we reached the turn-off for Jinghe. We took it, but almost immediately came upon a big police checkpoint. All of the motor vehicles were being stopped and we were no different, as some young policemen told us to lean up our bikes and proceed into a building. We did as we were told, and inside our passports were taken from us and we were asked to wait. I looked around, and saw that all of the locals also had to pass through this building. They were all filing through a turnstile, which would only let them pass with a successful scan of their Chinese I.D. cards. I knew something of the controversies of this part of China, that some of the native Uyghur people wanted independence from China, that the Chinese authorities were not going to allow that to happen. I also knew that some Uyghurs had resorted to violence and terrorist attacks to further their aims, and as a consequence of that came the high security everywhere, the x-ray machines at hotels and the blockades at the entrance to gas stations. But I hadn't realised until now how seriously the Chinese were monitoring the people here. Sure, there were security cameras everywhere, photographing every vehicle, but here it was the people themselves being recorded, every individual being time punched in and out of the town like some Orwellian nightmare.

It took a little while for the police officers, all of them young Han Chinese, to work out what to do about us. Recording the details of non-Chinese visitors seemed to be as important as tracking the locals, but nobody was quite sure how to do it. They were particularly interested in which hotel we would be staying at, but we didn't know until we got there, and eventually they gave up asking and allowed us to proceed.

The wide streets of Jinghe were decorated with red lanterns and fake flowers. New tower blocks were everywhere, Chinese writing over shop fronts at their base. People shuffled and slipped about on the frozen footpaths, while in the roads many people moved by motorised three-wheeled trailers, protected from the weather by giant pogies that extended out into big blankets around them.

We found our way to a hotel that we hoped would accept foreigners. We knew that the majority of hotels in this part of China did not, but we'd got the coordinates of this one from another cyclist who had stayed a couple of years earlier. His information proved to still be correct, and we were soon loading up all of our bags into the elevators and heading up to a warm hotel room that would be the scene for our rest and recovery for the next few days. Both of us had trouble with our knees that justified taking the time off to rest, and with Chinese hotel rooms being extremely good value (ten or fifteen pounds for a well-furnished en-suite twin room) there was really no good reason not to. We were now less than 900 kilometres from Mori, we had no more mountains to climb, and we had just about learnt to live with the cold. Things were starting to look good.

Another good thing about the Chinese hotels was that they tended to have excellent Wi-Fi connections, and thanks to the help of Andy, a friend I'd made when I stayed with him in Singapore a couple of years earlier, we had a good VPN that allowed us to circumvent the Chinese firewall that blocked the country's citizens from accessing half of the internet. That meant that I was able to get on Facebook, where I found some rather worrying messages from a guy named Markus, a fellow cyclist who'd come through this way a month or so before us. He'd had some considerable trouble with the Chinese police from the sounds of it, and that was certainly something for us to worry about, but in my present state I was too exhausted to think about it, and I fell into a most wonderful sleep.

I awoke early the following morning. Dea was still sound asleep on the bed next to mine, so I pulled my laptop up off the floor, intending to investigate Markus's information a little more thoroughly. But I remembered that I hadn't checked my e-mail account the night before, so I opened that up first. There was one new mail that caught my eye. I read it through, and then put the computer back down and just lay there staring up at the ceiling, my eyes welling up as I tried to process the information I'd just received. After a while I got up and went to the bathroom. I washed my face with trembling hands, then stared at my silent reflection in the mirror. I didn't know what to do with myself, so I went back into the room and started pacing back and forth, holding my head in my hands. Dea was awake by now and, sensing that something really wasn't right with me, she threw aside her duvet and came over to me. "What's wrong baby?" she asked, taking me in her arms and trying her best to soothe me. I opened my mouth to tell her, but the words wouldn't come out. Over her shoulder I could see that dawn was starting to light the Chinese street outside, and I wondered what I was doing here. "What is it, baby, what's wrong?" Dea asked again, but still I struggled to find the courage to say it out loud, because if I heard myself say it out loud, it would mean that it must be true.

"My mum's got cancer."

50

M y mum was standing in front of me. She was upset. We were in the back garden of the house in Newton Blossomville. The grass was green. Apples from our apple tree lay at my feet. Why was she upset? I must have done something wrong.

"You said a bad word didn't you?"

Had I? I couldn't remember.

"You know what it was, don't you? What your sister's knee was earlier."

I don't know why, but this was one of those random memories that had stuck with me from my childhood. Maybe it was because of my mum's refusal to let the word bloody leave her lips. As I lay sobbing on a bed in China almost three decades later, it occurred to me that I'd never in all my life heard my mother swear. In moments of near-profanity she always managed to turn it into shhh-ugar. Every single time.

That wasn't the only memory playing in my head. Mum was kicking footballs with me in the park, feeding the ducks with me, giving me a Kinder Egg on the way home for being a good boy at the supermarket. I felt like a child again now, weeping on the bed. My mum couldn't have cancer. She was my mum, this couldn't happen to her. She couldn't die.

After I'd got the tears out of my system I started to think in more practical terms. What could I do? What should I do? Should I fly home? I couldn't very well do anything to help her from the middle of bloody (sorry Mum) China, could I?

I went back to my laptop and started researching breast cancer. Mum's e-mail had said that it was only a small tumour and they had caught it early. With massive relief I discovered that the survival rates for such cancers was extremely high. There was a great chance that she would be able to come through this, but to get there would involve months of chemotherapy and then surgery. It sounded like Mum had a really tough road ahead, but I was encouraged by the survival rates and I was well past the crying stage by the time I got hold of my parents by video call.

"How are you doing, Mum?" I asked, with Dea sitting supportively at my side.

"I'm fine," she replied, almost cheerfully. Dad was next to her, and they both looked pretty happy under the circumstances.

"They actually found the tumour before Christmas and I was going to have surgery to have it removed without worrying you, but now they've decided I need to have the chemo, we thought we'd better let you know." My mum spoke casually, like it was not such a big deal. "It's going to be a longer process now, but we'll just take it one step at a time."

We went on to talk for a while about what was going to happen next, the effects of the chemotherapy, how it was going to make her sick, how my dad was going to look after her. And the idea that I should fly home was quickly shut down by my father: "Mum shouldn't have visitors anyway. The chemotherapy will weaken her immune system and make her susceptible to infection, so it's probably better if you don't come home while she's having the chemo." I chose to interpret this fatherly advice not as, "stay away, you disease-ridden homeless guy," and more as, "go finish what you've started, son!"

But it was so good to talk with my parents, to see them being so positive about things. It made me feel a lot better to know that they weren't being downbeat, that they knew what needed to be done to make Mum better, and that they were going to get it done. It had been a good conversation.

"Okay, bye for now, we'll talk soon," I said.

"Okay, good luck, and don't do anything silly," my dad said.

I was still in shock about my mum having cancer, but it seemed like they had everything under control and that was extremely reassuring. I knew my mum wouldn't want me to give up on my journey, not now that I was so close to the end, and I began to think that it was important that I carry on, perhaps even the most important thing that I could do for Mum. The self-inflicted struggle that Dea and I were going through with the Chinese winter was not exactly comparable with what she was about to endure, but maybe there were some parallels. Maybe by getting to Mori despite all that was against us we could provide some inspiration for her in dealing with her own long struggle. Maybe us carrying on and succeeding was the best thing we could do for Mum now.

I didn't know what else I could do.

51

Jinghe, China
20th January 2018

The most difficult part is from Jinghe to Kuytun.'
These were the words that troubled me as we set out from Jinghe in the direction of Kuytun. They'd been written by Markus, a cyclist who I'd been put in touch with by Liz. He'd passed this way a month or so before us, and his warning messages revealed that he'd been 'arrested' four times in this area of China and forced into police cars. I'm not sure if he really was arrested, but him being forced into police cars on four separate occasions was enough to confirm my suspicions that the police here represented a genuine threat to my mission. Markus had made some errors, like staying with locals, stopping at toll booths, and going to hotels that were not approved to host foreigners, but it felt like it was far, far too easy for things to go wrong with the police on this next stretch. As a result, Dea and I only planned to follow the G30 expressway for another 150 kilometres, until an alternative road would become available, which we could in fact use to bypass Kuytun completely in order to try and avoid having any encounters with the police there.

All of these concerns seemed unnecessary on our first day out from Jinghe, when we were passed by a grand total of one police car the whole day. In fact it was an uneventful day all round, and there's not much to say about it other than that we rode along on the expressway all day long, and it was awfully cold. At the end of the day we found some steps leading down the embankment off the road and through the fence. I went down them alone to look for a good camping place, walked off around a field, through some trees, up a steep snow slope, down a steep snow slope, across a frozen river, back across another field, and then finally found a great place to camp right under the road, just next to the steps where I'd started.

It was a cold night and a freezing morning. Packing away the tent and getting everything ready to go was always a horrible experience. Once we got on the bikes and cycled we could generate enough body heat to tolerate the extreme cold, although my right hand continued to suffer now, as one of my pogies had somehow fallen off without me noticing. And this day was much the same as the last; we just cycled on the G30 all day, with only one or two police vehicles passing us by, and without paying us any attention. Everything was going just fine.

Then a smaller road appeared next to the G30. This was the one we were planning to take, but we didn't use the first exit onto it, for I knew that would mean a toll booth and probably a police checkpoint. I'd done my research using satellite images on Google, and it looked like there was another exit ten kilometres further on that wasn't officially in use any more, so there'd be no need for us to interact with any police. It also looked like there was a big patch of trees at that exit that would make for a well-hidden campsite for the night.

The final advantage was that we could stop at a service station between the exits. It was the first one we'd seen all day, and we needed to top up our hot water. We walked inside through the security scanner that all public buildings had around here, and were met by three old security men in camouflage uniforms. They made us write our names in a book, then followed us over to the water machine, perhaps suspicious, perhaps only curious. They were all very old men. There were a great number of security personnel in Xinjiang, and it seemed as if they were all either very young or very old, retired people that needed to be given something to do. These ones were intent on following us, one of them even tailing me into the toilets, while another tracked Dea around the shop. They were a bit annoying, but they seemed harmless enough, and Dea and I laughed about it as we sat and ate a quick dinner. She had a Chinese pot noodle and I had a packet of cookies and a strawberry milk, while the security men watched us from the next table. Dea and I were both exhausted, and relieved that we only had a few kilometres to go before the exit where we could make camp and sleep. It was to be our final short ride on the G30, for the rest of the way to Mori there were alternative roads that we could take.

We said farewell to our three old minders and stepped back outside into the cold. I looked up and winced. Parked up next to our bikes was a police car, its lights flashing. This was really, really not a good thing to see. In it were two young officers, probably in their early twenties, one of whom stepped out and sort of walked over to us in a not very authoritative or confident manner. He didn't even really attempt to say anything to us, so I decided that the best thing to do would be to smile and nod at him, and then casually cycle off. Maybe they weren't even here for us. Maybe it was just a coincidence.

We rode across the large parking area and onto the slip road to rejoin the expressway, Dea just ahead of me. I looked in my mirror, and saw the police car was coming up behind us. It had its hazard lights on and it was driving slowly. *'Please just go past, just leave us alone,'* I pleaded, but it did not. It continued to follow slowly behind us up the slip road. I decided we needed to stop and see what was going on before it was too late.

The two young policemen both got out this time and tried to talk to us. Of course there was no common language, but it was obvious enough that they were telling us that we were not allowed to cycle on the expressway. "Can we cycle on the small road over there then?" I asked. They nodded. This other road was parallel to the G30, but unfortunately on the far side of it, so we couldn't easily get to it. But there was a way. Right at the start of the service station area, some 500 metres or so back, there had been a bridge that crossed the G30, which I was sure we could access on foot. There were some steps there up onto the bridge that we could carry our bikes up, I was sure of it. So I asked the policemen, via plenty of pointing, if we could go back, and get on the small road that way.

"No, no," they insisted, which of course left us in quite a difficult spot. We couldn't cycle forwards and we couldn't cycle back. This was getting serious now. This was the nightmare we'd feared. This was really happening.

The young guys seemed fairly clueless and were trying to get in touch with someone more superior to ask what they should do with us. It was obvious enough to me that the response they would get would be to put us in their car and drive us somewhere. I had no doubt that was coming, none whatsoever, so I decided I needed to act before that could happen. Some might describe what I did next as reckless, but I was a desperate man now. I'd come too far to lose it all. So I jumped on my pedals and began to cycle furiously back down the slip road towards the car park. Dea followed.

My hope was that the policemen would shrug their shoulders and just drive off on the G30, leaving us free to climb up onto the bridge and continue on the smaller road. For a second I even believed this was what was going to happen, but then I heard the sirens. The car had spun around and was pursuing us down the slip road. Oh God, was this what Dad had meant when he'd said don't do anything silly? We were in a f*cking police chase now.

The funny thing about this police chase, other than that we were on bicycles, was that the police tried to anticipate where we were going, and they overtook us and drove back over to the service station to wait for us there. A sensible course of action might have been to follow them, given that it was now clear that they were being quite serious about the whole thing. But, as I said, I was a desperate man, and so rather than following them to the building I stuck to the other side of the car park, and headed for the bridge, which I thought was surely our best hope of freedom. To her great credit, the ever loyal Dea was still right behind me, her desperate cries for me to stop lost in the wind.

One of the policemen got out of the car and began pursuing us on foot. Fortunately he wasn't much of a runner, but unfortunately the other one was still in the car, which was faster than us. The sirens returned, and the thrill of the chase was once again very much on. I think it was at this point that I started to wonder if, given that the only way I was ever going to get in a car was if I was actually arrested, it might perhaps have been slightly foolish of me to give these policemen such a very good reason to arrest us. But as the police car pulled over in front of our path and brought us to a halt, my objective was almost complete. We were now very close to a set of steps leading up to the bridge. It would be so, so easy for us to get up onto the smaller road from this position. All we had to do now was to convince our pursuers not to drag us off to jail.

The inexperienced officers still didn't quite know what to do with us, but one of them must have remembered some of his basic training, as he took our passports from us to deter any further attempts at escape. But they weren't putting us in handcuffs, and they actually seemed like pretty nice guys who, uniforms aside, bore no real resemblance to policemen. I asked them if we could just go up the steps and join the small road and continue our journey there. It was such a simple, logical solution, such an easy way for us to continue on without going near the expressway again, but every time I suggested it they just shook their heads and said, "No, no," like it was the worst idea in the world. One of them pulled out a smartphone and our conversation continued via a translation app, with them telling us that they were still waiting to hear from their superiors and would we mind all going over to the service station where we could sit in the warm. For a while I refused, believing that leaving the proximity of the steps would mean losing all hope of us getting away. It was growing late, and I knew that their superiors were going to tell them to put us in a car and take us to a tourist-approved hotel, the nearest of which was fifty kilometres away in Kuytun. With it starting to get dark and the policemen still in possession of our passports my hopes that we might be allowed to continue on alone by bicycle were pretty much gone. I began to feel defeated. I thought about my mum. She had cancer. What was I doing here? What was all this nonsense about? Everything felt like it was falling apart. I noticed the poor guys were shivering like mad in front of me. "Okay, let's go to the service station," I said.

I could barely look at the old security men, quite convinced that they must have called the police on us. We had been so close. A few kilometres from leaving the expressway for good, but now the worst had happened. We sat down at the same table we'd been eating at an hour or so earlier. The day was at an end, and it was quite impossible to imagine any way that we were going to be allowed to leave under our own power, but I couldn't give it up, not yet. I showed the policemen a message that I had saved on my phone. It had been translated into Chinese by our friend Jia, the Chinese girl we'd met way back in Christiansfeld, Denmark, and it explained my trip, how close it was to completion, and how very important it was that I not get in a motor vehicle under any circumstances. The men both nodded as if they understood, and for a moment our hopes were raised slightly, until they handed me a message, saying, "Our superiors tell us, you must come by car to Kuytun."

For some time we sat there exchanging messages, with them repeating many times that we needed to get in their car.

"But I've cycled ninety-eight percent of the way around the world. Please help me," I tried.

"Too dangerous to cycle now. We are concerned for your safety."

"But I cannot get in a car, so we must find another solution."

Another solution was not easy to find. We knew that we had to get to Kuytun, for that was where the nearest tourist hotel was, and it seemed obvious now that the police were not going to leave us alone in any other place, but Kuytun was over fifty kilometres away and the day was over. I knew there was no chance. Then the policeman handed me his phone with a new message.

"We go to Kuytun together. We drive, you cycle."

I laughed. It was so far away, and it was so late. It was absurd. But Dea looked at me seriously, "Okay, Chris, if that's the solution, that's what we'll do." And I realised she was right, it was a solution, and suddenly there was a glimmer of hope again.

We went outside and started to cycle back onto the expressway, which the cops had now decided was the best place for us after all. They drove their car next to us in the slow lane, with all of their lights flashing. We had a police escort now, and that was a pretty damn cool reversal of fortunes, but I remained worried. Surely this wasn't going to continue for fifty kilometres at our speed. They'd get bored, tell us it was taking too long, tell us it wasn't safe to be doing this after dark. I tried to pedal hard, to prove that we could cycle there quickly, but my legs were so tired. We'd just done a whole day of riding in subzero temperatures, a day that had left us both exhausted. How were we supposed to find the reserves of energy for this now?

After only a few minutes the police car pulled ahead of us and stopped on the shoulder, causing me to fear the worst. We were too slow, surely. One of them got out and showed me a message. "You are tired," it began, "stop and take a rest in the car for a few minutes."

I laughed, told him I wasn't falling for that one, and said it would probably be better to just keep on pedalling.

A few minutes later, and the car stopped once more, making me nervous all over again. But this time the policeman came over to me and pulled off his highly visible police jacket and handed it to me. Either he thought I wasn't visible enough, or he thought I was cold, but either way I put it on to keep him happy, and because the opportunity to wear a jacket with 'POLICE' written on the back wasn't something I thought I should pass up.

Dea refused the other policeman's jacket, and she was also wearing her balaclava against the cold night air, so altogether we must have made for quite a sight for passing traffic, who I could imagine were making comments along the lines of, "That criminal really should have picked a faster getaway vehicle."

Despite how nice the policemen were being to us now, we continued to try and go fast, still so fearful that they might change their mind, or get a message from their superiors telling them to stop being so utterly stupid and just arrest us. Annoyingly the road was going uphill a lot, and there was quite a bit of snow on the shoulder, and the policeman's jacket was incredibly warm. I hadn't taken my own jacket off, and I now became unbearably hot. It was minus twenty and I was sweating buckets. Yet I dared not stop, dared not give them any opportunity to rethink things. Well, they had plenty of time to do that, I suppose, as they crawled along the road at twelve kilometres per hour beside us.

It was too dark to see my cycle computer, but the kilometre markers at the side of the road counted our progress. It seemed to take an age for each one to come around. I was getting so unbelievably tired. After twenty-five kilometres I could take it no longer, and stopped briefly to drink some water.

"You know," I said to Dea, "if we gave them our bags we could cycle faster."

"No, that would feel like cheating," she replied.

I sighed. Who was this girl?

On and on we went, long into the night. As the kilometres slowly ticked by I began to feel like we might make it, like we might just pull this one off. The feeling grew stronger as the bright lights of Kuytun finally appeared out of the darkness. But every kilometre felt like agony and we were not home and dry yet. At the Kuytun exit another police car sat waiting for us. This was where our escort vehicle would switch over to the local police. Two new police officers got out and seemed friendly, and clear on the fact that we needed to cycle. Our original pursuers, after all we'd been through together, and having spent four hours driving beside us along the expressway, now felt like friends. At their request we all posed for photos together before I shook their hands and offered them my thanks. I really meant it too. They could easily have arrested us, and they would have been well within their rights to, but instead they'd gone out of their way to help, and as a result of their patience my quest was still alive, just.

Another thing that was only just still alive was my girlfriend, who was on the verge of collapse at this point. She'd just cycled fifty kilometres on nothing more than a pot noodle (had she had the cookies and strawberry milk, I suspect she would have been fine) and she could barely stand up any more. Luckily our new policemen were just as understanding, and they let her sit for a while in their car to warm up, eat something, and prepare for the final few kilometres. While I was waiting outside, jumping up and down to keep myself warm, one of the policemen came and showed me a message: "We go to police station first, then hotel."

Once Dea was revived we exited the expressway and followed the police vehicle into Kuytun. There was a certain sense of triumph to arrive on its wide boulevards and look up at its brightly lit sky-scrapers. It had felt impossible, but here we were, and I was absolutely freezing. I'd given the policeman his jacket back and my own was frozen solid with sweat, while my right hand felt like it was made of ice. Kuytun was quite a big place, and it took an agonisingly long time to arrive at our destination. Once there we were invited inside the police station. Dea, without noticing or caring for the irony, did so still wearing her balaclava.

The police at the station were as nice as all the others, and really were just following regulations to check our passports and record our details, while also being curious as to what the hell we were doing cyc-ling at this time of year. There was no really good way to answer that. But it was nice to warm up inside, and to take a moment to sit with a hot drink in our hands and try to piece together the evening's events. And it had been a long evening; a clock on the wall revealed that was now gone midnight.

We had one final escort, from the police station to the tourist-approved hotel where we could stay. The hotel was a fancy one, more expensive than we were used to, but by this stage it really didn't matter so long as there was somewhere for us to collapse and sleep. The police walked us into reception and in doing so probably facilitated the checking-in process, and then at long last they left us alone.

Dea and I went up to our room and closed the door behind us, falling into an emotional hug of disbelief and relief. Dea had been amazing. She had been so, so impressive, to cycle all that way with me, to do all that for me. It had been such a surreal experience, so close to the end of everything, but somehow, the dream was still alive.

52

Kuytun, China
22nd January 2018

After the exertions of the previous evening there was no chance of us getting up very early in the morning, and it was a bit of a struggle to even make it down in time for the complimentary buffet breakfast. This was one of the best things about the hotels in Xinjiang, the smorgasbord of cooked food we'd get to choose from in the mornings, much of it vegetarian and delicious. And this hotel had more than most. We loaded up our plates with mounds of egg fried rice and shredded potato and green beans and mixed vegetables, and then took a seat to stuff our faces despite the stares of the other guests. We took a couple of bites. "Ah, I need water!" I cried. It was horrendously spicy.

We decided to take the whole day off and stay another night in Kuytun. We both needed it, especially Dea, whose poor knee had become very painful as a result of our prolonged ride. It also fitted in with a new plan we'd come up with to try and stay in tourist-approved hotels every night, in order to limit the risk of another police-enforced disaster. Until now that hadn't been possible due to a lack of civilisation, but from here there were a chain of towns cycling-distance apart. And further justification for this idea was provided by the weather forecast, with temperatures predicted to fall even further in the coming days, dropping as low as minus thirty degrees Celsius (minus twenty-two Fahrenheit) at night. But the next town, Shihezi, was a hundred kilometres from Kuytun, and we needed this rest day before attempting what would be a challenging distance.

While Dea rested her knee I went for a walk around Kuytun and hunted for a pharmacy to buy her some anti-inflammatories. It seemed like a pretty normal town, so far as any Chinese town can be considered normal, and I wondered what all the fuss had been about with the police. There were lots of cars on the roads and people walking the streets, but with my black down jacket on and my buff pulled up over most of my face nobody paid me any attention, which was just fine by me.

I had just got back to the hotel and given Dea the random pills I'd bought her when there was a loud knock on our door. I went and opened it and found two young policemen standing before me. They were perfectly friendly and apologetic, as they asked us a few questions about what we were doing here, and took photographs of our passports. It was all just some routine checks they had to do, I supposed, but it was a bit silly given that all of this had already been done at the station the previous night. Still, there was nothing to do but cooperate, and they left us alone once they had what they needed.

We went to bed early, hoping to get a good night's sleep so as to be ready for the long day to Shihezi. Then at ten thirty we were disturbed by more loud knocking at the door. We pulled on some clothes and opened up, to once again find two policemen standing there. This time one of them was a bit older, and I wondered if perhaps the young guys hadn't done their job properly. Now we were asked the same questions by him, our passports were photographed once again, and this time they also insisted on taking mugshots of our faces too. "Sorry it doesn't look like my passport photo," I said, "but I've just been woken up."

Despite our late night disturbance we were awake at seven and raring to go, keen to get out of this town and leave the Kuytun police behind us for good. We also had a long way to cycle, of course, providing a further reason for us sneaking out of town in the dark. This time we ignored the expressway and joined the secondary road as the sun rose ahead of us. The shoulder was of course covered in snow and there were enough trucks to make the experience of cycling here not very comfortable, but we knew that it was our only option now, and hoped that it would at least mean there would be fewer police interactions to deal with.

Such hopes were dashed when we reached the edge of the small town of Shawan and came to a police checkpoint. Once again we were ushered inside and made to wait while our passports were checked. We understood that everyone was just doing their job, and all of the policemen and women had been thoroughly nice and apologetic to us, but our patience was severely tested when we were stopped again on the way out of town. This second checkpoint was just for traffic entering the town in the opposite direction, nobody else going our way was made to stop. We were both finding all this a bit too much by now, but there was consolation to be found in the thought that at least we didn't live here. It was my first time seeing such a police state in operation and I turned my frustrations into appreciation that I came from a world of such freedom, a world I was able to return to at any moment if I so wished.

We made it to Shihezi just before dark, and how nice it was to ride into town, for there were no police checkpoints in sight. Did we dare to believe that the worst was over now that we were past Kuytun? It certainly seemed like it when we took another rest day and not one single policeman knocked on our hotel room door. The hotel was a good one, even playing English movies on the widescreen television (nothing like a bit of *Mrs Doubtfire* to help distract from the difficulties of a Chinese winter), and the town itself felt much more relaxed than others we'd been to. We ate mountains of cheap, excellent food in a local restaurant, then walked in the park, where we heard music playing. We followed the sound and came across a dozen or more older people dancing in the middle of the park. They were twirling around together, appearing to be as free as birds, caring no more for who was watching them than they were for the cold.

Somehow the temperatures were still dropping, and the following morning was the coldest we'd yet cycled in. It was twenty-five below, and we were both wearing our balaclavas as we set forth for Hutubi, seventy-five kilometres away, where we'd managed to pre-book a tourist-approved hotel online. As we left town we passed many locals in orange jumpsuits, valiantly sweeping the roads and paths clean of snow with broomsticks. For many people here the winter was surely going to feel like a long one.

Not far past Shihezi we came to a police checkpoint on our side of the road, but we simply cycled straight through it this time, nodding at the police like we knew what we were doing and not giving them time to realise they should stop us. Halfway through the day, another checkpoint appeared on the opposite side, and this time a couple of policemen spotted us and ran over to point us over to the building. Waiting for us on the other side of the road was another young cop, this one cradling a large assault rifle. He shouted at us in Chinese as we approached. He seemed a little jumpy and I in turn became nervous that he might misjudge the situation. He had no doubt received little training, but surely we were a close fit as to what he'd been told to look out for, approaching him as we were in balaclavas and bulging jackets, ignoring his instructions only because we couldn't understand them. I ripped off my headgear as fast as I could and showed him my passport. His finger relaxed off the trigger, and pointed us into the building.

Inside a few more young officers made some phone calls and tried to work out what they were supposed to do with us. Eventually they took photos of us and our passports and let us carry on cycling. Pleased to have got that out of the way, Dea and I pedalled onwards for all of one kilometre, at which point another police checkpoint appeared, this one on our side of the road. We tried to cycle nonchalantly past, but we were of course stopped, and made to go over to yet another police building.

This time we were ushered through to a waiting room, where we were told to sit while our passports were checked. After two checkpoints in one kilometre Dea was beginning to lose her patience, but I tried to frame things more positively. At least we were being given the chance to sit down somewhere warm, and we were making pretty good progress towards Hutubi, so we could afford this little rest. As usual the police were very young, all of them under the age of thirty, and it was probably only their uncertainty about how they were supposed to do their job that caused all these delays. They seemed to all be Han Chinese, and most of them gave the impression they had been shipped in here from other parts of the country on some kind of work experience project. In any case, we had a tourist-approved hotel booked for the night, and we were no longer cycling on the expressway, so I was confident we were going to be allowed to continue on our way before too long.

A bespectacled girl who could speak a few words of English came and asked us what country we were from, where we'd come from, and where we planned to stay the night. I showed her the hotel booking, relieved that we'd come prepared this time, and she told us to sit down and wait a little longer. Quite a bit of time passed and I began to worry about how long it was taking. Hutubi was still thirty kilometres away, and it was after four o'clock by the time the girl returned with our passports. She gave them to us, but then told us to sit back down, and we were shut in again. The clock was ticking, and we wondered what it was that was taking so long.

Eventually several police officers, including the girl and a tall man we'd not seen before, entered the room. The man asked for our passports.

"He is here to drive you to Hutubi," the girl casually informed us.

"I had a feeling this might happen," Dea said under her breath, before addressing the crowd with a very forceful, "NO! We will cycle!"

I began fumbling with my phone, looking for Jia's magic letter, the one in Chinese explaining everything about my challenge, but it turned out not to be necessary. Dea's vehement protests appeared to have everyone convinced that, indeed, we were going to cycle. The police consented, but there was a caveat. The tall man still had to accompany us to the hotel, but, not wanting to drive at the speed of cyclists, he'd simply take our passports and meet us at the hotel. It was far from an ideal solution, but so long as it meant we didn't have to get in a car, it was what we were to do.

For the next three hours we cycled to Hutubi, worried that we would come to another police checkpoint or be stopped by a police car and be unable to explain why we were without passports. It was turning into another very long and stressful day. We both felt utterly exhausted, and it was with a great deal of relief that we found our way to the hotel without any further hassles. It was not our usual digs. The requirement for us to stay at the only tourist-approved lodgings in town meant that we would be paying a relatively large sum of money and staying in a massive, sprawling hotel full of pillars and chandeliers. We looked just a teensy bit out of place as we wandered into the giant foyer, trails of filthy slush dripping behind us. Of course the policeman was nowhere to be seen, and we couldn't check in without our passports.

We had been given his phone number, so Dea called it to try and locate him. She returned looking confused. "He didn't seem to know what I was talking about. It sounded like he was with some girls. At a party or something."

This was turning out to be a very long day indeed. All we could do now was wait and hope we would be reunited with our passports eventually. After about twenty minutes we saw the policeman's car pull up at the front of the hotel, and he came inside looking like a man keen to get back to his girlfriends. Together we went over to the hotel reception desk, where a helpful young lady translated his words to us with her smartphone.

"We cannot check you in now. You must first go to the community centre to register. Then we can check you in."

This was already enough to make my head throb, but it was set to explode when she added, "You'll go in his car."

That obviously was not going to be happening. I whipped out Jia's magic letter and showed it to the policeman. To his very great credit he read it through thoroughly, nodded, and suggested we walk instead.

So Dea, myself, and our new policeman friend stepped out for a walk across town in the freezing cold night. I was grateful to him for his patience. Like the others, he was only trying to do his job, and we weren't exactly making life easy for him either. After ten or fifteen minutes we arrived at a large building protected by a gate and a security guard. Inside it looked like some sort of police headquarters. The policeman sat down and began filling in some forms, copying information from our passports in what looked like a laborious process for him, and I found myself wondering if it wouldn't have made more sense for him to do that during the previous few hours that he'd spent waiting for us.

As we were waiting a chirpy woman named Julia, dressed in plain clothes but with the air of somebody quite important, came and spoke to us in broken English. She was nice, but our patience was really approaching breaking point, and when she told us she would need to keep our passports overnight I almost lost my temper. But we were in a police station in a foreign land, and there wasn't much we could do. She insisted it was the rules, they had to keep them, and she laid out a few more for us too.

"Don't leave your hotel, and don't take any photos."

What was this place?

"You should come back here in the morning to get your passports, okay?"

Our policeman escorted us back to the hotel, where we were finally allowed to check in. We'd first arrived at this hotel at seven o'clock, but it was nine thirty before we made it to our room, completely and utterly spent. There was nothing left to do but sleep.

We woke up early in the morning. All we wanted to do was get out of Hutubi and ride our bikes to Urumqi, now only eighty kilometres away. We hoped to find anonymity from all this nonsense in the big city, and Markus had said he'd had no trouble with the police east of Urumqi. All we had to do was get there. We'd been told to collect our passports after nine, though, so we had time for the hotel's breakfast buffet, which we ate all alone in a large restaurant. It all felt very reminiscent of a scene from a North Korean documentary.

"I can't believe she said don't leave the hotel, don't take photos," I said to Dea.

"I know, I wonder what happens here!"

Checking out of the hotel went smoothly and we made our way by bike to the 'community centre' where, predictably enough, the security guard refused to let us in. For quite a while he was trying to shoo us away with a broom, but eventually he relented and let us pass. Inside the building there was no sign of Julia, and no one else had any idea what it was that we wanted. Feeling exasperated, we took a seat, and waited some more.

"I'm worried they'll want to drive us to Urumqi," Dea said. It might sound strange given everything that had happened recently, but this thought hadn't occurred to my tired brain, which had optimistically believed we might just be given our passports back and set free. But as soon as the words left Dea's lips I knew it was true. Of course they weren't going to let us cycle. They'd kept our passports overnight, told us not to leave the hotel. They clearly didn't want us wandering around on our own. Of course they were going to want to escort us out of town. I put my head in my hands. I was running out of energy to keep fighting. This was so, so hard.

Julia appeared briefly, but there was no sign of our passports. She disappeared again into another room and we waited some more, absolutely convinced now that the delay was to give them time to organise our onward transport. Oh, this was so frustrating. I was so close to the end, so close to Mori, and it all just felt impossible. All I wanted was a fair chance, the freedom to keep my passport in my pocket, and to just ride my bike to the finish line.

Suddenly Julia was in front of us, holding out our passports. I couldn't believe it. I didn't dare to. Was she really going to let us go? We took them from her before she could change her mind.

"How are you getting to Urumqi?" she asked.

"Bicycle," we said in unison, making pedalling motions with our arms for emphasis.

"Bicycle!" Julia repeated, her eyes wide in shock. "It's so cold!"

"No problem," we said, desperately hoping it wasn't going to be a problem. Another policeman had appeared, and now fell into a serious conversation with Julia. I felt certain they were going to tell us that we couldn't cycle. There'd been a mistake, for sure. They would need our passports back. Julia turned back to us, and I winced, fearing the worst.

"Do you know the way to Urumqi?"

"Yes, yes," we reassured her.

"Okay. Good luck," she said, with a beaming smile.

We were free to go. We were really free to go! We weren't going to be made to get in a car. The idea hadn't even come up. It felt like a miracle! We hurried towards the door, as another policeman started talking with Julia. "Let's get out of here," I whispered to Dea as we neared the exit. We were almost there, Dea's hand was reaching for the door, when Julia's voice called out again.

"Wait a moment!" she cried.

We froze. I bowed my head. So near, so very, very near, and yet so far.

"Can we take a photo with you?"

53

H ow long will you be staying?" asked the receptionist, as we stood at the front desk of our Urumqi hotel. It was a good question. We'd only pre-booked a couple of nights, but as we stood there feeling exhausted, faces flushed from stepping in out of the cold for the first time in twelve hours, Dea's knee in pain, my bike breaking, our patience waning, there was no doubt it was going to be a lot longer than that. The ride from Hutubi had taken us all day. Thankfully there had only been one police checkpoint on the way and we'd been allowed straight through, but the traffic as we neared Xinjiang's largest city provided a different sort of stress, and this hotel, the only affordable tourist-approved option, was on the other side of town, meaning we'd spent the past two hours riding on busy footpaths in the dark. My chain was skipping a lot and one of my front panniers had a damaged clip and was falling off every time I hit any kind of bump. And with a police post on every corner there was a constant fear of something going wrong at any moment, but thankfully they paid no attention to us, and it seemed like we might be able to find the anonymity we craved in the midst of the big city after all.

Having told the hotel we'd be staying for five nights we made ourselves at home, appreciative of the warm bed and the breakfast buffet as we tried to rebuild our strength for the final push. The buffet was a good one, with coffee and fried eggs to go with the Chinese options, and each morning we'd load up with as much food as we could stomach, hoping to regain some of the weight we'd lost to the extreme cold. We were now less than 300 kilometres from Mori, but with Dea's knee in pain and temperatures still rarely getting above minus twenty outside there was every reason for us to take the time to rest up before attempting to cycle there.

Stepping outside of the hotel never failed to make me cough, the sudden shock of the cold air hitting my lungs producing an unstoppable reflex. We were in a busy area of the city, surrounded by tall buildings, a giant poster of David Beckham on the corner, a Pizza Hut across the street, and people bustling about everywhere. This was a modern city, and it certainly didn't stop for winter.

We were on the lookout for a supermarket when we stumbled upon a large bookshop. Short on reading material, we went inside to see if we could find any English books, and were pleased to find a collection of classics, being sold, perhaps not entirely legitimately, at very reasonable prices. We picked up a handful, as with a lot of China and a lot of desert ahead of us, even after Mori, we would be needing something to keep us entertained. Included amongst our selection was George Orwell's *Nineteen Eighty-Four*, a most appropriate accompaniment to our ride through Xinjiang, surely.

We had just paid for this handful of books when a local girl of about sixteen asked us if we wouldn't rather have a plastic bag to carry them in, and then procured one for us from the lady at the till. The girl, who introduced herself as Linda, seemed keen to practice her English, and fell into conversation with Dea as we exited the shop. The girls seemed to hit it off with one another, and walked arm-in-arm down the street together laughing, with me trailing along behind them. It was nice to see this friendship so quickly formed, in a country where such connections were often hard to forge. I decided to enter the conversation myself, and, with practical thoughts also on my mind, asked Linda if she knew where to find a supermarket.

"Yes, I will take you there if you want," she replied happily.

The supermarket was in the basement of a large shopping mall, and to get down to it required the use of a set of escalators. Naturally I couldn't take these, so I left the girls to go down without me, Dea having the awkward task of explaining to Linda why I wasn't accompanying them. I found the idea of just standing around waiting for them a little boring, though, and began to look for another way in. After a while I located a set of stairs that brought me in at the back of the supermarket, where a couple of security guards were sitting at a desk. They stopped me to check my bag of books, then allowed me to enter the store. I soon managed to locate Dea and Linda and I helped out with the shopping, taking particular delight in finding baked beans for sale. Once that was done I left them to pay and headed back to the stairs. Once again the two security guards called me to a halt, but this time for a much more worrying reason. It seemed that nobody was allowed to exit the store by these stairs, they were only an entrance, and I would have to go and leave via the escalators like everybody else.

'Dammit! Why did I take such a stupid risk?!' I asked myself, as my continuous journey once again found itself in slightly absurd peril, with me quite literally now trapped, in a supermarket. Well, there was no chance I was going to be getting on any escalators, so it was either I take the stairs or I settle in in the supermarket forever. I decided on the former, and, with the guards a little immobilised behind their desk, I bolted for the stairs. Once again I was on the run from the law, although my getaway was almost cut short when in my panic I couldn't remember if I was supposed to go up or down. Luckily I guessed correctly and ran back up into the mall. I hurried over to the top of the escalators, looking back over my shoulder nervously all the way for any potential pursuers. Dea and Linda appeared. "Let's get out of here!" I said.

Finding tourist-approved hotels for the remaining stretch was not as easy as we'd hoped. We checked online cycling blogs for other riders' experiences, but there were two routes east of Urumqi, and almost everyone took the other, more southern option. The major booking websites indicated that almost all of the hotels on our route

accepted only mainland Chinese citizens, and after a whole day of trying we had only located suitable accommodation in one of three
towns we needed it in. We even tried getting the front reception staff
to call possible hotels for us to see if they would accept foreigners, but
this brought no further success. Entering any of these towns late in
the day without knowing for sure that we could stay there brought a
risk of unwanted police attention that we couldn't afford. We simply
had to know where we could or couldn't stay.

Our salvation came in the form of Jia, the Chinese girl we'd met in
Denmark some eighteen months earlier. We were still in contact with
her, and as she was presently visiting family in the east of China it was
easy to video call. After explaining our situation, Jia said she would
take it upon herself to research our options for us. Working in the
tourism sector and being able to speak Chinese gave her obvious
advantages in this task, but it still must have taken her some time and
effort, for which we felt extremely grateful when she got back to us
with the names of tourist-approved hotels in Jimsar and Qitai to go
with the one we'd already found in Fukang. She hadn't managed to
find one in Mori itself, but that was alright. I remembered very well
where the hotel was that I'd stayed in last time, and I was looking forward to arriving unannounced and surprising Sunny, the sweet girl
from the hotel who had taken my photo by the sculpture and waved
me off on my mission around the world.

We were so grateful for all Jia's help, but she wasn't done with it
yet; hearing about Dea's ongoing knee trouble, she suggested a potential fix in the form of acupuncture. "It's very popular in China, you
should be able to find somewhere nearby. It works. It really works, I
think it will be very good for you," she insisted, and it was enough to
convince Dea to give it a shot. To make things even easier there was
an acupuncture clinic in the very same building, adjacent to the hotel,
and we soon found ourselves sitting in a waiting room where a young
woman named Claire was translating the words of the acupuncture
doctor. He was a man of about forty, dressed in a white coat, with a
bald head and a bit of a samurai warrior look to him. After examining
Dea's knee he said that he could do something to help with the pain,

but that for effective results it would require five treatments over the next few days, at a total cost of around 150 pounds. My personal scepticism about acupuncture increased significantly at this point, but the doctor must have sensed our hesitation, because he quickly added that he would do the first treatment for free and we could see how it went before deciding on anything more.

And so it came to pass that I was soon watching Dea, lying on her back in a pink robe, undergoing acupuncture treatment, which began with the doctor administering a heavy-handed massage to various parts of her left leg. Dea was wincing and almost screaming in pain with this tough treatment. It was quite different from how I thought acupuncture therapy went, and I was tempted to ask the doctor if this brutal massage was normal procedure. "Only for people who don't want to pay," I imagined he might respond.

After a while the massage was over and the doctor began what Dea would describe as the less painful part of the treatment, stabbing needles in her leg. They went in all over her left leg and foot, not just the knee, and they had to stay in there for quite a while too, working their magic.

Come the next morning Dea's knee was not feeling any better, and she was not planning to return for more rough treatment. But by chance she ran into the doctor at breakfast, and after telling him thanks, but no thanks, she soon received a text message from Claire. It said that the doctor was very sad she wasn't coming back, and he would be happy to do all of the treatments for free, because he wanted to help us succeed in making it to the end of our trip. It seemed like an extremely generous offer, and Dea decided she would take him up on it. The doctor clearly had confidence in his methods, and it seemed like it was worth a try. This time Dea went alone. She returned saying that the doctor had subjected her to fire acupuncture, a procedure which had involved inserting red hot miniature knives into Dea's legs, and I began to think he really didn't like people who didn't want to pay.

I make these jokes about the doctor in complete jest, for he was really a good man, one who only wanted to help us. He even took us out to lunch afterwards with Claire and another of his nurses. And even though the lunch included rotten eggs, that were black with a mouldy green yolk (a delicacy apparently), it was still great to get out and socialise with some local people. The Chinese were not always the easiest to get along with, but it was becoming clear that, break through the initial cultural differences, and they were as warm-hearted and generous as any people in the world.

With Dea continuing her treatments over the next few days I took the time to try and replace the drivetrain on my bike. I had the necessary components with me, having bought them in Almaty; I had been cautious that the bad weather and salt on the roads might accelerate the deterioration of the existing parts, and so it had proven. My chain was skipping so badly now that it was necessary to replace it, as well as the crankset and cassette. But as I tried to screw in the crank-removal tool I managed to destroy the thread on the crank, in so doing making it impossible to remove with the tool. This was a massive pain, and exactly the same predicament that had faced me back in Denmark, when I'd ended up bashing the crank off with Dea's father's biggest hammer. I didn't have Dea's father's biggest hammer with me this time of course, didn't even have his smallest hammer, didn't even have a hammer, actually. All I had was a wrench, and I took my bike to a quiet corner of the street, as far from any police post as I could get, to try and bash the crankset off with it. But it was to no avail, the crankset wouldn't budge no matter how hard I hit it. It was a frustrating situation, and one that would mean I would be leaving Urumqi for the final crucial stretch to Mori with a badly skipping drivetrain, and unfortunately now also with my front chainrings all badly misshapen, from having been bashed very hard with a wrench.

54

Urumqi, China
3rd February 2018

It felt good to be loading the bikes up again outside of the hotel, and not just to relieve the restlessness from what had turned into a whole week in Urumqi, but because the temperatures had risen so much. It almost felt like spring had begun, ready to heat our last few days to Mori as I adjusted things on my bike without even needing to keep my gloves on. It was simply wonderful, this sudden heatwave – probably about minus fourteen!

Before we'd got to the end of the street, however, things started to go wrong. It seemed my bash-my-bike-with-a-wrench method of repair had, against all the odds, done more harm than good. There were many things on my bike that had broken or stopped working over the years, including that little piece of plastic that sits at the bottom of the frame, under the bottom bracket, acting as a guide for the gear cables to run through. That had broken a long time back, and I'd replaced it quite ingeniously with a piece of grooved plastic cut from a water bottle, held in position with cable ties. Unfortunately not all of my wrench swings had hit their target, and I'd inadvertently broken some of these cable ties, which in turn allowed my rear cable to now slide out of position and jam itself into my crankset, rendering forward movement quite impossible. So I had to try and fix it, but as I yanked the cable free and set about readjusting it I noticed that the housing around the cable was damaged to the point of being useless. It was going to need a complete overhaul, but with a hotel to get to by the evening there was no time for that, so I settled for a quick solution and just fixed the rear derailleur in a middle gear. Luckily my bashing hadn't deformed the crankset as badly as I'd first feared, so I could still use both the small and middle chainring at the front, giving me a grand total of two gears to get me through the day.

At least getting out of Urumqi was a lot easier than getting in had been. Almost the whole way we had segregated bicycle lanes and, while these were also often used by cars, motorbikes, and pedestrians, they nevertheless kept us away from speeding traffic and provided a pretty nice way to escape the big city.

After twenty kilometres we were out of Urumqi and stopped to take a quick break. It was turning into a pretty good day. We were well on course for our target of Fukang and, for the first time in as long as I could remember, I was able to cycle without icicles forming on my eyelashes. We carried on and had a great, wide, quiet road to enjoy for a while. Unfortunately, things turned against us again when we moved onto a narrow road busy with trucks, where my chain started skipping so badly that one of my two gears was completely unusable.

We'd passed a couple of police checkpoints for traffic going the other way without problems, and we hoped we might get away with one hassle-free day on that score, but close to Fukang a checkpoint appeared on our side. We had to go inside and sit for a while as a man checked our passports and asked us where we were going, but there was no need for a police escort this time and we were soon free to go on. And the road grew wide again and the trucks all disappeared, and so we had a nice ride into Fukang in the end.

The hotel was a good one, and we decided to take another rest day here for a couple of reasons. The first was to give Dea's knee, which had indeed become less painful post-acupuncture, a bit of time to ease gently back into cycling again. The second was to give me a bit of time to try and salvage my bike. I took it over to a corner of the big car park out the front of the hotel and went to work. Bashing the crankset with a wrench had not worked before, so my new plan was to now bash the crankset with a wrench even harder. This didn't work well, so I refined the technique, and took a screwdriver, then bashed that against the crankset with a wrench. This also didn't have any immediate noticeable effect, so I alternated the two techniques back and forth for about half an hour with varying degrees of frustrated exertion. Then the crankset came off, which I have to say was pretty frigging awesome of it.

My elation at this victory was noticed by an odd young Chinese man who came over to talk to me. I indicated to him that I could not understand Chinese, and tried to demonstrate what I was doing with charades. But the man had come to talk to me, and talk to me he most certainly did. He stood there chatting for at least twenty minutes. I have not the first clue what about.

Defeating my crankset wasn't the end of my troubles, however, for my cassette proved itself a similarly tough opponent. Without a chain whip I had to employ more unorthodox mechanical techniques. I put my old chain around the cassette and affixed it to the rim of the wheel with cable ties in order to provide the necessary resistance to unscrew the cassette lockring. But this lockring was really not down for the plan, and stubbornly refused to be unscrewed. For half an hour or more I waged war with this damn cassette. At one point a stray puppy came over to me. It was ever so cute and I thought it was my friend, and it helped me to calm down and put things in perspective, at least until it picked up one of my cable ties and ran off with it. I was getting very frustrated. Several times the cable ties broke and I had to replace them. I really wanted to start bashing this damn thing with a wrench, but I knew that wasn't the appropriate course of action, not for this problem anyway, and with enough oil, patience, determination, and cable ties, the lockring finally came free.

With a new crankset, cassette, chain, rear gear cable, and cable housing my bike was in good shape again as we cycled away from the hotel at first light the following morning (first light, because all of China works to Beijing time, being twenty past nine). We had to get going early because once again it was a hundred kilometres to the next town of Jimsar. It was again not too cold, at least relative to what we'd been through, and I felt energised by the idea of making it to Jimsar. Do that and we'd be only two days from Mori, an almost unbelievable prospect. And the risk of not making it, and having to camp in the fields of snow, so open and exposed, where we'd be easy to spot by police or locals who might call them, offered even more motivation not to fail.

We took a smaller road which was actually more direct. It was a good one too, mostly wide and flat without too much traffic. The hours passed quite uneventfully. We came across a couple of police checkpoints, but both times we were waved through without even having to show our passports.

As the afternoon wore on Dea really began to look and sound tired, but she kept plugging away. With ten kilometres to go we took our final rest break. The sun was almost disappearing behind the mountains away to our right, but we were so close to Jimsar, we couldn't give up on it now.

"We're only 140 kilometres from Mori," I said to Dea. "If we can just get to Jimsar tonight, we'll have a good rest tomorrow morning in the hotel, a short forty kilometre ride to Qitai in the afternoon, and we'll be able to get to Mori on Wednesday."

Dea smiled.

"We can be in Mori in forty-eight hours!"

I'm not sure if this conversation inspired my girlfriend, but she certainly went off like a shot after that break, and I could barely keep up with her. More likely it was the two Snickers she'd eaten that had provided her the energy, but whatever it was, it meant that we made it into Jimsar just as day turned to night. We made our way to the hotel that Jia had recommended and to our delight we were allowed to stay, although it took a monumental amount of patience to get through the check-in process with the giggly teenage girl on reception. Sometime around eight we made it to our room, exhausted again, but another day closer to Mori.

It was so nice to enjoy a lie-in the following morning. With just forty-two kilometres to the next tourist hotel in Qitai we could afford to take it easy, and didn't set out until midday. We had to take a main road, the S303, but it was fine, with a big shoulder that was only partly covered with snow and ice. The first twenty kilometres went by quickly, after which we came upon yet another police checkpoint. For the third time in two days I got my passport out ready before we cycled up to the checkpoint, and for the third time in a row we were allowed straight through without anyone looking at it.

"I think I've got these checkpoints figured out now," I said to Dea as we sat down in a restaurant for some noodles a few moments later. "As long as I get my passport out of my wallet all ready to be checked, they don't bother."

After lunch we turned off on a smaller road to Qitai. With it being the last town, the final stepping stone, on our journey to Mori, it was here that my thoughts began to wander. The end was so close now. Until this point I'd not allowed myself to think too much about reaching the finish line. It had been too far off, there had been way too many things that could go wrong. Now there was less than a hundred kilometres to go, and it felt like I could start to imagine making it to the end. And then, interrupting my thoughts, another police checkpoint appeared on the road ahead.

I got my passport out ready. There was a long line of cars waiting, which seemed unusual given the quiet road, and I was worried that this would mean they'd take things more seriously here. We cycled past all of the cars to the front where the first policemen stood. I made eye contact, nodded, and kept moving forwards. They didn't try to stop us. For the fourth checkpoint in a row we'd gone straight through. Were our hassles with the Chinese police over?

We pedalled the final few kilometres and made our way to our hotel in Qitai. The process of checking in was once again a long one, with the receptionist taking an awfully long time over studying and recording our passports. We then had to carry all of our bags a long way over to another building where our room was. By the time all that was done I was dog-tired and just collapsed onto the bed.

"Do you want a sandwich?" Dea asked.

I did. I did want a sandwich, I'd been looking forward to a sandwich for a long time. But before I could take one bite, there was a knock at the door. I went over and opened it. No fewer than four policemen were outside, but not for long. One of them, who had surely seen too many cop shows, flashed his badge and then barged past me into the room. I sighed. Our hassles with the police were clearly not over. The other policemen all followed the first inside and questions were fired at us. Where were we from? Where were we going? What were our plans in Qitai? During all of this the keenest policeman, the once who had barged in first, was walking around the room and peering behind our curtains. What he thought he might find behind there, I could not imagine. Our passports were looked at and more questions were asked, with me just hoping that we weren't going to be forced to go anywhere, until eventually we were given our passports back, and left to our sandwiches.

It was a reminder that this wasn't over yet, that the police were still around, and that even with just one day of cycling between us and Mori, anything could still happen. It also made me think about how the situations we'd encountered with the police in this province seemed to be so much more difficult for us than they'd been for cyclists that had come through this way in the years before us. A follower of our blog had informed us that Xinjiang had recently appointed a new governor, a man who had previously held a similar position of authority over Tibet. That would go some way to explain the severity of the security clamp-down here, and things looked to be heading in just one direction. So much so that it was easy to imagine that in a year or two independent travel through Xinjiang for foreigners might well be impossible, as it already was in Tibet. That in turn made me realise how important it was that we'd come here now, rather than a year or two later, as we'd originally planned. There is surely some truth to the idea that everything happens for a reason, and while it had taken a while to discern any positives from Dea's horrible eye infection in the Pacific Ocean, in causing us to abandon our plan of cycling the Americas together, in forcing us to head east for Mori sooner, it might just have been the most important single event in bringing us here, just in time, to the brink of success.

55

Waking up in our hotel in Qitai on Wednesday the 7th of February 2018 I tried to think of it as just another day, just another bike ride. But who was I kidding? It was a special day. It was a monumental day. It was the day when Dea and I were going to try and ride the final eighty kilometres to Mori, that random Chinese town where I had restarted my attempt to circumnavigate the planet using only my bicycle and boats, three years and four months earlier. I walked over to the window and peeled back the curtains. It was still dark outside, the street empty. Not far away I could see the blue and red flashing lights of one of a great many police stations, a reminder that things could still be taken out of my hands yet.

Dea made us some breakfast and then we went downstairs to get our bikes. As I pushed mine over to my bags I noticed a piece of red material was stuck to the handlebars. "What the hell is this?!" I said, worried I'd ripped off a bit of the hotel's curtains or something. One look at Dea told me it wasn't the reaction she'd been hoping for. "Sorry, did you buy this?"

"Yes. It's a special day, red is supposed to bring luck."

I gave Dea a hug to show my appreciation for her gift. We'd been riding our luck for a while now, and today we could certainly use all the help we could get.

We started cycling around nine twenty, leaving Qitai on the S303 again. Straight away my mind was playing tricks on me, nervously worrying about what could go wrong. My hamstring felt tight, my knees felt painful. *'Not an injury, not now, please!'* It was all in my mind, I knew. What was not just in my mind was the creaking noise that was coming from beneath me, a noise that had been getting worse for the past few days, but that I couldn't place. It certainly didn't sound too good though, a bit like my bike might collapse on me at any moment. *'Please bike, not today, hold it together, please!'*

The shoulder on the S303 was good, so to drown out the worrying noise from my bike I put in my headphones and listened to music. The tunes soon carried me away on a tide of memories. I thought back over so many things. I thought about starting out from Paris over four years earlier, about how determined I was that I would do the whole trip only with my bicycle and boats, how optimistic I was, how full of anticipation about the world of possibilities ahead of me. I remembered my first ride across Europe and Central Asia, the wonderful people I'd met then, the memories I'd made way back in 2014. And I remembered getting to the border post in Siberia, that horrible feeling of being told I couldn't cycle across it, the face of the guards, the tears on my cheeks as the motor vehicle had carried me forwards. How devastating that had been, how crushing a blow it was to have lost it all after 27,000 kilometres. How I hoped and prayed that wouldn't happen again now.

My cycle computer ticked over to ten kilometres. Only seventy to go.

I looked at Dea in my mirror and smiled. *'Oh, how amazing she is!'* What a miracle it was that we found each other in outer Mongolia, just a few days after that disappointment at the Siberian border. Meeting Dea had only happened because of my decision to continue with my journey, to simply reset the circumnavigation somewhere in China, and carry on. Somehow she'd stuck by me and been with me ever since. Not always literally, but always in spirit, always supporting me, always believing in this mad project of mine. She'd given me the motivation to ride across China in 2014 only with the promise of seeing her again. And she'd given me a reason to ride across Australia in 2015 so that we could be reunited. Then in 2016, my motivation for crossing Canada had been to get back to her. And in 2017 she had been by my side, joining me on this ride of a lifetime, constantly impressing me with her determination and resilience as we conquered deserts and mountains together on our way back to China. It was so special to have been able to do all of this with her, and so, so special, so right, that we were finishing it together.

After seventeen kilometres we made a right turn off the S303 onto a smaller road south. The S303 would have been the most direct route to Mori, but back in 2014 I'd cycled down from Mongolia and joined the S303 some thirty kilometres before Mori. If we continued straight I would therefore connect with my line at some random intersection, a horrible dirty crossroads if I remembered it right, hardly the place for special moments. Taking the small roads from here would instead lead us into Mori from a slightly different direction, meaning that I would only reconnect with my line in Mori itself, at the park where I had stood in front of a sculpture and told Sunny that I was off to cycle around the world. I had a picture in my mind of this perfect ending, where I cycled into the park with the Sigor Rós track *Hoppi-polla* playing in my ears, mostly because it was the song they always played at the end of *Extreme Dreams with Ben Fogle*, which was one hell of a television show, by the way. And here I was now, on the verge of achieving my own extreme dream.

Twenty kilometres cycled. Sixty to go.

The small road took us south and was going slightly uphill and into the wind. It felt like a bit of a struggle, but it was put in perspective by my thoughts turning to my mum and what she was going through. Her chemotherapy was due to start the very next day. Her world was about to change completely, and I only hoped I was going to be able to give her some good news before it all began. I'd been talking quite a bit with my parents over the past couple of weeks, making use of the Wi-Fi in the hotels to video call with them. It was the most frequently we'd talked in years, and I only found it a shame that it had taken my mum getting cancer to make that happen. We were such different people, me and my parents, but as I rode along through the snowy Chinese landscape something occurred to me. "I don't know where he gets it from," was a common thing for my stay-at-home parents to say about me and my travels, but I suddenly realised, I got it from them. Maybe not the sense of wanderlust, but the stoic resilience my parents had shown to my mother's diagnosis, the optimism, the subtle, stubborn determination to overcome adversity, these were the traits I'd inherited that made all this possible. And then there was the way that my dad stood by my mum, a steady, calm rock, ready to spend the next six months driving her to the hospital and looking after her in between. And it was the same way that he'd looked after his family his whole life, going to work every day to make sure that my sister and I would want for nothing in life. When I'd started out living this way I'd refused to take anything from my parents any more. I'd wanted to prove my independence, to show that I could do this on my own. I'd felt like I didn't want to owe them anything.

But I owed them everything.

Thirty kilometres cycled. Fifty to go.

We made another turn and were heading east again. The road was flatter, we had a tailwind, all we had to do now was to cycle and this road would take us all the way to Mori. I kept listening to my music, in my own world. I was riding in the Australian outback alone under a zillion stars, I was cycling across the Uzbek desert with Alex, the Kyrgyz peaks with Liz. I was in Turkey and Bosnia, beside the Rhine and the Panj, I was lost in Indonesian palm oil plantations with Tom and crossing the Canadian prairies with Vivian. I was everywhere all at once. I wasn't just cycling the last eighty kilometres, I was cycling every single one of the 46,000 kilometres I'd cycled since I'd last seen Mori.

Forty kilometres cycled, forty to go.

We stopped and ate some sandwiches, sitting at the side of the quiet road, looking out over the white fields. It was a calm day, not too cold. The weather had done its worst, but it wasn't going to stop us now. We didn't say much. I was still thinking. Thinking about all the people I'd met along the way, many of whom had daily struggles and problems in their lives I could not have guessed at, but almost all of whom had, given the chance, helped or supported us on the way, if only with a smile or a wave. I was indebted to so many people, it would simply not have been worth doing this journey were it not for the incredibly good-hearted nature of most of the world's citizens. As we continued and passed through a small town I wanted to wave at and thank all of the people that we went by, though they could not have guessed at the magnitude of the moment that was fast approaching.

Fifty kilometres cycled. Thirty to go.

There are times riding a bicycle when everything just feels right, and this was most certainly one of them. We were flying along now, aided by a strong tailwind and a road that was flat and had hardly any traffic on it. The sun was out, the temperature was quite comfortable. Everything had turned our way, literally everything, and with music filling my head and Mori fast approaching I began to feel utterly euphoric. For the first time I became absolutely certain that we were going to make it, absolutely convinced. Then I heard an Alsation bark aggressively at me, and I looked to my right to see it flying towards me. But it snapped back on its chain. I smiled. It really felt like the world had thrown everything at me that it possibly could, but there was nothing that was going to stop me, nothing. I was going to make it.

And then we came to a police checkpoint.

We tried to pass by with just a nod, but the officer manning the road was on the ball and made us stop and show our passports. Then another policeman, this one with a large rifle over his shoulder, came out of the building, took our passports, and told us to follow him back inside. We were told to take a seat, while he tried to work out what a foreign passport was.

"It's going to be fine," Dea whispered to me, but she could not know that. How many foreigners did they get out here on this small road? Surely none. What were they going to do with us? I twisted my hands nervously. My fate was no longer in them, it had been snatched back by the hands of the Chinese police. Phone calls were made. More phone calls were made. The police ate some cookies and coffee. More phone calls were made. This wasn't looking good. It was taking way too long. Something was wrong, I knew it. Half an hour passed, maybe forty-five minutes. The number of police officers behind the desk had grown from one to six, but no information was forthcoming from any of them. All we could do was wait; wait and hope that the news would be good.

Then, finally, one of them translated something into English on his smartphone and handed it to us. I looked at the screen and my heart sank.

"Something happened in our county. Prepared for state of readiness here. Cannot allow you entry. Sorry for the inconvenience."

'Sorry for the inconvenience? Sorry for the inconvenience? I just cycled 46,000 kilometres around the world, and you're blocking the road with twenty-five measly kilometres to go, and you're sorry for the inconvenience?!'

I always knew this was going to happen. It was surely the most inevitable of endings. If ever I thought about it enough, I knew, deep, deep down, it would end like this. It was simply my fate. To try so hard, to get so close, yet to succumb at the last, just like all the historic British nearly-men, Robert Falcon Scott, George Leigh Mallory,

Timothy Henry Henman, and the rest. Oh, why had I got cocky? Why had I allowed myself to believe I was going to make it? China was just too difficult. Of course it was going to stop me somehow. Of course it was.

"You must return to original road."

And with this new message thrust in front of me there was suddenly hope in my heart again. They weren't going to put us in a car. They were giving us our passports back. They were going to let us cycle away. Not in the right direction, true, but it was enough, as I excitedly realised that all we had to do was retreat slightly and find our way back to the S303, and the dream could somehow still yet come true. And we didn't even need to get to Mori now, not really. All I had to do was to get to that intersection, that ugly crossroads where I'd come down from Mongolia. It wouldn't be the fairytale finish, but it didn't need to be. I just had to get to that crossroads.

We checked the map and saw that there was a road heading north from the small town we'd passed through, and it looked like it led directly to the very intersection I needed to get to. I was pumped up now, adrenaline coursing through me like never before as we sprinted back past the restrained Alsation. This was still very much on. The road north was all downhill and I was so determined to get there I was just flying along once we got to it. I wanted to get there as fast as possible, before the police could come along and tell us that they'd made a mistake, that we weren't allowed to cycle here at all, that we'd have to go with them. Roadside markers counted down to the junction. Ten kilometres. Nine, eight, seven. I was pounding along at more than twenty kilometres per hour, Dea in my mirror doing her best to keep up, music still ringing in my ears as the adrenaline kept firing and I kept pounding down on the pedals for all I was worth. Was it really it this time?

We passed an expressway exit and the quiet road suddenly became overrun with quarrying trucks. This wasn't particularly pleasant, but indicated that we were closing in on the right junction, as the one thing I remembered about it was all the trucks. The end of the road drew nearer as I dived out of the way of a recklessly overtaking truck.

Things could still go wrong. I was expecting to see the inevitable police checkpoint at any moment, but none appeared. There were only three kilometres to go, then two, then one. I put on Sigor Rós and I just kept right on pedalling. This was it, this was really it. The junction was ahead of me, there it was, there it was, and suddenly I was there, I was there, bursting out into the middle of the crossroads and it was the most incredible, surreal feeling of my life. It was a feeling I had never felt before. All of the trucks, all of the traffic, had just vanished, there was nothing else there for a moment, leaving me free to float into the middle of the crossroads, guaranteeing that I crossed the line I'd taken when turning east here having arrived from the north all those years ago. With Sigor Rós's inspiring melody in my head I felt euphoric, I felt like I'd achieved something, here in this, the most horrible of settings. It was a disgusting place really, with filthy red trucks parked up everywhere and litter strewn about, smoke pouring from a skip. Yet what I experienced here was a once-in-a-life-time feeling. A feeling that comes from achieving a dream after fighting so hard for it for so many years, but a feeling that was simultaneously being tempered by only being ninety-five percent sure that I'd actually done it. I was not absolutely certain that this was the right place. I felt like there was a chance that I'd got to Mori by a different way, that I had made a terrible mistake, that I had this all wrong. Even as Dea caught up to me and hugged me in congratulations there was still a doubt in my mind as to whether I'd really made it. "We'd better keep going to Mori," I said.

So we continued east on the S303. Mori was still thirty kilometres away and there were only a couple of hours of daylight left, but I had some kind of summit fever, and I had to try and make it there still. On we rode, me a mess of emotions, believing that I had finally made it around the world but still just not being quite sure. I wanted to get to Mori, I wanted to make certain. I was thinking now about when I'd met John in Nicaragua, when he'd told me that unless you do it all by bike and boat, you haven't really cycled around the world, and I thought about what my reaction had been, and my reaction played over and over in my head. I was still cycling so fast, desperate to get to

Mori, but Dea was falling behind. We needed to stop and eat something, we'd hardly had anything to eat all day. I noticed a short section of crash barrier and lent my bike against it. As I did so I looked up at some houses nearby and I saw something amazing. It was the world's worst basketball court. The two baskets were old and broken, they didn't have nets, and they weren't even facing each other. It was a terrible example of a basketball court, it really was. But that wasn't what made it amazing. What made it amazing was that I had seen this basketball court before. I remembered it. I remembered photographing it. I remembered chuckling at it for being such a dire example of a sporting arena. And looking at it again now was amazing, for as I did so I knew, with one hundred percent certainty, that I had been all of the way around the world using only my bicycle and boats. A rush of emotion overcame me once again. I kicked at a pile of snow, I punched at it. I didn't know what else to do. Sigor Rós was no longer playing. New Found Glory's punk-pop classic *Hit or Miss* was in my ears now, and I knew that from this moment on it was going to be one of my favourite songs. It had been one of my favourite songs before this moment, for one thing, but now it was even more special, now it was the backdrop to one of the best moments of my life. Dea arrived, worried something had gone wrong having seen me attacking snow, but nothing was wrong. I hugged her and told her I'd done it. We had done it.

But nobody has ever done that!

They had now.

56

Xinjiang, China
7th February 2018

I suddenly felt completely and utterly exhausted. With my goal achieved there was no longer any very good reason to get to Mori before nightfall, and my body had no enthusiasm for the idea whatsoever. We weren't going to make it before dark and the odds of there being another checkpoint seemed high, so we decided to call it a day and make camp under the road in a small underpass. We had not been planning to camp and did not have a lot of water. "Don't worry, I've got a litre and a half of liquid here," Dea said, pulling out a big bottle of champagne. "Congratulations. I'm so proud of you."

I popped open the champagne, which turned out to be weak red wine, and Dea and I toasted the success of the day. And what a day it had been, and what a journey, and looking at Dea I knew there was no one I would rather have done it with, and no one I would rather be celebrating beneath a road in subzero temperatures with, than her. She had been amazing throughout the whole thing. I was inspired by her, by the way she had come back from her eye infection and her repeated knee problems, the way she had overcome every obstacle, and by her ultimate determination to make it to China with me. This special moment wasn't mine, it was ours.

We arose from our hiding place the next morning, keen to ride the final few kilometres into Mori. Even though I had technically been around the world by bicycle and boats now, it still felt like we had to make it to Mori to complete the challenge. It had been our stated mission for a long time, and getting back to the park that I had made my official starting point was very important to me.

So you can imagine my dismay when, only two kilometres into our day, we came upon a police checkpoint. Once again we had to go inside and hand over our passports, and once again we were made to wait for a very long time. There were a lot of phone calls made, a lot of looking at our passports, and then the heartbreaking message was once again passed to us that we would not be allowed to continue into Mori. I sighed. Why was this so hard?! We were now only fifteen kilometres away from the park, from the sculpture where I'd officially started, the place I so badly wanted to get back to. But these policemen were serious, and stood firm against our protests. They simply were not going to let us through.

We didn't back down either. For one thing, if we didn't get through here the only other way for us to continue our cycle across China was to go all of the way back to Urumqi in order to take the southern route, a 500 kilometre detour. But we had to get to Mori. We just had to. I showed the police the address of the hotel that we planned to stay at, the one I'd stayed at three years earlier.

"Do you have a reservation?" asked the policeman's smartphone. We did not, but a thought now struck me. If Sunny was still there, and if we could get hold of her, maybe there was a chance she could help us. I asked the policeman to call the hotel and ask for Sunny, and he did try, but it didn't work. Sunny was her English name, her Chinese name was different, and no connection could be made.

For over an hour we were in that police building, our passports on the policeman's desk, our bikes waiting outside, Mori fifteen kilometres away and a million miles out of reach. But we didn't give up. Dea had a great idea, and called Claire, the English-speaking girl from the acupuncture centre in Urumqi, to ask her to call the hotel for us in order to explain the situation and try and get hold of Sunny. Claire agreed to try and help. People were still being so nice, so good to us. The drama continued, with people in the station asking us questions, making phone calls. Then the senior policeman shouted out,

"Chris?" and I knew there was only one way he could know the shortening of my name. He passed me the phone.

"Sunny?!"

It was her. We'd made contact and it was so good to hear her voice again. She remembered me well.

"You told me you would come back, but I didn't believe it!" she said, sounding, well, disbelieving.

We chatted for a little while, then I explained our circumstances, and asked Sunny if she could talk with the policeman and try to convince him to allow us into Mori. She agreed to try.

I handed the phone to the policeman and he talked for a while to Sunny. Actually he talked *at* Sunny for a while, and then hung up the phone. I couldn't believe he did that, without passing it back to me to hear what he'd told her, but some time later Sunny was back on the phone and I got to talk to her again.

"He says you can come to Mori," she said, raising my hopes for the briefest of moments, before adding, "but you have to come by bus. He says you can come by bus, or you can go back to your own country. I'm sorry, it is the only way."

This was not what I had been hoping to hear. I couldn't do it. I couldn't come all this way around the world and then take a bus to the finish line. What a pathetic ending that would be. There was no way it was going to end like that. We would have to go back. I thanked Sunny for her help and said goodbye. It was so, so sad. We were not going to get our reunion after all.

I went to hang up the phone, but the policeman grabbed it from me just before I could, and began to speak with Sunny again. Dea and I looked at each other.

"I can't go into Mori on a bus, Dea."

"I know Chris."

"We'll cycle back to Qitai and figure out what to do from there."

We'd given it our best shot, argued our case for hours in this police station, but the gig was up. There was no way through, it was time for us to retreat again.

The policeman hung up the phone again, and handed us back our passports. We turned for the door.

"Go Mori," he said.

"What?"

"Go Mori."

"By bicycle?"

"Yes, yes. Go Mori."

We were in shock. We did not know what had just happened. The policeman seemed to have had an inexplicable 180 degree change of heart. There was no explanation for it, but we didn't hang around to hear one. We vaulted onto our bicycles and started pedalling towards Mori as fast as we could. It felt like one final miracle. Surely this was just meant to be, it really was.

It had started to snow gently, but that didn't matter. We just pedalled and pedalled for all we could, until a police car came up behind us, lights flashing. I held my breath, but it zoomed straight past us. I just kept going, kept turning the pedals, moving forwards. The town of Mori came into view. It was not an especially distinguished townscape, but after 46,000 kilometres and all the trouble we'd had getting to it, it felt like the most beautiful sight in the world to me.

We crossed a bridge into town, and found ourselves heading down the busy main street. I knew that the park was still a few kilometres away, and there seemed to be police cars driving everywhere, something that had not been the case on my last visit. One of them kept slowing down next to us. *'Please don't stop us, please don't stop us now!'* I thought, fearing we might be dragged off to some 'community centre' or told we couldn't cycle into the town centre, or some such nonsense. I saw a policeman take a photo of us out of the car window, only increasing my fears, but then it sped away. Our route was clear. On and on through the town we went, Sigor Rós in my ears again, until finally, there in front of us was the sculpture that I recognised, my start and finish line. And wouldn't you just know it, but the whole park was blocked off, surrounded by a new fence topped with razor wire.

We phoned Sunny. Her hotel was just around the corner, and she was with us within a couple of minutes. I gave her a hug, so pleased to see her again, and so unbelievably grateful for all of her help to make it here.

"Can we go into the park?" I asked her.

"No."

I was so close to the finish line, so very, very close.

"Not with the bikes. Pedestrians, yes."

"That's okay! We'll leave the bikes here."

"Okay, let's go."

And Sunny led us through a security gate, past an uninterested guard, and into the deserted park.

We walked over to the sculpture, its silly silver wings gleaming in the winter sun, until we reached the place where one thousand two hundred and twenty-six days earlier Sunny had taken a photograph of me and my bike. My bike hadn't quite made it back (nice try, bike) but that was alright, I had someone much more special (sorry bike) to hold this time. Sunny took a photo of Dea and me in front of the sculpture, our arms raised in triumph, and an ambition I'd held in my heart for so long was finally realised. I had done it. I had really, actually done it. My journey around the world entirely by bicycle and boats could now be deemed a one hundred percent complete success.

The three of us walked to Sunny's hotel, where we sat down and chatted, with me feeling truly relaxed for the first time in a very long while. Sunny was such a sweet girl, she really was. She told us about her life, her boyfriend, how things had changed a lot here, but how important it was to concentrate on the positive side of things. I showed her a copy of my first book, and pointed out the bit with her, when I'd been in Mori the first time. I wanted her to understand how much all this meant to me.

"This is amazing!" she said, looking close to tears. "I can't believe all this. I still can't believe you came back."

I told her that she could keep the book, and she asked us both to sign it. She helped us come up with Chinese names for the purpose, mine translating as 'King Travel', and Dea's as 'Queen of Enlightenment and Elegance'. It was all such great fun, and as we headed out for a celebratory lunch with Sunny I realised that this was what really mattered – the way our travels brought us together with people, created friendships and formed these special connections.

I had set myself a massive challenge, so big that at times it had seemed impossible, and now at long, long last I had succeeded. In demonstrating that it is possible to go all of the way around the planet without using motor vehicles I felt like I had achieved something worthwhile, but I knew that I wouldn't have got close to achieving anything without the help of others. I knew that the real reason why the journey was a success was because of the people along the way; because of Hardy delivering us pizza in Germany, because of Nurseit looking after Dea's bike in Kazakhstan, because of Merdan giving us a bed for the night in Azerbaijan, because of Alex bringing us bike parts from Dubai. It was a success because some old man in a flat cap in Uzbekistan knew how to weld, just as competently as some old man in the Australian outback had. It was a success because of the Caspian Sea official who walked with us to Passport Control instead of forcing us onto a bus, because of the Chinese policemen who drove with us for four hours instead of arresting us. And it was a success in the end because of the doctor who insisted on fixing Dea's knee in Urumqi, because of Jia taking the time to find us the hotels we needed, because of Claire for contacting Sunny, and ultimately because of Sunny, and whatever the hell it was she said to bring the policeman round. And the really amazing thing was that none of these people had anything to gain by helping us, they had no stake in my mission, they had no reason to be so nice; they just were that nice, they just wanted to help out of the goodness of their own hearts.

I had finally achieved my goal, true, but in the end, the real achievement was surely theirs.

Progress Report
Mori, February 2018

1. Circumnavigate the planet

Completed

2. Do so using only my bicycle and boats

Mission accomplished!

3. Pass through antipodal points

...and I ended up where I started!

4. Visit all of the inhabited continents

Still only four, but got to leave something for the trilogy.

5. Cycle at least 100,000 kilometres

75,640 kilometres completed. 24,360 to go.

6. Cycle in 100 countries

Sixty-one, leaving thirty-nine more to explore in Part Three.

7. Return with more money than I start with

Well you bought this book, didn't you? Anything is possible...

The adventure continues:

www.differentpartsofeverywhere.com

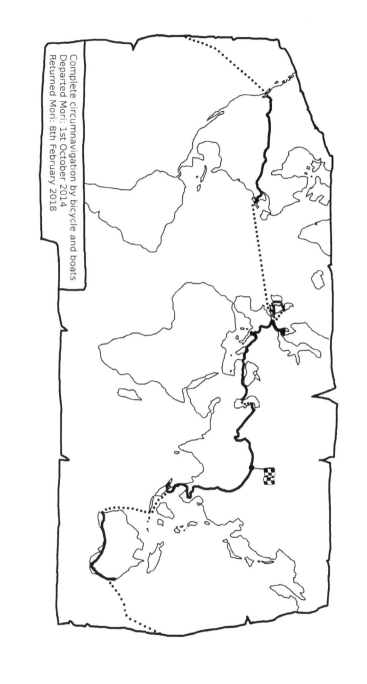

Complete circumnavigation by bicycle and boats
Departed Mori: 1st October 2014
Returned Mori: 8th February 2018

ACKNOWLEDGEMENTS

I must once again start by offering a huge thanks to the people of the world, for the support and generosity that made this trip possible, and worthwhile. The number of people who have contributed something to our journey literally numbers in the thousands, and to name you all would require a whole other book. But please know that it really is massively appreciated.

Special thanks go to Rachelle and Ned Johnson, for being especially fine examples of the good-hearted people of the world. In offering and organising us places to stay these past couple of months, you made the writing of this book possible. Thank you. On that note thank you also to Hal and Tracey, and Lynda and Craig.

To all of you out there for buying this book, and the previous one, thank you. And special thanks to those who have taken the time to offer me positive and/or constructive feedback – thank you for encouraging me to keep going with the writing, and for giving us an income so that we can keep travelling this way.

Unbelievable thanks once again for my lovely girlfriend, Dea Jacobsen, for giving me the support, the companionship, and the inspiration to make this journey. There really is nobody else I could imagine having done all this with, and I doubt I would have succeeded without you. Thank you so much for being you.

And lastly I have to thank Mum and Dad.

For everything.